MEMOIR

OF

BISHOP MACKENZIE.

BY

HARVEY GOODWIN, D.D.

DEAN OF ELY.

"I heard the voice of the Lord, saying, *Whom shall I send, and who will go for us?* Then said I, *Here am I; send me!*"—ISAIAH VI. 8.

CAMBRIDGE:

DEIGHTON, BELL, AND CO.

LONDON: BELL AND DALDY.

1864.

The profits of the sale of this Work are given to the Funds of the Universities' Mission to Central Africa.

TO THE RIGHT REVEREND

SAMUEL, LORD BISHOP OF OXFORD,

LORD HIGH ALMONER TO HER MAJESTY,

AND

CHANCELLOR OF THE MOST NOBLE ORDER OF THE GARTER.

My Lord,

When the request was made to me by the family of the late Bishop Mackenzie, that I would undertake to write a Memoir of his Life, the request was accompanied by the expression of two wishes.

The first was, that the profits of the sale of the book should be devoted to the furtherance of that cause, in the attempt to advance which the Bishop died. Concerning this I could have no hesitation.

The second was, that the book should be dedicated to yourself. To this also I gladly acceded; and it was highly gratifying to me, that, in reply to my letter asking permission to dedicate the book as the family desired, you not only gave your consent, but assured me that you should deem it an honour to have your name associated with that of Bishop Mackenzie.

I now present to your Lordship the Memoir, upon which during the past year I have been engaged. The Bishop's family, and some of his friends, have freely placed in my hands his more private letters, and other materials from which the story of his life could be gathered, leaving the use of the documents entirely to my discretion. The plan which I have adopted has been to make the Bishop, as far as possible, his own biographer. I have printed nearly one hundred of his letters wholly or in part, and I trust that they will help to convey to the minds of those who read this book an impression of the exceeding gentleness, cheerfulness, and simplicity, coupled with manliness, strength of purpose, and unwavering faith, which belonged to our departed friend and brother.

My Lord, I once took occasion, as we walked together into Ely Cathedral, to say to you, that although I had known Mackenzie intimately for a long time, and had been with him under a variety of circumstances, I had never seen a cloud on his brow, and had never heard him say anything which I could suppose he would wish to recall. I did not exaggerate when I so spoke, nor, indeed, could I easily give what would seem to me to be an exaggerated view of the excellence and sweetness of his character: but in this memoir I have refrained as much as possible from dwelling on my own opinion of his goodness: I have endeavoured rather to exhibit a simple picture of his life, and then have wished the reader to form an opinion for himself.

It has been a melancholy pleasure to be permitted to pay this tribute to the memory of our deceased friend. The pleasure will be enhanced, if I can venture to think that through this memoir Bishop Mackenzie can yet speak, and infuse into some of us that spirit of faith and love, which in so conspicuous a degree animated him. No one would have shrunk more than himself from the notion of a book being published, which should be to him a mere laudatory epitaph; but if the memoir of his life should tend, by God's grace, to incite Christians to dare and to do for Christ's sake, then the publication of it is a tribute which he would have at least excused, because it would have been regarded by him as the means of carrying out after his decease the dearest wish of his heart.

I am, my Lord,

Your Lordship's obedient Servant,

H. GOODWIN.

THE DEANERY, ELY,
Christmas, 1863.

ADVERTISEMENT.

In this Volume the name of the African tribe with which Bishop Mackenzie was chiefly associated has been printed *Mang-anja,* in order to guard against the pronunciation *Man-ganja ;* the name is pronounced as if the word *hang* were followed by the word *and.*

The river *Shire,* which in some works is printed with an accent upon the final *e,* is to be pronounced as if it were written *Shirry,* or nearly so.

The views of Mount Zomba, the Missionary settlement at Magomero, and Lake Shirwa, are taken from sketches made by Dr Meller.

DIRECTIONS TO BINDER.

CONTENTS.

CHAPTER VII.

CHAPTER VIII.

CHAPTER IX.

CHAPTER X.

CHAPTER XI.

CHAPTER XII.

CHAPTER XIII.

MEMOIR OF BISHOP MACKENZIE.

CHAPTER I.

BOYHOOD AND SCHOOL-DAYS.

CHARLES FREDERICK MACKENZIE was born at Harcus Cottage, Portmore, Peebleshire, on the 10th day of April, 1825, and was baptized by the Right Reverend Daniel Sandford, Bishop of Edinburgh. He was the youngest of a large family, of whom six brothers and five sisters survived at the time of his birth[1].

As a child he exhibited great natural power with regard to figures, and thus gave indication of future mathematical ability. He appears to have possessed nc other mark of great mental superiority. As a child also he is said to have exhibited a gentleness of dispo-

1 The eldest was the late William Forbes Mackenzie, Esq. of Portmore, who was secretary to the Treasury in the Ministry of Lord Derby in the year 1852. His name is popularly connected with the law for regulating the sale of spirits in Scotland, commonly known as the "Forbes Mackenzie Act."

sition, which was entirely in keeping with that wonderful sweetness and nobility of character, to which I can testify as a friend of his manhood.

I find it recorded of him, that, when a very little boy, he was accustomed to amuse his elder brothers with the exhibition of his arithmetical powers. Charlie was placed upon a table, and examined by these same elder brothers; hard questions were put to him, which he puzzled out in his head by some method of his own, and answered correctly, though without being able to say how he reached his results. His examiners had slate and pencil to help them, but he generally got to the end of the sum first, without any such help. Strange however to say, when he went to school, and was compelled to write his sums upon the prosaic slate, his great superiority for a time disappeared, and it was only when he reached the higher level of algebra that his real mathematical ability made itself manifest.

He lost his father when only five years old, and the education of himself and of several of the younger children devolved to a considerable extent upon the eldest sister. As this sister is gone to her rest, and as to her wise superintendence much of the subsequent excellence of Bishop Mackenzie's character appears, under God, to have been due, it may be right in this place to allow him to express his own feelings. Writing from Liverpool, on the eve of his first departure for Africa, he says to this sister: "I cannot go, as we are to do to-morrow, without sending you a line to say that my regard and affection for you are deepened, instead of being lessened, by this separation. I feel so strongly that my aptitude for what is good, has been, under God, so entirely due to your judicious training of me, that I cannot say how much I am indebted to you. Dear ——," he proceeds, "let us hold on in the right way. Let us press toward the mark of our high calling in Christ Jesus. In due season we shall reap if we faint not. That God may bless you and yours is my earnest hope, and I would fain have it my constant prayer."

On the death of the father in 1830 the family removed to Edinburgh, and here the education of the boy Charles was carried on regularly till 1840; first in a private school, and then at the Academy. His talents at this period, as before intimated, do not appear to have been in an extraordinary degree conspicuous; that which chiefly distinguished him was a singular guilelessness, great simplicity of character, and most scrupulous conscientiousness. Some persons might have said that he was not manly enough, too girl-like, too soft, too ready to allow his tears to flow on a slight provocation; but there was nevertheless the real manliness, which is ever considerate of the feelings of others, and which shrinks from everything mean and unworthy. On one occasion Charles and his companions were competing for a prize; the prize composition was an essay on some school-subject, and it was a question whether books of reference might or might not be used; the other boys used them freely, but Charles doubted, and abstained; he lost the prize, but the gentleman who gave it, and who heard the circumstances under which Charlie's essay had been produced, marked his approbation by an extra prize.

I think I shall be pardoned if I introduce here two or three short extracts from a journal kept by the sister of whom mention has been already made, as they will not only throw a light upon the Bishop's boyish days, but also shew that even then this keensighted sister saw the shadow of her brother's future superiority.

"G—— (a brother older than Charles by six years) came with me to do some arithmetic, and seems sincerely anxious to improve, but was obliged to defer a satisfactory solution of his difficulties till Charlie should come home. G.'s affectionate respect for Charlie's talents and character is really beautiful, and often strikes me. When I first proposed a few days ago to call in Charlie's assistance at the arithmetic, and gently expressed a hope that G—— would not have any uncomfortable feeling about it, he exclaimed, Oh dear, I would not scorn to learn *anything* of Charlie."

Again: "Charlie is much occupied about learning Hebrew. I consulted Bishop Walker on his behalf: he has taken a desire to learn it systematically, and has been for nine months devoting a portion of his playhours to it; he is anxious to have a grammar, and to do the thing methodically. His reasons were very sensible: 'At present grammars are no drudgery to me, on the contrary I should feel it rather an amusement, and could easily give half an hour in the evening to it. If I were to wait until I am obliged to learn it, the taste for grammars may perhaps have worn off.'"

I apprehend that in this boyish desire to learn Hebrew we may trace, not the mere love of language, which did not at all belong to his mind, but the conscientious wish to fit himself for the Ministry, to which he looked forward as his calling from a very early period.

Again: "His selection of books to take to the Highlands is what one would not expect a boy to choose for the holydays: Euclid: his prize (a book on science): Mental Improvement: Bible: Prayer-book: an elementary book of science which he has studied long ago and wishes to revise......He is most keen about Euclid, and it is a characteristic trait of him, that after returning from the Exhibition (receiving his prize and aiding in applauding others who received theirs), he quietly told his news, and then sat down to study Euclid."

Here is a peep at another side of his mind.

"He is rather defective in imagination. In scenery he requires to be urged and reminded to admire the beauties of nature, and from want of habit lets them pass unobserved. His turn of opinion is calculating, and naturally his observation is directed only to subjects giving food for such reflections. Fine mountain views he admires when pointed out, but they do not of themselves strike him. He himself told me in the most simple naïve manner, 'Only think of my stupidity; when I went to the top of one of the high hills near Inverie, I quite forgot to look at the view which I went on purpose to see; but I just sat down a little and ate my cake, and came down again.'"

Speaking of his rapid improvement at school, the sister says:

"Certainly his mind is wonderfully acute, and he

has the happy faculty of conveying information with the same clearness as it has to his own mind....His remarkable modesty of disposition deceives those who do not know him intimately....His ever active mind never seems to tire, but even when his body is weary, he is still equally keen to work. When S——[1] is not disposed to work longer, he goes to A——, who is anxious to improve in arithmetic; if she fail him he goes to work problems on the globes with ——; yet there is a total absence of pretension and a perfect equilibrium."

One more extract from this journal.

"Charlie's eyes so bad; confined to bed. S—— sat with him in the forenoon, working problems in algebra, &c. Charlie's mind fully occupied in assisting in their solution, and not a murmur because his blind condition prevented his having the power of writing them or drawing the figures. At present these problems are the greatest source of interest that he has."

These notices of the Bishop's boyhood, it will be observed, are not *ex post facto:* they are memoranda made at the time, and they agree admirably well with the character developed in later years, as known to myself and others: the same gentleness, the same simplicity, and the same activity of mind, shewing its real superiority, in boyhood as in manhood, chiefly in the direction of abstract mathematical reasoning.

In 1840 Charles was sent to the Grange School near Sunderland, then under Dr Cowan. Here his mathe-

[1] A sailor brother, seven years older than himself, lost at sea in 1842.

matical tastes and powers appear to have been still further developed, and it became more evident that Greek and Latin were not the subjects in which he was most capable of obtaining University distinction. It was finally determined that he should proceed to Cambridge. I have before me several letters written home during this school period, but they contain nothing sufficiently striking or characteristic to persuade me to pause upon them. Neither have I been able to recover many stories of his school-days; but I have met with one which appears to me sufficiently characteristic to be worthy of a place in this memoir: of its general truth I have no doubt, though I have endeavoured in vain to obtain a version, for the accuracy of which in all particulars I can vouch. The story is as follows:—A smaller boy having on one occasion offended Mackenzie, and committed some act of aggression for which according to the usual code of schoolboy law he deserved "a licking," Mackenzie quietly took the boy aside and remonstrated with him, pointed out to him how much in the wrong he had been, and by his gentle behaviour at length moved the offender to tears.

Dr Dawson Turner, now head-master of the Royal Institution School at Liverpool, but a master at the Grange School in Bishop Mackenzie's school-days has favoured me with a letter, from which I will give an extract. After remarking that Mackenzie's talent was almost wholly mathematical, and that he never could have been made a very good scholar, Dr Turner adds, "In divinity, with me, Mackenzie always did very well, and gave promise of future ability. I remember him most as a very pleasant, good tempered, jolly sort of boy, very fond of athletic exercises, and one of the best oars in the two four-oars I got up and taught the fellows to row in, during my mastership at the Grange. He was a very good foot-ball player too. As I did not myself reside in the school-house, I saw but little of him except in school-hours and in the play-ground; but this much I well remember, that he was one of the very few, out of the very many with whom I have worked my hardest and best, that ever shewed any gratitude for the pains taken with them, and took the trouble of keeping up a kindly acquaintance in after years with their former schoolmaster. Some time after I had left the Grange School, Mackenzie, with one or two other old pupils of mine at Cambridge, sent me a present of books, and I have still a large and handsome knife that he gave me on getting his scholarship."

I conclude this chapter with a reminiscence which has been kindly furnished by the Rev. J. Erskine Clarke, vicar of St Michael's, Derby, and a contemporary of Bishop Mackenzie at the Grange School. It will be observed that there is a little discrepancy between the recollections of Dr Turner and Mr Clarke on the subject of athletic exercises; but I give them as they have come into my hands, observing that the discrepancy is apparent rather than real.

"I remember well Charles Mackenzie at the Grange School, Bishopwearmouth. He was not however a hero among school-boys, though he afterwards proved himself so true a hero among men. He lacked that dash and self-assertion which are requisite to give a boy a leading place amongst his fellows. Moreover, Mackenzie was no cricketer; nor indeed much given to athletic exercise at all.

"My own most vivid remembrance of him is that of seeing him walking up and down by a hedgeside in a remote part of the playground with his arm over the shoulder of his cousin John Forbes, and often with some younger lad walking on the other side of him listening to their talk.

"At the same time when he did join in any games, he did so with a right goodwill. I can recall him to my mind making vigorous rushes at foot-ball, or working hard in the Fives Court, and he was always one of every party of bathers.

"At lessons he was always studious and attentive, though his diffidence and shyness prevented his doing himself full justice in the class. He was one of the editors of a school-magazine, but the two volumes of it contain only a few lines by himself, and they are of a mathematical character.

"The example that he set during his stay at the Grange was thoroughly good. I never remember hearing him found fault with, and (what could not be said of many of his contemporaries) I cannot remember his doing anything which if known would have deserved rebuke. I have no doubt that Mackenzie's society influenced to their highest good those boys who were much with him, and I believe that even the most graceless lads, who would have spoken of him as rather *soft* and very *slow*, would have acknowledged and in their hearts have honoured his gentle goodness and his unfailing kindliness of temper, always ready with a smile to make his own pleasure give way to that of others;—the germ of that self-sacrificing love which afterwards deprived the Church Militant of one of the most faithful of her soldiers, and gave to Africa another Martyr's grave."

CHAPTER II.

COLLEGE LIFE—UNDERGRADUATE.

IN the year 1844 Mackenzie removed from the Grange School, and came into residence as a Pensioner of S. John's College, Cambridge, in October. S. John's has, as all Cambridge men know, a high reputation for mathematical vigour, and was selected on this account as Mackenzie's College. He found however, when he came into actual residence and was made acquainted with the rules of his College, that as a Scotchman he would labour under great disadvantages, and would in fact be ineligible to a fellowship[1]; he consequently made up his mind to "migrate" to Caius College, which he did in the Easter term of 1845.

I was myself a fellow of Caius College, and holding office as Mathematical Lecturer, at the time of Mackenzie's migration. Rumour told us that a very clever Johnian had come amongst us, and there was I think a little jealousy excited by the news: the College

[1] This restriction is now removed. The Cambridge Calendar informs us that "the Fellowships and Scholarships are open to all British subjects without any restriction or appropriation."

was itself stocked with very promising freshmen, as was demonstrated by the final result of the Senate House Examination in 1848, and there was a natural tendency to look with dissatisfaction upon the arrival of a man from another College, whose accession was understood to be due to the fact that Scotch blood excluded him from the emoluments of S. John's. This circumstance would hardly be worth recording, except for the sake of appending this remark, that if any jealousy of the new comer did exist it rapidly vanished under the influence of his genial presence. Mackenzie soon became a favourite in the College, as he well deserved to be.

In speaking of my own personal knowledge of Mackenzie I may here state by the way, that going out of residence in the summer of 1845 I had little opportunity of becoming intimately acquainted with him as a member of the College. I examined him at the end of his first year, and remember well the decided superiority which he evinced in his treatment of a problem paper, which it fell to my lot to set; but owing to circumstances, which it is not necessary here to explain, I saw little or nothing of him again until the period of his B.A. degree.

The story of Mackenzie's undergraduate life cannot therefore be given from personal recollection; but in truth the most important portion of it will be told by himself; he was in the habit of writing with great openness to his sisters, especially to the eldest sister, spoken of in the preceding chapter, and from some of his own letters the reader will be able to gather more surely than from any other source an account of his inner life and feelings. The reader will also see how early and how earnestly he looked forward to the sacred office to which he had devoted himself, and how anxious he was to lose no time in preparing himself for it.

LETTER I.

(*To his Eldest Sister.*)

MY DEAREST ——,

Many thanks for your kind and most acceptable letter. After I had sent my letter to the post, I began to wonder what you would think of it, and half to wish to have it back again. Soon after I left home to go to Grange I began to think that I must learn to rest on One higher, and more constantly present, than any one on this earth could be, for sympathy and assistance in the struggle of life: and this led me to what I now think an error, trying to avoid to a certain extent any communication, especially correspondence, on religious subjects. For I don't know whether I am of a more sympathetic nature than other people, but I do think that as long as I am in the body I must be influenced very much for good or ill by intercourse with others; and why should I shut all the avenues of the former only to give the full advantage of the influence to the other?

As to books, I have taken to Leighton again, in consequence of the high praise which a friend gave him the other day, and I like him quite as well as ever. Also I have asked the loan of Manning's sermons.

* * * * *

My mathematical studies are getting on pretty fairly now, though not quite perfectly. The fact is, I sometimes think I have lost that engrossing interest in the subject which I once felt. But then, again, I am not sure that it may not be as well that this should be so: for other things of greater importance will soon become my daily business, and it might have distracted me.

And now to come to the next subject of your letter.

* * * * *

[His sister had recommended him to make application to a clergyman to allow him to assist in pastoral work: and he accordingly made application to a Fellow of the College, the Rev. W. B. Hopkins, now Vicar of Wisbech, who then held a curacy in Cambridge.]

* * * * *

He at once said, "Oh you wish to go among the poor, do you? then I think I can give you a little work to do;" and he went on to describe a set of little houses in the suburbs[1], where a number of old women live, who are supported by a benefit society, and who are a long way from their parish-church; and when I afterwards said that my idea was to go with some Clergyman, he offered to let me go with him some day. So I thankfully accepted his offer, though it had never occurred to me to ask him.

This morning he told me to come to him at eleven, and we went to see a woman who had a very bad cough, and had been in bed for a year. When we came out again, I had quite made up my mind that it was not a mere accident that I had asked his advice on the point. He was so kind and shewed me a book giving practical directions on the subject of pastoral visitation, and promised to give me a copy. Altogether I must bless God, and thank you for the suggestion of what will I am sure by His aid be a most useful and instructive and corrective exercise; and by Hopkins' account of the poor old women (about whom, however, he is to make more particular enquiry), if I go once or twice in a week and read to them, it will be giving them what they have no means of getting at present.

* * * * *

[1] The Victoria Asylum. The description of the Asylum, given in the letter, is not quite accurate.

This plan for the visitation of the aged inmates of the Victoria Asylum was carried out with the consent of the clergyman of the parish, and was a source of great comfort to the old people and great satisfaction to Mackenzie himself. The following is his own modest account of his early labours.

LETTER II.

(To the same.)

My dearest ——,

* * * * *

What I wanted particularly to speak to you about is, the reading at the Asylum to the old people. I fancy what you thought of was, my going on a week-day into a house, and being quiet and simple; but somehow Hopkins seemed to think that going up on a Sunday afternoon and getting them all together, (there are twelve sets of rooms, and very often a husband and wife, at any rate more than one in a set of rooms, so that the number is about twenty,) would be a good plan, and at the time I left it quite in his hands, and agreed to whatever he thought best. The consequence was, that, after having been up once without and once with my Bible in my pocket, I went up last Sunday at two. But it was so new a position, and I could not feel, (what I imagine must be a great support in the pulpit,) that I was God's appointed servant, only doing my duty in being His ambassador. On the contrary, it seemed as if I had undertaken it of myself, and I could not fancy that anything I could say would be of any use. I had spent some hours in preparation before going there, on the two previous days, and on the Sunday morning itself; but when I got there, though the number was small, in consequence of all that could get out to church having gone there for the Sacrament, yet I got quite red in the face, and after reading the chapter (S. John xiv.), I went over it again, throwing in a few remarks where I could. Then we knelt down, and read some of the collects and prayers from the Prayer-book. On the whole, I should have felt perfectly miserable, if I had not remembered, that lame and wretched as my endeavour had been, it was better than nothing; for I had read the words of the Bible and used the prayers of holy men, and that if I had not gone, no one else would; so that I was not stepping in any one's way. But the worst of it all is, that this week having determined to go on Wednesday to see one or two of the old people quietly, when the time came I felt disinclined, and went out for a walk instead, though my conscience told me that I was robbing God of what I had devoted to Him. * * * It was curious that I perceived, or fancied I perceived, a change come over me soon after, and that night and the next morning I was quite out of sorts and disinclined for duty of any kind. * * * To-day I cannot have been altogether alone in fixing my resolution to go up. And when I got there, I went to a very nice family, an old man and woman, and two young women their daughters: we went through the 32nd Psalm; and I came away, not much happier, but thankful that I had been spared the pain, which I am sure I should have felt, if I had quenched the resolution to good which was just formed within me. My dear ——, pray for me, that my faith may be strengthened and my love warmed, for that is, I think, my great want.

* * * * *

I will ask the reader to note an expression in the foregoing letter, which may possibly have escaped him, but which he will find to contain the motive principle of Mackenzie's conduct in the higher path of duty to which he was afterwards called: *if I had not gone, no one else would:* there is not the hint of a feeling that in ministering to the poor folks at the Asylum he was doing anything extraordinary, or doing his work better than others could have done it: on the other hand, he is very humble indeed as to the work and the way in which it was done, and only takes comfort from the thought that if he had not done it, *no one else would.* It will be found hereafter that this same thought, the thought that there was work to be done for God and apparently no one ready to do it, impelled him to leave all and follow Christ into foreign lands.

It will be judged, from the anxiety which Mackenzie felt to be doing something in the way of humble ministration, that he kept his eye steadily upon that work of the ministry for which he considered himself to be in a state of preparation, and towards which he desired all his reading and study to converge. At the same time he did not forget that University work was his principal work while *in statu pupillari,* and he was wise enough to perceive that it is a short-sighted policy to neglect the full training of the mental powers under the tempting notion of doing God service. I suspect however that, like many other earnest young men, Mackenzie sometimes felt himself pressed by his feelings in this direction: in one of his undergraduate letters he writes thus:

Mr R.'s letter arrived * * * It was quite general, recommending strict and full attention to the University course. I answered it as well as I could, trying to throw in a spirit of acquiescence in his principle, that a young man's chief object up here should be his degree. This I presume is because it is supposed to be the best preparation for his profession; for I cannot see how it is else. However, *prac-*

2

tically I am convinced it is: that is, my theoretical doubts, if they exist, do not, I think, interfere with any wish and intention to work hard, as in my case at least it is plainly *a* duty, even if it is not the chief one.

Accordingly he worked hard; and when I have said this, and have tempered the view of a man given chiefly to mathematics by the qualifying thought of those old people at the Asylum with their kind reader and ministering friend, I have said almost all that is necessary of Mackenzie's undergraduate career. I will, however, throw in a few extracts from his letters, which will, as I believe, be not without interest. The letters are all addressed to sisters, and are written in the tone of confidential intercourse. The portions which are here preserved may be regarded as straws, shewing the direction of the stream of Mackenzie's thoughts at this period.

* * * * *

Your letter has given me great pleasure on a second perusal, and indeed, dear A——, if we could only see the things which are behind this temporal universe, and which will be made manifest to us when it is dissolved, how trifling should we account those things which now occupy so much of our attention; and how very different those things look, when we try to look through them, and when we allow the light and glory of those things which are naturally unseen to beam through them! And if the glory of the unseen world is such as to illuminate earthly beauties with such a heavenly radiance, how surpassingly glorious will be the vision, which shall assuredly burst upon our eyes, when death shall have dissolved the thick film which now prevents our seeing clearly.

* * * * *

There is little doing here different from what I have already described. I have picked up the beginning of an acquaintance with one of my fellow-pupils, C—, and expect to find in him a friend. We agreed one evening in lamenting the fact that a man is constantly hoping that he has found perfection in an acquaintance, in whom on after and further knowledge he finds just faults enough to spoil the delightful delusion: and I have been endeavouring to moderate my hopes of his own perfection by this very maxim.

* * * * *

There is the chapel-bell going; so I shall not attempt to finish this. I missed going to chapel this morning for the first time since I came up. The fact is I had a very slight attack of cold. There is the chapel-bell stopping.

This is to-morrow evening, and we have just come out of hall; so I'll go on. I truly sympathise with you, my dear E——, in your regrets on the shortlived effects of God's dispensations to us, whether of warning and pleading as in sickness, or of mercy and love in revealing His mercy to us. We might almost be tempted to think it would be better if we were not such frail fallible erring creatures as we are. But all things are in His hands, and all these things are working together for our ultimate good. And what, I think, we should do, is neither to sit still and fancy He will do all for us, (for though it be true that except the Lord keep the city their labour is but vain that guard it, yet He will not guard those who are careless themselves,) nor must we be utterly discouraged, though Satan will often whisper that God has forsaken us. But let us look to Him as a loving Father, who occasionally allows us to withdraw our hand from His, that we may know and feel how weak our tottering steps are, and how helpless we are without Him.

And now do not fancy that I am preaching to you in a Pharisaical spirit. But my idea is that since we are so often reading things which draw away our minds from God, and as our intercourse with society generally has this tendency, it is well occasionally to try and help each other on our heavenward course, instead of throwing entanglements in each other's way; and (unlike the literal case) this assisting each other will give ourselves a "fillip" instead of detaining us.

* * * * *

You know the prayer for the Church Militant in the Communion Service. We have it every Sunday in the College Chapel, and on my more attentive days I do enjoy it so much. I know none which give such a delightful view of the communion, in feeling at least, between the Church Militant and the Church Triumphant.

* * * * *

Since my return I have not been killing myself with work. I have been reading a little in the morning, taking good exercise in the afternoon, when I could, and playing chess all the evening. The latter we have been playing under a curious modification: a *four* game: two and two partners, playing round in turns, each with his own set of men on an enlarged board. If one man is checkmated, he does not play any more, and his pieces stand on the board and cannot be taken, till his partner takes the piece which checks him, or forces its owner to withdraw it, when the dead man is restored and plays on again all right. The games are very long and sometimes tedious, especially if you are mated. We had not time to finish a second the other night between six and twelve! It is rather a waste of time perhaps, but then this is the vacation.

* * * * *

I am going to set to work for the evening in a few minutes, but I think a word or two to you first would be pleasant. This has been the first week of work this term, and at the beginning I set myself a sort of scheme of what I was to do all the term; and in looking back I find I have lost about three or four hours of mathematics, no chapels, no exercise, and no sleep: so you see that is pretty well. I am not at all inclined to work to-night, but I suppose there is no help for it.

* * * * *

I need not say how fully I feel for and with you in your account of your own distress, and I think one consolation which you evidently had in your mind is, that this world is appointed as a scene of warfare and struggle. Though Keble's lines apply directly to acting clergy alone, yet the argument is the same to all:

> But chiefly ye should lift your gaze
> Above the world's uncertain haze,
> And look with calm unwavering eye
> On the bright fields beyond the sky,
> Ye, who your Lord's commission bear,
> His way of mercy to prepare:
> Angels He calls ye: be your strife
> To lead on earth an Angel's life.
>
> Think not of rest; though dreams be sweet,
> Start up, and ply your heavenward feet!
> Is not God's oath upon your head,
> Ne'er to sink back on slothful bed,
> Never again your loins untie,
> Nor let your torches waste and die,
> Till, when the shadows thickest fall,
> Ye hear your Master's midnight call?

And then think of the short, the very short, time it can last. How we shall wish one day that we had some further opportunity of working in this life for our Master's glory! I do not know what the commentators say, but it struck me the other day that this might be the meaning when it is said in the Psalms, "No man praiseth Thee in the grave, and shall the dust give thanks, or shall it declare Thy truth?" For we shall give thanks to Him in the grave, but not declare His truth to man. However, this may be straining the text.

* * * * *

I look forward now a good deal to being at work in a parish. I have seen a very little of the sort of thing, and this my present work [at the Asylum] is as good a preparation as anything I could do in the meantime. But it will be much greater and much grander than anything we can conceive.

* * * * *

In January 1848 Mackenzie graduated with Mathematical honors; in Cambridge language he was second Wrangler, the Senior Wrangler being Mr Todhunter of S. John's College. With this amount of success he was abundantly satisfied, and it only remained that he should obtain one of the two prizes, called Dr Smith's prizes, which are given to two of the most distinguished mathematicians of the year, in order to complete his honours. This prize, however, he was not fortunate enough to obtain. As it happened that I was myself one of the examiners, acting as deputy for the then Lucasian Professor, Dr King, President of Queens' College, I may perhaps be permitted in a few words to explain the manner of Mackenzie's failure. Three papers were set, one by Dr Whewell, Master of Trinity College, another by Professor Challis, and the third by myself. No one of the examiners had any doubt as to the propriety of assigning the first prize to Mr Todhunter; but with regard to the second the results of the papers were not unanimous; in one Mackenzie was admitted to be first, in another Mr Barry, fourth

Wrangler, was allowed to have surpassed him, and in the third the examiner was unable to say which of the two was the superior; under these circumstances, the examiners, having had two meetings and taken time to re-examine the papers, considered that the case was one in which they were bound to act upon a provision in Dr Smith's will, by which in case of equality he desires that men of Trinity College shall have a preference for his prizes. The second prize was accordingly adjudged to Mr Barry. Immediately on knowing the result Mackenzie wrote a most friendly letter to his successful rival, and remarked to one of his sisters that "he felt it was much better for him that it should be so: one was so apt to be elated and hurt by too much success."

The following is his letter to Mr Barry.

LETTER III.

HARCUS, *Tuesday.*

MY DEAR BARRY,

Your kind note which reached me this morning was the first intimation I had of the result, and I must confess that at the moment a shade came over my face. But when I came to consider the matter, I came to the conclusion that it was very much better as it is. For myself I am convinced that what I had already gained is enough for my weak head to stand, though some people might fancy it was not much turned by it; and this now sets you in your proper place, and shews openly what all in Cambridge would believe without it.

Do not fancy that I think myself a disappointed man in the smallest degree: the prize itself is of course nothing;

the being bracketed second is as good in reality as being second with a gap below one; and I think my consideration for others, though it is not always so great as it should be, may well lead me to rejoice in sympathy with you.

I am really very much obliged to you for writing. It reproves myself; for I left many letters unanswered when I left Cambridge, on the plea of being busy with examinations. And now, my dear fellow, let me encourage you for the next examination[1]. If you don't think of the happiness we are having, who have done with this kind of work, you will long for it less, though certainly I am transgressing my own rule in thus reminding you; and finally let me excuse myself for the length of this epistle, on the score of a natural clumsiness of expression,

And believe me to be

Your sincere friend,

C. F. M.

An amusing anecdote may be recorded in connection with this Smith's Prize examination. Mackenzie had gone from Cambridge before the result of the examination was known, leaving word with his friends to telegraph the result to York, where he would inquire for the message, while himself *en route* to Edinburgh. Arriving at York he went to the Telegraph Office and asked anxiously for the message; he was informed that a message had arrived, but was of so strange a character that the clerk had telegraphed for a repetition of it, thinking that there must be some error. "Let me see it," said Mackenzie. Whereupon the clerk handed him the following charming piece of English. "The Muffs have postponed the decision till to-morrow—Keep your tail up."

[1] The examination for the Classical Tripos, in which Mr Barry soon after gained first Class honours.

I am not sure that the second word of the message was not spelt in a somewhat unusual and eccentric manner, namely, *Mough.* Anyhow the telegraphic official was puzzled; but Mackenzie relieved his mind by assuring him that *he* understood what was meant, and carried away the facetious but unsatisfactory message.

Another anecdote connected with this period of Mackenzie's life will here find a fitting place; and I the rather record it, because it is highly illustrative of his character and the principles of his conduct. It so happened that the year of Mackenzie's Bachelor of Arts' degree coincided with the 500th Anniversary of the foundation of the College: it was a fortunate coincidence, for Caius College had done itself in that year very great credit: it numbered no less than nine wranglers, the 2nd, 8th, 10th, 11th, 12th, 18th, 25th, 34th and 38th out of a list of thirty-eight, an achievement I believe unexampled in the history of any of the smaller colleges. The 500th Anniversary of the foundation of the College was the cause of a grand dinner, at which many pleasant toasts were proposed, as befitted the occasion. Amongst them the then Bishop of Norwich (Dr Stanley) proposed, in a very warm-hearted speech, the health of Mackenzie and the other wranglers who had just brought so much glory to their College. Whereupon Mackenzie was compelled unexpectedly to make a speech; and the speech he made was very short and very blunt, but so thoroughly to the purpose, and delivered with such simplicity and such beaming good-nature, that it elicited thunders of applause. He said that "the Bishop of Norwich had spoken of his fellows and himself in terms far too flattering: that they did not deserve the praise he had been kind enough to award them: for *they had only done what was natural under the circumstances,*"—the remainder of the speech, if remainder there was, was lost in a torrent of jovial cheering and approbation, and Mackenzie found to his surprise, that instead of blundering in his part, as I doubt not he had expected to do, he had made one of the most successful hits of the evening. He spoke however in jest what was true, so far as he himself was concerned, in sober earnest: it was always his way to do what was natural under any circumstances in which he found himself placed: he never strove to seem anything that he was not, or to do anything which it seemed beside his duty to do: he was always easy, always natural, and herein lay the secret of that great charm of his character to which I am confident that all those who knew him well would bear the most abundant testimony.

Mr Barry has kindly furnished the following personal recollections of this period of Bishop Mackenzie's life.

"I first became acquainted with Bishop Mackenzie in October 1845, when we were undergraduates together at Cambridge. I do not think that I enjoyed in his case that special intimacy, which is given only to one or two friends, and which, at that time of life especially, makes those friends the sharers of almost every thought or feeling in a man's mind. But, from October 1845 till January 1848 we met constantly in Mr Hopkins' mathematical class. In that class (which in our year included the first four Wranglers) we had daily opportunities of judging of each other, not only as to intellectual powers, but also, to some extent, as to temper and character; and the two Long Vacations which we spent together at Cambridge naturally threw us more upon one another for companionship. All this gave opportunity of mutual knowledge; and Mackenzie's character was one which made such knowledge in his case both easy and attractive.

"I should perhaps leave Mr Hopkins to speak of his mathematical powers; but there may be some peculiar interest in the opinion formed of a man by his contemporaries, and of that I can certainly bear my testimony. What we were struck with was the union in him of great quickness of conception with an unusual comprehensiveness and solidity of understanding. I never remember to have heard from him a single answer which betrayed ignorance or misconception of a principle. He had the true mathematical faculty, the results of which are often simulated in examinations by great powers of memory and judgment; but which, unlike its counterfeit, has real capacity for origination and discovery. In fact, that very quickness and originality seemed to us occasionally to turn him out of the beaten track which leads to the Senate-House. It was not in his way to despise regular system; but he seemed to forget or to ignore it, and would obtain results without that regular evolution of intermediate steps, on which Cambridge Examinations naturally and rightly insist.

"Except in relation to mathematics, I do not remember to have been impressed by his ability. He was no great talker on general subjects; I do not think that he ever spoke at the Union, or took part in the discussion of the great religious questions which excited most of us so strongly. In the ways, therefore, which most bring out a man's ability independently of the course of University study, he did not shew much of what was in him. It was a subject of some surprise to us that such was the case. I hardly know now to what cause to refer it. In general intercourse we were most struck with the remarkable simplicity, sincerity, and kindliness of his character, the utter absence in him of anything like conceit or presumption, or that straining after effect which every University-man knows as the common temptation of the leading men of a year. But I do not remember to have noticed in him any decided line of opinion or thought; or to have been strongly impressed by evidence of any marked and predominant influence of religion upon his life. Such influence may have existed, and been kept in reserve; certainly we always thought of him as a religious man, and the groundwork of a true Christian character was to be seen in his almost childlike simplicity, honesty, and kindliness of heart. But it did not, so far as I know, shine out clear above all other influences, as it did in after life. I heard of his devotion to the missionary work with some surprise, surprise (that is) that the impulse to it had been received, but not surprise that he should count cheap his own gifts and labours in any cause which he had once taken up. I heard afterwards that the impulse had been given through the sermons of one not unlike himself in simplicity and practical earnestness. But by whatever means received, it, and the train of thought which led to it, seemed to make a wonderful change in his whole character."

The reader who has perused the portions of letters printed in this chapter may perhaps regard with some astonishment the statements made in the preceding paragraph. But I have thought it well to give the two testimonies side by side: his own letters shew what was going on within, and prove that a strong impulse of religious activity, which had in it the germ of missionary enterprise, had already touched Mackenzie's heart: the reminiscences of his fellow-student shew how modest and unobtrusive his religious feeling was. Some persons may say that it would have been well that his light should have been made to shine more distinctly: possibly this may be true; but the point is not worth arguing, since my purpose must be to represent Mackenzie, not as he might have been, but as he was: yet this ought to be said, that the retiring modesty and unobtrusiveness of his religious character was probably that which, more than anything else, gave him an influence for good: there was nothing to repel: all was brightness, and gentleness, and sunshine: and it was scarcely possible to be in his society without coming to the conclusion, that he had found out the secret of life, and that it would be well to be like him.

CHAPTER III.

COLLEGE LIFE—HOLY ORDERS.

I HAVE not said anything hitherto of Bishop Mackenzie's personal appearance. As we have now arrived at a period of his life, when his outward man had become very much what it continued to be during his brief sojourn upon earth, it may be well in this place to devote a few lines to the description of his person, for the benefit of those amongst my readers, who will know him only through the imperfect medium of this memoir.

He was tall, nearly six feet high, and very well made. He had great muscular strength, and remarkable power of endurance. The portrait given in this volume gives a fair representation of his face: it was not in any critical sense handsome, but it was such a face as one loves to look upon. There was in it an exceeding gentleness of expression; indeed it appeared to be a face which could not frown: it was withal very thoughtful, and had a certain quiet air of deliberation, which his friends will well remember. His eyes were not large, or rather they were too small, but they were very bright, and had a pleasing expression quite peculiar to themselves. A great deal of courage and determination was expressed by his mouth. His voice was very musical and pleasant, with a little of the Scottish accent, especially when he was animated. His forehead was fine and well developed, but perhaps somewhat exaggerated by his early baldness. On the whole his outward appearance suited very well with his inward character; strong, manly, active, enduring, yet gentle and preeminently free from guile. He was rapid in his movements, a very fast walker, fond of violent exercise, especially of boating; calculated by his good health, powerful frame, and excellent spirits, to enjoy life physically as completely as it can be enjoyed. He sometimes overtasked his strength, and appeared for a while oppressed and weary; but he soon rallied, and never lost his calm placidity of temper. During his residence in Cambridge I believe his good health never varied, and his bodily strength (as will appear in the sequel) underwent little or no diminution during life. In his last sojourn in Africa he allowed his beard to grow; a very necessary precaution in the prospect of the life which he was to lead.

After taking his Bachelor of Arts' degree, Mackenzie followed the course into which a number of young men are tempted year by year in Cambridge; that is to say, he soon became a fellow of his College, worked as lecturer or assistant tutor, and employed a certain portion of his time with private pupils. Meanwhile he never allowed himself to look upon this kind of life as anything but a temporary and preparatory arrangement; he ever kept his eye fixed upon the Christian Ministry as his work and calling, and endeavoured to fit himself for his future character, both by study and by practical assistance in such spiritual works as he found lying in his way. Thus he undertook the management of a Sunday school, he took an active part in the working of a Mendicity Society, served as secretary to the Cambridge Board of Education, and helped to carry on the Cambridge Industrial School. In fact, any one who had a work of Christian love and practical usefulness in hand knew always where to look for help: Mackenzie was always ready to take a part, and though in some respects his habits were not those of a man of business, being deficient in orderly arrangement and economy of time, still there was a heartiness and simplicity of purpose, and an unfailing supply of good humour, which made him a delightful comrade in any work, whether secular or religious.

When I speak of his habits as being in some respects not those of a man of business, I only say that to which he himself frequently bears testimony in his letters. In one of them he alludes humorously to a saying current amongst his friends, to the effect that he had a marvellous facility for getting into "gigantic messes," and an equal facility for getting out of them. The fact is that he was always ready to consent to undertake any kind of useful or benevolent work which was pressed upon him; and not unfrequently the engagements which he contracted were incompatible, or so nearly approaching to incompatibility, that it would seem impossible that they could be all fulfilled. Yet somehow he contrived to do what he promised, and to perform works which men technically more business-like would perhaps have failed to accomplish.

Correspondence was not his strong point; at least, his correspondence was not regular and not systematical; and as a minor defect I may mention that the greater number of his college letters are not dated as to time, so that they cannot be quite certainly arranged. A considerable number of letters, written to his sisters, have however been placed in my hands, and I shall endeavour, as far as may be, to make them tell the main tale of this portion of his life. The tale will be very simple and uneventful, and will be chiefly interesting as exhibiting the quiet and modest manner, in which the great purpose of leaving all and following Christ gradually ripened in his soul.

The following letter addressed to his eldest sister will shew something of the inner workings of his mind soon after the period of his B.A. degree. Bearing in mind the peculiarly close relation of love and confidence in which Mackenzie stood to this sister, as already mentioned, the reader will believe that he has in this letter a genuine peep into the writer's heart, and will probably be struck with the honesty of purpose and the humility which it reveals. The letter, though undated, may be assigned from internal evidence to April 1848. On May 4 of that year Mackenzie was appointed one of the secretaries to the Cambridge Board of Education, in the place of the Rev. J. J. Smith; he held the office until 1855, when he was compelled to resign by his departure for Africa. This is the appointment to which allusion is made in the letter.

LETTER IV.

CAIUS COLLEGE. *Friday.*

MY DEAR ——

I have been very remiss in my correspondence with every one this term, and perhaps with you it may partly have unconsciously arisen from my not having got quite into the sort of reading we thought of. This has arisen partly from my wishing to get on with my Hebrew, there being a class which I joined and found myself of course quite behind the rest; and I felt it due to them to work as hard as I could, to get up to them as soon as possible. But, besides this, I have not given nearly so long to divinity as we spoke of; for at first it was some little time before I got into the way of my work, and then when I had got started fairly boating soon began, and that occupied not only the middle of the day when we actually rowed, but the morning also, for we breakfasted together; and so I lost not only my hour of divinity or Leighton in the morning, but I am sorry to say sometimes even my time for reading and prayer; and that very soon cast a gloom and deadness on my whole life.

Still all this time I was obliged to give my energies during four hours of the day to my pupils.

* * * * *

It was strange that my work at the Asylum never became a drudgery or a trouble to me. Indeed, one day I put myself and the whole crew to considerable inconvenience on purpose that I might go up. But I think I was partly led to this by a lurking feeling of pride that I must not be remiss in a piece of business which I had voluntarily undertaken, and of which a good many people knew.

And now one consequence of all this has been, that I

have got the vaguest ideas of what is a man's duty and what is not. One thing I clearly see, that it is a duty to study the Bible; but I am losing interest in it. Then as to prayer, I often don't know what to pray for; and I feel sometimes as if I had no object in life. Now this looks, I think, very much like the state of a man who has not done his duty, and as if I ought to look at the text, "If any man will do His will," &c. But then the question comes back,—what *is* His will? I am not breaking any external law: I am going regularly to Chapel: and probably no one would find any fault with me who looked at me from without,—unless they charged me with a little indolence. But it is in the heart that the mischief lies, and I don't know what to do. I have not been thoroughly happy for some time, and have felt lowspirited for a day or two.

Sometimes I think that the preaching I hear here is too much about the feelings—talking about love and faith and hope—without speaking of duty.

* * * * *

Sometimes I feel almost inclined to repine at my lot because it is so prosperous, and to wish that I had some of those afflictions which are so often spoken of as necessary for men: but then I doubt whether it may not be that I should be unable to endure, and that God is sparing me till my strength is greater.

I do not think that the respect which is paid to "a good degree" is good for me. The other day, Smith, our late tutor, offered me an office which he had held, namely, one of the Secretaryships to the Cambridge Board of Education. At first I declined it, as mixing me up with men so much my seniors, and as pushing myself forward. But he overruled this objection by saying, that my *position* in the University was quite sufficient to justify it, and so by Hopkins' advice I accepted. I mention this to shew what I consider the idolatry of Mathematical and Classical talent which exists here.

* * * * *

If my poor head could stand it, it would be all very well as increasing one's influence over others.

I mentioned the fact of the vagueness of my ideas of duty and of the object of a man's life to —— and ——, two of my companions. The one said he believed it was common at our time of life to have doubts and difficulties, and they would wear off. The other became metaphysical, and got into the subject of the purposes of temptation, which he said was a mystery too deep for us to fathom.

On the whole I am inclined to think that I have taken my religion too much on trust; and I have trembled to think how little foundation I have laid to confront any doubts of the inspiration of the Bible, if such should arise in my mind. I have often laughed at the idea of doubting it, as if I could ever be such a fool; and I am half inclined to go into the question now.

* * * * *

Of the year 1848 I have hardly any other record beside the preceding, but I find in a letter to a sister the following pretty passage:

Do you remember the story of ——, on seeing the moon after his long journey, saying, *Eh! hoo far she's comed!* That has sometimes suggested to me the very consoling thought, that not only the sun and the moon, but a far greater than they, is as much in one place as in another; and that in the silent chamber, when the eyes are shut, one may make a home of every place: and surely that is the time when one more apparently and certainly breathes a true and real life. If the spirit of such moments were spread over our whole day, we should make a home wherever we went, or at least get glimpses of a home that is as near one place as another.

The following year is a still more complete blank as regards correspondence; at least, nothing has come into my hands serving to illustrate the general fact which I know from other sources, namely, that Mackenzie was leading a quiet, amiable, and useful life in College, lecturing most conscientiously, working vigorously with private pupils, taking his share in the work of the college-boat, and setting an admirable example to the young men above whom he was just one step removed in University standing. It is difficult to exaggerate the usefulness of such a life in Cambridge, while at the same time there is very little to be said about it. And there was this special excellence in the life and example of Mackenzie, that they could not fail to make piety popular; it was, I believe, impossible not to like him, and it was equally impossible not to respect him; and it may be said, without fear of contradiction from those who know the habits and atmosphere of Cambridge, that a young man of acknowledged intellectual ability, who is able to join together, without effort or ostentation, the reading of the Scriptures to aged people in an Asylum, or the teaching of a Sunday school, with the exercises of the river or the cricket-field, is beyond all others likely to influence for good the young members of the University.

The next letter belongs apparently to the summer of 1850; it refers to the "late interest in the Examinations," which must mean the College Examinations in the month of May, at the conclusion of the work of the Easter Term; and this consideration would seem to place the letter somewhere in the Long Vacation of that year. But Mackenzie's unfortunate carelessness in dating his letters makes it uncertain even to what year it belongs; the point is however of no great moment; it may suffice to say that he seems not to have accepted the offer made to him, the records of the school shewing that he never was actually superintendent. Pray observe, readers, the modesty with which he expresses a doubt, whether, if Mr Titcomb had known all, he would have offered him the situation. The letter is to his eldest sister.

LETTER V.

CAIUS COLLEGE. *Monday.*

MY DEAR ——,

* * * * *

The immediate object of my writing is to tell you of a proposal which was made to me the other day.

One of the suburbs of Cambridge, called Barnwell, is very thickly inhabited, and by poor people. There are two schools attached to the parish, and in one of these I taught for three or four Sundays this summer, when most of the teachers were gone away, for in it almost all the teachers are University men. This made my name known to the clergyman, Mr Titcomb, and about a fortnight ago he offered me the superintendentship of the Girls' school. He made the proposal to me verbally through Hopkins, who got me my post at the Asylum. Hopkins seemed inclined to dissuade me from accepting, because I should then have to leave the other—I mean the Asylum. But Mr Titcomb wrote me a very strong letter, requesting me to think of it. He asked me to breakfast yesterday morning, and then we went to the school. The duties are to be there twice on Sunday, to oversee the whole, and I suppose to take a class occasionally, and to conclude with a short address. Then during the week there would always be some children to see after, and some houses therefore to go to, and this would give a taste of parish visiting.

Now I want your advice. * * * * I will just give you my own ideas, and if you could manage to write soon, I should really like to hear what you think. I should not move from my present position, which I am getting to like better, without some positive reason. As far as I am concerned myself, the Sunday work would be longer. * * * * But then there would be the additional advantage of an insight into the working of a Sunday school. As to the week-day work, it would be about the same in time, perhaps a little more, but different in this respect, that there would be more going among people whom I did not know, and who did not know me, and would so far be more like my final parish-work. At first I thought this an advantage, but now I almost think it better to practise with people whom I have got to know a little, and not to dive at once into the full difficulties of visiting. Then as to whether I should be fitted for the position: Mr Titcomb thought at first that I had taught for a good while in another school, and perhaps if he had known, as he now does, that it was only for three or four days, he might not have made the offer.

So far it seems to me the question is pretty nearly balanced; and when I come to consider the two claims upon me as duties, it seems still pretty nearly equal. For I am engaged with the one at present. Yet Mr Titcomb is very pressing. He wishes to have a Bachelor of Arts, and not an Undergraduate; and it is not very easy to find a resident B.A. who would be willing to undertake the work. He says, if I decline, he has no other satisfactory course to fall back upon: the present superintendent has just been ordained, and has got a curacy. On the whole I am in great doubt. I had declined, you see, and now it is brought before me again. If an Undergraduate can be found to take my place at the Asylum, I almost think I shall go: and yet I am getting very fond of the old people, and I really think most of them like me; they might be shy with another, at any rate at first.

I am sorry to say that the late interest in the Examinations has too much directed my thoughts from other things. I never perceived at the time very distinctly that I had almost entirely discontinued reading Leighton, or anything of that sort. And then too they stopped morning Chapels, and that made my attendance then both less regular and less profitable: for it is a very different thing going to Chapel straight from your bed-room before breakfast, and coming away from a merry meeting of friends after dinner for the same purpose: and, as I always find, everything else went wrong at the same time. I did not regret that I could not see my old people during the Examination week: but now that the stress of that is over, I hope to be a little more regular; though I sometimes think, what is the use of a religion which yields in time of difficulty, and cannot keep straight except in time of ease and peace?

* * * * *

In the autumn of 1850 he made a tour in Switzerland, his first and only tour in that glorious country. Notwithstanding the natural deficiency of taste for scenery, of which he seems to have been accused in his younger days, he manifestly enjoyed this trip exceedingly. Several letters are before me, written with all that enthusiasm which a first acquaintance with the grander features of nature is almost sure to beget: there is in them, however, nothing so characteristic as to make me think it desirable to transfer their contents to these pages: Mackenzie performed no gigantic and unprecedented feat of mountaineering, but enjoyed himself in the well-worn path, which so many travellers tread year by year; visited Interlaken and the valley of Lauterbrunnen, passed over the Wengern Alp, and enjoyed Grindelwald, intended to go over the Strahleck and did not do it, slept on the summit of the Faulhorn, &c. &c. I may observe, however, that the letters give the impression, which I have had confirmed by actual testimony, that Mackenzie was a first-rate travelling companion: few things are more trying to the temper than partnership in travel: very good friends fall out under the influence of the small annoyances and unavoidable differences of opinion incident to this kind of partnership; and I have heard of two persons, who during a succession of summers started together for a pleasure trip, but never returned in company. Perhaps, therefore, this may be a not unfitting place for bearing testimony to Mackenzie's perfect serenity of temper in small things. I have seen him in many different circumstances, sometimes very annoying and trying, but I never upon one occasion saw his temper ruffled, or observed the slightest cloud of annoyance to settle upon his countenance. I may add, that in his Swiss letters one of the most prominent points is his anxiety about his travelling companions: no pleasure which he experienced himself seems to have made so much impression upon him as his regret at being compelled to be behind his time in an appointment to meet a friend in Lucerne, and his sorrow that the same friend should have been compelled through him to descend the Faulhorn in the dusk.

The year 1851 was the important year of ordination.

I have observed that from early youth Mackenzie had looked forward to holy orders as his final destination; he ever kept his eye steadily upon this goal; and he regarded his general education as valuable chiefly in the light of a preparation for the high office of the ministry. Consequently I find in his letters no doubts concerning the choice of a profession; his only question was how he could best prepare himself for an office for which he believed that he was chosen, but for the duties of which he felt himself inadequate and unworthy. He was ordained deacon on Trinity Sunday, by the Bishop of Ely.

The following is an extract from a letter to one of his sisters, shortly before his ordination.

LETTER VI.

As to myself, I am afraid, dear ——, there is much between what I am and what I was. And it arises I suppose from forgetting that "the violent take the kingdom by force;" for in a busy life like mine one must insist with oneself on having time for thought, and in this I have fallen into my natural defect of acting on impulse, and not on method and plan. I know you have warned me of this often, and I am writing now to make myself fancy you are speaking to me. It is not that my time goes away utterly wasted, for it never does that here, at least seldom, but that active employment for the mind has a greater charm for me than quietness and meditation; but I will try by God's aid to mend this.

I am in full swing at the school, and as I have not been out of Cambridge on Sunday since I came up in January, I have had little interruption.

* * * * *

It was about this time that my own intimacy with Mackenzie ripened; we were thrown much together as fellow-workers in the Cambridge Industrial School; this school was established for the purpose of rescuing poor boys from the dangers of idleness, and has proved, by God's blessing, a more efficient instrument of reformation and improvement than its first promoters had even ventured to hope. Mackenzie entered into the scheme with all his heart, and won the affections of master and boys by his genial kindness. A boy from this school accompanied him on his first voyage to Africa; the boy had had only slight opportunities of making his acquaintance, but when asked by the master whether he would be willing to go, he replied at once, "O, I would go anywhere with Mr Mackenzie." But I must not anticipate, and I will recall myself to the year 1851, by inserting an extract from the last letter which I can find written to his eldest sister before his ordination.

LETTER VII.

I am now looking forward to an end of my labours for this term. The College Examination begins on Monday and will be over on Friday the 6th, and then I shall have a few days to think of the Examination that is coming. I have to thank you, dear, for your sympathy with me now. It is indeed a time of important change, like an outdoor servant taken to live in the house, and give the whole attention instead of only a part to the Master's service. Not that I contemplate leaving College yet. I am convinced that much good may be done here, if one can only consider it as one's parish, and as this is not a very common light to regard an ordained fellow in, I am the more inclined to remain, as seeing some work to do.

I have been laying myself out this last half year to get intimate with the boys, and have pretty well succeeded; principally I suppose because the occupation accorded with my wishes and gave me pleasure; and this is, I think, a very great source of influence. However, I am rather speculating too much, and after all I am daily more and more convinced of the permanent duty of taking care of oneself: I mean, avoiding the delusion of thinking of others, while oneself is going down hill; and to this I find myself prone.

* * * * *

The reader will observe that in the above extract Mackenzie speaks of "getting intimate with the boys," by which name he designates the Undergraduates. I believe that few men have been more successful in this work. He was amongst them precisely as an elder brother, influencing them for good without obtruding advice, and impressing by his presence a high and pure tone. The remark was made to one of them, who loved him well, on the occasion of the news of his decease reaching England, "You must feel as if you had lost a brother." "Ah," was the reply, "no brother was ever to me what Mackenzie was."

We now enter upon Mackenzie's clerical life. The change was not in his case, as indeed it ought never to be, a sudden and violent one. He continued his old works of usefulness, and he seems, in the first instance, to have looked forward to a lengthened stay in College as a clerical fellow. Here is a part of a letter, which, for a wonder, is dated, and which expresses his views at this time.

LETTER VIII.

CAIUS COLLEGE. *July* 9, 1851.

I am unwilling to leave College. I can hardly conceive a more useful and important place to be in; and though there are influences for bad here, in the shape of clergymen who do not think it necessary to act as parish working clergy would, (I am putting it in the extenuating language they would use,) yet there are very many who are not so, and I don't think the "atmosphere" so unwholesome as that of ——, for instance. I am writing coldly I know, but I do not think I am letting selfish considerations overbear higher ones. I should like to live here as a clergyman, with such of the Undergraduates as I could influence as my parish, and to throw up private teaching altogether.

I have begun my clerical duties by reading prayers, but have not preached yet. I intended to have done so on Sunday next, but find my assistance will not be wanted.

* * * * *

He very soon however felt a craving for more directly ministerial work than any which he could find in College; an offer was made to him of a curacy in Shropshire, which would have taken him altogether from Cambridge, but this he declined; and almost immediately afterwards an opening occurred which seemed exactly to meet his views, namely, a curacy in the neighbourhood of Cambridge, which would enable him to have regular parish-work, and yet not remove him from a sphere in which, with all his modesty, he must have felt that he was making himself very useful. The offer of this curacy is communicated to a sister in the following letter, in which he also alludes to the curacy in Shropshire and to his having declined it.

LETTER IX.

CAIUS COLLEGE.
Friday, July 26, 1851.

DEAR ——,

Thank you for writing, and thank you much for writing what you did. I have no hesitation myself whatever; though differing from ——[1] is a strong step; and I don't think I should have felt so easy about it, but that I am sure she does not know the position of things here, and therefore that I can judge better than she can. I had a most kind letter from ——, offering, in a neat way, if I took this and wished her to come to me there, to come at once: but I had made up my mind. I must write and thank her, however. Luckily for me the thing was put out of the question at once by my having agreed to be one of the Examiners in the University Examination next January; and that I could not well put off. Besides, I should not like to leave my place in College in a hurry, as they would need to appoint a successor: but your notion of the work I might do here is quite my own, and I believe for a time that will be best.

I have been offered a sub-curacy (if I may coin the word) about five miles from Cambridge. The curate is virtually rector, and I should be his curate. The population is about 900, I believe, and in winter I should have the principal weight of it on my shoulders; but on the Sunday I could always get help.

* * * * *

The next letter, written to his eldest sister from a place in which he was taking temporary duty, again refers to the curacy near Cambridge, the duties of which he had now arranged to take after the Long Vacation.

[1] His eldest sister.

LETTER X.

LITTLE WALTHAM, ESSEX.
August 7, 1851.

DEAREST ——,

I dare say you do not know what I am doing. You know I have taken the duty once or twice for a friend in a stray way already, but I like better being resident as I am now. A friend, a man of my own year at Cambridge, is the curate here; and finding his throat inflamed, he asked me to relieve him for a week or two. So I came here on Monday, and shall do his duty in Church and a little visiting for a fortnight. It is next best to having a parish of my own; and that I have arranged to have in the neighbourhood of Cambridge, as soon as I go back in October to College, as you have probably heard from Harcus. * * * The Rev. W. Clark is to be my Rector, though he is only Curate himself. * * * As far as working the parish is concerned, I am clear it will not be so satisfactory as if I had nothing else to do; but as Mr Clark knows my position exactly, and can get no one better for his purpose, part of the disagreeableness is removed, and I do really wish to remain in College for a time.

* * * * *

I find it difficult to write sermons, not so much for want of something to say, as from the temptation to ramble. I am afraid too that those I have written are hardly understood by the poor people. However, I suppose if one tries always to get simple, it will come in time. My object ought to be, I suppose, to catch attention, and then preach the simple doctrine of Christ crucified: at least, if that is not the principal topic of the second half of my sermon, ought it not to come in somewhere? At any rate, when I have but two Sundays to preach to this congregation, I think I ought to be very distinct in this: perhaps in my own curacy it may require a little variety; and there are other things of importance doubtless besides this one, but it is never difficult to turn the subject to this.

I have been taking a good deal of interest in Cambridge in a Mendicity Society there; but I think I must have told you of it.

* * * * *

In the Mendicity Society, mentioned in the foregoing letter, Mackenzie was most active, taking (as usual with him) the most laborious share of the work. The purpose of the Society was, and still is, to prevent the encouragement of systematic mendicancy, which in a place like Cambridge is liable to grow into a fearful evil. It has been said, and I believe with truth, that beggars have been in the habit of coming to Cambridge in term-time, and seeking other pastures during the vacations, as regularly as the members of the University. In order to stop the bestowal of alms upon such unworthy recipients, and at the same time relieve the truly unfortunate, a house was opened in Barnwell into which poor travellers could be admitted by tickets signed by subscribers. The house was put under the charge of a constable, whose wife acted as matron; all cases were examined; and the genuine poor travellers were supplied with a clean lodging for the night, with supper, and with breakfast before starting next morning. The working of this machinery has been found exceedingly satisfactory in Cambridge, and I believe in other places also; but in order to give the right tone to the establishment, and to turn (if it might be) the short sojourn of the poor travellers to some spiritual profit, it was necessary that some one interested in the work should go up to the mendicity house in the evening, speak a few kind words to the inmates, and conduct evening prayers. Mackenzie was one of the volunteers for this work. On one occasion I accompanied him, and was much struck with the manner in which he accomplished his task. I was sure that he would succeed in making his presence agreeable to the poor travellers, but I was not prepared to find him so successful as he proved himself to be in conducting the family worship. He read a chapter from the Scriptures, and then made a short comment upon it with a simplicity and earnestness and readiness, which made the lesson as well adapted for its purpose, in my judgment, as it could be. The prayers were from the Book of Common Prayer, which seemed to him to be for all purposes a sufficient manual of devotion*.

In the summer of 1851 he conducted a mathematical examination at Eton. Some of his impressions are contained in a letter to a sister.

* I subjoin a characteristic circular, printed by Mackenzie, and given to Members of the University:—

"It is better to give One Shilling to the Mendicity Society, than Two Sixpences or Twelve Pence in indiscriminate charity; for by this Society relief is given in a shape in which it cannot be abused, and in which it does not suit the tastes of professional beggars; and there is an additional advantage attending this form of charity, viz. that one night of perfect order and peace is secured to the recipient.

"In order to divert into this more useful channel the money which is constantly given to beggars, and which in most cases does harm instead of good, I shall be very happy to receive at *any* time, any sum, *however small*, and shall keep a special purse in my pocket for the purpose: the amount so obtained will be entered in the Subscription List of the Society as small donations from Caius College.

"If any one wishes to see the working of the Society, and will call on me a little before Seven any Evening before the end of this month, I shall be most happy to take him with me when I go to admit the applicants.

"C. F. MACKENZIE.

CAIUS COLLEGE, *Nov.* 15, 1851."

4

LETTER XI.

* * * This is by way of explanation of my silence. So you are to put yourself back a week, and then read on. You have seen my declining of the curacy, and I hope no one is distressed at it. I have no doubt myself I am doing what is best on the whole; but I want to thank you for the kind way you proposed to accompany me. It would, I fully believe, have been very pleasant, and the people seemed nice people from the little we knew of them.

* * * * *

My visit to Eton was pleasant enough. I think a Public School is the finest thing I ever saw: at least my ideal of it is. I think they are trying at Eton to work out the system, and make the most of it: I mean, to keep up a good spirit of gentlemanly feeling among the boys, and I dare say of Christian feeling too; though I was there hardly long enough to see this attempt so distinctly as the other. What a field of occupation! 600 picked boys out of England! I went to chapel twice, on Sunday and on Tuesday. They were very well-behaved. What an opportunity for any of the masters, by their manner, to give solemnity to the place, and keep up the home-reverence, which is a little apt to be lost, if chapel is made frequent. I think,—at least I thought while on the spot,—that no life could be so charming as that of a master there; I said so, and they agreed, but said there were dark pages now and then too. I think you will enter into my feelings on this point better than any one else.

In the October term (1851) he commenced his work at Haslingfield, which he continued until the time of his first departure for Africa. It was very laborious, and few men could have borne the effort; but with him it was a labour perpetually lighted up by sunshine, and the effort was not apparent. As a general rule he combined his parochial duties at Haslingfield with college-work, but in the vacations he several times left his college-rooms, took lodgings at the house of the village schoolmaster, and gave himself up unreservedly to the work of his parish. On several occasions I have spent a day with him in his village-home: very pleasant and bright those days were: but days always were pleasant and bright in Mackenzie's company.

The date of the following letter is December 1851, when he had had a few months' experience of parish-work.

LETTER XII.

(*To a Sister.*)

I find college and parish-work very heavy together, but hope before the time of my present engagement is out, namely, next October, to have discovered how to combine them without overworking myself. I meant to have given you a journal of my work to shew you that my neglect has not been intentional, but perhaps you will believe me without.

I have never been able to get out to my parish, Haslingfield as it is called, more than once during the week, and as you might conceive, have not been further than the visiting of the sick. This vacation I shall be a good deal occupied with preparing for the Examinations next month: but that is a kind of work which is in my own hands more than lectures: I can work *double* one day, and *none* the next: so I shall get out at least twice a week, I hope.

I have been reading Evans' *Bishopric of Souls.* He has given me a great longing for a country parish and nothing else to do: but I believe I am more useful as I am.

* * * * *

My ordinary practice has been to walk out to my curacy in time for the school, which is at half-past nine. I take a class of a dozen; but the remaining thirty are all in the room, and I have some difficulty in hearing or being heard. However, I have the advantage of letting the master get away for a quarter of an hour, to practise the hymns with the girls, who sing in church. Then at half-past ten service begins, and Mr Clark or I do the whole. This lasts till about a quarter to one. We dine at the vicarage, which is Mr Clark's house, and go into church again at half-past two. About a quarter of an hour after we have come out I set off and walk home. It is five and a half miles, and I generally take an hour and ten minutes, or an hour and a quarter. So you see the grass does not grow under my feet. When I get home, which is before six, I have tea or cold meat; and at a quarter past seven I go out to one of the churches, ——'s, and hear the sermon only; the fact being, that neither Mr Clark's sermons nor my own are quite to my taste, and I like to hear one good sermon in the day. Then I come back and have tea with ——, where I usually meet three or four or five friends, and go to bed tired.

In the January of 1852 Mackenzie was for the first time Examiner for Mathematical Honours. I was myself Senior Moderator on the same occasion, and the preparatory work for the Examination was therefore, according to custom, chiefly done at my house. Thus I was brought into a new relation with Mackenzie; I found him as agreeable a companion in an examination as he had proved under other circumstances; modest, cheerful, amiable. He expressed much good-humoured surprise at the trouble which the preparation of questions for the Examination cost him. The practice in

Cambridge, and it is a very wholesome one, is for each Examiner to submit to the whole Board each question which he intends to propose to the Candidates for Mathematical Honours: and each member of the Board, when a question has been read, makes it his business to criticise it with the utmost severity. No ordeal can very well be more searching; and before it is finally approved, every question is thoroughly sifted both as to its principle, its difficulty, and the mode of its expression. Mackenzie had not prepared his questions with the prospect of so severe a test; and I remember well the good-humoured regret with which, after much discussion and hearing a variety of objections, he finally abandoned several of his questions, with the remark, "Well, the fact of the matter seems to be, that it won't do any way."

The examination interfered with Haslingfield ministrations for a time, but when it was over he returned to them with renewed satisfaction. The following letter seems to have been written in the beginning of March 1852.

LETTER XIII.

(*To a Sister.*)

CAIUS COLLEGE. *Tuesday.*

DEAR ——,

Your letter threw a shade over the day I got it. Not because you had scolded me, but I thought I could see you look cold at me through the pen and ink: at least part of your letter gave me that "feel:" others were like your own good kind hearty self.

*　　*　　*　　*　　*

It is indeed as you supposed. I have not had much

work which required to be done at a given time, and so have been always in arrear: making frantic efforts to get up at five, and so get a start in the day, which has probably ended in my being sleepy for an evening or two afterwards.

I fancy sometimes I feel the evil of not taking exercise *regularly*, as I did when an undergraduate. There are some of my duties now which must be done between two and four in the afternoon, which is the universal time for exercise here, and then on those days I perhaps get none, while on another day I have a great deal. On Sunday I have always my eleven miles walk, besides the duty, which is fatiguing. To-day I shall be at a meeting of the Mendicity Society's Committee at two, and as chaplain at the Hospital at three: so I shall certainly have no walk.

* * * * *

I am greatly disappointed with our boat this year. They are pulling so badly, and are losing places day after day. Poor Caius is not the place for "pluck," (do you know the word?) and yet by the bye we have some good cricketers now.

* * * * *

You understand I hope that I am penitent about not writing to you and every one else, and that I have written this not under compulsion, but only because I did not dare delay longer.

C. F. M.

Amongst other duties Mackenzie, as intimated in the preceding letter, took his turn as chaplain of Addenbrooke's Hospital. It was characteristic of him not to be content with the ordinary duties of the office, but to be ready to promote in every way the comfort of the patients. The arrangements for the out-door patients were at that time very incomplete; these patients saw the physicians, received their prescriptions, and then were obliged to wait until they could make their way to the little window of the dispensary and receive their medicines; not always a very easy task, the waiting hall being quite full. The effect was that the weakest were attended to last, and those who could with least inconvenience remain were first served. Moreover, the confusion and discomfort were very considerable. Mackenzie took the matter in hand, and by means of a system of tickets, the working of which he personally superintended for some weeks, he speedily introduced order, and banished much of the inconvenience which had been previously felt. This may seem a trifling feat, and hardly worthy of being chronicled; but, in truth, it was this spirit of active kindness, this readiness to help in little things when the comfort of others was concerned, which caused much of that warmth of affection with which Mackenzie was regarded by his friends.

The next letter belongs to the beginning of the Long Vacation, and looks forward to the stir created for a few days in the quiet dulness of the University by the Master of Arts' Commencement. The description is put out of date by recent changes in the University; and the dulness of the Long Vacation now knows no break. The old arrangement, doubtless, had inconveniences; but the meeting of men, who had known each other as undergraduates, after several years of actual contact with the world and its work and its cares, was very pleasant, and frequently not without profit.

LETTER XIV.

(*To a Sister.*)

CAIUS COLLEGE. *Thursday.*

DEAR ——,

Your letter on Sunday morning was a great delight to me. I feel such a disinclination to write after a long silence, that if you take courage to break it, it is a great relief to me.

It is very true what you say of difficulties, apparently insurmountable, giving way to the influence of time and circumstances. I always connect such cases with that of the women at the sepulchre—*who shall roll us away the stone?*

* * * * *

You have had great doings with your twenty-five-persons luncheon party. D—— was in my rooms when I was reading your letter, and when I told him, he said, "What a happy family you seem to be, always so glad to see each other, and to be together:" and so I think we are; at least I am coming to think that no one is so well treated by his own people as I am.

You are quite right, dear ——, in praying that I may be kept humble in this place of literary excitement. I don't know what would become of me, if I had not the parish to draw my mind to better things: I am never happier than when out there. Just now I am pressed by making papers for the Examination of a school in London. I make the papers here and send them up, and they send me down again the answers of the boys. And besides this, men are continually coming up to college just for a day, and they consider a settled man like me as their lawful prey, and I too am glad to see them, but it takes up time; and more than that, distracts one, (like the elephant that does more damage to the forest by pushing through, than by all he eats, ten times over).

R—— was here on Monday and Tuesday; he was one of my two or three greatest friends before we took our degrees; and now we don't meet more than once or twice in a year. Then on Tuesday evening F—— came here and went next morning; he has been abroad for fourteen months, and of course had plenty to say. Then this morning D—— came in just when my breakfast was done, having arrived by train: so I gave him breakfast, and this afternoon an aunt of his is coming up for three or four hours, and I must have a lunch-dinner with them. This evening I have promised to go to J——'s rooms. H—— too is coming up to-night, and will be in my rooms every morning, no doubt. Then on Saturday M—— and a heap of others will come up and stay till Tuesday, taking the degree of M.A., and I shall give them a breakfast party or two, and take walks with them separately, and so on; and then I look forward to a fortnight or three weeks of peace, in which, no doubt, if I write to you, you will find me grumbling at the dulness.

I think I never described such a thing to you before. Observe, it is an extreme case; partly because in term-time half of one's duties are inflexible, such as lectures, and so a little amusement for the rest of the day is pleasant enough.

*   *   *   *   *

In the course of the Long Vacation he got away from college, settled himself down in his quiet lodgings at Haslingfield, and from thence wrote to one of his sisters as follows:

LETTER XV.

HASLINGFIELD, CAMBRIDGESHIRE.

DEAR ——,

Here you see I am arrived. I have taken a couple of rooms in the schoolmaster's house.

* * * * *

I got here at ten o'clock on Monday night. I had sent my portmanteau by a carrier, and intending to walk I was easily induced to remain by little things that had to be done in Cambridge. H—— walked half-way with me, and then I came on alone over the fields. It was a strange feeling on two accounts. Partly, I was coming to live in a strange place as a home, a thing I have not done since I came to college, and since I went to school,—which has on the two former occasions brought desolation, but not on this. The other reason of strangeness was that now I was beginning what will take place when I am a placed minister, a thing which I think will be very delightful.

I have the schoolmistress as my waiter, assisted by her daughter, a child of eleven or twelve, who is very shy, having never waited on a gentleman before. The next morning, after coming in with the eggs, and asking if I wanted anything more, (which she had evidently been told to do, but as evidently had not been told to listen to my answer,) she stood (on one foot, I suppose, or some other uncomfortable position,) for an instant, and then darted off through the door.

* * * * *

I have already spoken of Mackenzie's residence at Haslingfield: I will only add here that he set himself vigorously to work to make personal acquaintance with his parishioners, and, as I have heard incidentally, with great success. The memory of him is still cherished in the parish. It was quite to be expected, however, that he should feel disappointed with his own efforts: every honest and earnest man is doomed to this feeling of disappointment: it is only when the aim of a Christian minister is contracted and his standard of excellence low, that he can feel satisfied with what he has been able to do. Hence I am not surprised at the tone of the following letter, which I find from the post-mark to have been written in the beginning of August.

LETTER XVI.

(*To a Sister.*)

HASLINGFIELD. *Thursday.*

DEAR ——,

* * * * *

I propose being ordained priest on the 19th of September by the Bishop of Ely, and think of coming north at once after that.

* * * * *

I find this living in the country not so profitable as I expected—I mean that I don't get so well to work as I hoped. I find great difficulty in writing a sermon here; partly I think from the want of books, partly from the novelty of the place. And I have not been so active in visiting. There was something very definite in walking from Cambridge to see those who needed to be called upon; but now that I am among them, I can do it at any time. Then I never forget that I have problems to make for January, and I cannot do much of that work out here.

However, I have seen more of the school a great deal than before. And even of the people I have seen more than I should have done had I been in Cambridge.

* * * * *

The "Problems for January," spoken of in the above letter, were Senate-house problems, which it devolved upon Mackenzie to supply as Moderator. He was Senior Moderator in January 1853, and again in 1854. Those who did not know Mackenzie personally might be surprised, that having so ardent a love of the work of a country parish-priest, he could allow himself to undertake so many other occupations and duties. But the fact is he delighted in work, and his good nature and desire to be useful were so strong that he found it impossible to refuse, when requested to undertake to do anything of real importance which required to be done.

He was ordained priest at the time proposed, but I find no special reference to the event in any of his letters.

Mackenzie was not by natural gift an orator. He had no great flow of words, and no fervour of imagination, such as enable a man to throw an interest into a subject in itself dry and uninteresting. When it became necessary for him afterwards frequently to address public meetings, and when he had an important theme upon which to speak, his earnestness and simplicity made all that he said very impressive; and his active self-devotion gave more emphasis to his words than any mere eloquence could have supplied. Here is an extract from a letter, in which he speaks with characteristic modesty of his first attempt to make a speech. The letter belongs to the latter part of the year; the school spoken of is the Cambridge Industrial School.

LETTER XVII.

(*To a Sister.*)

CAIUS COLLEGE. *Tuesday.*

DEAR ——,

* * * * *

I am very happy in having lots to do, which is become necessary to me now. I enclose you a copy of some speeches made in the Town Hall last week, one of them by me. It is my first real attempt at the thing, and is not a first-rate one, but I have got over the nervousness of getting on my legs pretty well. I thought little of it before, and knew not a great deal about the school, though I am one of the Committee; it takes a while to get a good knowledge of a plan of the kind. Next time I hope I shall know more about what I am saying, and make a better show.

And this will be a proper point at which to finish this chapter, for the next year will open to us a new view of Mackenzie's life. Hitherto, it will be observed, college-work and parish-work have entirely filled his mind; in the next chapter we shall see how it pleased God to open his mind to a severer view of his duty, and to commence his education as a Missionary.

CHAPTER IV.

FIRST THOUGHTS OF MISSION-WORK.

THE year 1853 began, as we have seen, with a Senate-house Examination. While engaged in this laborious and responsible work, Mackenzie very wisely obtained regular help for his parish: in fact, his friend the Rev. W. W. Hutt, then a fellow of Caius College, undertook the whole of the duty, as he did previously in 1852, when Mackenzie was Examiner, and again in 1854, when he was Senior Moderator. When Mackenzie left England, he had the satisfaction of leaving his flock in the hands of this faithful friend.

This will explain Mackenzie's long absence from his parish, as mentioned in the next letter. That letter is the only one which I find in the beginning of this year, previous to the very important communication which follows it, and upon which I shall have a few words to say presently. It will be seen that at the end of February his heart was still full of Cambridge; no thought of foreign service had apparently then crossed his mind; he was evidently quite happy in his work; indeed they who remember his joyous countenance and unmingled cheerfulness and readiness for work in those days cannot doubt of his happiness. Hence the letter which follows will, I think, appear all the more remarkable; and different as the first letter is from the second, (the letter of Feb. 24 from that of April 23,) I do not know that a more striking introduction to the second could be supplied than that which is contained in the first.

LETTER XVIII.

(*To a Sister*).

CAIUS COLLEGE,
Feb. 24, 1853.

DEAREST ——,

We shall really be ruined if we go on writing to each other the moment we get a letter; and if by any accident an additional letter were written there would immediately be a double fire. This is all *à propos* of my having just read your letter.

Thanks for all your news, and above all for your few words about ——. Is'nt it strange how people get drawn together when they are all drawn toward Christ? You know it is their common attraction to the sun that keeps the planets within sight of each other.

I was at Haslingfield last Sunday for the first time since November. Do you know I had a dislike of going there again, and thought of giving it up; but, as indeed I knew it would be, when I had been there I was quite happy.

* * * * *

And now I must bring before the reader the turning point of Mackenzie's spiritual life. The immediate cause of his attention being called to Missionary-work was, as will be seen, the establishment of a Mission at Delhi, by the Society for the Propagation of the Gospel in Foreign Parts. It would be out of place to say much concerning that Mission, but I may observe that the Rev. J. S. Jackson, who was the first missionary, was of the same College as Mackenzie, and three years junior to him in standing. The opening of this Mission was very promising; but very soon came the Indian mutiny, and the mission was for a while swept away under most tragical circumstances. Mr Jackson's companion in labour was murdered; he himself was absent from Delhi at the time of the outbreak, and was thus preserved. In the "Colonial Church Chronicle" for June 1854, I find the following notice: "The Rev. J. S. Jackson and the Rev. A. Hubbard arrived in Delhi on February 11, after making a short stay at the Colleges at Calcutta and Benares. They found the nucleus of a mission consisting of a score of native Christians, who are assembled every Sunday in the Station Church by a teacher in the Government College." In the number of the same periodical for August 1857, there is a letter from Dr Kay of Bishop's College, Calcutta, which contains the following: "The Delhi Mission has been completely swept away. Rumours to this effect were current from the beginning of the outbreak, but we kept on hoping that some of the members of the Mission might have escaped. Two native Christians succeeded in escaping to Agra. One of them says that he saw Mr Hubbard fall....And Mr Jackson has been spared...."

This, in few words, was the history of the mission which first inspired Mackenzie's mind with missionary thoughts; the Mr Hubbard spoken of as having lost his life in the outbreak, was the man whose place he was desirous to have filled. The manner in which the Delhi Mission was brought prominently before him, so as to lead him to wish to give himself to the work, will be best told in his own words. He communicated his views fully and honestly to his eldest sister in a letter, which I am now about to lay before the reader. This letter is the pivot, so to speak, of Mackenzie's spiritual history. I do not know how it may strike the reader's mind, and I do not pretend to be a quite impartial judge. I confess to a degree of reverence and admiration for the writer, which may have led me to over-estimate its character; but I do not hesitate to speak of it as being, in my opinion, one of the noblest and most touching compositions that I have ever seen.

LETTER XIX.

CAIUS COLLEGE,
Saturday, April 23.

DEAREST ——,

We have spoken before now about the advantages of my remaining in College, and whether it would not be better for me to find some more directly clerical work elsewhere. I have been thinking about a change lately, and should like before definitely making up my mind to have your opinion on the matter. This will probably be a longish letter, and as I don't know at what hour you may get it, or what you may be doing, I wish you would lay it aside till you have half an hour quiet.

I don't think you ever quite liked my staying here; at least, if you did, I think it was more in deference to my opinion than from your own conviction. What I have said has been that it is a mistake to say this is a place in which

5

nothing clerical can be done, and I still think that a really good man, if he were liked here, might do much good: indeed I can hardly think of a more important place in England, except perhaps the head-mastership of a school, and even that falls short of this place in one respect, that without doubt a considerable number of the Fellows do not consider their responsibilities but may be induced to do so by a few good examples; and so a little leaven leavening the whole lump, there would be a great increase of good influence brought to bear upon the flower of England's upper classes, at an impressible age, and one at which character is *set* for life.

I say all this to shew that I still think I have been right in my theory that this is a place particularly adapted for a good man to do good: and if nothing now presented itself except a curacy in some part of England I should not, I think, hesitate to remain here. But there is another field open, for which it is very difficult to find labourers. A great friend of mine, called Jackson, my junior by three years, has been induced to undertake the position of chief of a new mission at Delhi, and has been for some time anxious to find a companion to go with him. At first a friend of his, of his own standing, agreed to go; but he has since declined, I don't know why. Jackson applied to me among others to try and find some one to go with him; and I spoke to one young man, an undergraduate of this college, who had once said something of having an uncle in India, who was very anxious he should go out to India as a missionary. However when I came to speak of Jackson's going out, I found he had no settled intentions himself, and so the matter dropped.

I remember when —— used to speak to us about going out as Missionaries, he used sometimes to say, he had been asked why *he* did not go himself, and though he said he was too old, and that he had duties in England, I used to think his defence not very strong. I remember too, when some years ago the subject of medical missions excited interest —— saying to me, "Why should not *you* go? they want *men* very much," and my answer was, "I am not going:" I would not admit the idea into serious contemplation.

And when Jackson came to Cambridge a month or two ago, to try and find a colleague, I thought once or twice, why should not *I* go, but said nothing to him, as I thought that would be unfair before I was more definite myself. I spoke of my feelings to one or two Cambridge friends, in a general way, saying that I could not see any reason why one of us should not go, and I was afraid it was because we could not make up our minds to the self-denial, and that there was no good reason, but ended by saying, "Don't be alarmed, I'm not going;" and so it passed off.

But on Thursday Jackson came again and we chatted quietly about his prospects, and the opening there was, and how he wished he could find some one; and after he left me I read a bit of Henry Martyn's life before *he* left England; and I determined for the first time, and prayed God to help me, to think what was best to be done, and *to do it.* I thought chiefly of the command, "Go and baptize all nations," and how some one ought to go: and I thought how in another world one would look back and rejoice at having seized this opportunity of taking the good news of the Gospel to those who had never heard it, but for whom as well as for us Christ died. I thought of the Saviour sitting in Heaven and looking down upon this world, and seeing us who have heard the news, selfishly keeping it to ourselves, and only one or two, or eight or ten, going out in the year to preach to His other sheep, who must be brought, that there may be "one fold and one shepherd:" and I thought if other men would go abroad, then I might stay at home; but as no one, or so few, would go out, then it was the duty of every one that could go to go. You see I thought of the pleasure and the duty, and I think they were both cogent reasons. So I determined to sleep upon it; and in the morning, when I thought about it, the more I thought the more clear I got. I thought of my duties here, and how I had been in the habit of considering them superior in importance to anything else; but then that was in comparison with posts for which there was no lack of persons to be found; whereas this was a thing which it seemed no one could be found to do. I thought too of what I have considered the qualifications for usefulness in Cambridge, namely, my good degree, and the way people don't dislike me, and my pretty large acquaintance: but then I thought, these things will not be lost, for though it would be no argument if there were no other arguments, yet it removes the objection to my leaving Cambridge to say that the better I am known the more interest will be raised in the missionary cause. Then I thought too of Jackson, and how disheartening it was for him, his first friend leaving him, and every one else saying, "I wish I could find some one to go with you," but no one thinking of going; and I thought, what right have I to say to young men here, "you had better go out to India," when I am hugging myself in my comfortable place at home.

So I determined to tell Jackson what I was thinking of, and found he would like me to go with him, and his only difficulty was that he thought I was useful here. Now the consideration of this was one thing which further induced me to go. For though I may say I have tried sometimes to be useful, yet it has been far too much with me a matter of intention and hope; and the day when I was to do good has always seemed to retire before me. I am now twenty-eight, and it is high time I was doing something. I have given this place a good trial, and am thoroughly dissatisfied. I can't go into details on this point.

I took a long walk that day, and thought it well over, and made up my mind that God would approve of the change, that Christ would approve, and that the Holy Spirit would help me in it. I thought my dear mother would have smiled through her tears at the plan if she had still lived, and that she would now rejoice without grief. I thought you would give me your solid and sober judgment upon it, and I thought that your opinion would be in favour. I was not so sure of ——, but I thought she would be willing that her own heart's comfort should be made known to those who now have no means of hearing. I thought —— would at one time have thought of coming with me, but I feared she was not strong enough; but I was sure she would be glad. I could not so well tell what the rest would think. I thought —— would be surprised, and would soon forget it. I thought too of my work here as Lecturer, and arranged in my mind who there was that would take my place. If there had been no one, there is a kind of College spirit that would have urged me to stay here.

I thought of my future prospects, and saw that by keeping my Fellowship I should have nearly £200 a year besides the salary of the Society, which would be I suppose between £100 and £200; this would be more than enough for me there; and I should either stay there for the rest of my life, or, if compelled to return, should have my offer of a College living to fall back upon.

All this I have put down to shew that though I have not had much time, yet I have not omitted the necessary considerations. Indeed, the general question of the advantage the duty and the pleasure of going out I had considered before, first in advising Jackson to close with the offer that was made to him, and again in looking for some one else to be his colleague. And all that I have had to think of these last few days has been, whether there was anything peculiar in my own case that should prevent me from going.

And I freely confess I can see nothing except my own unfitness. I am rather afraid of my own instability and want of method and perseverance, habits which have been increasing with me of late. I am rather afraid of their injuring the cause I am going to undertake. But at the same time I hope that the having one main object in life may assist in steadying me: at present I have scores of interests all claiming attention. And I do trust that if I go forth boldly trusting in God, He will not fail to help me.

I have not much time to write more, yet I must tell you something about the work I am going to. At Delhi there are of course a great number of young men of good talents, and likely to have great influence as they grow up. There is a Government school, to which they come in great numbers, but at which they receive no religious instruction: yet the general knowledge they get shakes their confidence in their own system, and they are in danger of becoming infidels. That is the general state of the case, and is I fancy common enough in India. There is a considerable spirit of inquiry among them; and the Chaplain on the spot has encouraged this, and has already gained the confidence of some of them, who have listened to his message and have been baptized. These are from among the higher classes of society. There is no mission at the place at present, and the Propagation Society have determined to establish one, and to send out two young men from this country for the purpose. Jackson and I, I hope, will be the two. He has settled with the Society some time ago, and was directed to find a companion if he could. So I have no doubt of being appointed, if I make application. He is to sail in September.

Now dear ——, I have always looked to you as my mother and early teacher. To you I owe more than I can ever repay, more than I can well tell. I do hope you will pray for me, and then give me your advice. I am still free, and will listen carefully to what you say.

My own main argument is this,—we may, it is true, serve God, and shew our love to Christ, in one place as well as in another, (and I am trying to avoid the notion that by going out I shall be free from weakness and sin,) but no one else will go, so I will. There are plenty in England: there is grievous need there. Jackson is a first-rate fellow: I never knew so firm, so conscientious a man, that I liked so well. * * * I confess the feeling of my heart that most distresses me is, that I cannot look forward with composure to the risk of his dying, and leaving me behind. But though in this I am "otherwise minded, God will reveal even this to me."

Since if the whole plan were to fall through, and I were to remain in this country, it would be unpleasant that the idea should have got abroad, you will exercise your judgment and tell what I have said to whom you please. I shall write to no one else till I hear from you.

Ever your affectionate brother,

C. F. M.

Notice, reader, the honesty of this letter, how determined the writer is to practise what he preaches, and not to ask any one to do what he is not prepared to do himself: notice his humility in being ready to go as second in command to a man three years his junior: notice his modesty in seeing no objection but his own unfitness: and above all notice the argument, which was the ground of all his subsequent course of action, "no one else will go, so I will."

Here is another letter written to the same sister two days afterwards.

LETTER XX.

CAIUS COLLEGE,
Monday, April 25, 1852.

DEAREST ——,

I wrote hurriedly on Saturday night, and had not time to read over what I had written. I think there must have been many things which I ought to have said; so now I take my chance of remembering them.

First, I am anxious to hear from you, if you are well enough and strong enough to write, for I am deferring my absolute determination till I hear from you.

I am very anxious to impress upon myself that this is not so great a sacrifice, as it once was, to go out as a Missionary. There are many Europeans at Delhi; and above all other worldly comforts, I go out with a friend whom I highly esteem and value, and greatly love.

My chief feeling about it all is that Christ needs servants in various places: some in this country, and some elsewhere: and that the greatest want is abroad. It seems to me that England is bound to do all she can for her subjects abroad; and as others will not go, I will. The only thing, I think, which has prevented my doing so once and again, has been a tacit resolution not to put the case to myself as possible: for as soon as I did that, the case seemed clear.

As to my qualifications for it: I must learn Persian and Hindustani, I suppose, but I have hardly found out yet what is to be done; but these things would have to be learned by any one going there: so I am as good for the purpose as they. And as to the character of the Mahomedans and Hindus one will have to deal with, every one would have to learn that by experience. The only thing that seems deficient is my own religion, which I know is very weak: in that I seriously think I am far inferior to many others who might go out. But all I can say is, if no one else will go, I shall be better than nothing, and I do trust that as my day is so shall my strength be.

Dear ——, you will think of me when I am gone; and we shall meet, I know we shall, in the kingdom above. What matter where we spend the remainder of our life? The time is short: "it remaineth that they that have wives be as though they had none, &c."

I heard a sermon last night on the text, "If any man will come after Me, let him deny himself and take up his cross daily and follow Me." And I think this is my path. I never could swallow the notion of voluntary self-denial, as a discipline: but I think self-denial in the service of God and for an object is what we ought to practise.

But I am growing prosy, and it is getting late.

Now don't think I have taken a mania on the subject: though these two letters have been mainly on this matter, yet I was out at dinner this evening, and took as much interest in a discussion about derivations of words as any one else. They said "wig" came from "periwig," and that from "perruque," and that from a Gothic Latin word "pellucus," and that from "pilus," Latin, a hair.

Your very affectionate brother,

C. F. M.

The following, to the same sister, was written about a week later.

LETTER XXI.

CAIUS COLLEGE. *Thursday night.*

DEAREST ——,

It is late, but I write a line to thank you for your very kind and excellent letter.

I shall write, I dare say, to-morrow: but I may say that on consulting two of my best friends here, I find they are opposed to my going. Goodwin decidedly so: Hopkins, rather so.

However it is for myself to decide.

Your very affectionate brother,

C. F. M.

I have allowed my own name to appear in the preceding letter, and have not supplied the place with a blank, as I might have done, because the position which Mackenzie has here assigned to me as one of his advisers seems to give me a right to say a few words upon the question of the propriety of his leaving Cambridge as a Missionary. Mackenzie has stated that I was decidedly opposed to his going, and this is quite true. My opposition was in fact too decided, for it gave him the impression that I had not sufficiently considered the subject; and I think when I told him that he must not go, I detected upon his countenance the nearest approach I ever saw to dissatisfaction. But my opposition was based upon two grounds. In the first place I did not think that the Delhi mission was the best for him, even if he determined to go out as a Missionary; his power of languages was not great, and the peculiar openness and simplicity of his character seemed to me not suitable for dealing with the accomplished civilized infidelity of well-educated natives. But this view did not carry to my mind so much weight as the argument derived from the positive advantage of his presence in Cambridge: this he was sure to underestimate, but as a looker-on I thought it could hardly be over-estimated: it was not the removal of an ordinary man whose place could be easily filled; but the loss of one who combined in himself a number of qualities, which made him to be of singular value and very hard to replace. Hence I still think that I did right in opposing his departure. By doing so I gained, as will be seen afterwards, greater influence in deciding his departure for South Africa. On that occasion I assented to his wish to go; but it was only because I then found that the missionary spirit had laid hold upon him in an unmistakeable way, and that the question really was, not whether he should go at all, but whether he should go to that particular mission.

The result of the representations made by his family and those of his intimate friends whom he consulted, was that he declined to offer himself as a Missionary for Delhi; but it will be seen from the next letter that, although declining at this time, he distinctly reserved to himself the right of going abroad on a future occasion.

LETTER XXII.

(*To a sister.*)

Saturday Evening.

DEAR ——,

You took my plan much as I expected. I have now to tell you that I have resolved *not* to go to Delhi. Whether 'twas right to distress you in Scotland, and at such a distance, before consulting College friends, I almost doubt; but I half feared to make up my own mind and then have to bear the brunt of arguments against the plan, coming from home. I am afraid I have dishonourably thrown the pain on you, but I know you will not be inclined to blame me at present.

The hopes expressed in your letter, that the work to be done at home is more important than the other, and that it is more adapted for me, were stated as facts by men on whom I could rely for judgment and honesty. And now the matter stands thus. A more suitable post abroad may spring up at a time when my ties of duty at home are less: in which case I shall consider myself at liberty to go.

I cannot write more. Shew this to ——, next time you meet, though I have just written to her.

Yours truly,

C. F. M.

After this letter Mackenzie dropped once more quietly into his round of duties. In a letter written probably in the May or June of this year, he says, "I don't wish that my projected plan should be thought of any more. I want you all to forget that it was proposed." And then he goes on to speak of his work at Haslingfield, and of a prize which he is busy in adjudging for proficiency in knowledge of the Church Catechism.

In the summer of this year he took up his abode, as in the previous one, at the schoolmaster's house in Haslingfield. Here is a letter which gives some account of his proceedings. The reference to the College examinations shews that it belongs to June.

LETTER XXIII.

(*To a sister.*)

HASLINGFIELD, *Monday, the 13th.*

MY DEAR ——,

It's sorry I am to have been so long in writing. I am debating whether an apology or a confession will be best. I have been far from idle lately. Our College Examination ended on Thursday week; the next day I came out here: and though under no actual pressure of engagements, yet there is always much to be done.

One thing has taken up a good deal of my attention lately: a class of nearly thirty candidates for confirmation. The confirmation was held at the adjoining village on Friday last: and I confess I have been much interested in the young people. It is a very important age of course, but besides that I half feel that the respect for the rites of the Church in the Parish depends a good deal upon me. I think Mr Clark looks at his parishioners as individuals, each of whom he earnestly desires to be saved: I rather look upon this as part of the universal Church, and wish not only to benefit this generation, but to keep up the customs of the Church and to gain for her the love of her children. As it has happened this time, Mr Clark has been very unwell for three or four months, and thus the responsibility of improving well the minds of these young people has fallen on me.

I have been trying very hard to induce them to come to the Holy Communion. You would be surprised if you knew how few do attend here, and none I think of the younger people. If I could only break the ice this time with one or two, I should be abundantly satisfied: of course the more out of the twenty-eight the better, but I hardly hope for more than two or three. But that would be a beginning.

* * * * *

I have been delighted beyond measure by your last two letters: and would, I think, write twice a-day rather than lose your correspondence. So now you know how to get a letter out of me. Seriously, I regret much being so irregular in my duties of affection: and as I am in a course of general amendment, I shall hope to include this.

* * * * *

I have arranged my days very methodically: three days a-week on one scheme, and three on another. My occupations are—

Sermons,
Bible and concomitant studies, such as the study of the question of inspiration,
Hebrew,
School,
Visiting,
Exercise.

All this falls between breakfast at eight, and dinner at six. After dinner I am on varieties, Logic, Shakspeare, History, &c., and I suppose letter-writing must come in then, for there is no other time,—which may partly account for my not writing since coming here.

One whole day last week was spent in hearing the Church Catechism for a prize, said with the strictest accuracy. I was so tired at night.

Your very loving brother,

C. F. M.

The following is to the same sister.

LETTER XXIV.

CAIUS COLLEGE, *July* 11, 1853.

DEAREST ——,

I torment myself from week to week, because I don't write to you. So as I have just finished a very kind sisterly letter from you, I think it kindest to myself, in the most selfish point of view, to sit down at once, and write to you.

* * * * *

We are indeed a frail family, and here am I as strong as a horse, hardly sympathising with the rest of you. Certainly sight goes a long way towards convincing one of the realities of things: I mean that when I come home and see you all, and see how far from well some of you are, I always feel more for you all, than when I am here, with work and amusements that have no association with home. I believe I feel more sympathy for a slight ailment, a fit of ague, that will be gone in a week or a month, than I do for the continued sickness of a loved sister like —— ; I hope you will not think me a brute for all this; I believe it is natural, but that I have it in excess.

I am at present an amphibious animal; partly resident at Haslingfield, and a little in College. The Long Vacation work has begun; that is to say, the Students have begun to come into residence to work, and the Chapel service must be kept up. The tutor has a Church of his own to attend to, and is wisely afraid of over excitement on Sundays: so he takes the service in Chapel through the week, and I on Sundays. This brings me into Cambridge on Saturday evening. I go out to Haslingfield for the services, and return to College again. Yesterday I found no more serious consequence than an inclination for bed at about 10 o'clock, and I expect to be able to go on with this as long as is required.

* * * * *

Also I must make a stay of two days at Canterbury, to see the last of Jackson before his going to India. I told you, I think, of his having found a companion to go to India with him: Hubbard by name.

* * * * *

The October term came, and Mackenzie resumed his College work: the only letter that has come into my hands is one bearing a post-mark of December 6: from this I give one short extract.

LETTER XXV.

(To a sister.)

* * * * *

I cannot tell you how much I feel the good of having sisters to be writing to me and thinking of me and praying for me in this busy place. It is a slippery road we are upon, and we might almost despair, were it not for God's gracious encouragements: it is our Father's good pleasure to give us the kingdom, and I do confidently hope that we shall indeed reach that happy place where all evil is excluded.

In January 1854 Mackenzie was Moderator, as I have already mentioned; and the hard work brought upon him by this office, in addition to his ordinary routine of business, will probably account for a total dearth of letters to his family. Nothing has come into my hands belonging to the early months of this year; but the following letter will shew that as soon as the Easter vacation allowed him to absent himself from Cambridge, he again betook himself to his Haslingfield lodgings, and endeavoured to realize for himself the character of the parochial Clergyman. The letter is to his eldest sister.

LETTER XXVI.

HASLINGFIELD, *April* 12, 1854.

* * * * *

Other things are going on tolerably smoothly. I am growing more methodical in my habits, and I am trying hard to be determined and fixed in character: for I think I am easily led. At least I very easily form my opinions according to the company I am in: or if I do not form my opinions afresh, I am very apt to seem to agree with the person I am with. (A friend of mine sometimes says of another, who has this weakness to a considerable degree, that he *smells of the person he has been last with.*) I have been trying to overcome this, and find it beginning to grow easier.

Term ended about a week ago, and I have been rusticating here, enjoying the quiet of the place very much. Though I spoil it by often having to go into Cambridge, where the associations of the place make me feel as if it were term-time again.

* * * * *

I have heard from Jackson from Delhi. He had just arrived, and looked round him with very great interest at the scene of his future labours. He says the two natives of most note among those who have been baptized are very intelligent, and he wishes to gain a few other native converts that they may not stand alone. He says how much he would like —— or myself to be with him, but speaks of his companion Hubbard as a great comfort.

I have seen lately a journal of Archdeacon Merriman, the Archdeacon at the Cape of Good Hope; very interesting reading I thought. If you can lay your hands on it, I think that you will like it.

* * * * *

It will be easily believed that so earnest a feeling concerning the duty of missionary work as that which was called forth by his thoughts on the Delhi mission would not be likely altogether to slumber in a heart so honest and single as was that of Mackenzie. The principle involved in those emphatic words of his, "No one else will go, so I will," coupled with his very modest view of his own usefulness in Cambridge, could hardly fail sooner or later to come to the surface, and impel him to missionary enterprise. How he was led, in God's wise providence, to take the great step, will be seen in the following chapter.

CHAPTER V.

LEAVES CAMBRIDGE FOR NATAL.

ON November 30th, S. Andrew's Day, 1853, were consecrated at Lambeth Parish Church, the first Bishops of the newly formed dioceses of Graham's Town and Natal, in South Africa. These two dioceses had previously formed a portion of the diocese of Cape Town. The zealous Bishop of this enormous diocese, having made a very remarkable journey through its whole extent, and taken a measure of its spiritual necessities, returned to England in 1852, and succeeded in making arrangements for the subdivision of the diocese, and for the maintenance of two new Bishops. Dr Colenso, who was chosen to be Bishop of Natal, left England soon after his consecration, in company with the Bishop of Cape Town; he made a rapid inspection of his diocese, which he embodied in his interesting narrative, entitled "Ten Weeks in Natal," and then returned home, arriving in England, May 27, 1854, for the purpose of pleading the cause of his diocese, with the advantage of some personal knowledge of its wants, and obtaining assistants in his work.

Just about the same time, arrived another colonial

Bishop in England. On the same page in the "Colonial Church Chronicle" which announces the arrival of the Bishop of Natal, I find also the following notice. "The Bishop of New Zealand has reached England after an absence of twelve years from his native land. This brief period, marked by hitherto unexampled labours to spread the Gospel, and to found the Church among heathen races, must at some future time become an epoch in the history of the Church of England. And the record will not be inglorious, at least if wisdom, prudence, untiring courage, rare self-devotion,—all directed with a single eye to the honour and glory of our blessed Redeemer,—are worthy of a remembrance in the annals of mankind." The feeling excited in the minds of English people by the news of Bishop Selwyn's return was very striking and also very cheering to every Christian heart. The missionary was expected with something like the feeling which belongs to the return of a great general from a successful campaign; and the mind of England was probably more generally turned to missionary thoughts, and more open to impression concerning the great work of evangelizing the world, than it ever had been at any previous period. Of course Bishop Selwyn was seized upon to speak and preach upon all possible occasions, and few who heard him will ever forget the simple and modest manliness of his eloquence. In no place was he more heartily welcomed or more thoroughly appreciated than in his own University, and in November 1854 he preached a course of four sermons in the University pulpit as select preacher.

These four sermons were published at the request of the Vice-Chancellor, under the title, *The Work of Christ in the World.* I shall venture to extract from them the concluding passage: it is striking to read,—how much more striking to hear!

"And if," said the Bishop, "it please God to call you to a more peaceful lot, to the work of the ministry in England,—in the colonies,—or in the mission-field, you will learn to think all things light, which you can do or suffer for the cause of Christ, when you see what the service is which the world exacts. And yet our work also has no narrow compass. I go from hence, if it be the will of God, to the most distant of all countries—to the place, where God, in answer to the prayers of his Son, has given Him the heathen for His inheritance, and the uttermost parts of the earth for His possession. There God has planted the standard of the cross, as a signal to His Church to fill up the intervening spaces, till there is neither a spot of earth which has not been trodden by the messengers of salvation, nor a single man to whom the Gospel has not been preached. Fill up the void. Let it be no longer a reproach to the Universities that they have sent so few missionaries to the heathen. The Spirit of God is ready to be poured upon all flesh; and some of you are His chosen vessels. Again, I say, Offer yourselves to the Primate of our Church. The voice of the Lord is asking, 'Whom shall I send, and who will go with us?' May every one of you who intends, by God's grace, to dedicate himself to the ministry, answer at once: 'Here am I, send me.'"

I now return to Mackenzie. In the autumn of 1854, I think in the beginning of October, the Bishop of Natal proposed to him that he should go out to Natal as archdeacon. So far as I can remember he had not made known to his friends that any decided change had taken place in his views with regard to home work, but I suppose that his previous conduct with regard to Delhi pointed him out as a man who might not improbably accept a foreign appointment if offered to him; indeed from one intimate friend he had extracted a promise, on relinquishing the Delhi scheme, that any fitting opening which might afterwards occur should be mentioned to him. In the latter part of the summer of this year he spent a few days with my family and myself at Felixstow in Suffolk, but I do not remember that he conversed with me upon the probability of his going out as a missionary. However, the proposal came from the Bishop of Natal, and the following letter shews the manner in which he received it. The letter is to his eldest sister; it is undated, but internal evidence refers it to the month of October. He speaks in it of having been "named for the Caput." The Caput, or more fully, the Caput Senatus, was a body consisting of five persons, upon whom devolved the duty of approving of Graces before they were submitted to the Senate; it was abolished in 1856. I find by reference to the records of the University that Mackenzie was not only nominated a member of the Caput on October 12, but was actually elected at a Congregation holden on October 18. I cannot tell when he resigned; Mr Romilly, the late Registrary of the University, informs me that "the practice of the University never was to make a second election in the year after the resignation of a man duly elected: so there is no record of Mackenzie's resignation." It will be seen, however, that the date of the letter must be certainly subsequent to October 12. We are thus brought very near to the month of November, in which the Bishop of New Zealand preached; of which more presently.

LETTER XXVII.

CAIUS COLLEGE, *Monday.*

DEAR ——,

Read the enclosed at some quiet time when you can command it.

C. F. M.

A year and a half ago I was asked to go to Delhi, and on the advice of most of my friends, I declined.

Now I have another offer. The Bishop of Natal (one of the two new Bishopricks at the Cape) wants me to go with him as Archdeacon, and to be second to him in the Diocese.

The Bishop was with W. B. Hopkins on Friday, and Hopkins told him he might ask me, at any rate, to go. So I conclude that Hopkins is favourable. I shall write, however, and ascertain this point.

I have consulted Goodwin, and he says that much as he would regret my going, he must advise me to go.

My own feelings are very strong in favour. For the last two or three months I have quite had my mind made up, to go somewhere abroad, as soon as home claims left me free. When I left this place in August, I fully intended to have spoken to you on the subject: but other plans, you know, prevented me; for I did not wish to complicate the matter, and I should have thought the scheme we spoke of, a tie to this country of considerable strength.

But now I look upon that as laid aside for the present; so that I think other ideas should return with full force. To neglect one way of being useful, because another way may become feasible, would be absurd.

My *positive* reasons are simply that there is difficulty in getting men to go out; and I have no reason to give against going; therefore I ought to go. Like labourers in a field, each should go where he is most wanted.

I look upon Goodwin's approval as most important. He was so strong against the other, that his sincerity and disinterestedness are proved. He does not deny that the College will miss me, but he says he could more easily find a man to fill my place here than one willing and able to do the work there.

* * * * *

I have only a few minutes now before the post goes.

I have so far made up my mind to go, that I shall at once disengage myself from some duties which would interfere with my going. I was named for the *Caput* a day or two ago, but by declining at once, I shall give less trouble than if I were to wait for a week or two: I shall therefore do so. Also I shall at once find some one to take the office of Examiner in the Senate-House next January[1]. I should have told you that the Bishop will sail in January or February, and would like me to go with him.

* * * * *

I said I had almost made up my mind: I have not a shadow of doubt of your approving: indeed, I feel sure that this opening and my accepting are but the fulfilment of your hopes since I wrote about Delhi. I am more anxious to hear what —— says: but I have just read over his letter to me about Delhi, and though the remarks apply nearly as well to this as to that, yet I cannot say they change my views. Still, if he has anything to say, I shall be glad to

[1] His place was taken by Mr Ferrers of Caius College.

hear from him, most thankful indeed for anything that will help me to come to a right final conclusion. I shall write this evening more full particulars of what I know already of the work.

* * * * *

It will be observed that the above letter throws a considerable responsibility upon the editor of this memoir. In explanation of the advice which I thought it right to give to my dear friend, I have only to say this. It seemed to me quite clear, and I think the tone of his letters will prove, that Mackenzie's mind was fixed upon missionary work. The Delhi scheme had been abandoned in deference to the opinion of his friends, and here was the same desire breaking out again. Might not his friends, if they still insisted upon keeping him, be fighting against God? I confess that when he mentioned the subject to me a second time, I thought that I had no right to oppose upon the general principle, but only upon the conviction that the particular sphere of missionary work to which he was looking was unsuited for him. Now it seemed to me, that if go he must, the Natal opening was a very suitable one. I thought that his fine temper and irresistible loveableness would tend to smooth the difficulties, to which an infant Church in a colony must inevitably be subject; and so far as Heathen work was concerned, I knew that he could condescend to the simplest of his fellow-creatures, and I thought that he would be happier in planning missions amongst the untaught Kafirs, than in dealing with the objections of acute Hindus. It will have been seen that in the first instance, rightly or wrongly, I did my best to keep him for what seemed to me to be peculiarly his sphere of work; I did not dare to act in the same manner a second time. How much it cost me to think of losing him I will not say.

For the present, however, the offer of the Bishop of Natal was declined, apparently in deference to the wishes of his family. The immediate cause of the ultimate determination to go to Natal is to be found in the sermons of the Bishop of New Zealand already referred to. At these sermons, it was noticed by Mackenzie's friends, that, contrary to his practice, he was regularly present. He usually, as we have seen, spent the whole Sunday at Haslingfield, walking home in the evening: but during the month of November he was to be seen each Sunday afternoon in Great S. Mary's Church, and his intimate friends, who knew all that had passed, concluded that his attendance was significant. Certainly to a mind that was at all leaning towards missionary enterprise, nothing could be more likely to give the final movement than the sermons of Bishop Selwyn: eloquent and forcible in themselves, they were a hundred times more eloquent and forcible when regarded as the testimony of a man, who had himself done so much, and done it so nobly. The next letter will shew their effect upon Mackenzie's mind. Like the last, it is to his eldest sister.

LETTER XXVIII.

CAIUS COLLEGE,
Monday, Dec. 11.

MY DEAR ——,

I hope, though you may be surprised, yet that you will not be seriously sorry, when I say that I have reconsidered my decision about Natal. I have offered to go with the Bishop in the capacity he proposed before, and I have been accepted. So now the whole thing is fixed, and I shall sail with him in February.

Soon after coming to the determination of staying here, I began to doubt the rightness of that conclusion, and then Bishop Selwyn, of New Zealand, preached in the University pulpit in November, and he revived in my mind the conviction, that a man's going from home is like a branch being cut from a tree to be planted somewhere else, and that the other branches will spread, and very soon no gap will be seen. At this time the Bishop of Natal wrote to me about another man, a friend of mine here, and asked if I thought he would be a good person to go. I wrote to say, I thought he would be a good person, if he were free to go; and it ended in this man and myself discussing his case, and our deliberations ended, rightly I believe, in his declining. Then I wrote to the Bishop, that if he was still free to offer it to me, I would accept; and he writes me that he most heartily welcomes me as his brother and fellow-labourer in the work.

In all this I have acted on my own responsibility, having changed my mind without the advice of any earthly friend: but I do humbly trust, that what I have done is according to the will of my heavenly Master.

* * * * *

So far I have spoken of myself, though I have been of course speaking to you. Now comes ——'s case. She writes me that —— recommends a warmer climate. Natal is a beautiful climate, and I fancy —— would not wish for a better escort than mine. So I am writing by this same post to propose to her to come with me in February.

* * * * *

I hardly know what more to say. On the point of going or staying, I consulted no one; but on the point of Natal or elsewhere I again consulted Goodwin, and he is most clear on that head. So I willingly agreed.

Dear ——, good bye for the present. Commend me to ——'s kind thoughts. Commend me to God's care.

Your very affectionate brother,

C. F. M.

Of course there need be no secret about my going: it is fixed.

The next letter is to another sister: it gives no additional information, but is too characteristic to be omitted.

LETTER XXIX.

Caius College,
Dec. 11, 1854.

Dearest ——,

It is long since I have written to you, and though I began a letter a few days ago, on receiving one from ——, which spoke of your being again in Edinburgh, yet I did not get it finished, being interrupted; and the attempt found its way into the fire.

And now dear —— I have something to tell you, which I fear will vex you. I suppose it may as well come out at once: I have made up my mind to go abroad. I am going to the colony of Natal, with the Bishop of Natal, to be his second in command; to help him to put in order what needs arranging there, and to commence schemes which may, I trust by the blessing of God, lead to the conversion to civilization, to Christianity, to happiness here, and to the hope of glory, many of the simple natives of the place.

I shall have to go in February; but on that very account I must see you all for a while before that time. So I propose coming to Edinburgh on the 23rd.

I hope you will be enabled to look at this move of mine in the right view, as a short separation that we may be united for ever; as a noble work with which my Master has entrusted me, for the due performance of which you must help me with sympathy and prayer. My dear ——, I used to form my judgment a good deal by yours: those days are gone by: but it will be unspeakably comforting to me, if we can heartily join in giving up our own will to God's, and rejoice in that which may best tend to set forth His glory and to hasten His kingdom.

It is late, and I have other letters to write.

Good bye, dearest,

Believe me to be, now as ever,

Your affectionate brother,

C. F. M.

The next is also to a sister, and inserted for the same reason as the last.

LETTER XXX.

CAIUS COLLEGE,
Dec. 11, 1854.

MY DEAR ——,

I have been very remiss in not acknowledging your letter. I can speak to you however on the subject to which it refers when we meet, as I hope we shall before long, for I am looking forward to being in Scotland at Christmas this year.

The fact is, I have given up my Examinership this year, because I have been asked to go out to the colony of Natal with the Bishop, as his second in command, to help him to make arrangements in his diocese, at its first starting; and I have accepted the offer. It is only proposed that I should go out for five years, but though of course I may come home before that time, or after it, yet I have at present no intention of coming back, except perhaps for a short visit.

This will, I believe, surprise you as much as any one; yet I feel confident it will not distress you. The Lord hath need of him, is a sufficient answer to all questionings, Why should I go? My reason is very simple. There is in the colonies a lack of men; there is none at home. Therefore let all that are free go cheerfully to that other part of the field, where their labour is more wanted than here.

This is a very simple view of the case; one which I believe will at once commend itself to you, even though the fulfilling of the duty it brings were to you like the cutting off a right hand or the plucking out a right eye.

Please tell —— what is in this letter, and say that as I hope to be down so soon I may perhaps not write to him, as I should certainly have done, had not you been in his house. I hope he will not think me utterly mad; I hardly hope he will approve of the step I have taken: a step, concerning which I have no hesitation myself, having deliberately arrived at my present conclusion after more or less deliberation during two years.

* * * * *

My acquaintances in Cambridge, of whom I have a goodly store, are a good deal taken by surprise by my resolution: my best friends congratulate me.

Now dear —— it is late, and to-morrow evening I shall spend with my Bishop in London: so I must not be sleepy, or perhaps he will say I may stay at home.

In short, good night.

Believe me to be, now as ever,
Your affectionate brother,
C. F. M.

The following short letter speaks for itself.

LETTER XXXI.

(*To a Sister.*)

CAIUS COLLEGE,
Dec. 19, 1854.

MY OWN DEAR ——,

I cannot tell you how your letter affected me. It was one of my first thoughts when I wrote to —— in

October, How would *you* feel it? and now I see that, bitter as the parting may be, yet you are supported by Him who is a sure Refuge in time of trouble.

Let us remember that the time is short. It remaineth that we must be separated from every earthly tie, in order that such bonds as are holy may be renewed.

I shall not say more just now. I shall hope to see you on Saturday.

Your affectionate brother,

C. F. M.

The result then was, that it was finally determined that Mackenzie should go out with the Bishop of Natal, in the character of Archdeacon. His own family did not offer any strong opposition, indeed opposition was manifestly useless; many of his Cambridge friends acquiesced in the scheme, seeing how clearly his own mind was made up; but some expressed their opinion very strongly that his proper sphere of action was Cambridge, and that he ought not to move. In one point all agreed, namely, that his departure from Cambridge was as simple and genuine a sacrifice of self as it was possible for a man to offer upon the altar of God. *Others will not go, so I will,*—this principle, and no love of roaming, no weariness of home quiet, no enthusiastic belief in his own power of working missionary miracles, took him away from England and gave him to South Africa. Of the scene of his future labours, more will be said hereafter.

The Christmas of 1854 was spent in Edinburgh, with his family, and it was soon arranged that the invalid sister, referred to in page 90, should go as his companion to South Africa. He mentioned it to me, if I remember aright, as a singular support to him, and a sign of the correctness of his choice, that after having made up his mind to go to Natal, the next post brought him a letter informing him that a warmer climate had been prescribed for this invalid sister.

On his return from Scotland, there was plenty of work to be done in the way of preparation for an early departure. I have only one letter which belongs to this period. Here it is.

LETTER XXXII.

(*To a Sister.*)

CAIUS COLLEGE,
Jan. 29, 55.

MY DEAR ——,

Your present[1], reaching me a few minutes before I left ——, went at once into my pocket. So when morning dawned, before we got to London, —— and I could read, each to himself, for there were others in the carriage, our morning psalms.

I cannot help blaming myself for the weakness of our parting. For surely it is a glorious prospect, that is before me, doing the work of my Master, (faithfully, I hope,) here, and waiting for His return. The idea has sometimes crossed my mind, if in heaven we have work to do for Him, (as doubtless we shall have,) still shall we not look back on the work we might have done for Him here, and which we have neglected? For this time will never come again. We may serve Him *then* faithfully for the future, but *the past* —this world which will then be past will never come again; and as our love will be so much warmer, so our sorrow for neglected opportunities of serving Him will be

[1] A small Prayer-Book to carry in a waistcoat pocket.

the keener, if indeed sorrow can be there. I felt something like this on leaving school to come to College: though a new sphere of usefulness was opened before me, it never could make up for the one that I left; and now I feel something of the same kind: great as are the means of serving Him to which he has now called me, I have had great means here, and these opportunities I have too often neglected. The future has its own responsibilities which will correspond with its opportunities, the past is gone. These thoughts, at such a change of life as the present, seem to me to be presages of the thoughts that will vex one on a deathbed, or perhaps beyond the grave.

I must stop for the present. When I write again, it will be, I dare say, in a more hopeful strain.

I have made out the accounts of the Board of Education, have preached my last sermons at Haslingfield, and am advertised to preach next Sunday in one church, while the Bishop is preaching in another.

* * * * *

It was eventually determined that the Bishop of Natal and his mission party should sail from Liverpool in the beginning of March in the barque, Jane Morice, which was prepared specially for their accommodation, and made as convenient as so small a vessel could be made for so large a party. A brother-in-law of the editor of this memoir, residing at Oxton, near Birkenhead, invited Archdeacon Mackenzie and his sister to take up their abode at his house while the preparations for the voyage were in progress; this they gladly consented to do, and I offered to accompany them. Owing to this arrangement, I had the pleasure and privilege of seeing the very last of my dear and honoured friend.

He was perfectly cheerful, as he always was; and several times he said to me, as we were busily engaged in Liverpool, making arrangements for the voyage, "I cannot help thinking how different all this would have seemed, if you had not come with me." A few days before the sailing of the *Jane Morice*, there was a farewell service in Trinity Church, Birkenhead; and on March 7 the missionary party embarked.

The parting scene is strongly impressed upon my mind. We waited upon the pier at Liverpool for a steam-tug which was to convey the party to the vessel, lying in the river. The party was all assembled; the Bishop with his family, the Archdeacon and his sister, two clergymen, a German professor of languages, several missionary ladies, two catechists, a farmer and his wife, a few labourers and mechanics, and several boys, in all about 30 or 40 persons. It was a solemn quiet scene. There was plenty of time for last words, and the moments seemed very precious to us. At length the steam-tug came alongside; the party was soon on board, and the last thing which caught my eye was the happy countenance of the boy from the Cambridge Industrial School, who was eating an orange with all the appearance of entire absence of care.

I may refer the reader to page 2, for a short letter written by Mackenzie at this period to his eldest sister, in which he acknowledges gratefully all the care and kindness he had received at her hands; I here add another, written on the day before the sailing of the *Jane Morice* to another sister equally dear to him.

LETTER XXXIII.

(*To a Sister.*)

OXTON HILL, BIRKENHEAD,
March 6, 1855.

DEAREST AND SWEETEST ——,

We sail to-morrow; so I write to-day to say Good bye, and to bid you cheer your heart, as I know you are doing. We are, at least I can speak for myself, and I believe —— will say the same, in the most cheerful and happy frame of mind. We have a good deal to do, which seems to occupy our minds, and the extreme kindness we have received from our friends here beggars all description.

* * * * *

So you are getting better, dear ——. If the accounts of your health are good, it will be the *best news*, I speak advisedly, that I can hear from home: I mean the news that will give me most selfish pleasure: of course one ought to feel that the *best news* is, the success of the Master's kingdom.

Ever dear ——,
Your affectionate brother,
C. F. M.

The voyage of the *Jane Morice* was most prosperous, and as little unpleasant to the mission party as so long a voyage in so small a vessel could be. The Archdeacon shall tell his own tale of his life on board ship in a letter written to the editor of this Memoir.

LETTER XXXIV.

THE JANE MORICE,
March 15, 1855.
Lat. 37°. Long. 13°. W.

DEAR HARVEY,

My first letter after parting is, I think, due to you. Thanks many for your continued kindnesses in Cheshire not that your late kindnesses have obliterated former ones from my mind, but our intercourse lately has been more tender and brotherly, I think, than before.

But you will probably care more for some account of what has been going on, than for any long accounts of my feelings.

This is the eighth day of our voyage, and it has seemed both long and short. I was frequently sick during the first two days, and hardly touched a thing: but I am thankful to say that I had no headache, and was able to run about as much as ever: this was lucky: for with the assistance of a lady, Miss ——, (or rather she with my help,) waited on the steerage passengers, nearly all of whom were ill, and all very downhearted. It was hard work, but has ended in making a very friendly feeling between the two parts of the ship. You would have laughed if you had seen me, in a little cabin with four berths, quite dark; I making the bed for some person, man or woman, who sits upon a box talking Suffolk: or standing outside the ship-kitchen begging the black cook for some "fresh water boil" to make arrow-root, (I can make it famously now): or going from one part of the ship to another, helping Miss —— to walk on the slippery decks, each carrying two cups of arrow-root, I with a pocket filled with a brandy-flask, a tumbler, a bottle of raspberry-vinegar, and two eggs. Then we had great confusion about the luggage. And besides, I have been down in the hold seeing the stores weighed out to the steerage passengers; and in the morning I am either running for the breakfast for the children, or holding one while the nurse dresses another; and we are together keeping the other two quiet.

I write these particulars, that you may see how fortunate it is that I had not mounted my official coat before leaving England. On the whole I have selfishly enjoyed the voyage very much. There has been plenty to do, and I have had strength to do it.

* * * * *

We have had short morning and evening prayers in the cabin, and in the steerage, every day. On Sunday morning we had a short service.

* * * * *

This is the first day on which I have begun any work for Natal, namely, the grammar for an hour this morning. I have told the lads that they, and any others that like, may read with me for an hour in the morning: we are to begin to-morrow. I go to bed always at ten, and lately have not got up till seven; the fact is, one's nights were broken at first, and even now I think the motion of the vessel injures one's rest. We have had a capital run so far. The wind was against us on the second day as we came down the Channel, but on the Thursday night a fine breeze sprang up, which lasted till about yesterday, and has brought us well on our way. One night I got up at about three, and walked on the deck till four, enjoying the magnificence of the scene: fine waves foaming beside us, and the ship breasting them famously.

It is difficult to give you any idea of our party without being personal.

* * * * *

Our day now is as follows. I get up between six and seven, and at seven I have the four lads to read the Bible; at eight the steerage passengers breakfast, and the cabin passengers begin to emerge from their cabins at the smell of cocoa, which comes hot and excellent from the kitchen. Till breakfast, which is nominally at nine, but is ofter nearer ten, we sit and read or walk on deck. Breakfast consists of coffee, bread baked that morning, toasted captain's biscuits, cold saltish beef, and perhaps a fowl or a duck or a tongue. Immediately after breakfast we have prayers on deck, not the full morning service, but parts of it: I read, and the Bishop gives a ten minutes' lecture on some part of the second lesson. Then we have our Zulu class, in which we have read the fifth chapter of S. Matthew, besides a good deal of grammar. Then we play for a time: (I often go up the shrouds, or arrange some of the things which the Bishop has entrusted to me, or heal up an incipient quarrel amongst the steerage, or take a turn at the wheel, or run up to the main-top yard): or else work at the Zulu till dinner-time, three o'clock, often four. Dinner consists of soup, pair of fowls or ducks, or some mutton, pork, or corned beef, and a pudding. After dinner we are on deck again till tea, about eight; then prayers in the cabin and steerage separately, with a hymn; and then reading, or writing, (as now,) in the cabin, in nearly perfect silence, or sitting on deck, admiring the stars: I never do this latter. Then at ten talking is forbidden, and before eleven we are all in our berths. I find I lie most steadily on my back; I learnt this from a tin case of arrow-root, which used always to tumble over until laid on its larger face. It is close upon eleven: so I must stop. We are now just passing S. Antonio, one of the Cape Verd Islands.

March 28. You see how seldom I take up my pen, and for how short a time. We are now in lat. 11°: yet the day has been very cool, except in the direct rays of the sun. We have an awning, stretching forward from the hurricane cabin, so as to protect us from the sun. We are getting on famously: we ran 200 miles between noon on the 26th and noon on the 27th, and about as much in the next twenty-four hours.

The Zulu gets much easier. We are in the 7th chapter of S. Matthew now. The grammar is very good.

We are longing to be at Natal; not so much, I believe honestly, on account of the annoyances of shipboard, as that we may get to work. I suspect the affairs of the mission are rather at a stand-still for want of us.

April 16. Lat. 20°, S. Long. 29° or 30°, W. We have a vessel in sight a-head, and hope to send letters by it. We are still progressing in the most favourable manner, and hope to make the voyage in about ten weeks.

* * * * *

During this hot weather we, the gentlemen, have been enjoying a new mode of bath. There is a fire-engine on board, which is used every morning for flooding the decks in the operation of washing them: there is no nozzle, but an open tube an inch and a half in diameter: this is turned upon us, and the result may be conceived better than described. Another more refined enjoyment we have had in these tropical regions. The sunsets have been most gorgeous, and the sunrisings even better. Yesterday and today many of us were up at a little after five feasting our eyes for an hour or more. I forgot, strange to say, to mention, that I am writing with Mrs Goodwin's pen, which is excellent. My best and kindest remembrances to her.

* * * * *

As for myself, I have not a shadow of regret at the change of occupation: on the contrary, I am full of thanks to Him who gave me the good will, as I cannot help regarding it, and gave me strength to carry out the purpose, and has so fully recompensed me for any sacrifice. I could not help thinking last night, if there were nothing else than the increased pleasure of singing the hymns in our service, thinking of the words all the time, (a habit which I began in your church, I think,) I should have richly gained. This last paragraph I have written, as you will believe, to encourage others who may be thinking of coming out.

* * * * *

I give the conclusion of the voyage from Miss Mackenzie's journal.

May 20th. Yesterday morning we were roused very early by being told the land of Natal was in sight. For many days previously we had been nearly becalmed, an unusual occurrence on this coast so near the Cape; but a strong and favourable breeze had now sprung up and we had made more than 200 miles during the last twenty-four hours. The coast was a very pleasant sight, rising in hills, and increasing in beauty as the sun rose, and the lights became varied. There were dark woods running along the shore, and green patches of underwood on the rising ground. There was a general feeling of joyous thankfulness among all, for our voyage throughout has been a most prosperous and peaceful and happy one; no storms to alarm, no sickness among the party, and all has been harmony; the few necessary discomforts of so long a stay on shipboard being nearly all forgotten amidst the many blessings of the present, and hopes of the future, when our duties and occupations are begun. I myself felt a little regret at the even tenour of our life being ended, and the pleasant intercourse and constant accessibility to any one whom I wished to speak to, being changed to the usual restraints of life, and the busy world; but in this feeling my brother was the only one who sympathised with me.

We made very slow progress this day, but were so close to land that we did not feel the monotony as we had done in the midst of the ocean; but to the Bishop the delay was very trying, as he hoped to cross the bar (which is passable only at high tide) in the evening, and got ready to go to Durban and officiate this forenoon. In the evening a rocket was sent up to announce our arrival and give warning to the pilot: but it was not seen, and he did not arrive till eleven A.M. I wish I could write in the glowing strain I could have done at that time of day; the land looked so beautiful, the rising hills so refreshing to our eyes, the sun was so bright and warm, and the sea so smooth, the air so balmy, while the whole service for the day was so suitable to our excited feelings; and I believe all joined with heart and voice in the 103rd Psalm, ascribing praise and blessing to God for all His mercies, which the Bishop took for the subject-matter of an excellent short sermon he gave us.

About four P.M. we crossed the bar, where the waves roared and broke with white foam; but within Durban bay it was like a lake, the water quite green and placid, and the banks most beautiful and covered with evergreens and flowering shrubs.

The Bishop went on shore and is to return to-morrow, when he has made arrangements for the accommodation of his large party; and we shall then take a final leave of the good *Jane Morice*, the Captain and all the crew. The recollection of the time passed on board her, and of this my first voyage, will ever be one of the bright points in my life. The quiet to-night, while we are lying at anchor, seems very strange, and the ship looks unlike herself with all her sails furled; and I doubt not the sailors are enjoying the unwonted luxury of undisturbed sound sleep, which indeed will be equally welcomed by most of the party. I feel confident all will unite in private, as they have done in public prayer, in thanking God for all the blessings He has vouchsafed us, and for His protecting care of us during the voyage.

On reaching Natal the Archdeacon committed to paper some miscellaneous reflections upon the voyage. I subjoin a few extracts.

May 20, 1855. *Sunday.* After a most prosperous voyage of seventy-four days from Liverpool, we are now lying in the harbour at Durban. Before writing what I have to say about the voyage, I wish to record my strong feeling of the very great mercies we have received during this time from the hand of our most gracious Father, both in outward protection and comfort, and in the pleasures of kind and Christian society.

There are not many facts to be recorded of the voyage, that bear upon the interests of the Mission. Most of the members of the Mission-party have devoted a good deal of attention to the study of the Zulu language: the effect of which has been a certain amount of acquaintance with the regular forms of the grammar, (very little progress has been made in the knowledge of the idioms,) and a translation of S. Matthew, made by the American missionaries, has been read through, and most of the constructions thoroughly understood. In this work the missionaries have been instructed by the Bishop, who has given up a good deal of time for the purpose: and the Bishop has been assisted, and in many instances himself instructed, by Dr Bleek, a German linguist, who has been engaged to assist in methodising the language, and in further translations. I have said that little progress has been made in the less usual idioms of the language: for the Bishop and Dr Bleek were not sufficiently deep in their knowledge to enable them to take us much beyond the simple and more common forms of expression: and besides, the book which we were translating being itself a translation, and one made probably by persons who had only an imperfect knowledge of the language, we could not expect to find in it anything but simple forms of language, frequently repeated. However, some ground has been gained, and we are certainly in a position to pick up the language from actual communication with the natives.

Another good result of the long voyage has been the acquaintance we have thus had an opportunity of making with each other. For instance, I have had many opportunities of conversation with the Bishop, from which I have derived much advantage, and which has, I think, shewn us that we are so nearly alike in opinion and feeling, that we may confidently hope to work harmoniously together. Then again, others of the party have had opportunities of making friendship together, quite as well if not better than on land. This I think worth mentioning, because it seemed at first as if the ten weeks of the voyage would be thrown away. I looked upon this as a necessary and unavoidable loss arising from the scene of our future labour being in a distant land: I now look upon it as having been highly useful to our work. One other good purpose the voyage ought to have had; but I must confess that I did not turn the time to profit in this respect; I mean that one ought to have used the time for reading and prayer and meditation, so as to grow in grace and in the knowledge of our Lord and Saviour Jesus Christ. If this should fall into the hands of any person who is about to follow across the waters to this or any other mission, I would suggest the necessity of distinctly striving to make this use of the voyage. No doubt there are difficulties in the matter: one being the obstacles which exist on board ship to solitude.

In the earlier part of the voyage we had a good deal of sickness on board; not more, I dare say, than usual in such cases. This, which might have appeared an unmixed evil, did, on the other hand, afford to those who were well an opportunity of sympathising, and in many cases of alleviating the distress of their neighbours. This cannot have failed to have drawn to each other by the cords of love those who were afterwards to work together. Another aspect of the voyage I must mention. We have not been, as some may have expected, and as some may even think we ought to have been, a gloomy, sombre party. We have been as cheerful as possible. To be sure, we have had a good deal of young blood among us, more than many missionary parties: but I think even the elder ones among us have felt that religion and cheerfulness, far from being incompatible, are productive the former of the latter: the good gifts of our heavenly Father being intended to be accepted as from Him, and that thankfully.

As to events during our passage, which have not affected the interests of the mission. Our course was more to the Westward than I expected. We ran as far as 30° of W. Longitude. The reason of running to the West is that the N.E. trades are thereby made available to the fullest extent, while after running across the S.E. trades, keeping as much to the South as possible, the longitude which has been lost may be gained again in the temperate zone, where the prevailing winds are from the West. But I believe the main reason is, that on the Western side of the Atlantic the belt near the Equators (between the N.E. and the S.E. trades), in which the winds are variable and calms frequent, is narrower than on the eastern side; and it is considered to be worth while to incur a certain addition to the length of course to be run, rather than risk an indefinite detention in this region of variable winds. In our case the Captain intended to cross the line about longitude 19° West, but was driven as far West as 25°.

We saw several kinds of birds. One of them was caught, an albatross, with a baited hook. He was allowed to walk on the deck for some time. I was struck by the want of muscular strength in the wing. He was a heavy bird, considerably heavier than a swan; yet the wing yielded to one's hands without much resistance, when we bent one of the joints of it. This may be, because the bird, though very much on the wing, does not require to give violent blows with the wing, and needs muscles capable of exertion for long periods, rather than capable of exciting a powerful force for a short time.

The heat on crossing the line was considerable, but not so excessive as I expected. Some of us indeed were put out of sorts for a few days, but I found it only slightly enervating: and it made it necessary for us to remain a good deal under the awning. (We made jokes at the time about the connection between *awning* and *yawning*, which may shew the weak state of mind and body to which we were reduced.)

This day we crossed the bar, and are now lying at anchor in the bay. Yesterday morning at daybreak we saw the mainland of Africa for the first time.

* * * * *

The party being now safely arrived at their destination, this Chapter may suitably close with the following testimonial, taken from a letter written by Miss Mackenzie on the voyage.

I am very happy and all the passengers are agreeable, owing (the Bishop told me) to my excellent brother, whose peace-making qualities we know of old; he is also the life of the party, the sunshine of the steerage, and the director of everything, from the boxes in the hold to the preaching and teaching of all on board.

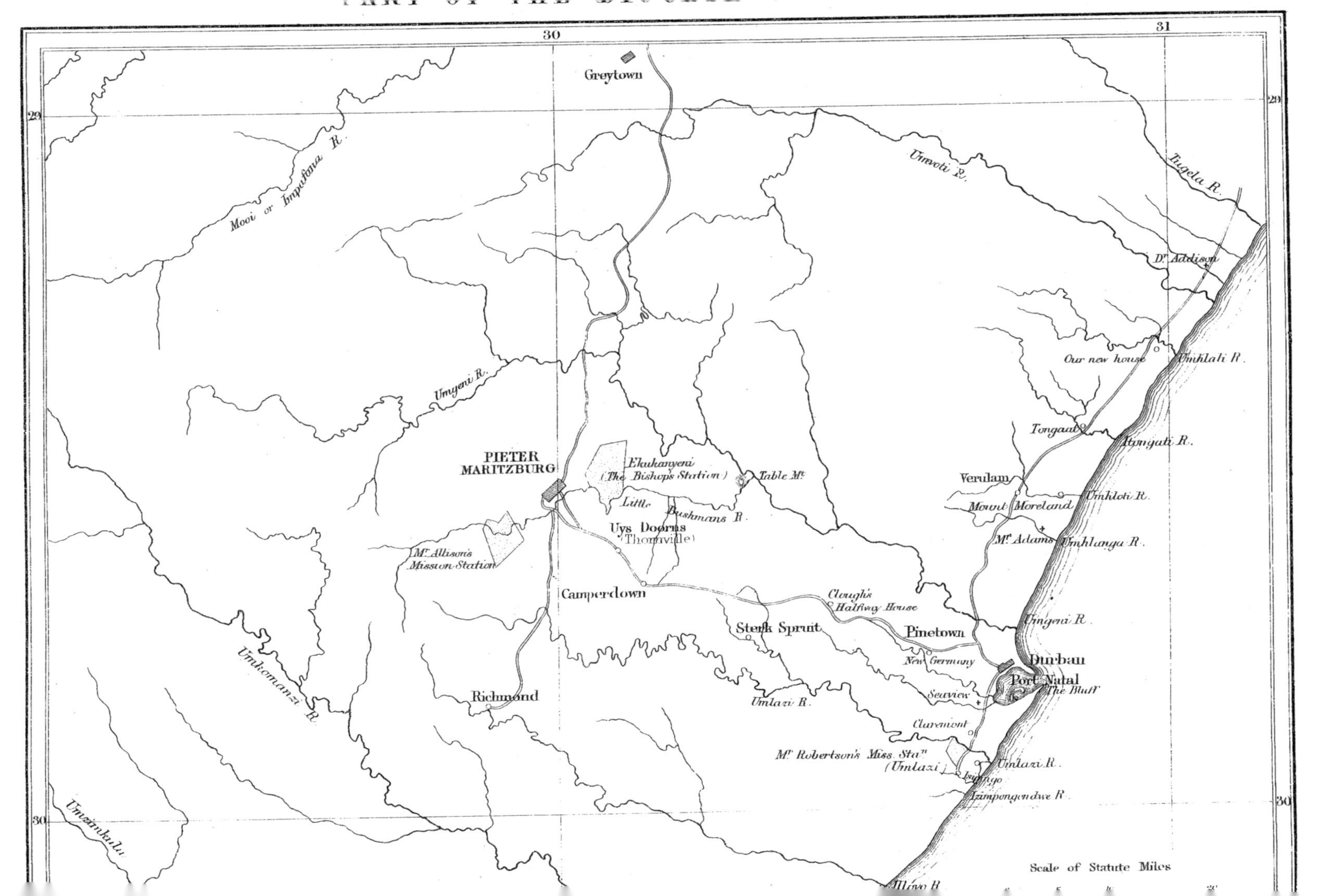

30
31
29
Greytown
Mooi or Impafana R.
Umvoti R.
Tugela R.
Dr. Addison
Umgeni R.
Our new house
Umhlali R.
Tongaat
Tongati R.
PIETER
MARITZBURG
Ekukanyeni
(The Bishop's Station)
Table Mt.
Verulam
Umhloti R.
Little
Bushmans R.
Mount Moreland
Uys Doorns
(Thornville)
Mr. Adams
Umhlanga R.
Mr. Allison's
Mission Station
Camperdown
Clough's
Halfway House
Sterk Spruit
Pinetown
Umgeni R.
New Germany
Durban
Port Natal
The Bluff
Umkomanzi R.
Seaview
Richmond
Umlazi R.
Claremont
Mr. Robertson's Miss. Sta.n
(Umlazi)
Umlazi R.
Isipingo
Izimpongondwe R.
Umzimkulu
Scale of Statute Miles

CHAPTER VI.

RESIDENCE IN NATAL. DURBAN.

AN interesting historical sketch of the colony, which is now for several years to be the home of Archdeacon Mackenzie, will be found prefixed to Bishop Colenso's *Ten Weeks in Natal.* The colony has been so much before the eyes of English Christians, as an interesting and hopeful scene of missionary work, during the last seven or eight years, that it might perhaps be taken for granted that the readers of this memoir would be already sufficiently acquainted with the position of Natal, both geographical and religious. I shall think it right, however, to suppose that there are some to whom a few words of explanation will be acceptable, and for them the following paragraphs are intended.

"Natal lies upon the South-East coast of Africa, in latitude 29 to 31 degrees. It derives its name, *Terra Natalis,* from the fact of its having been discovered by the Portuguese navigator, Vasco di Gama, on Christmas-day, A.D. 1497. Its extent of surface is about 18,000 square miles, or just one-third of England and Wales. The country may be described, generally, as rising rapidly from the coast of the Indian Ocean, in four distinct steps or terraces, each about twenty miles in average width, and each having its own peculiarity of soil and climate. Along the coast the heat is greatest, and though scarcely, in the height of summer, to be called 'tropical,' it is yet sufficient to allow of the growth of cotton, sugar, coffee, pine-apples, and other productions of the tropics. There is a good deal of woodland and park-like scenery in this region; but further inland, as the country rises in elevation, the temperature is diminished, and the air is clear and refreshing, except when the hot wind blows from the North-West, from the sun-scorched centre of Africa. The second range of land is almost bare of trees, but excellently well adapted for grazing purposes, besides furnishing abundant crops of hay, oats, *mealies*, or Indian-corn, and barley. The port-town of Durban, with its population of 1100, lies in the former district, and Maritzburg, the city and seat of government, with a population of about 1800, including the military, in the latter. Beyond this, the hills again rise, and we come to a region in which is found plenty of forest-timber of considerable size, and of very superior quality. And still more inland, immediately under the foot of the Kahlamba, or Draakenberg mountains, the soil is well adapted for growing wheat and other European products[1]."

Natal was recognised as a British colony in 1845, and became a separate diocese in 1853. Ecclesiastically speaking, it is of the nature of an island, being separated from the diocese of Graham's Town by Indepen-

[1] *Ten Weeks in Natal.*

dent Kaffraria, while to the North-East it is bounded by the heathen country of the Zulus. Some years before it became a British colony, an attempt had been made to evangelize the natives under the auspices of the Church Missionary Society. In August 1837, the Rev. T. Owen, with his wife and sister, landed at Port Natal, and shortly after commenced missionary operations. In the beginning of the following year, however, a terrible massacre of Dutch boers, who had settled in the country, and who were murdered in cold blood by order of Dingaan, the native king, and the manifest probability that Mr Owen and his family would sooner or later share the same fate, made the missionaries determine to accept the offer of escape, which the king made them, and to leave the country.

This massacre was amongst the dark recollections of the colony, when it was put under the care of a Christian bishop. Bright days seemed to have dawned: the steadiness and equity of British rule had caused a considerable immigration of Zulus, glad to escape the tyranny of their native chiefs, and the Bishop reckoned the native population at the time of his first visit as being from 100,000 to 120,000.

The Zulu Kaffirs are spoken of as a noble race of people, very superior to the Hottentots,—some one has described them as "magnificent savages"; they are honest and independent, capable of thinking and judging for themselves, and they speak a language of considerable refinement, and almost of Italian delicacy of pronunciation. Their chief fault seems to be that which belongs to all unchristianised races, a want of appreciation of the dignity of women; polygamy is the law of the country: and each new wife being purchased with a certain number of cows, the multiplicity of a man's wives unfortunately becomes, to a certain extent, a measure of his wealth and his social importance.

To this short notice of Natal, which will be enlarged incidentally as we proceed, I shall only add, that the reader will find at the beginning of this chapter a map of a portion of the colony; it includes all those places which are more immediately connected with Archdeacon Mackenzie's work and journeyings, and is copied from one which was made under his own direction, for the information of his friends at home.

For the account of Archdeacon Mackenzie's life in Natal, I shall depend to some extent upon his own letters, written from time to time, but in no great abundance; in addition to these, I have carefully read through a very large number of letters, written to friends at home by the sister who accompanied him, and by another sister, who (as we shall see) joined him afterwards. The extracts which I shall think it right to make from those letters will give only a faint notion of the life of earnest Christian work which they reveal, a life darkened sometimes by troubles, and those troubles not slight, but lighted up with the quiet light of practical godliness and charity. Admiration for their brother's character is not the least conspicuous feature of this very interesting collection[1].

[1] I have sometimes wished that a series of letters, taken from the collection here referred to, could be published. I think they would make some Christians at home in love with a Missionary life.

I now give two letters written by the Archdeacon some months after arriving in the colony, the first to myself, the second to his eldest sister.

LETTER XXXV.

DURBAN, *July 27th*, 1855.

DEAR GOODWIN,

* * * * *

For the first week after landing we all remained here, that is, at the town of Durban, about two miles from the mouth of the bay where we landed. I was chiefly employed in seeing that the goods came on shore, and were safely stowed in the warehouse; partly in seeing that the rest of the party were comfortable. About a week after landing the order was given for the mission party to proceed to Maritzburg, which is (as you know) fifty-two miles from this. We went in ten waggons, each of which was drawn by twelve or fourteen oxen. The particulars of the journey I shall not enter into, except one point. On the last night of the journey, shortly before we went to bed, we heard a considerable noise in a Kafir cabin close to us. Several of us went to see what was the matter, and found some four or five Kafirs sitting round the fire, which burned in the middle of the hut, on the ground of course, singing. I fancy it was a war-song. Every now and then, at the crisis in the song, one of them struck the tent-pole, which was about as thick as the calf of one's leg, heavy blows with his knob-kerry, with a ferocious or rather malicious expression of face. Then at other times they all joined in a curious noise made by panting with all their might, and at each expiration making a groaning noise, at the same time shaking the whole body. This amusement they continued till they were quite tired. We often hear a noise in the town of Durban, which betokens that the Kafir servants of some two or three families have got together, and are having a night of it in this sort of way. It is very horrible to see, but I sometimes doubt whether it is much more barbarous than the noises I have sometimes enjoyed making at a boating tea, or than the fantastic dancing performed by the best society. I assure you I think they are all very much on a par, and must all of them be accounted for as the ebullition of ex*h*uberant spirits (I wonder where that word got its *h* from; I know I ought not to have put it in). At Maritzburg I remained three weeks, preaching on Sundays and learning Kafir on the week-days.

About five weeks ago the Bishop determined to employ Mr —— (the Colonial Chaplain, who has been taking the duty at this place for the last four or five years,) in forming and taking care of scattered congregations on the coast. I see now how it is that dissent seems naturally to take the lead in a new place: the ease with which some one with the gift of language starts up in a little settlement where there are six or seven families, and conducts service on Sunday, is not comparable with the difficulty of getting a man in Episcopal orders to be minister in such a place, or even in two or three tolerably near each other. As to the amount of good done, that is a different thing; but dissent steps in very often among a set of people heartily attached to the Church, and by degrees steals their hearts. I suppose the remedy must be the ordaining men deacons, and letting them study for a few years longer, while in charge of such places, before admitting them to priest's orders.

Well; the result of this appropriation of Mr ——, for which his acquaintance with so many people in the colony admirably fitted him, left the town of Durban without a pastor. Accordingly I have been placed here, and think it possible I may remain here for a year, or perhaps two or three. It is not exactly the work I came out to do. At the same time the *principle* on which I came out is in no way broken; namely, I came out because so few were willing and able to leave home. And after all, I am perhaps exercising as great an influence for the good of the natives, if I be allowed to exert a good influence on the whites here, who will again act on the natives. Nothing can so interfere with missionary operations as the presence of a white population uninfluenced in heart by Christianity. Then, too, if I can get on with the language, there are as many coloured people as whites in the town, acting as house-servants. They do not stay for very long periods at a time; two or three months to eight or nine; never a year, without spending a month or more at home, after which they very often do not return. However, if I knew (or rather, when I know,) the language, I can work among them to my heart's content. The church here is complete as far as the fabric goes, walls and roof, but is not free from debt.

* * * * *

The people here are, I am thankful to say, well disposed towards me so far. Some little opposition exists to the custom (not an innovation, as you say,) of having baptisms in the service. I have to-day filled a sheet of paper in answer to a letter containing arguments in favour of letting the custom remain as it was under my predecessor.

* * * * *

I have just begun having service on Saints' days: prayers in the morning, prayers and sermon in the evening. I have about twenty in the morning, and fifty in the evening. The music in the church is very good.

* * * * *

As I was coming down from P. M. B. (Pieter Maritzburg) a fortnight ago, when I had got about half way, I thought I would take a short cut by a Kafir path. I had heard of the short cut, and had observed where I expected the cut to come into the road again. So I went off the road, and trudged away, my path being by the side of a little stream, with hardly a trickle of water in it: but the bed was in many places twelve feet deep and twenty wide, and there were evident signs of overflowing the banks in the wet

8—2

season. I had left the public-house about six, with a cup of coffee for breakfast; as I went on the path I began to think it was longer than I expected, and at last I could not find any track at all; so I concluded that I had lost my way. I climbed to the highest ground near, and I thought I recognized a hill; but on going some miles towards it I found I was wrong. By this time I had lost any notion of direction I might have had. Unfortunately your compass was still packed up in a zinc box at Maritzburg, (I have it now,) and the sun was not visible,—the first and only day I have missed him, I think, since landing. I was at fault about the points of the compass, when I saw an atom of a rainbow (not more in length than its own breadth) on the horizon. I stopped, marked its position, and noted which side was red and which violet; and taking it for granted it was the primary bow, I estimated the position of the sun, and looking at my watch I made out the North. Aha! said I to myself, I wonder how long it would have been before his knowledge of Homer and Cicero would have helped —— out of a place like this. Now, said I, Durban to which I am going lies S. W. of P. M. B.; so if I walk towards the S. E. I shall get back to the road in the least possible time. Off I set in high spirits, and went on for half an hour, when I suddenly remembered that Durban is S.E. of P. M. B., and that I was walking parallel to the road instead of at right angles to it. By this time it was about eleven, and I was getting very hungry and tired, when I saw a Kafir kraal; so up I went, and asked one of them, "Shew me the way to Pine Town." The man understood and nodded; when he was ready, I said, "Give me to eat:" so he made me go with him into his hut. You have to crawl in on hands and knees; the hut is about fifteen feet in diameter, quite circular, and about six feet high in the middle. They are *all roof*, as one of our party described them, with a strong post in the middle to support the centre. They are made of reeds wattled. Well, in I crawled, (as I had done a dozen times before, but never having been the only Englishman,) and two of them with me. One called out loudly to his wife, who brought in a vessel of sour milk, *amaci*, thick stuff, but not too thick to drink; so I put it to my lips with considerable satisfaction; and then gave my guide a shilling, which he perfectly understood. The other fellow then gave him his purse containing some five or six shillings in silver, in order, as I supposed, to make some purchases, and finally took off his shirt, and gave it to my guide, who had only an old coat on; this was taken off, the shirt struggled into, the coat put on above; with the exception of these articles of dress, my guide had only a Kafir full dress, which consists of something like the Highlander's purse, (without the kilt,) and sometimes a strip of cow's hide with the hair on round each ankle. Then we started, after my guide had taken several whiffs of hemp, which they smoke instead of tobacco, tobacco being used solely for snuff. The pipe was curious. It consisted of a cow's horn, with a hole on one side, into which the bowl was inserted. The bowl is of wood, I think. The man puts his mouth into the large end of the horn, which he manages to fill up, and then draws in his breath, receiving thereby the smoke from the bowl.

* * * * *

Well, we set off at last. After walking two or three miles, we came to a hut: my friend threw down his stick and assegai, and crawled in. I threw down my stick and followed. The hut contained a man, and four wives, some with two or three children, some apparently without. I went out again when we were ready, back foremost; partly I believe from a courteous dislike of turning my back upon them: they were very much amused. We reached Pine Town, on the way to Durban, about 2 o'clock, instead of 10, as I had promised. So I determined not to try a short cut again, till I knew better how to prevent it becoming a long one.

* * * * *

LETTER XXXVI.

DURBAN, *July* 30, 1855.

DEAR ——,

I cannot remember for certain, and my memory (that is A——) is not here to remind me, whether I wrote to you on landing. I think I did; and sent the letter by the Mauritius, in which case you must have got it some two months before you get this: however, I will call this No. 1.

* * * * *

We came to anchor, Sunday, May 20; landed next day; started for Maritzburg (written P. M. B.) Monday, May 28; arrived on Thursday, May 31. * * * I started for Durban on Thursday, June 21. The Bishop had been at P. M. B. for a fortnight or so, but had returned to his family; they left Durban for P. M. B. on Tuesday, June 26. As to the time of the journey, an old colonist, or a good rider, will go through in a day, twelve or thirteen hours: one like myself will go through in two days: a waggon takes three, that is, sleeps three nights on the road, arriving about the same time of day as they started: they are not able to make the journey by sleeping two nights, because they cannot by any contrivance, or under pressure, start early in the morning.

* * * * *

I do not know whether —— has described waggon travelling. The body of the waggon is not unlike an English one, only narrower, and I think longer. From the sides there springs a roof, supported by semicircular arches of wood, and consisting of canvas. The sides and roof are very strong, as indeed they had need be. There is a pole, and six or seven pairs of oxen, constituting a "*span*," draw it by means of yokes. The yoke is a piece of a pole, about four inches in diameter, and long enough to reach across the necks of two oxen; then there are two pieces of wood stuck into it at each end, which pass down on each side of

the neck of each bullock, so as to keep the top-piece in its place. These pieces are about as broad and thick as your hand. They pass in front of the shoulder; and I thought at first the beast pushed against them in drawing, just as a horse pushes against the collar with his shoulder; but I soon found that their only use is to keep the top-piece from slipping off the neck, and the draught arises from the pressure of a hump above the shoulder against the said top-piece or pole. The Cape oxen have all of them this hump, without which they could not be used for drawing, at any rate not half so well. Well: you have perhaps seven such yokes, with a pair of oxen *under* each, (we hear of oxen putting the neck *under the yoke,* you would not so speak of a collar), and a strong chain, or a rope made of thongs of skin, passes forward from the end of the pole and is fastened by a short rope to the middle of each yoke: so when the driver says *Trekk,* (or *Trek,* it should be, I believe)—for the waggon-terms are most of them Dutch—the oxen go on, and the waggon follows. He is provided with a long whip, which gives very severe cuts sometimes. They make no difficulty about going over stones very much larger than one's head, so that the jolting which ensues may be conceived to be considerable. They are generally provided with large clumsy *shoe* drags, and I am told that sometimes three wheels are dragged in going down a steep hill: they would drag all four, only they say that the waggon would be unmanageable, and might twist round so as to stand across the road, in which case it would upset. The oxen have no means of holding back in going down hill, so the only thing to be done is to run to the bottom as soon as possible, and try to keep on the road. We had one instance on our way to P. M. B, when both R—— and I thought we should have been upset: he said quite coolly, "I think we shall have an upset; but it will not be a bad one!" But they say the road from Durban to P. M. B. is a prodigy for goodness: I have not yet seen any other.

The main advantage in using oxen here is, I imagine, because their feeding costs nothing. The country as you go along is quite open, and generally covered with grass; and the oxen are simply turned loose to graze in the morning before starting, and at the halts which they make once or twice in the course of the day. The land belongs to some person, but there is very little cultivation indeed; you see an acre or two with forage growing, and then you go on for two miles without seeing a house, or a sign of life, except a Kafir kraal or two on the side of the opposite hill. But you will say you have heard enough of waggons and oxen.

My present work is the parish of Durban, or rather the town, for at present the parish extends, I suppose, twenty-five miles in one direction and fifty in others. The town is said, if I remember right, to contain about 1000 white people, and I suppose there may be as many Kafirs acting as servants. The church, the only one in the colony that has a roof on, is not yet completed; but owing to arrangements that have been made since the Bishop came out, it is now progressing. It will hold about 250 persons: it is built of brick; the roof is open, and the beams are shewn. There is no east window: I mean the east end is built up, without a window in it: they say it would have been too hot in summer, if the morning sun had once got in. The floor is of wood, and the seats are at present plain white deal benches with backs and ends. There is a very nice instrument (a seraphime I think it is) and a voluntary choir, who sing very fairly, almost too well for the congregation: one of them has proposed to train a set of boys, which offer I have thankfully accepted. We have Jackson's *Te Deum* every Sunday, and the music for the responses at the Communion is prettier I think than any I ever heard. When I said to the organist that I had never heard it before, and that I liked it, she said, "Very likely not, Sir; it is my own composing." The church is tolerably full in the morning, at eleven, and nearly as full in the evening, at half-past six. These hours suit the people here, who commonly (universally, I think) dine in the middle of the day. Besides the English church, there is a Wesleyan chapel, and a Congregationalist. The former has been built some time; of the latter the foundation was laid the other day; there has been a congregation however for some time.

When I left England, it was, as you know, with the expectation of being stationed on the mission ground: but we have found things less advanced than we expected, and it seems it would be premature to be building a house on the ground yet. Besides, the Bishop was anxious for several reasons to put a new clergyman here at Durban. One of them was the fitness of the man who was here, the colonial chaplain, for forming and making up new congregations of colonists in the outlying and thinly-peopled districts of the colony; and he had no one that suited his purpose so well to be placed here as myself; so he said to me that he thought of placing me here for a time, and I said at once that I would do anything he liked. It has occurred to me once or twice that this was not what I came out for: but then I have remembered, and it has perfectly satisfied my mind, so that I do not think the objection will return,—I came out here, simply because there was a scarcity of people that could and would come: I did not come *because* I thought the work more important than what I was leaving: though I did and do feel the importance of the work here very strongly; but I came because so few would. I left plenty in England; and my coming abroad has left the place open for others. So I am quite satisfied, and am convinced that I am doing best by being at the bidding of the Bishop. You may be surprised at my saying all this; but I know you are interested in my being satisfied, and I like to tell you honestly what I think.

To return to the question of an abode. It is very difficult to get a house to suit. There are plenty of houses with three rooms, a sitting-room and two bed-rooms, and one or two little outside rooms, built in the verandah; but these are hardly big enough.

* * * * *

Do you know I found myself, the other day, persuading a mother to send her eldest son, a gentle boy of 11 years old, to school: she said he was very closely bound to her: nobody's advice or opinion was so good as mamma's. I told her I had a sister, to whom I sometimes felt disposed to write for advice still, because I used to feel very much towards her, as this boy did to *her:* and I said the wrench at leaving home at the age of 15 was so great, that I never failed to urge mammas to send away their boys earlier than that, unless they thought they could keep them with them altogether. My own sister, it is very comforting to look forward to meeting again: it may be in this world, or it may be in another; but it will be some time.

One of the peculiarities of this place is the utter absence of old people. The church-clerk, who is also sexton, is a man of about 55 perhaps, and I suppose there are one or two others like him; but the great number of people are young, and the number of children is wonderful. Another peculiarity is the smallness of the incomes: not above two people in the colony have above £400 or £500 a-year: not above fifty, I dare say, more than £200. It is not easy to get money from people who have not much.

Two of our number, Dr Bleek and Baugh, are at a Kafir kraal, living among the natives to learn the language. That is the proper way: I wish I were with them.

* * * * *

It will be seen from the preceding letters, that soon after arriving in the colony Archdeacon Mackenzie was settled down as the parish priest of Durban; it will be seen also that his own judgment somewhat questioned the arrangement, but that he acquiesced on the general principle of submission to superior authority, and satisfied himself that all was right by reflecting upon the reasons which had induced him to leave home and devote himself to foreign work. Without venturing to express a positive opinion in a matter in which local circumstances require to be thoroughly well known in order to enable any person to form a valuable judgment, I may perhaps say that it was a considerable disappointment to his friends at home to hear that Mackenzie was appointed to the parochial charge of Durban; they had rather looked forward to the influence which his fine character and Christian spirit should exercise upon the whole diocese, and had regarded him as the companion and friend of the Bishop, rather than as the clergyman of a small white population. Hence, when troubles arose in Durban, in no way connected with missionary labours, but of a kind which might have happened in any parish in England, there was certainly amongst his friends at home a disposition to grudge him to such work, and to question more than ever the wisdom of his choice in determining to go abroad. These Durban troubles I would gladly pass over altogether, the more so as I believe that many who were much opposed to the Archdeacon at the time learned to see his worth, and did not fail to testify their altered feeling towards him when he visited the colony a second time: but it would be impossible to speak of this portion of his life, and to describe his ministry at Durban, without alluding to the disturbances which arose from the differences between his parishioners and himself. The fact is, that at the time of the Archdeacon's appointment to Durban the minds of many persons were in a state of irritation concerning Church matters: preaching in a surplice appeared to some to be only Popery in disguise, the Offertory an innovation to be sturdily resisted, the public administration of Baptism a dangerous novelty, and true Protestantism was regarded as bound up with all the careless fashions introduced in careless times. This kind of feeling, for which allowance ought on many and very good grounds to be made, was not confined to England, but extended to the colonies, and Durban was influenced by it.

It may be stated perhaps that with regard to internal management, the infant Churches of the colonies are in one respect more favourably situated than the Church at home, and in another less so. On the one hand, the congregations in the colonies are newly gathered, and have no bad habits of long standing to break through; on the other, there is a feeling of independence in the colonies, which is likely to extend to the Church, and to make it more difficult for the minister to lead his flock, in matters not distinctly ruled by law or custom, than in England. It may be added, that there is a corresponding temptation in the colonies to get rid of bad habits which have crept into many of our English congregations, and a corresponding danger of such efforts leading to misunderstandings between minister and people. In the case of Durban matters stood thus. The congregation in that place was the oldest in the colony, and differed in some of its habits from those more recently established: especially there was no Offertory, as a regular part of the Church service, although the practice was universal elsewhere throughout the diocese. The attempt to introduce uniformity, an attempt to which he was first led by his confidence in his people and belief that they had confidence in him, and in which his feeling of submission to his Bishop led him to persevere when his own judgment prompted him to desist, was the origin of troubles which constituted the most painful chapter of his life. I remember well the intense sorrow with which his friends at home regarded the vexations which he had to endure, and the admiration with which they noted the saintly manner in which he bore them; for myself, the subject was so exceedingly painful that I could not bear to open the packets of local newspapers which were sent to me from the colony, and which contained the history of vexations and annoyances which I could not alleviate. Beyond doubt this was part of the discipline and education by which God was fitting His servant for a more difficult and trying post.

Having made these remarks upon the Durban

troubles, I shall introduce a portion of a letter in which he unburdened his mind to the editor of this Memoir. It is the only sorrowful letter I ever received from him; the only one that I have read in which his noble heart seemed to be at all bowed down by the weight put upon it. The letter, as will be seen, was strictly private, and in one paragraph he gave strict injunction that nothing taken from it should be published: the reasons assigned however were of a temporary character, and do not apply now; I trust that I shall not have violated the spirit of the injunction by printing a portion in this volume. I have omitted everything which in my opinion Mackenzie would have desired to withhold.

LETTER XXXVII.

Loose slip: to be read first.

You will soon find that this must be a very private letter. I must have some one to unbosom myself to, and though I do so to a certain extent to some here, yet there is no friend to whom I can so fully speak as to you.

DURBAN, *Feb.* 8, 1856.

DEAR GOODWIN,

I have received your very acceptable letters. My sister has written home in some letter to somebody, that the delight of reading a home letter is quite as great as it has been described, though she was sceptical on the point before she came out. I quite agree with her, and I think it only right to our friends at home, that they should know the thrill of pleasure with which we hear that there is a vessel outside, (that is, not yet entered the harbour,) then that she has an English mail on board; then that she has seven or eight bags of letters which have been landed, and that letters will be delivered at three o'clock in the afternoon; finally, the discovery that the half-crown sent by the Kafir has come back reduced to three threepenny pieces, indicating that we have seven letters, of which perhaps three are for the Robertsons, to whom we immediately send them, while we (unless it be Saturday afternoon) sit down to the full enjoyment of our own.

I have dated this letter "Durban," as usual, though I am at present out on one of my clerical tours. I left home on Thursday (yesterday) morning, at half-past seven A.M., having intended to be off at least an hour earlier, but having lost that time in seeing that the horse was fed, that the fire was lighted and the coffee made, and in putting up the shirts and papers I should take with me. I was on my sister's horse, having sent my own the day before, by my own Kafir groom, to the house of a friend, fifteen miles on the road. I have a little capering about, and am nearly on the neck of my horse, as soon as he discovers, by the direction of his head, and the saddle-bag at his side, that he is off on a journey. I come, after four miles riding along a flat road, to the river Umgeni. There is no bridge, but a great floating stage, known as "the punt at the middle drift;" but as the depth of the water is not sufficient in all parts to float me and the horse as well, though in general it carries loaded waggons across, I take off the saddle and lead my horse behind me, he having to swim in the deepest part. I pay 9*d.* and lose a quarter of an hour in this operation. I proceed along a sandy road through the bush, sometimes along glades covered with long grass, sometimes along a road cut through the bush, (which stands here for *jungle,* and consists of trees thirty feet high, and bushes matted together in the most beautiful way with masses of convolvulus and other creepers,) till I come to the river Umhlanga, on the other side of which is the house of my friend Adams. In one place the road, which is a waggon-track, is so overgrown with grass from side to side, that it reaches as high as my head while I sit on horseback. This part of the road has not been travelled by waggons for a few months.

It is now a quarter past ten. I stop at Adams', and have breakfast. The bread is made of mealies, and tastes to me much as oatcake does, I suppose, to an Englishman, who has not the good sense to appreciate it. I find here my horse, and send back my sister's by the Kafir who brought mine. About 12 we start. The sun about 10^{0} from the zenith. We follow narrow paths, not waggon-tracks, across the river Umhloti; we call upon the little merchant of the neighbourhood, and tell him that I have every hope of being able to keep my appointment by holding service in the house of one of his neighbours at half-past three next Sunday, and beg him to let his friends know. This knot of people is called Mount Moreland. There are some ten or twelve families, dotted about on grassy knolls, in a space of about six miles by three, the majority of whom are members of the Church of England, to whom a Wesleyan preacher comes from the adjoining neighbourhood of Verulam every Sunday morning. This Wesleyan service is attended by most of the Mount Moreland people. All that we are at present able to do is to offer them a service once in three weeks, and it is on this duty partly that I have come up.

We arrive at seven o'clock at the house of Mr ——, the resident magistrate of this district, which is called the Umhlali, from a river which runs through it, at a distance of about forty-five miles from Durban. I carry with me a surplice, which I shall leave in this neighbourhood, and three copies of the last S. P. G. Report, which I shall also leave in various places.

So far I have written in a common way of what might interest any common friend. But I must in this letter try to give you an idea of the position of things here, of which you may have heard something. We have had great trouble and annoyance from the opposition of the people here, some few violent persons especially, to the Offertory. I knew on coming to Durban that it was the Bishop's wish to introduce the Offertory, and I proposed to him, on our way to church the first time I preached here as incumbent, that I should begin at once with my surplice, as the people had been very anxious to have me here, and I thought they would take me quietly with all my faults, of which they would consider this to be one. He advised me not, but to wait till I had gained the confidence of my parishioners. Unfortunately I fancied I had done this in about three months, and then proposed to the Bishop to introduce surplice and Offertory. He said, "Well, do so, if you think you can: only do not consider that I order it: I only sanction it." When I mentioned here to one of the churchwardens what I was going to do, he said, "You don't know what a storm you will raise—I, for my part, cannot collect the Offertory, in defiance of the feelings of the people." I said, "O, that will all die away again in a week or two; if you will only do your duty and make the collection, it will be all right." Unfortunately I gave ten days' notice of my intention: they called a vestry meeting, and unanimously requested me, in the chair, to waive my intention; their avowed reason being that the surplice and Offertory were connected with a party in England with which they could not agree, and they were afraid if this were allowed to pass, something more would follow. I refused to waive my intention. The meeting broke up in great disorder. On the Friday the churchwarden told me that they intended to organize an opposition, to leave the church, and get a clergyman from England, who would officiate in the way to which they were accustomed. (They objected to my baptizing during the service, as well.)

The reader will here see the elements of a quarrel and disturbance of much bitterness. I shall omit the greater part of the letter, which describes all the particulars of the storm, because it might give pain to some under whose eyes these pages may come; it must suffice to say that the breach between minister and people became wider and wider, until at length it amounted to an actual separation and to open war. I ought however to add, in justice to the Archdeacon, that he did in the first instance waive his intention, and that it was only upon finding that concession did not produce confidence and harmony that he was induced to carry out his original scheme. I now resume the letter.

All this is very unpleasant. I used to say, I did not know why God had given me so sunshiny a life. One or two people used to say, that I did not need tribulation: but this I never believed. Others, such as you I think, used to say it was because my nature was good-tempered, and I did not think things to be painful which others did: but even so, this was the gift of God. I now think that He has answered my prayer which used to be for pain and annoyance, when He thought it wise: and I thank Him, and only hope He will "fit me for perfect rest above:" perhaps that rest may be made more sweet by annoyance now.

* * * * *

My present position has driven me to feel the necessity of prayer for the whole state of Christ's Church Militant. In this respect I am still very deficient, but I trust to be improved.

My hope is, that God may work a cure out of the very violence of the disease; that true churchmen, being true Christians, will rally round the Church; and that the opposers of the Bishop being now, as they are beginning to be, joined by those who would claim for all a vote in vestry, and by those who would level the Church on the plea of religious liberty, may become encumbered by their friends.

Thus our enemies may be drowned in the act of pursuing us into the sea. I have much comfort in reading of the old days, when the Church was in worse difficulties than this, yet out of them all the Lord delivered her.

* * * * *

I have not a great deal of time for reading, but as much I believe as I had in Cambridge. I am preaching four times a-week: three times in my own church, and once at a week-day service for some people four miles off. This makes me feel the necessity of reading more than I used to do when Haslingfield was my field.

* * * * *

It is now May 3. I really hope I may never keep a letter on the stocks for three months again. All I can do now is to close this and send it by the mail which goes to-day.

* * * * *

Times are troublous here still. I am holding service in a large building hired and licensed for the purpose, while one of the churchwardens encourages a service, read, by his directions, by a layman in S. Paul's church. The Bishop is prepared very soon, I think, to go to law to prevent the building from being used, when closed by him. I do not seriously blame myself for any part I have taken in the whole matter, though I think I might have acted with more judgment once or twice.

Yours very truly,

C. F. M.

The next letter is to his eldest sister, and belongs to nearly the same date as the conclusion of that which precedes.

LETTER XXXVIII.

DURBAN, *May* 22, 1856.

DEAR ——

It is now more than a year since we landed here. The time has passed very quickly: so quickly that if it keep up its present rate, we shall very soon arrive at the end of this changeful world of separation, of care, of conflict, and be joined together in peace and happiness; and this quick passing of time will, I think, continue, so long as health and strength give leave for constant employment. I have sometimes thought of the peculiarity of God's dealings with me, that for so long a period (since I went to Grange at least in 1840, and how much earlier you will remember better than I do—since I had the scarlet fever, I suppose) I have had no illness of any kind. I do not attempt to account for this, but wish to leave the matter in His hands who knows best.

* * * * *

You speak, I see, in your letter of Nov. 12, which A—— has just given me, of the possibility of my coming back, and finding my place at Cambridge open. No: that's a mistake; Cambridge, above all places that I know, soonest fills up the place of one that goes; and those who go so soon lose connection with so fluctuating a society, that it *never*, I think, works well for a man to return. But besides this, the principle which made me leave College (and it required a clear principle to make me break a resolution which I often used to express, that I would not leave my *then* work for any position I could conceive,) still exists, and is likely to continue as long as I live, namely, the small number of persons able and willing to come out as clergy to the colonists, or missionaries to the Heathen. I say all this, not to give you pain, but because I think it is better not to encourage, even by silence, a hope which I feel sure can be realised only by my utterly losing health, and becoming unfit for work, (which, by the way, I have not the smallest intention of doing at present). I think my friends would have been pleased, if they had seen me on Tuesday, at our Sunday-School treat, playing and enjoying the games as much I believe as any of the children.

As to the work here, it is, as you know, in some respects less satisfactory than it was. My congregation is, I suppose, from eighty to a hundred, instead of two hundred, as I dare say it was: still I feel that these are braving the danger of persecution, which was at first so real that I thought it quite as likely as not that one or two of those who attended my church would be ruined, by the majority of the people withdrawing their custom. This must I think do good: to suffer in a good cause is very strengthening: it is a thing which seldom happens at home; and as I really hope that things are slowly mending, I am far from dissatisfied with my present work. I am resolutely refusing to give up the Kafir evening school, ill-attended as it is, for two reasons: one, that if once let down, it will be so difficult to get it up again. Besides, we do not know when God will put it into the hearts of these heathen boys to come in great numbers. There are, they say, about 1000 in the town as servants. But besides this, I am anxious to keep up my slight knowledge of Kafir, and to improve. Now each night I read them half a page from a book compiled from the Bible, and then talk to them about it, constantly saying, "Is it correct to say so?" and this will, I hope, be a less frequent interruption as I go on. The Kafir prayers I know pretty well now, and can read them quite intelligibly and intelligently too. So, as I said to A—— last night, when she was arguing that it was lost labour, I decline to abandon the school. The UmFundisi (as we call Mr Robertson, that is, *teacher,*) comes in every Sunday to preach to them; and I hope the week-work may help his congregations. I do so look forward to the time when I shall be able to talk fluently.

The thing I regret more than anything else at present is my bad judgment in the choice of instruments: and this is a very serious defect in my position. I think I am not bad at urging others to work and finding work for them, but I sometimes get taken in, and appoint a man unfit for the work. I say *sometimes*, but in fact I am thinking of a particular example.

* * * * *

Archdeacon Mackenzie's ministry in Durban continued for nearly a year and a half; during the greater part of that time his life was much embittered by the dissensions already referred to and the troubles connected with them; nevertheless he worked on quietly and faithfully, believing himself to be in the path of duty, and trusting that light would break in upon him at last. Nothing interfered meanwhile with the perfect peace and happiness of his home: the various little annoyances of colonial life, I need hardly say, did not trouble him, and even the great and real vexations which he endured have scarcely left a trace upon the pleasant picture which his sister's letters contain. From these letters I shall now make a few extracts, for the purpose of conveying to my readers, in the best manner possible, a peep at Archdeacon Mackenzie's life in Durban.

1855. Sept. 3. You would rejoice to see Charles here, so much liked and respected. He often looks pale and worn, but —— assures me that he has a brighter look since I joined him, and have made him a comfortable home, looking after his meals, and seeing that his coat is brushed. I have improved his horse also, by being head-groom, and seeing that his and my own are properly fed and cleaned. I am perfectly happy in being here with Charles, but was sorry he was appointed here. When I asked him which he liked, he said he never asked himself the question.

Sept. 4. We are in a confusion and bustle, moving out of a borrowed house we have occupied during the fortnight I have been here. We have no view of the sea, which is a drawback, and our verandah touches the street; no little garden in front; and people take pleasure in telling us how bad the situation is; but we could not get another to suit us, and we are not disposed to make or find difficulties in what is irremediable, and I think my perhaps over-punctilious fastidious nature is done good to, and does good to Charles's perfect indifference to comfort or appearances. He looks paler than at home, but is very active both in mind and body.

Oct. 15. You would all be pleased above measure to see Charles, how much he is looked up to and respected, and how very sensible and firm he is, and such an excellent preacher. He is adored by all the sick and young of his flock. I am convinced he is doing far more good than if directly employed in converting the heathen, for he is influencing and teaching the white people, who by being the masters are the practical teachers of the Kafirs, and he speaks very plainly to them of their duties to the native population.

We had not taken possession of our new house when I wrote last. It is a very comfortable one, except that the white ants dispute the possession of it, and raise mounds on the floor, and eat up our mats, and would eat into our boxes if we let them alone. We poison them with arsenic, but nothing effectually removes them except digging till you come to the white-ant queen, a most disgusting animal; but our colony is so large that her palace is at too great a distance to make it possible.

Mr Robertson, the Kafir missionary here, works very hard, reading Greek and divinity with Charles part of the day, and besides taking every opportunity in the course of his walks and rides of proclaiming the Gospel. He has a Kafir class and service every evening, which is tolerably well attended; and though we see as yet little fruit of his labours, it would be wrong to be discouraged or to doubt God's power of bringing many to the knowledge of Himself. There are a great many nominal Kafir Christians, but they have not a good character, and I am afraid deservedly so, being much less honest than their heathen brethren, and acquiring Christian vices along with the outward civilization of European dress.

Mr Robertson has only baptized two converts as yet, and, as far as we can judge, they are sincere. One of them is our servant, and we always treat him as a Christian; and as he is not more free from faults than all other people, and was unwilling the other day to do as I desired him at the moment, I reminded him of the duties of servants in the Bible, and it was touching to see the humble reverential way in which he bowed his head as I did so.

Oct. 17. Panda, a Kafir chief, and brother of the monsters Dingaan and Chaaka, of whom you will read in Gardiner's account of Natal, is so cruel; his subjects in great numbers leave him and come to us for protection, and he demands that we give them and their cattle up to him to be put to death or enslaved; and some think we should agree, for fear of irritating Panda. A bargain has been made that the cattle be given to him, and this has been done; but there is still a ferment whether the poor people should receive protection or not; so Charles, in one of the best sermons I have heard him preach, took for his text, "Except the Lord build the house, &c.," and while disclaiming to give any private opinion, he urged the duty of trusting in the Lord, and not doing what was wrong to secure present safety; and ended by begging help for the Kafir school lately established, in money, and by making arrangements so that the Kafir servants should be able to attend. Many, I know, were struck with his remarks.

Nov. 1. Charles is remarkably well, but overpoweringly busy. On Sunday he breakfasted a little after 7; read the burial-service at the cemetery, which is at the far end of the town; then he read the full service to the troops for Mr ——, who is ill; then the usual service at 11; the Sunday-school for an hour and a half at 3, and evening service at 6.30.

Nov. 8. Charles has just returned from Maritzburg.

The Bishop sent for him and Mr Robertson to meet the Governor, Sir George Grey, who seems to have taken all hearts by storm. They rode the 52 miles from hence to Maritzburg on Monday, and 30 miles on Tuesday with the Bishop and the Governor and a large party to visit Ngoza's kraal; a mission-station is to be founded there. They rode back the 52 miles to-day with the Governor.

The missionary work thrives apace. The Kafir school is increasing weekly. Charles and I are paying all the expenses of it at present, the first outlay of repairing and thatching the building, buying forms oil and lamps. Mr R. talks to every Kafir he meets, and invites them to come to school: so one morning a small chief with two attendants came to beg him to visit his kraal, and preach, and teach his people. The chief was dressed in a red blanket, but took his hat off, and gave it to one of the Kafirs to hold. He was very ceremonious all the time of the interview, but the moment Mr R. left them, the chief and his attendants jumped like schoolboys over the fence, and were gone like a shot. Mr R. would like to have a mission-station there.

Charles is very well and strong; the exercise he takes and the fatigue bodily and mentally he goes through are wonderful, and yet he cannot overtake half of what he has to do. Whenever he goes from home I occupy myself in tidying his room, arranging his books, and killing spiders and fish-moths, very destructive creatures to muslins, paper, everything.

Nov. 9. I have just had the honour of a visit from the Governor, Sir George Grey. He paid us a very long one, more than half an hour; and this is his only day in Durban. We had a good deal of talk about missionary work. He is very zealous and enthusiastic, and is sure he could do anything with the Zulus here; they are so superior in disposition and circumstances to the frontier Kafirs.

1856. January 14. Mr Robertson's work in the town we call the Scotch mission. In Christmas-week we resolved to give them a feast: so an ox was purchased for 10*s.*, killed about eight hours before it was to be devoured, cut up and boiled in a large caldron, while part was cut into thin slips and roasted in the fire. We had another large caldron, in which coffee and a great deal of sugar was boiled; and we had a large basket full of loaves. You would have laughed at the helpings, as 5 lbs. per head was the average eaten. When the repast was finished the Archdeacon exhibited his magnificent magic lantern, with dissolving views, many of them astronomical, which greatly pleased them, especially every one which shewed the moon; she being the regulator of their term of work. They seldom engage themselves for a longer time than a moon, and talk of the moon being dead when the time of payment comes; but many will remain in this way for fourteen or twenty moons without a break. We limited our feast to those Kafirs who had attended the night-school and the Sunday services. They are very fond of learning, and sounds of a, b, c are constantly heard, and I am constantly caught by strange Kafirs, as well as our own, to read or explain a sentence they cannot make out.

Feb. 9. This morning we had early service at seven A.M., which Charles means to continue through Lent, but the clerk is ill, and the friend who is doing his duties forgot to send the keys of the church, and Mr Robertson mounted my pony to get them. He failed: so there was nothing for it, but for him to break in at the window and let us in, and then he had no surplice; so he read prayers without one. The windows on one side are only of calico. They are putting glass and pretty carved stonework up, but the work gets on very slowly. I have a letter from Charles this morning, and expect him back to-morrow. He says he is getting more confidence in speaking to the natives, and that one considerable chief whom he had seen begged that a Missionary might be sent to teach his people "to walk gently." He writes that he has been trying to get refugees to work on Mr Robertson's mission-station, which he is founding ten miles from Durban.

Feb. 25. Charles is very well indeed, and as active in mind and body as he used to be at home, and his influence is very decided for good on a wide circle round and below him; his good judgment temper and patience never fail him. I am very sorry that he cannot have the work he came out for, missionary work, I mean, among the Kafirs; his whole heart and affections are with them, and his progress in the language, considering his opportunities, is wonderful. If more clergymen would only come out, he might be relieved of Durban, and have plenty to do as Archdeacon and Missionary. It is astonishing what he gets through, and kind friends are always warning me that he will not be able to stand it long; but he is not the man to be persuaded by a sister that he is overworking himself, and I can enter into his feelings, that a pleasure ride would be no relaxation to him, while he feels that there are many of his congregation he ought to visit, whom he has not time to call upon.

The position of Mr Robertson's mission-station will be seen by reference to the map. This mission specially interested Archdeacon Mackenzie; he had great confidence in Mr Robertson's powers and qualifications as a missionary, and he spent many happy days at the Umlazi, assisting in the mission work, and at the same time studying under Mr Robertson the Zulu language, and the art of dealing with and influencing the natives. The accommodation which Mr and Mrs Robertson could offer in their mission quarters was doubtless of a rough and simple description, but their hearty hospitality and their manifest zeal in their work made the visits paid by the Archdeacon and his sister specially delightful, and the Umlazi a pleasant place of retreat from Durban. In order to give some notion of life at this mission-station, I shall introduce an extract from a letter written by Miss Mackenzie.

Ekufundisweni. June 8th. This is the name of the mission-station, established about three months ago, about ten miles from Durban, of which Mr Robertson is the missionary, and the Archdeacon the superintendent. The name signifies "a place of teaching," and Mr R. as well as all other clergymen is called UmFundisi. The situation is a very good one, both as regards beauty, fertility of soil, and numerous Kafir kraals in the immediate vicinity. As I sit in the verandah of the temporary hut in which the family dwell, I look out on the winding river Umlazi, an extensive plain (on which we hope one day to see sugar, arrow-root, and cotton growing), and very pretty low hills covered with natural wood at the foot, and above grass dotted with picturesque clumps of trees; in the distance is seen Durban bay, the bluff or promontory which forms it, and the white surging waves of the Bar make a constant music. Further to the South we see the river Umlazi fall into the sea, and we hope to make an excursion one day to the shore there, and to pick up shells, which are much more perfect than what we find on the beach at Durban. The huts built for present use here are of the simplest and roughest construction, but Mrs R. has a magical wand by which she gives a ladylike look of refinement to all she puts her hand upon. The largest or family hut is twenty feet by fourteen, divided by screens into three rooms, bed-room, study or dining-room, and sitting-room. The mode of building is to stick thickish poles into the ground at a short distance from each other, and to do the same for the verandahs by putting poles in front of the others all round. In this land of heavy rains verandahs are almost indispensable to keep the walls tolerably dry. Sloping beams to the roof are added, and a few horizontal ones to strengthen them. The thatch composed of grass is now put on, and the intervals between the poles are filled up with reeds, to complete the walls. It is pitched outside with clay, which soon dries. The doors and windows were brought from Durban, and the whole expense was under £5. A kitchen is built separate, but it has neither fire-place, chimney, nor grate. There are two round huts, built for the Kafir boys and women-servants, and a very nice one for friends, which I inhabit; also a large one for the Archdeacon, which he and the Bishop shared when they were here. In honest truth, these huts are not to be compared to houses at home for poultry or pigs, far less those for cows and horses.

I must give an outline of how our days pass here. The sun rises at seven, but an hour before all are roused by the ringing of a large bell, hung on a tree. This is heard by families on the plain at a great distance. At about eight Mr R. has Kafir prayers for his own servants. Then we breakfast, and our prayers follow. Before they are ended many Kafir children have arrived to be taught. We have now eight who come regularly. We teach them the alphabet, as in Infant Schools, making them sing and clap their hands, march, count, &c. The children like coming so much, that in some of the kraals, where the parents keep their children to work, to nurse the infants, or watch the cows, they make them hide when they see us coming to invite them.

From the data now before him, the reader must picture to himself the Archdeacon's life to the end of the year 1856. The head-quarters Durban; some time spent at the Umlazi mission-station; occasional journeys to Maritzburg, and the more distant parts of the colony; with a great deal of work in outlying stations where no minister was resident. It was doubtless a very laborious and anxious life, but would have been a very happy one, and would have completely satisfied Mackenzie's mind, if his peace had not been broken by the troubles at Durban. These oppressed him grievously, as we have already seen; his own perfect integrity made it extremely painful to him to be regarded as one desirous of introducing unauthorized innovations into the service of the Church, and his kindly disposition made discord and strife most uncongenial; there were also other circumstances of a deeply painful kind which added much to his trouble, but of which I deem it unnecessary to preserve any record. Suffice it to say, that his residence in Durban was by far the most trying portion of his life, and that he could hardly fail to rejoice when the time of his departure came. The change took place at the end of the year 1856. On being relieved of his charge, the Archdeacon went to Maritzburg to take the duty of a brother clergyman, and in the following year, as we shall see, he entered upon a new and very interesting field. Thither I shall be glad to follow him; but before doing so, I will insert a few letters written during the period of his ministry at Durban. It will be observed that the first has been written at intervals, and does in fact carry us into the beginning of the following year.

LETTER XXXIX.

DURBAN, *August* 18, 1856.

DEAR GOODWIN,

I made a tour on the coast North-east of this ten days ago, of which I think a short notice may be interesting to you. It was to the same places to which I remember describing a former journey, six or eight months ago; but what gave especial interest to this recent visit was the fact that the Holy Communion which I went to administer had not been, so far as I know, celebrated before by a minister of the Church of England in these parts.

On Friday, August 8, I left Durban at about three o'clock P.M., intending to cross the Umgeni, to call at the house of a friend, a good churchman, and a Scotchman, Adams, about fifteen miles from this, to hear some details of the plan he has been preparing for a church at Mount Moreland, and to proceed thence by a hill-path to Verulam. On reaching the Umgeni, about four miles from Durban, I was overtaken by a lad named Galloway, who was looking for three oxen that had strayed, and for want of which his father was delayed in starting with a loaded waggon to trade in the Zulu country. They had been seen North of the Umgeni, and he had ridden out to look for them.

The Umgeni is about a quarter of a mile broad; a strong flowing stream; in some places deep enough to reach the saddle-flaps, in most places not higher than the horse's knees. There were still very distinct traces of the flood, which did so much damage in all the great river-valleys last March; withered flags and floating rubbish of all kinds, that had been caught by the branches of trees, shewed that the stream had been some thirty feet higher, and twice as broad as at present. It was impassable for horses for about a month, and for some time after this very dangerous from the soft shifting sand at the bottom.

About ten miles from the river my road to Adams' house turns to the right. Just at the fork of the roads stood a house which was in course of building at the time of the former journey which I described to you. Since then it has been burnt down, and the walls of wattle and daub are black and mouldering, the floor being strewed with the ashes of the fallen roof. I happened to pass it on the morning after the accident, on my way to Durban, after riding up the coast with the Bishop last June. I found three little children, from five to ten years old, whom their father and mother had saved from the fire, with nothing but the slight night-dress in which they had been sleeping. I promised them a supply of flannel from Durban, and unbridled from my saddle the warm jacket which I used to use at home for railway travelling; this I lent them for protection on the following night, as far as it would go. I knelt down with the little family, and used a few of the prayers in the little book of Common Prayer which I constantly carry in my waistcoat pocket, judging that whatever might be their ordinary custom, the unusual character of that morning might very probably have deprived them of the blessing of family prayer. All this was last June. I was now riding past the blackened ruins at about five o'clock, a short hour before sunset.

April 6, 1857. It is really quite disgraceful that this letter should have remained so long untouched. I shall not now attempt to go on with the account I was giving you, though I was coming to the important fact, that having dismounted that evening, and driving my horse before me, because he was (I thought) too tired to carry me, and too lazy (as I found) to follow without dragging in a tiresome way at his bridle, he walked away, trotting when I quickened my pace, and led me many miles out of my way, till it was quite dark, when I caught him at a house. I should not have liked to have lost him altogether, for he is a very useful horse; nor even for a time, for he had on him the saddle which the Master and Fellows of Caius so kindly made a part of their very liberal present to me. I determined not again to drive my horse before me, even if it were troublesome to make him follow.

* * * * *

I want to interest you particularly in the Umlazi mission; but first I ought to say, that your wish that I should be freed from Durban is accomplished; and the other, that I should be employed in Mission-work, will (I hope) be accomplished soon. * * * I cannot help hoping that some good may have been done to individuals during my seventeen months' ministry. There were some fifteen persons confirmed last June, and I hope some good seed may have been sown in this and similar ways.

* * * * *

But to come now at last to the Umlazi mission. Robertson is a most satisfactory missionary: his heart is so thoroughly in his work. His Sunday services are attended on an average by 200 persons. Many of them sit on the logs of wood which serve as seats, with the chin resting on the hand in earnest attention. None of these has yet professed a wish to be baptized; and this, I think, is well. I should dislike above all things going too fast: but I hope that when one has done so, many may follow. The grand stumblingblock is polygamy, which is woven in with all their customs and habits; so much is this the case, that I can easily believe they think it impossible for a black man to live without having, or hoping to have, several wives. Well: it is in the hands of God, but in part it depends on the Government, who may (I think) do something to restrain polygamy for the future. Our school thrives: there are now about fifty children every fine day, and that is at least five in every six. The first class has lately improved much under the regular teaching of my younger sister, who is devoting herself to Kafir work most assiduously. They can read in Kafir, when divided into syllables, and can write very fairly. There are three or four other classes; one taken by Mrs Robertson, another by my other sister, and one by "Boy," as he is used to be called, but now known as "Abraham;" a trustworthy Kafir, who with his wife and children has been baptized, and is regularly employed as a teacher at the Umlazi. They also sing: the Bishop has at the end of the prayer-book which he has prepared printed some Kafir hymns, and has written music to suit them. But their most satisfactory lesson is the Old Testament history, which Robertson has been teaching them.

They know and remember the history from the Creation to the Captivity of Joseph, and express their approbation or the contrary of the several acts of which they read.

The school lasts in this way from about ten till one. The afternoon at the Umlazi is commonly spent in visiting the kraals. Robertson especially visits any who are sick. Perhaps you may have heard of a man, who, a little before Christmas, being very ill and sending specially for Robertson one morning, asked earnestly if he might come to live with him and to die at the station. Of course no difficulties were thrown in the way, and he remained in one of the huts on our hill, (which the Christian Kafir servants gave up for his use), for two or three weeks; and then, seeming to have profited by R.'s teaching, he was baptized, and soon after died. He was buried in the ground set apart for our future churchyard, by the side of the grave of a woman, a Kafir, who had also been baptized by R., the wife of a white man who was employed on the station.

And this mention of a prospect of a consecrated churchyard leads me to speak of our wish to have a church at the Umlazi. Hitherto the Kafir teaching and preaching has been held either in a clearing in the bush near the house, or in a broad verandah in front of it. * * * I want to have a special collection for this object in Cambridge, for which purpose I will send you, as soon as they are ready, the plans of the whole, together with an estimate of expense. We are making a similar effort amongst our friends in Scotland. I fancy we shall want about £400 or £500. If we can build it for anything like that sum it will be far cheaper than any building of its size in the colony.

* * * * *

LETTER XL.

(To a Sister.)

LADISMITH, *Oct.* 20, 1856.

DEAREST ——

I don't know how long it is since I wrote to you, or any one at home. I think a duty neglected presses less heavily, instead of more heavily, as it ought to do, each day it is neglected. Certain it is that I constantly say to myself, I ought to write home, and that I have considerable pangs of conscience on the subject. A—— often reminds me of it, but I am afraid that advice only hardens me. Well, here I have begun: I will write this letter, and try not to let it be so long again.

One secret of my writing to-day is that it is raining, so that I am not able to prosecute the journey on which I started seven days ago. What! you will say, afraid of the rain? No: but afraid of crossing the rivers, which have been swelled by heavy rains during last night.

On Tuesday last, the 14th, I left Maritzburg with Mr Green to visit this northern portion of the diocese. I had never been north of P. M. B. before. So when the Bishop found that he could not come up this way, as he had intended, I very gladly agreed to go with Green, and try to fill his place as well as I could. This is not very easy, as one thing which makes a Bishop's visit acceptable in this part of the world is the hope that he will do something in the way of church-building, or placing a minister; and we were not empowered to act in this way. Still we were sure the people would be glad to see us, as there is no clergyman above P. M. B, and we should therefore be able to administer the sacraments after a vacancy of fully three months.

We started about noon, having been detained by business: the thermometer at 92° in the shade, and I have heard since that it rose to 101° that day. This is much higher

10—2

than I have known it to be before. We spent an hour and a quarter in climbing the steep ascent out of the town; very severe work for the horses. We tried to mend a broken-down tree-cart in the charge of two Kafirs, but failed for want of a linch-pin, or any substitute for it. Came on to the Umgeni waterfall, said to be 300 feet high. Slept at the house of a farmer: arranged to hold a week-day service in that neighbourhood on our return, we fixing the day, consulting about the hour, and leaving our hosts to arrange about the place of meeting and to give notice. On Thursday (to omit Wednesday, on which nothing occurred, except our riding along the road, and discussing many points, ecclesiastical and private), after seeing two farmers, one a well-to-do man, who is "entering pretty largely into sheep," the other a man with three or four strong sons, who has some thirty-nine or forty acres under the plough, and just now covered with fine looking bearded wheat; he has also a grove of orange-trees, not large, but certainly more numerous than any I have seen in the colony; I dare say there are sixty or seventy trees, of eight or nine years old, covered with sweet-smelling blossoms:—after all this we got to Doornkop, the farm of George Moodie, Green's brother-in-law, where a large family live. They gave us two or three strawberries, the only ones I have seen in the colony. Next day, after some delay in consequence of the Kafir with our small luggage not having arrived, we started about noon. We passed the house of an old boer, about ninety, who asked us our names all round (we were accompanied by one of the Moodies), and then began again, having forgotten the first when he got to the last. About 3 o'clock we parted, Green going on with our guide to cross the Drakenberg, and be at Harrismith on Sunday; I cantering quietly to this place, which I reached in about two hours.

* * * * *

I spent Saturday in calling upon most of the people,

and had satisfactory clergyman's conversations with one or two of them. I think it is easier here to get at people's inner thoughts: either we are drawn together by being so far from home; or the infrequency of a clergyman's visit makes confidence obviously necessary; or else perhaps the fault in England was my own, arising from the mixture of my occupations. However, I have very much liked what I have seen of this place: it is about a hundred miles from P. M. B., and about fifty hence to the Berg, that is, the Drakenberg, or Dragon Mountain, which is the boundary between this and the sovereignty. There are perhaps sixty houses, many of them well built of stone; four or five shops, or stores, as they are called; a magistrate, two or three persons connected with Government, such as clerks, clerk of the peace, postmaster, gaoler, a physician, five coopers (there is a large manufacture of butter in this grazing country: a man said to me to-day, "We have not much money, as our business is done a good deal by barter and on credit, but if a church could be built *of butter*, or for butter, there would be no difficulty,") a smith, a builder, two carpenters, and one missionary. We had a good attendance at service on Sunday morning, about sixty, though only eleven communicants, and a collection of £2. 10*s.* 4*d.*, which is very good; but of course we cannot expect so much every time. The magistrate is giving us all the help he can; it is very satisfactory to have for the Church the support of the influential people in the colony.

* * * * *

On the whole there is much to cheer in our work, as well as much to make us despond; but I encourage the former feeling and repress the latter. I think our Mission-work is really good on the whole: of course, connected as I am with the Umlazi, I cannot say less than that it is the best: but seriously, I think there is religious Christian teaching going on there. One young Kafir will I hope soon be baptized; and the children that come to the daily school must, I think, be receiving impressions from what they see of the life of a Christian family, if from nothing else, which will never be effaced: and even if we are only preparing the soil for future missionaries, it is very good to be allowed to do anything for Him: He knows best when the fruit should appear. At the Bishop's station, Ekukanyeni, the thirty Kafir boys have certainly made great progress in reading, &c. When I was there ten days ago I heard the first class, consisting of seven, read the Psalms for the day in Kafir, each taking a verse, more fluently than would be done in most village-schools in England. It is true that the language having only recently been made a written language is perfectly phonetic, and therefore it is easier to learn reading Kafir than English: but it is a grand thing to have thirty boys sitting as orderly as in an English school, learning reading and arithmetic. There were no men or women at the Ekukanyeni mission; nor are there likely to be any: but these boys, if any of them become true Christians, will be very useful.

* * * * *

LETTER XLI.

(Accompanying the preceding.)

LADISMITH, *Oct.* 20, 1856.

DEAR ——

I inclose this in a more public letter, because I hardly know to which of all my friends to write first.

I do often think of you all, oftenest I think at morning and evening time, and very often of you in particular when I am riding: for on a long journey, when I am alone, I very often take your little Prayer-Book from my waistcoat pocket, and learn one of the Psalms for the day. I have found great good from this. Some people think that thirty-one is too old to be learning by rote; but I like it, because I always find new beauties in what I learn in this way. I like too to look at the pencil-marks at the side of particular verses which have struck you.

I very nearly lost that little book one day. It was Sunday, and I was riding from one place to another to hold afternoon service. We got a little off the path at one place, and met some Kafirs. I was riding with S——, the colonial secretary: a few miles further on he stopped at a house to rest his horse, and make a call, saying he would join me in the evening. At night he asked me what I had lost: I said at once, "a little book, which I value as much as any in my library:" so he gave it to me, saying that it had been picked up by those Kafirs and brought to the house where he had stopped.

Dear ——, there are many things to dishearten here, but there is much to cheer, and most perhaps this,—that all the work is for our Master, who knows all things, who suffers with us, yet is always victorious, who rules all things after the counsel of His own will, and who will shortly come to receive us to Himself: and then there will be no partings! God bless you, my dear sister, and give you joy and peace, ever increasing, in believing.

* * * * *

LETTER XLII.

EKUKANYENI, *Nov.* 12, 1856.

A—— has just put a pen in my hand, and told me to write down the account I gave her last night of the untoward commencement of my last journey to Durban about ten days ago.

I left the mission-station on a Friday, in the middle of the day, to spend an hour or two in P. M. B. and then start for Durban. I was very anxious to be in Durban early on the Saturday, as I had matters to arrange before Sunday. I intended originally to ride halfway on the Friday, but as time went on compounded with myself, and said I would get to Camperdown, about 15 miles, before dark. Dr S—— said to me, "Do not be later in starting than 4 o'clock: it will be a very dark night." Well: I was in Mr Green's house: it was looking dreary and drizzling: I had to step across the street to see ——, and I had to close my portmanteau, and then to talk over matters with Green. So I let time pass, till it got to be about 6 o'clock. Then at last I left his house, and went for the horse I had in my eye to hire. (My own horse has a sore back, and I have not been able to ride him for weeks.) But the horsedealer said his foot was chafed, and I could not have him: so I had to send elsewhere for one. Time was lost in this way, so that it was eight o'clock before I was riding on the top of my horse, (as the Kafirs say,) and fairly leaving the town. The animal was evidently not accustomed to gentlemen who had a fancy to wearing very long plaids, and started a little as I unfolded the huge one —— gave me; but he got used to it by degrees. In a quarter of an hour he came to a dead stop, and I could just see before his nose the wall that had been put to stop people from going on the broken bridge (which fell last April); so we turned and crossed safely the temporary bridge a few yards off. Now, thought I, the river is crossed, it's all right. From this place there is a tedious hill to climb, with three or four sluits, that is, small streams, to cross. My horse pretended to have conscientious scruples about cantering in the dark, making one or two stumbles by way of demonstration. So it ended in our agreeing that if he would keep on walking, I should reserve a quicker pace for next day. After we had been out, as I thought, about an hour, I saw a light ahead in the distance. I first satisfied myself that it was not a firefly, of which I had seen several; and when a second appeared, it flashed upon me that it was Maritzburg, to which my horse was slowly returning! I said at once aloud, Come, this is too bad! and turned him right round, falsely concluding that the opposite of wrong must be right. I could remember, for about two miles, that I had just passed over this part of the road. Well, on I went: it was very dreary, and I could see that there was mist before me into which I was entering: when at last I came to a house, apparently new built. I addressed the inhabitants both in English and in Kafir, and dismounting found there was no one there: but thus much I learned, that I was certainly on a wrong road, for I knew there was no such house on the right one. I crossed a little stream with some difficulty, and got at last to a Kafir kraal. There was a salute of dogs barking to welcome me, and on the owner shewing himself, I asked where the waggon-road was, and who would go to shew it to me. They said it was a long way off, over there (pointing). It was too far for any of the boys to go, but they would lead me to a Dutchman's house—what would I give? If it had not been for my horse, I would as soon have stayed with them till morning: but he, poor fellow, could not have crept into a hut as I could. So I offered sixpence for a guide to the Dutchman's. I had offered sixpence, and then a shilling, for a guide to the road, but the man seemed afraid to trust his boys so far in the dark. Two little boys accordingly ran before me, each in a blanket, and we knocked up the Dutchman. He said the canteen (public-house) was not far off, and one of his Kafirs led me thither. I found it was one o'clock, and I was nine miles from P. M. B. I turned into bed, being very wet, desiring to be called the first thing in the morning: not, however, without wishing many happy and good returns of the birthday of my very dear sister, of whose birthday one hour had elapsed.

CHAPTER VII.

RESIDENCE IN NATAL—UMHLALI.

In January, 1857, Archdeacon Mackenzie with his sister returned to Durban. This was for a short time their home, although the Archdeacon had ceased to be the minister of the place; his work was now of an unsettled kind, partly along the coast, partly at Pine Town; it was still to be determined where they should permanently fix themselves, and devote themselves, as they desired, to Mission-work.

The wandering life of her brother, and his constant absence from home, made a residence in Durban, which would otherwise have been quite delightful, somewhat desolate to Miss Mackenzie; and towards the end of January she again went on a visit to the interesting Umlazi mission-station, while her brother was obliged to go to Maritzburg.

I mention this visit to the Umlazi, because it was during the visit that the Archdeacon's party was increased by the arrival of a second sister, who proved a most valuable addition from a missionary point of view, and also added much to the happiness of the family circle. Of this lady it would manifestly be improper to say much in this memoir; I will simply remark that she appears to have given herself at once to missionary work with wonderful zeal and considerable success. Mackenzie was wont to distinguish her as his *black* sister, in consequence of her enthusiastic love for the native race.

It was at the end of February that Miss Alice Mackenzie arrived. The Archdeacon was at the Umlazi, and was prepared, on hearing of the ship, to go down at once with Miss Mackenzie to welcome the new comer, and bring her up to the Umlazi. Unfortunately, just before the arrival of the vessel, Miss Mackenzie was taken ill, and was unable to perform the journey, but the Archdeacon, not being able, as his sister remarks in relating the incident, to see difficulties, started for Durban as soon as the news of the *Admiral's* arrival was made known, and brought his sister up immediately, in the dark, to join the party at the Umlazi. It is amusing to find her in a letter to friends at home describing this nocturnal journey with great enthusiasm: at one time her horse lagged behind in the middle of a river to drink: "it was wonderfully pleasant," she writes, "to be sitting alone in the dark in the middle of an African river; the reeds higher than myself on either side of the water; the sweet soft air blowing gently round, full of the chirping of strange frogs, and the fire-flies glancing round in all directions." Speaking of her brother in the same letter she says: "He is very much what he was in face: looks rather older, but strong and well, and his bright look, his ready merry laugh, and his winning ways are much as of old. His kindness to both children and natives is also pleasant to witness. His tenderness both to A—— and me indescribable."

An amusing incident was connected with the landing of Miss Alice Mackenzie. The Archdeacon requested that a telegraphic signal should be made to the ship, to the effect that his sister should come on shore at once. A difficulty however suggested itself, namely, how to distinguish the lady by any telegraphic signal: fortunately there was a signal corresponding to the name of a ship, the *Sir Alexander Mackenzie;* and the message was duly sent, that Sir Alexander Mackenzie was to come on shore in the first boat. The message was understood, and under the imposing title of Sir Alexander, Miss Alice Mackenzie landed in the country of her adoption.

Here is a passage from a letter in which Miss Mackenzie speaks of her sister's arrival, and which I introduce chiefly for the sake of the mention of the Kafir woman's kindly feeling: "I cannot express the grief it was to me to be ill and unable to go and meet her, and being very weak I could not help crying; for besides the uncertainty when we should meet, (I never imagined she could ride ten miles, the last part in the dark, and a large river at the end of the journey,) I was disappointed that her first impressions should not be in our own home; but it has all ended well. In the morning, when the tears were running down my face, Pangela, my dear Kafir woman, came into the room, and kneeling at a chair, she began kissing my hands, and in her own language saying, (it was so like poetry,) "Hush! dear Inkosazan: hush! your sister has arrived: hush! hush! dear Inkosazan, hush: she has passed the dangers of the sea: she is now on the land: hush, dear Inkosazan: it is good to pass from the sea to the land: hush, hush, Inkosazan, hush!"

It would be deviating from the chief purpose of this memoir, to go into details concerning the Umlazi mission, which, though specially dear to Mackenzie, was not his own principal work: but I think I shall be justified in giving the following picture of the work going on there, and in which both the Archdeacon and his sisters took their shares.

"I have just returned," writes Miss Alice Mackenzie, "from my first Kafir Sunday service, and my heart is full. The service took place in a clearing in the bush. Trunks of felled trees served the people for seats: the men, about sixty or seventy, on one side; the women, thirty or forty, on the other: the school-children ranged in two rows in front. The two clergymen in their surplices stood on a rude framework of rough wood. I had a place close by. The rest of the company were higher up the bank, behind the congregation. The prayers began with the sentences and confession: the twenty-third Psalm was sung: also a sweet thing beginning *Jabulani*, 'Rejoice ye,' and very rejoicing and sweet it did sound. Another hymn was sung to my dear old friend *Martyrdom:* and the effect was curiously beautiful, the more so, as I had just before said to Mrs Robertson that the scene and the gathering might have represented a meeting of Covenanters in the days of old. A lesson from the Bible was read. It was on the Resurrection: but I am sorry to say I missed the thread of it, and could not make out what it was at the time. The sermon was much easier, for each sentence was repeated again and again, either in the same words, or with but a slight difference, so that I could understand a good deal of it. He said he was going to speak to them of the love of God, and repeated again and again how men love their own children, bad as well as good; that God in Heaven is the Father of us all, and loves us all so much that He sent His only Son to die for us all. He repeated to them again and again the last two verses of S. Matthew xxviii., (the Bible lesson he had read before,) and then spoke to them of the privileges of those who are baptized, becoming members of Christ, &c., and then went on, 'and we are sent to tell you of these things; to baptize you, that you may not perish, but have everlasting life.' The whole was interspersed with earnest exhortations: 'Listen, my children: the words I speak are not mine, but they are the words of our Lord and Saviour Jesus Christ. He who believeth and is baptized, shall be saved.' His earnest look to heaven when he said this was most touching. Then he shewed how everything on earth and of earth must pass away and perish and return to dust; but the heart within us that thinks and remembers and loves will not pass away: the things of heaven will never perish. And then again, to the little school-children: 'Listen, listen, my children:' urging all to love God, to love one another, to believe and be baptized. It was very beautiful, and all sat so quiet: only now and then a little restlessness among some of the small children, stilled in a moment by his gentle admonition. The Archdeacon read part of the prayers, and chiefly led the music. After a few more prayers the elders were for the most part dismissed: the children, the Christian men and women, gathered round the pulpit to be catechized. They were asked and answered at once, Who made them? Who saved them? Who sanctifies them? and they were taught to repeat the first verse of the 100th Psalm, then to sing it; then a few more Collects, winding up with 'Lighten our darkness, &c.' and the Lord's Prayer; and then the blessing, 'The Lord bless us and keep us, &c.;' and I did feel that God's blessing must and would rest upon such loving earnest labours."

This life at the Umlazi was sufficiently pleasant, but still was uncertain and unsettled. In the beginning of March I find Miss Mackenzie writing, "I shall be very glad when we have a home of our own again; and this state of uncertainty is very trying. We do not in the least know whether we are to have a mission-station, or to go back to Durban, or what; and the worst of it is, it all depends so much on circumstances, that we are not likely to be wiser for a long time." However a plan was arranged at last: the Archdeacon went to Maritzburg to assist at an ordination, and on April 1 he returned to the Umlazi with the news that the Bishop had consented that he should take a post now vacant at the Umhlali, about forty miles north of Durban. It was uncertain in the first instance whether this would be a permanent arrangement; such however it proved to be, and the Umhlali continued to be the Archdeacon's spiritual cure until he left the colony of Natal.

With characteristic energy Mackenzie undertook without delay to reconnoitre his intended abode: he arrived at the Umlazi one night unexpectedly from Maritzburg "wet, weary, and cold," and after a day's rest started again to pioneer the way to the new settlement. The reader will understand its position by reference to the map. The station combined several opportunities for usefulness. In the first place, the district, which was to be the parish, comprised a considerable number of scattered English congregations, which could only receive an adequate supply of spiritual ministrations from a man of Mackenzie's strength and energy. In the second place, the station was in the immediate neighbourhood of the camp, and the soldiers would fall under his charge. And in the third place, he would have abundant opportunities of carrying on the work of evangelization amongst the natives. In fact, there would be abundance of occupation for himself and for his sisters, both *black* and *white*.

The Archdeacon found that it was necessary to build huts at the Umhlali for himself and his party. This necessity occasioned some further delay before the migration could take place, for though hut-building is not a very serious process, still it requires some time. Accordingly May arrived before all things were ready. All this while the Archdeacon had been tenant of his old house in Durban; and here his goods and chattels had been stowed away, very much, it is to be feared, to the benefit of the white-ants and fish-moths. A fortnight before coming to the Umhlali the sisters made an attack upon the old house, and had a grand turn-out, packing, arranging, and cataloguing, preparatory to the migration. Meanwhile poor Mackenzie had literally no home, but wandered about, doing his work as best he might, and living as best he could. Here is a passage from a letter which will bring the whole state of things before us.

"Dear Charles is leading a very wearing out and rather unsatisfactory life at present, both to himself and his horse (which is however in much the worse condition of the two), but I hope it will soon come to an end. We are preparing to join him at the Umhlali, which is forty miles from Durban, and fifty from the Umlazi. He has five services on Sunday, and one of them is eighteen miles from another; these eighteen miles he has to ride hurriedly in the mid-day sun, and for the last several weeks he has ridden to the Umhlali on Saturday, and returned here on Monday: this he does not like, as it interferes with his parish-work of visiting, but at present it is absolutely necessary. I hope at the Umhlali he will have more time for writing, for I have a letter which he began to Mr ——, last August, and he will not be able to finish it for this mail. I must make you a plan of our house when we are settled there; we are each to sleep in a round bee-hive Kafir hut, but Charles is indulging me with a small window of four little panes. I told him I had never heard of a kitchen, or any place except the sitting-room, where our dinner could be cooked: so he said, "O! a cook-house can be put up in half a day: there is no difficulty in that." Whenever we discuss whether it will be feasible to stow away things, such as boxes, books, &c., Charles always says, 'O! we can sling a shelf from the roof for them,' which has grown into slinging the articles themselves; and to-day, when we were admiring my beautiful gilt vase, Charles suggested that it should be made a substitute for a chandelier."

The first of June found the party at last more or less settled at the Umhlali station, some of the members of the family "hutted" for sleeping purposes, and all occupying in common a small house, which also served the purpose of a church. The life was rough enough, and besides the usual inconveniences of white-ants and fish-moths, and the depredations of rats, I find frequent notices in the home-letters of such additional discomforts as the following: tiger-cats constantly stealing the poultry, puff-adders and such like venomous beasts finding their way into the huts, toads in the washing basins, and huts flooded by violent rains[1].

[1] Here are a few little passing notices by way of illustration. "I saw," says Miss Alice Mackenzie in one of her letters, "a small scorpion for the first time on Sunday. I could not help laughing when my sister, who was looking at it, said to the Archdeacon, 'It is not so large as that which I found upon your whiskers!'" "It is a curious specimen of our manner of life here that the frequent breaking of glasses and cups is apt to leave us short. Yesterday Mrs. A—— said to me after dinner, 'I have only two wine-glasses: all the rest are broken.' To which I answered, 'We have only one; our last but one was broken yesterday.'" "A tiger-cat has visited us two nights and carried off a hen, the last of the three we took such care of in London, and another great pet, a cock of the Spanish kind."

Moreover the site of the house and church was not well chosen, and the station had not the advantage of a picturesque view; this however was subsequently remedied, though in a very unpleasant and expensive manner, as will be seen. But home is home though never so homely, and no home could be more peaceable, happy, and even joyous, than the Archdeacon's home at the Umhlali. In one of his sister's letters there is an account of an especially disagreeable person, and the remark is added, "I think Charles as nearly dislikes her, as it is possible for him to dislike any one." With such a disposition, with his time fully employed upon a great work, and with a consciousness of doing all for Christ, how could Mackenzie be otherwise than happy?

"Here we are," writes Miss Mackenzie, "settled for the present at our new quarters, and very funny ones they are. Mr Adams, who has been our only visitor, and who was helping me to shut a drawer, was in despair at my room, and said it was only fit for lumber. Alice is in a Kafir hut, an oval shaped one, with a grey Kafir blanket hung up at the doorway, and an open space for a window, which when she is cold she fills up with a plaid. Both door and window are ordered; but nothing in this colony is done in a hurry. The ground of her hut is the earth, covered with mats. The Archdeacon's hut has only the framework made, and I don't know why the Kafirs are not thatching it. He sleeps for the present on the sofa in the sitting-room (an iron bed, with a chintz covering over it). It is not a large room; about twelve feet square. * * *

The rest of our house is a long room about twenty-eight feet by twelve. This is the church of the district, till another is built, and Charles uses the sitting-room as a vestry, and enters the church by a door opening from it. The congregation have a door for themselves. There are two verandah rooms Mine is about five feet by ten, and Jessie's, which is also the pantry, about five feet by twenty. They are very rough indeed, and what is worse, the roof slopes less than the church; so they do not keep out the rain : but we have still two months of dry weather to reckon upon; and I am so thankful to have mine, for it has an opening at the top of the wall to the church, for the sake of ventilation; but when I am ill and in bed I can join in the service in the church."

In the same letter there is the following notice of the Archdeacon's work.

"At present I fear there will be no change. His Sunday labours are very intense. He has short early Kafir prayers, then breakfast at half-past seven. Full service, at the camp, for the soldiers at nine. It is about two miles off. As soon as he comes back the congregation is assembling here, and his horse is saddled for him to mount as soon as the service is over. He has another service at Mount Moreland, about sixteen miles off, at three P.M. In coming here he shewed us the spot where his horse always knows he may walk instead of trotting, to allow him to eat his dinner of sandwiches. This ride in the hot sun is very knocking up, both for him and his horse. He told us he was in similar circumstances to Elijah, as the brook he used to drink from was now dried up. His horse is again ready for him when this service is over, and he rides to Verulam, either four or six miles, I forget which, where he has service at six P.M. in Mr ——'s house. He goes to sup with a kind Dutch lady, and spends the night with Mr ——. This is Monday, and it is getting dark, and he has not returned, and he tells us perhaps he may not always return home till Tuesday, but do parish visiting work at that end of his parish while he is there."

The work in which Mackenzie was now engaged was undoubtedly very arduous, and seems to have told somewhat on his strength. Some months later I find his sister writing thus:

"I am beginning and trying not to think so much either of likes or dislikes, but how we may make the best use of all our talents under present circumstances; but still nature says, without my asking it, that this is the least pleasant part of Natal that I have been in. By and bye if we are allowed to see more of the fruits of the Archdeacon's work, I shall be thankful; but whether we see it or not, God cannot fail to bless his earnest and singleminded labours; here however as everywhere the harvest is so great, and it is not much that he can do with either the black or the white people. All last week he was at P. M. B. He went up to the consecration of the cathedral, but business of other kinds detained him till Friday at five P.M. He rode all night to Durban, fifty miles, where he had more business, which detained him till the afternoon, and he did not reach this place till Sunday at two A.M.

We had supper on the table all ready for him, and the sofa arranged as his bed. He was very tired, but was up again for Kafir prayers before seven. We had a short talk with him during breakfast, and he left us again as usual after church, but promised not to be late in coming home to-day."

The complaint concerning the situation of the house at the Umhlali, which occurs incidentally above, is repeated not unfrequently in the home-letters. "Certainly," writes Miss Mackenzie, "our house is placed where no Kafir would have planted his kraal; far from wood, bush, water, and hills, in a bleak bare plain, and a cold visible mist rises from what is called a *fley*, or wet valley, near, which we sometimes see coming towards us, and a cold damp shiver comes over me, and a pain in my bones and eyes; and this succeeds probably a broiling sun, which nearly drove me distracted with headache a few days ago." However, the situation had the advantage of being very healthy, and the medical man attached to the camp assured the Mackenzie party that the daily average of sick soldiers was only $\frac{5}{31}$ of a man.

Amongst the white population the soldiers were some of the Archdeacon's most interesting parishioners. His manner and bearing were peculiarly suited for winning the hearts of soldiers, and there is reason to believe that they thoroughly appreciated his efforts on their behalf. His great desire was to fill up their leisure time and tempt them away from the canteen. For this purpose he opened a room for them in the evening, which he supplied with such amusing books and papers as he could, and the evenings were sometimes enlivened by popular lectures.

It will be understood that the work of influencing the natives by going amongst their kraals, and persuading them to send their children to be taught, was constantly carried on; but in addition to this, the Archdeacon and his sisters opened a school for the white children, of whom a considerable number were within reach. And thus the time of all three was thoroughly occupied, and notwithstanding the rough and laborious character of the life which they led, time passed pleasantly enough. "Is not this a happy life?" writes one of the sisters enthusiastically, after describing in a letter the details of one day's employment.

Towards the end of July in this year a sad calamity happened to the Umhlali Missionary party. The house which they occupied was thatched, and the thatch was exposed inside the house as well as outside; a careless person placed a candle upon a shelf with the flame under the thatch; the result was immediate, and in a few minutes the house was on fire. The materials, being very dry, burnt with great rapidity; and it required much effort to save any considerable portion of the effects. The kindness of the Archdeacon to the soldiers now served him in good stead; some of them were coming to the reading-room when the fire broke out; the alarm was given, and soon fifty soldiers were on the ground, working with all their might. Much was saved, some property was lost; but all was borne cheerfully. One of the Kafirs came to the Archdeacon to know where they were to sleep, as they feared lest the sparks should set fire to their hut; "There is my house," said the Archdeacon, pointing to the ruin, "you may take possession of it if you like." "O Inkos," replied the Kafir, "I do not know how to laugh to-night." The fire began about five P.M., and within three hours they were all assembled in a hut which had survived, enjoying their tea and a cake which had been saved from the fire: then they joined in their evening service, and returned thanks for all God's mercies to them.

The fire was however for a long time a source of considerable annoyance. In one respect it was a benefit: having to build a new house it was as convenient to build it upon a good site as upon a bad one, and the disadvantages of the old situation, which have been already alluded to, were remedied by the purchase of a plot of ground in a much prettier neighbourhood, nearer the sea, in the midst of the native kraals, and in the centre of the Bush. But after having obtained the ground, it was not so easy to get the house built. The plan was soon made, and was sufficiently simple; but some of the materials had to be brought from a distance, and it is very difficult in such circumstances as those in which the Mackenzies were placed to get work regularly performed, and to keep contractors to their bargains. And so it came to pass, that the house progressed very slowly, and it was not until the beginning of the following year, 1858, that the party entered upon their new house, which was even then in a most unfinished state. Meanwhile, they lived as well as they could in huts and tents: the soldiers were permitted by the commanding officer to work for them, and the huts and tents were made as comfortable as circumstances would permit. Nevertheless, that hut-life possesses some minor inconvenience may be judged from such passing notices as the following: "Dec. 9. Our candle is being constantly put out by large moths; I have an enormous locust wrapped up in my handkerchief; and the table is covered with beetles; but mercifully we have very few mosquitoes."

The accident of the fire did not prevent the Archdeacon from exercising hospitality. When the party was reduced to residence in huts, the female portion considered that all visits of friends were out of the question, were altogether beyond argument. Not so the Archdeacon, who never saw difficulties in matters of this kind, or in much greater ones. A young friend had been engaged to come and see them; and by shifting beds, mealie bags, and barrels, accommodation was provided, Mackenzie erecting an extemporaneous bed for the stranger in his own tent. Having got thus far, it was considered possible to lodge their friend Mr Adams. Next came the Dean of Maritzburg. And so by a course of gentle progress, Mackenzie prepared the minds of his sisters for a visit from the Bishop, which accordingly took place in August, after having been voted impossible and absurd.

Meanwhile the economic arrangements of the party were somewhat peculiar. They were paying rent for two houses, one at Durban still on their hands, and that which was burnt, while they were themselves inhabiting two huts and two tents, and rejoicing in the proprietorship of four or five acres of land, upon which they found it impossible to expedite the erection of the more permanent and comfortable dwelling for which the contract was taken. They bought the land moreover, and contracted for building, with the feeling that in all probability before the house was inhabited they might be under the necessity of moving elsewhere. However, all was sunshine with the Archdeacon at the head of affairs: it was, as I can testify from experience, impossible to be down-hearted in his gentle and joyous company; and accordingly, all the inconveniences and vexations were laughed at, and the real work of the Gospel went on unhindered.

I cannot refrain from inserting here a description of his character as it appeared to one of his sisters during the residence at the Umhlali. "Your letters came yesterday, after Charles was gone; and he is not to be back this week, as he is going on a round of services in desert places, and will be back on Monday night, this day week. He sometimes says he wonders he is never ill; but I think his heavenly spirit does not need the discipline. It seems to me, we are all like those creatures that play upon or live in the water. Some never need go down into it, but skim over the top, their wings always free, and they always breathing the upper air. These are they whose lives of retirement, in a sick room or otherwise, save them from mixing with the temptations and trials of active life. Others, again, are by circumstances hustled a good deal, and have to come up every now and then to the top of the water to breathe. But he is like those creatures, which live in the water, but carry their own stock of air down with them, (water-spiders I think they are, which carry down the air and live as if in a divingbell). He mixes with the world because he must, and he leads such an active life as would be distracting to most people; and yet he carries his own heavenly atmosphere around him, and breathes the air of Heaven as freely and purely as though he never went down into the water at all. And his influence is telling here. One man, a careless person enough himself, said the other day, 'If the Archdeacon does not succeed in carrying any of the Umhlali people with him to heaven, at least he is sure of going there himself.' I liked to hear it, as a symptom of the impression his character makes. But the attendance at church is so improved, and it is encouraging to see the increase in the number of communicants; and then I always remember that influence in a place like this is like training a little twig, which will one day grow into a strong great tree."

Mackenzie was never (as has been remarked before) a good correspondent; but this portion of his life is more than usually bare of letters. No doubt the constant moving from place to place in his large parish interfered excessively with opportunities of writing. The letters written home from the Umhlali by his sisters contain a great amount of matter most interesting with respect to the general work and daily life at the station; but so far as Mackenzie himself is concerned, they are too frequently filled with lamentations concerning his absence, and the intensity of the work which he thought it right to undertake. I have, however, some letters before me, which belong to this date, and from them I will here introduce two or three which will be rendered intelligible by the narrative which I have already given.

Here is a scrap of a letter written from the Umhlali to one of his sisters at the Umlazi.

April 23, 1857.

His love, if we could enter fully into it, is indeed enough to satisfy us. His work enough to occupy us. His care enough to assure us of safety and give us peace. Would that we were always resting on Him, and not letting listlessness or sin of any kind, or any earthly love or allurement, come between us and our love! Happy indeed we may and ought all of us, far and near, to be in Him. And if we are seeking this peace, He will, whether we attain to it rapidly or not, be making us at least to grow. I am thinking of myself when I say this.

LETTER XLIII.

(*To a Sister.*)

DURBAN, *Aug.* 10, 1857.

MY OWN DEAR ——,

I hope you have got safely my letter, written at Ladismith, and I would now give something to be able to insert a letter in each of the mails between this and you. I must try, however, not to get again so neglectful as I have been. It has really not been want of time, (though, to be sure, the exact time in which it would be best to write a home-letter never seemed to come,) so much as that objects close at hand seemed always to claim attentiou.

I spent three hours this morning with our excellent

friend Adams, (whose name you are sure to know,) arranging the details of our new house. It is to have five rooms :

each twelve feet wide, the middle one sixteen feet long, the others ten and nine, and a verandah all round. The walls are to be nine feet high, of *green*, that is, sun-dried bricks. I stipulated this morning for a piece of timber to be built into the wall, all round each room, at a convenient height for nails; else we should have knocked down our walls by driving nails into them. The whole is to cost when plastered, (but not floored, by the bye; I have forgotten about that,) certainly within £90,—the rent for one year, I suppose, of many a house in Edinburgh. And if you say that a house in Edinburgh is so high from its situation, I will back our situation against any in the town, for a view, and for the advantageous visiting of our parishioners, black and white. We have the sea before us, with swelling, undulating hills for two miles between us and it, clothed with natural wood, and studded with kraals, while our white population is all behind us, on the cleared but less beautiful ground on which we have ourselves been living for the last few months.

But neither the house nor the view are worthy of the inhabitants, (of course the present company,—I am alone,—is excepted,) I mean that the view inside, when I sit with my two sisters, far surpasses the view outside.

* * * * *

I expected the Bishop from P. M.·B., but he has altered his plans, and is not to be down till Wednesday. We had a laugh on Saturday night about the spare bed in my tent. At first after the fire, A—— was impressing on me the impossibility of having visitors. I was in one tent, with many boxes and some stores. Another tent was occupied by stores; and the two huts by the females of our establishment, then five in number. So I said little: but when Frank Galloway was to come up for his sister Polly, though I knew A—— expected him to come and go the same day, I arranged for him to sleep, as we had originally (before the fire) intended. I borrowed a *cartel* to support a mattrass for him, and so his bed was made in the tent. Then Mr Adams was coming to see us: where could he sleep? O, what did for Frank would do for him. So it was. Then we expected the Dean. A—— proposed to take up her abode in the tent, and give up the drawing-room with its two sofas to him and me: but I would not hear of it, and when the Dean and I arrived on a Saturday about midnight, we stowed ourselves away very happily in the tent; having first partaken of a slight supper, each sitting on his own bed, and the loaf, beef, bottle, &c. being on the box that served as a basin-stand. And now we expect the Bishop on his visitation tour: and I have had no difficulty in persuading them that he can surely sleep where the Dean did. They used to speak in Durban of the *thin end of the wedge.* I think Frank Galloway certainly was that.

I am so glad to get the bill for £37. 6*s*. That will go well on towards finishing the chancel of the Umlazi church. The Dean and I spent an evening in arranging the dimensions and materials of a church for the Umhlali. It is to be 57 feet from end to end, and to cost (say) £140, and hold over 100 people. The civil population is now about fifty, and nearly fifty of the troops attend regularly. Besides these buildings, the bricks are on the ground to build a little church at Mount Moreland, to cost about £50 or £60. I think you must admit that the churches under my eye have not been extravagant. Pine Town, built; all finished, except the plaster inside; cost about £210. Claremont, a wooden-building, with seats for about forty, cost about £35: this has been in use for more than a year. The Isipingo, in use, cost £55: not quite finished. The Umlazi church is to cost about £90. This will be larger than any of the others. We want it to contain 400 persons.

I hope you will not think this too business-like an epistle. It is almost too near the time of the closing of the mail to let one write freely; besides, I have still about me the feeling that I have not hitherto written so often as I ought. Still you will believe me when I say that it is a pleasure, a great pleasure, to write: and I need not tell you what a pleasure it is to hear from you.

Your ever loving brother,

C. F. M.

LETTER XLIV.

(*To the same.*)

UMHLALI, *Nov.* 5, 1857.

DEAR ——,

Many happy returns of your birthday to you, my own dear sister. We drank your health on the first, and I rejoiced more than ever before at its coming on *All Saints' Day.* It is very happy while we are wishing you all good gifts in His good providence, to be thanking Him too for His saints that have gone before: the great multitude which no man can number, of all people nations and languages, praising God! Dear ——, may we all be joined to that blessed company, and may we now be learning the language and the manners of the heavenly Jerusalem.

I don't think I have written to you since I sent from Durban the stick which —— gives to ——, along (it is now Nov. 9) with a common stick of my own, which is for you. I have often trudged with it through the sands of Durban, and was using it that very morning, on which I despatched the rhinoceros stick for ——. So I thought it would serve the double purpose of helping to save and strengthen the precious stick, and also of conveying to you a good shake of the hand. I think it would probably have some sand on it when it arrived; at least I know there was a good deal on it when I packed it up; I rolled it up just as it was, with the same feelings as actuated those who buried Sir John Moore.

I have been carried on so far by the paragraph which I *began* four days ago. I write now specially to catch this mail, as being an opportunity I think I never had before, of writing to you when you had not written to me. Your letters are such a treat to us all, and you are so constant and regular, that you will understand my joke of catching so special an occasion to write to you.

You speak of our being at the Umhlali as a thing in which you can acquiesce, in the conviction that we shall soon be moved from it. But really I think we are useful here, and I am sure we ought to be happy. You know that we came here at my especial request to the Bishop, and with the full approval of the Dean, who quite confirmed my own notion that it was the proper place for me. You have heard by this time that we have got into Kafir work here; though perhaps the latest letters may have given you the impression, (and if so, I must confess it would be a true impression,) that the Kafir work is rather going back at present. But we are looking forward to increased opportunities when we get to our new house on the hill. The white work, however, in this district is really important. My only regret is, that I cannot make more of my Sunday than I do. I wish I could say like Joshua, "Sun, stand thou still!" There have been four sudden deaths in the last few weeks: one up the country, and three on the coast. One at the Umlazi; Fea, the white man who built our buildings there, and who was making bricks for the church: one in Durban: and one in my own district or parish, a Mr ——, who met with an accident while riding on a Sunday, and died on the Tuesday. He had not had an opportunity of going to church nearer than ten miles, since he went to his farm, more than a year ago; and, I fancy, had neither been at church, nor received the Holy Communion (though a communicant), during that time. I am very anxious to establish a monthly service, if nothing better, in his neighbourhood. He, poor man, (as we say,) is gone; but there are others. It will be, however, at the expense of a service somewhere else; I almost fear, at the expense of the Umhlali.

I was stopping for a few moments just now, having been writing like a steam-engine, when Guafu, who was laying the cloth for dinner, enquired politely, "Do I stand in your light?" I said, "No." He is a fine fellow. I wish you could be present at our morning or evening prayers sometimes, to observe how well (compared with the others at least) he remembers what we have been reading about lately. We are at Acts xii. just now. When we came to the death of James, I told them the names of Simon and Andrew, John and James, as the four chief Apostles. He and Bafuti can remember the other three, but always forget the name of S. Andrew. I think they are struck with the endurance even unto death of the early teachers.

Good bye. God bless you now and evermore.

Your affectionate brother,

and friend and fellow Christian,

C. F. M.

LETTER XLV.

(*To his Eldest Sister.*)

UMHLALI, *Jan.* 6, 1858.

DEAR ——,

* * * * *

Your letters are not only very pleasant, but very good for us. They sometimes keep up spirits that have been flagging (not mine), and they bind us very closely together. I often think of you in my long rides: last night, for instance, I got home about half-past eleven, having had Orion and Jupiter as my companions, as well as our glorious Cross and Centaur: and I was thinking which of them would be visible at the same moment in England. I came to the conclusion, that what was right over your heads, your *zenith*, is always on our horizon, and similarly our zenith, (the star which is just over our heads,) will at the same moment be on your horizon in a direction a little East of South, probably between S.S.E. and S.E. by S.; also that at every moment either you or we might say, Half of what I now see of the sky they see also, (unless the sun is above the horizon). If you at any time want to know what we can see, think of a line stretching from about E.N.E. right over head to W.S.W.; all the stars that are S.E. of this line are at the same moment visible to us. In short, if you had a wall with an exposure to the S.E., or between that and South, then sitting at the foot of it looking forward and upward, you would see half of the whole sky: *that* half we see also. We see, besides, another half below your horizon, but we do not see what is behind the wall. If you want to see these stars in the *same position* as we do, you must lie on your back, with your feet to the wall, which must be so high as to seem right over your head. The top of the wall is our horizon; and by looking up through your eyebrows you will see what is over our heads; what is on your right hand is on our right hand also, what is on your left is on our left: in short, you are just in the position in which we are when we stand looking about N.N.E. There's the result of my conversation with Orion and Jupiter last night.

* * * * *

As to your plan of my staying at home one Sunday every fortnight, I'll think about it; but prejudices are against it. Even with my present attempts there are one or two places very much neglected. I am just arranging to give a Sunday service to a place between Verulam and the Umgeni. This would entail my absence from home the whole of that Sunday. I propose to do this about once in two months. I have for the last three weeks had a Monday evening service at the Tongaat, and this will want a Sunday now and then to keep it alive, and for the more solemn administration of the Holy Communion. Fancy white people, who used to live in London, communicants, firmly attached to the Church of England, who have never received the Communion since they came out, five or six years ago. I know such a case. Again: a man had a fall from his horse, and died in three or four days: he also was a communicant, but had not received the Communion for a year and a half. I heard of his accident, and was on my way to his house, on my return from a summons to Durban, but he had been buried. These are strong cases; and I feel strongly that we shall do no good to the blacks by neglecting the whites. And till I have a curate, (which God grant soon!) I don't think I can possibly give up any white service on Sunday. I am really well; and though both Sunday and Monday are hard days, I was out of bed by six this morning, (Tuesday,) and am as hearty as possible.

And now my own dear sister, (dearer though less written to than even in Cambridge days,) good bye. And may the God of all peace and grace give us every blessing, more than we deserve or desire, through Christ our Lord.

Your ever loving brother,

C. F. M.

The next letter refers to a Church Conference, concerning which I shall have more to say presently. I introduce the letter in order to shew the spirit in which he engaged in the work, and his own humility concerning his fitness for it. His opinion of his own incapacity for this kind of business was however founded in truth: he was not the man for a consultative body, was too easily led, and as regards a Church synod too little read in ecclesiastical history and ecclesiastical literature generally, to be capable of exercising a great amount of influence.

LETTER XLVI.

UMHLALI, NATAL, *March* 17, 1858.

DEAR GOODWIN,

* * * * *

We are to have a Church Conference here next month as a preliminary to a regular synod. It is to advise the Bishop whether to call a synod; how to constitute it, and whether to apply to the legislature for an act confirming it. Yesterday was the day for electing lay representatives: and I don't think any parochial district, (we have no actual parishes,) will turn out a better man than my people did. * * * For my own part, I have a very strong feeling of my incapacity for such business. My comfort is, that I did not come out here with any idea that I was peculiarly qualified for the work, but simply because there were few labourers here in comparison with home, that others would fill my place at home, and I should be taking up the place of none out here: and so, if one does but do one's best, He for whom we are working will excuse the performance. But it is a matter of considerable responsibility, to be one of the leading members of the first Diocesan Synod (for so it is virtually). God grant us wisdom. I wonder now sometimes that I was bold enough to come out. I don't think I should now. Or if I did, not as Archdeacon.

* * * * *

Your affectionate friend,

C. F. M.

The Church Conference took place at Pietermaritzburg, on the twentieth of April, and following days. As I am writing a history, not of the Church in Natal, but of the life of Archdeacon Mackenzie, I shall not think it necessary to give a full account of the proceedings.

It must suffice to say that on certain important points the Archdeacon found himself in a minority, and that upon ascertaining that the views, which himself and those who voted with him considered essential, were negatived by the majority, he retired with the Dean of Pietermaritzburg and some other clergymen from the Conference. The matter under discussion was the future constitution of a Church Synod, and the point upon which a strong difference of opinion was manifested was the status which should be granted to native congregations. Should such congregations be put on a footing of equality with regard to representation with the white congregations? did the equality in Christ of members of His Church imply equal rights in all matters of church-membership? There was also the additional question of the proper method of dealing with the soldiers; some holding that a camp congregation should send a delegate to the synod, others holding the contrary opinion: but I apprehend that the real point in the discussion was the position of the black congregations, and that the high view of the privileges conferred upon all men, whether white or black, by vital union with the Redeemer, which the Archdeacon held, made him regard his own presence at the Conference as useless, and indeed impossible, when that view appeared to be negatived by the opinion of the majority. I should not be honest if I did not state my own opinion that Mackenzie was in error. Doubtless the question of dealing with a Church composed of two different races in different conditions of civilization must involve many difficulties; and it seems an easy mode of disposing of those difficulties to say that all are one in Christ; but Christian equality does not involve equal fitness to deliberate and make rules for the government of the Church, any more than the equality of Englishmen in the eye of the law involves universal suffrage; and it seems to me that in the infancy of such mixed Churches, the more advanced and more civilized portion must assume to some extent the guardianship of the weaker and less intelligent, looking forward to a time when such guardianship shall be no longer necessary, and can be safely abandoned. In fact, the question appears to me to be one of expediency and not one of principle, and I cannot but regret that my dear friend was induced to take a course, which, without leading to any important result, deprived the Conference of the advantage of his presence.

Yet even here, if he was in error, as I think he was, the error was a noble one. It was the love of the weaker race, the strong feeling of the dignity of the lowest of mankind when elevated by the knowledge of Christ, the fear of the native being trampled upon by the colonist, that made him protest in the most emphatic manner that seemed possible to him, against that which he deemed to be unsound in principle.

Whatever may be the true view concerning Mackenzie's conduct, there can be no doubt that this was a very trying time to him, and that he returned with great delight to his pastoral labours at the Umhlali. He felt himself out of his element in the conflicts of opinion stirred up in a deliberative assembly, and I have reason to believe,—the feeling is in fact expressed in one of his letters,—that he was conscious on such occasions of the need of a more definite theological training than he had received, and of the evil of the practice of passing so rapidly as many Cambridge men do from mathematics to holy orders; he was most in his element when he was ministering to the wants of others, and exhibiting the real depth and value of his Christian principles by going about like his Master, and doing good.

The Conference was opened, as we have seen, on April 20; on April 22 the Archdeacon retired, and on April 23rd, Friday, he seems to have left Pietermaritzburg. The following extract from a letter of Miss Mackenzie's will bring him home, and give a picture of his life at the Umhlali at this period.

He did not leave P. M. B. till one P.M. on Friday. He meant to have started early, but was obliged to call on the Bishop first: then he remembered he ought to call on Dr and Mrs ——. While he was with them the cathedral bells rang, and he could not go before service, and so it was one o'clock, and the roads dreadfully slippery with the rain, before he got fairly away. I knew his ways too well to expect he would do anything else, and tried to keep in patient trust that all was well with him, but I could not help thinking of poor Mr ——, who was thrown from his horse on his way to P. M. B. and very severely hurt; but in spite of darkness, bad and slippery roads, a tired horse, and swollen rivers to cross, he was preserved in all dangers. He slept at the half-way house, breakfasted next morning at Pine Town, did some business in Durban, reached Verulam at eleven P.M. and went to bed; but was up very early, and was here a little after eight A.M. on Sunday morning. He let his horse, Spring, wander away by accident at P. M. B., and, trusting to his usual good luck, did not take so much pains to recover him as he would otherwise have done, and rode the ninety miles on his new horse, which is still called Bob. The Archdeacon had less than an hour to dress and breakfast before he was at the camp, for service at nine. He has a church-meeting at Mount Moreland and elsewhere to-morrow; so he does not return till the afternoon. I am thankful to say the hour for his Monday service at the Tongaat is changed from seven P.M. to four; so he will be at home in future in much better time. He is wonderfully strong. It is vain to ask him to do less. Did I tell you of my once writing to him from the Umlazi to beg he would release Mr R. from a service at the Bluff? His answer at first overjoyed me, quite agreeing that it was a total break-up of Mr R.'s Sunday; but I stamped my foot when I read on, and found that he meant to add it to his own duties. So the thinking what he could leave out of his duties here after reading your letter, made him add a quarterly service at the Umhlanga, when he is away from the Umhlali all day, and the Saturday also. I was quite thankful to him yesterday for giving us less music than usual; it is a great fatigue to his voice. It is pouring and blowing hurricanes. We have still no windows in. Part of a partition wall fell down to-day from the badness of the bricks it was built with, and I don't know when our house will be finished.

In the next letter, one of the last written by him to his eldest sister, who died in the latter part of the year, he appears again to allude to the approaching Conference.

LETTER XLVII.

UMHLALI, *April* 3, 1858.

DEAREST ——,

* * * * *

We are having divisions and searchings of heart here in church-matters. You know how unfitted I am for such things. Pray for me, that I may be guided right, and may not injure my own soul, that I may be honest and true, yet loving and gentle. There are such men: the Bishop of Cape Town is one, I believe. My comfort, when I feel that I am in water too deep for me, is that I did not come out because I thought myself peculiarly fitted for the work here, but simply because so few would come. And I think we may feel the comfort that a party would, chosen by lot from a regiment, that they were of God's selecting, that a man's skill and pride had not chosen them, that they went forth like Gideon's three hundred in the name of the Lord.

* * * * *

About this time Archdeacon Mackenzie was appointed chaplain to the soldiers, who were encamped in the neighbourhood. He had indeed been virtually chaplain for some time; but he was now regularly appointed with a salary, which though not large was important as enabling him to obtain assistance in his widely extended parish. For some time he had felt the need of a fellowlabourer. He was very anxious that a young Cambridge friend, to whom he was much attached, should come out and work with him, and he sent a very pressing invitation; on due consideration the invitation was declined, and as I believe on good and solid grounds. I here give the letter which Mackenzie wrote on the occasion, and I would especially call the reader's attention to the temper with which the disappointment was received, and the manner in which he endeavours to direct his friend's mind to an important field of work nearer home.

LETTER XLVIII.

UMHLALI, *June* 3, 1858.

MY DEAR ——,

Your letter gave me great pleasure, coming from your affectionate heart, and telling me so truly what you thought about coming here, and not coming here. I am quite satisfied that you have done what is right in following your own judgment in the matter, and not coming out simply because I wished or advised you to do so: and I have no reason (certainly I have no right, if I had reason) to blame you for deciding as you have. The way I look at it is this. There is a great deal to be done at home, (and perhaps no work is so important, though few so difficult, as that of a clergyman among and over the Undergraduates); there is a great deal to be done abroad, and fewer in proportion to do it. I take this last for granted, without any accurate calculation, and I may be wrong; but I think so. Well: every one must decide for himself where he can best work *for the Master's cause*, after clearly making up his mind that *that* must come first, before private inclination, and even before other ties, (except so far as they involve duties, and so are part of the Master's cause). If you think that you honestly did and do determine to do what you impartially and conscientiously think right, then of course you may feel quite at ease. I should not doubt this, but for one or two expressions in your letter; on the whole I believe you did so determine, and therefore I am satisfied.

But if you in your own heart are not sure that you would give up all for Him, and think you did not decide this particular question (of coming out) on that principle, I would say, take this instance as a test sent by God to shew yourself to you; try to purify your intentions by thinking more of His Infinite Love, and our relation to Him as His children; and pray that you may come nearer to the blessed state of the saints above, who have no will opposed to His. And, my dear fellow, when you do so pray, pray for me too. It is very sad, how changeable we are; how easily we forget the high office to which we have been called, and the purity and singleness of heart required to enable us in any degree to fulfil our mission.

* * * * *

I am very anxious about the college-servants. Just before I left, I had some talk with —— about them; I mean their being cared for, as persons capable of religion, by us their masters, being clergymen. —— told me of the appointment at Oxford, (in Magdalene, I think), of one of the fellows to the office of chaplain to the college-servants. I dare say your arrangements at —— may be better than ours; but ask —— when you see him, whether anything has been done in Caius about bringing good influences to bear upon the servants. I was reminded of it the other day when defending the practice of daily service; I quoted the excellence of the habit I, with so many others, had in college of going regularly in the morning: my opponent said, "Yes, and the bed-makers, what did they do?" I admitted that I had enjoyed the privilege myself, without their joining in it. I forgot by the way to say, that I did try hard to get my gyp to come to my rooms at 6 A.M. for prayers, promising not to keep him above five minutes: but he always said, they were so bustled, they could not come. So you see, I tried something; but without success. I think if in each college those who are anxious to do good would talk the matter over, they might do something. When men leave college they feel a responsibility to their servants; and why should not the same feeling exist in a house established for religious as well as intellectual education?

* * * * *

I think if I were back in College again, I should try to impress upon those of the Undergraduates who now neglect it, the need of studying the Bible, and other first books of divinity, if they are thinking of being ordained. Part of Sunday might well be given to this.

I have mentioned in every letter I am writing this mail, that I have got a curate. I am as pleased as a father at the birth of his first child. Nay, but seriously, I am very glad. I shall now give a Sunday afternoon once a month to a Kafir service, and we shall bring two more congregations of white people, one at the little Umhlanga, the other at the Tongaat, into regular Sunday services. I shall not myself pass many Sundays in the year without celebrating the Holy Communion: I have been administering it more than once a fortnight for several months. I believe this to be itself a privilege. At the Conference at P. M. B. in April, we had the Holy Communion every morning, and I don't think I could have got through the trials and difficulties of the week without it. By the way, that was another thing I wanted to know from you and ——, whether you have Communion oftener than once a term. Why not on the first Sunday of every month? or, if you like to regulate it more academically, say three times in the term? Now don't say, (you and ——), "What has he to do with us, giving us orders in this way? has he not enough to do in his own Archdeaconry?" No—I know you will not.

* * * * *

And now, my dear fellow, good bye. Whether we shall meet on earth is in God's hands, and will be as He wills: but we may trust to a meeting above in His time; how soon we know not; only let us ever stand with our lamps burning in our hands. God bless you!

Your affectionate friend,

C. F. M.

The new curate alluded to in the foregoing letter was a great satisfaction to the Archdeacon's mind, not (as will be easily believed) because he would be able to relax his own efforts, but because the aid of a brother clergyman opened new fields of activity. The stipend was partly supplied by the Bishop, partly by local resources, and it gave the Archdeacon great delight to find that his people responded heartily to the appeal which he made to them, and that there would be no difficulty in supplying the guaranteed amount of salary. He instituted a monthly collection in his five churches, namely, Umhlali, Tongaat, Verulam, Mount Moreland, and the little Umhlanga, and found it answer so well that he determined to adopt the same system of collection for the support of education in his district. I here introduce a scrap of a letter, in which he expresses his satisfaction with the new arrangement.

LETTER XLIX.

(*To a Sister.*)

UMHLALI, *June* 30, 1858.

* * * * *

The new curate works well. Every one is pleased with him, and whereas I told the Bishop I thought we could raise £40 a-year in the district towards his support, this month has just about produced its share. We shall each have service three times every Sunday on an average, and there will not be many Sundays in the year on which I shall not celebrate the Holy Communion. I do feel very grateful for being allowed thus to feed His sheep in the wilderness; and I trust that the outward forms of His service may be the means of grace to the souls of His people, and that His glory may be shewn forth.

* * * * *

There is a great dearth of letters in the latter half

of this year, 1858. The reader, however, will be able to fancy to himself the Archdeacon's regular course of laborious duty, and his happy home now rendered almost comfortable; in fact, I find Miss Mackenzie writing towards Michaelmas in this fashion: "We were burnt out of house and home about a year ago: but there are advantages in every trial; and whereas we were living in a very uncomfortable ill-built house, situated in a bare desolate-looking field, with no pretty view from it, now we have built a mansion for ourselves, with eight small rooms in it; and we have such a glorious view of the sea, separated from us by beautifully wooded hills and valleys; and our ground being our own, for we have bought between twenty and thirty acres, it is both pleasure and profit to plant fruit-trees, pine-apples, bananas, &c.; and the rapidity with which everything grows is astonishing."

I shall be pardoned if I take advantage of this absence of anything of especial interest connected with the Archdeacon personally, to introduce two or three notices of collateral matters, which will nevertheless tend to illustrate the story of his life in Natal.

In page 177 there is a specimen of Kafir politeness; here is a specimen of Kafir passion. "I was in the sitting room," writes Miss Mackenzie, "when I heard screams, and then saw Jessie (the maid) running. I joined her, and saw Uskendi crouching under a tree where he had fallen, while Bafuti was close by with a long stick in his hand, and Umzanga was trying to hold him in. As soon as I joined them, Uskendi made his escape, and I took hold of Bafuti's arm, but he shook me off, and said in English, almost foaming with passion, 'You like that boy bite me? you like that boy beat me?' I said, No, it was very bad, but he must not beat him when in a passion. He *roared* out in Kafir, 'Leave me, don't touch me.' So I said very quietly, 'Bafuti, is that the way in which you speak to the Inkosazan?' Then I told him Uskendi should certainly be punished, but that it was not good for himself to beat him while he was so angry, and I reminded him of UmFundisi's teaching. * * * Umzanga now came and tried to take the stick by force from him, but this was beginning to make him furious again; so we told him to desist, and I said that I would not take it from him, that I knew he would not use it now, and that, if he promised, we would trust him entirely. * * * Poor Bafuti! his whole body shook, and I could see his heart beating, while the tears rolled down from his eyes; but with an effort he threw away the stick of his own accord, and walked away; but he was very angry, and he seated himself at the corner of the house, as if to watch for his prey. * * * He was very grave all the afternoon, but when I asked him if he would like me to speak to him, he said, 'I wish it.' Then I reminded him of the evil spirit taking possession of a man, and about Cain and Abel. At night at prayers, when the Archdeacon asked them all what were the sins we were tempted to commit, Bafuti answered, 'Being very angry;' and he seemed quite humbled at the remembrance of his passion."

I hope the reader will see in the story which I have just given, evidence not only of the strength of

Kafir passion, but of the influence of Christian teaching and example. I hope he will also feel that such conduct as has been described, if it betrays something of the savage, does at the same time indicate a nature capable of being trained to higher things; the fact is, that few races appear more hopeful than the Kafirs of South Africa; the great obstacle to their improvement is (as I have already had occasion to remark) polygamy, and the custom associated with it, according to which a man has the absolute power over his daughters, and can sell them for their price in cows under any circumstances; hence I find the Mackenzie missionaries occasionally complaining that any young girl taken by them, educated, even baptized, is liable to be sold for a few cows, as third or fourth wife to some heathen husband. The English government has thought fit not to interfere with the native law in this respect; and possibly it may have been politic to take this course; but certainly to the missionary, and to every wellwisher to the native race, the consequences are very deplorable.

This bargain concerning women even affects their children sometimes, as will be seen from the following: "Our domestic troubles," says Miss Alice Mackenzie in one of her letters, "are curiously different from those at home. The boy Umabokwe was visited the other day by his father, who was in a great excitement, and spoke to us so fast and with such a torrent of words, that we could not follow him. Umabokwe was summoned to tell us what it was all about; and he explained, (in Kafir, only he spoke gently, so that we could understand him). 'A man is coming to take me away.' It seemed that his mother, when she married his father, had not been paid for: at least not the whole price of cows. She is dead since, but the man who owned her before her marriage now claims her son. The Archdeacon is gone to the magistrate about it."

Then there is superstition standing as an obstacle to the faith and to the improvement of the people, and the stories told of the "witch-doctors" are very strange. Mr Shepstone, whose name is well-known to all acquainted with Natal, always spoke of the knowledge of these men as something which he could not explain; and that which was a mystery to him may well be a source of tremendous influence upon the minds of the natives. The magistrate at the Umhlali spoke of the witch-doctors in the same way. He told the Mackenzies the following story. He was leaving home, and only two boys were left in his house. He shewed one of them, whose name was Usfile, a revolver pistol which was in its case, and desired him not to touch it. When he came home it was broken. Both the boys denied any knowledge of the accident, and Usfile said he did not like to be suspected, and wished a witch-doctor to be consulted. There was one, come quite lately from the Zulu country, who knew nothing of European ways, or houses. This man being applied to first chewed some medicine, and then went raging about to get himself into the proper state of phrensy; then he threw himself on the ground, saying there was a snake inside him, and groaned horribly. By a kind of "magical music" he discovered what was wanted from him: they never told him what they wanted to consult him about. He said, "You do not want to know about cows." The people assented. Then he said, "No: it is not cows: it is something in the house." The people assented again, more loudly than before. This went on for three hours, the witch-doctor always coming nearer to the truth, till he ended by describing the case with the pistol in it, the table under which it lay, how the boy had tried to unscrew it, and that there was another boy with him, and then he pointed to Usfile as the culprit, who confessed.

Stories, similar to the preceding, and of great interest in themselves, might easily be multiplied; but I must leave them, in order to return to that which more definitely concerns the life of Archdeacon Mackenzie.

Throughout the year 1858 I find constant sorrowings on the part of Miss Mackenzie concerning her brother's severe work, long rides, sometimes in a hot sun, sometimes in drenching rain. She has chronicled also some minor inconveniences: as when upon one occasion his horse was troubled with a sore back, and being unable to ride upon it with a saddle the Archdeacon called at the house of a parishioner to ask if the good woman of the house could in any way assist him: she very benevolently lent him her *ironing flannel* to serve as a temporary saddle, the Archdeacon promising to return it before the next ironing-day.

Under date December 21, of this year, I find a notice which I think the reader will pardon me for introducing as it stands. It illustrates at once the effect of Mackenzie's character upon those about him, and the roughness of the life which he was accustomed to lead. "I do feel," says Miss Mackenzie, "the responsibility so great of being allowed to live with Charles. It is not only that his temper is so unvaryingly even, amidst provocations both great and small: it seems as if he could not fail there: but he grows in holiness, and in devotedness, and such utter self-forgetfulness! It is a great comfort to me that he takes care of his health without neglecting what he thinks his duty. I never can be reconciled to his long Sunday rides in the hot wet season; but he thinks it is right, and that he is planting the Church. On Sunday, after service, it was desperately hot, quite enervating, even to me, and he started off on a twenty-five miles ride. He had the misfortune to lose his flask of wine by the way; so he had only the hot water of the river to drink. In the evening the heaviest of our Natal rains came on, and next morning the country was in a flood. He was much wished to stay, but he said he would try to return. The river Ninoti was very high; and it has a slippery stony bed. A Kafir was told to go in and see what state it was in, but he could not keep his footing. A white man told him that a little higher up he might swim through himself, but not his horse; so he left him in the charge of Mr ——, as well as his waterproofs, which would only encumber him in the water. He had to swim another river which is only a brook in ordinary times. The Umvoti was not higher than his knee, but it was very wide, and he said he compassionated horses more than he had ever known was necessary; it was so fatiguing to walk through the water. He arrived dripping at Dr A—'s, for it had been raining all day. He found them at dinner, and they gave him dry clothes and lent him a horse; but he arrived here about half-past nine pretty wet, as the Umhlali was high: so he did not stay to give us any news, but went straight to bed, and he is quite well this morning."

The year 1859 opened with a very heavy trouble, the loss of his eldest sister, who has been already described in this Memoir as intimately connected with Mackenzie's early education, and the formation of his character. The next three letters, which are nearly all that have come to my hands of this year's correspondence, refer to this event. The first is to the sister herself, the second to another sister, his chief correspondent in England, and the third to his brother-in-law. They are dated from Seaforth, the name given to the new house at the Umhlali.

LETTER L.

SEAFORTH, *January*, 1859.

DEAR ——,

I have just finished copying for A——, and for very shame must write you a few lines myself. My dear one, it is indeed, as A—— says, the first real home anxiety we have had, except ——. Dear one, I trust you trustfully in His hands, who watches over Israel, and slumbers not nor sleeps.

* * * * *

The more I try to obey the rules of the Church, the more of beauty and truth and reality I see in them. I never used the Visitation service in England, and I do not use it here quite as it is directed, but I have looked more to its prayers than before; and they are very beautiful.

Then the having the Communion at a marriage is so good, when both are real Christians,—a solemn binding of them together, and with all true members of the Lord, present and absent. I feel a far more general meaning in the Communion than I used to do, not only the strengthening and refreshing of our souls, but the union with the Church, His body, the blessed company of all faithful people,—however men may differ as to who are to be included in that phrase. He knows His own, and keepeth them every instant.

Dear ——, you may be now among the members of the Church in Heaven, who have washed their robes and made them white in the blood of the Lamb. If so, we shall never meet again on earth. But what a meeting in heaven! Any two of us to meet so would be more than we can conceive,—we made perfect, and never more to part: and then to think of the many! Dear mother, with so many of us, I trust, and with her own brothers and sisters; and each to see in the others the reflexion of their own joy, and to feel the joy of others to be their own!

God grant us grace to arrive at that blessed ending, for Christ's sake. Amen.

Your affectionate brother,

C. F. M.

LETTER LI.

SEAFORTH, *January* 29, 1859.

DEAR ——,

* * * * *

We are looking anxiously for the mail to hear of our dear ——. Well, wherever she is, her Father is with her. Those who do not know *Him* think that a cold thing to say, and imagine that *faith* makes people indifferent to the sufferings and misfortunes of others. God knows it is not so, but that rather we are bound together the closer by His great Fatherly overshadowing wings.

Feb. 2. Dear ——, the news came yesterday. I heard it on my road home, through Miss ——'s kindness, she having heard it here. Well, dearest one, when I heard it, I said at once, "I'm very glad." I could not help thinking first, she is over the fever: she is through the grave and gate of death. Then I thought of poor ——. I do feel for him. They say none can know a widower's or a widow's grief: perhaps not: but one can tell what her loss to him would be. I remember how her telling me she was to be married shot through me such a pang as I have seldom felt,—never, I think,—far worse than this present one: for now is she not there, whither we are all hastening? God grant we may all arrive safe in His time.

* * * * *

LETTER LII.

SEAFORTH, UMHLALI, *Feb.* 2, 1859.

DEAR ——,

It was very kind of you to write to us yourself, at a time when your heart was so full. God has, I trust, supported you with His everlasting arm, and that you can now look forward past the bounds of time and death to the kingdom where there shall be no partings. May He of His infinite mercy bring us thither, where we shall be safe for ever.

We have indeed all of us owed much to God through her. And it must be grateful to you, though adding to the sense of your loss, to feel how much she was looked up to and respected and loved by all. I at least, for one, know of no one who did not so. And surely we ought not to think it strange if the brightest gems are sometimes removed from the workshop to the immediate presence of the Great King. What a comfort it is to feel sure that He is able of His infinite wisdom to think for all and to provide for all, to whom the influence of a single event extends. No doubt each one of your children had just as much of her direct influence as was on the whole best. There comes a time when the sapling that has been supported, trained, and perhaps shielded from the storm, should stand alone and gain strength by being buffeted by the winds, learning to cling more firmly to the solid ground, from which ultimately all support must come. Then too, she being dead, yet speaketh; they will often remember her words, which will sound more solemnly than ever.

I believe there has been a strong influence for good on me from my father's character, described to me by various people, by none, I think, more vividly or effectively, than by you my dear brother,—thank you for doing so. And will not the example, which they have had before their eyes, live in their memories, and draw them after her?

But, in the mean time, it is sad—most sad—to us, who are left behind. Though we are so far from home, we live always in the prospect of perhaps being allowed, were it but for a time, to see you all again. And now one bright and beautiful face will be wanting; one Christian spirit that would have welcomed us back, and bid us God speed out again, has fled. But O how blessed the teaching of the Spirit, to say, "His will be done: He doeth all things well." There was a needs be! She is part of our treasure laid up in heaven, making it the more natural and easy for our hearts to be where our treasure is.

I have been led lately to think, how His excellence and loveliness and beauty are shewn forth to us—weakly indeed, but so only could it be to us—by the excellences of His creatures. And if a mortal being, a creature, confessedly with imperfection, can so engross our affections, what will be the bliss of the open vision of the King in His beauty!

My dear ——, I never, I think, spoke or wrote in this way to you before. But I feel her presence, above us all, such a bond of union, that I have not been afraid to speak in this way to you who are so much older, and so much more fit to tell me these things than I you.

God bless you all.

Your affectionate brother,

C. F. M.

I have only one more letter written from the Umhlali, which I insert here, not so much on account of any special interest connected with it, as because it is the last.

LETTER LIII.

(*To a Sister.*)

SEAFORTH, *March 6*, 1859.

DEAR ——,

You called your letter (of December and January), just received, a short one. It was shortish for you, but not for me: I mean, if I had written such a one, I should not have called it so very short.

I am so very glad at all you say about the Church Service. It is a bond of great power to knit our hearts all together, by knitting them to Him. I remember in my first term at Cambridge, when I first had the opportunity of attending daily service, not making full use of it: either going as seldom as I could, or not attending much while there,—I forget exactly. I remember talking to dear —— about it, and her advising me to try and get good; and I went on liking it more and more from that time. In my third year I was offered the chapel-clerkship, which required my attendance twice a day, and that made me like it more, for I got into the way when that year was over of attending always when I could. And I believe it was the General Thanksgiving, in Caius College chapel, which influenced me for good more than any other earthly means. I like to remember this, because it is another case (of the many) in which I may trace mercies received from Him through her who is gone to His presence.

*　　*　　*　　*　　*

To-morrow is the first day of Lent. I feel somehow not ready for it; but, in fact, that tells me I am the more ready for it as a time of self-examination, humiliation, and prayer.

I have come to think of it out here more as a time for inward private work than I used, and not only as the established season for additional services in Church. God grant that it may be blessed to me and to us all, though it will be passed before you get this.

* * * * *

In the February of this year, Mackenzie was ill for the first and last time, so far as I know, during his residence in Natal. On the first of February he was out on one of his long expeditions, and the day was extremely hot: he drank some cold water, which quite deranged him, and when he reached a friend's house, he found himself really ill. Cold cloths upon his head and rest however soon restored him, and the next day he was able to come home. At first it was feared that he had received a sun-stroke; this happily proved to be a mistake; but for some time after he was more or less of an invalid, and forbidden by his medical adviser to do all that he had been in the habit of doing before. In the beginning of March he was well again, and resumed his long Sunday journeys.

In March, after much negotiation concerning exchange of duty, an arrangement was made, which enabled the Mackenzie party to visit Maritzburg. Change was becoming necessary, and on March 28, they started in an ox-waggon upon their journey; the Dean of Maritzburg relieving the Archdeacon from his work at the Umhlali. In the beginning of April they were comfortably settled at Maritzburg, where the Archdeacon, in addition to other clerical work, undertook the cathedral school. The following is the only letter which has come to my hands at this period.

LETTER LIV.

(*To a Sister.*)

P. M. B. *April* 9, 1859.

DEAR ——,

*   *   *   *   *

I am looking forward rather to the next few weeks. My sphere of duty is more confined. I could walk in half an hour from this house to any part of my parish, and that is a new idea to me. At the same time I find the school somewhat fatiguing and harassing: there are seven classes, all to be kept at work at once. As to parish-work, I shall have to set myself to it more steadily next week than I have done hitherto.

The cathedral daily service is a great help, and we have Communion every Sunday. Certainly, while we live in the flesh, outward things are a great help to the spirit.

*   *   *   *   *

During this stay at Maritzburg, it was arranged that the Archdeacon and his elder sister should visit England. I think I cannot introduce this new turn in their history more appropriately than in Miss Mackenzie's own words. On May 9 she writes: "There is a plan for Charles and me to sail for England by the next steamer. My heart is full at the very thought of it. * * * I cannot tell you how I feel. I am in a flurry of joy."

The cause of this arrangement I will endeavour to explain. For some time there had been a scheme for sending a missionary Bishop with some clergy into the Zulu country. Who was to be the missionary Bishop? Mackenzie's name was very naturally suggested, and

I believe it was all but determined that he should be the leader. It was with reference to his consecration as a missionary Bishop to the Zulu country, that his trip to England was first planned. The Bishop of Natal, however, thought that it would be well that he himself should undertake this new missionary work, and, in order to undertake it, he was prepared to resign his own See and go to the wilder and more difficult field. Eventually it was proposed that both the Bishop and the Archdeacon should go as far as the Cape, and there take counsel as to what was best to be done. At the last moment, the Bishop's engagements would not allow him to leave Natal, and consequently it seemed almost useless that either himself or the Archdeacon should go, it not being clear that Mackenzie had any definite business to transact when he arrived in England. However, the arrangements had been made; and therefore, somewhat against his own judgment, Mackenzie was persuaded to come home. Accordingly, with his elder sister, he left Natal in June, and arrived in England at the end of July, 1859. The reader will see hereafter why I lay stress upon the circumstances under which Mackenzie returned to this country.

CHAPTER VIII.

MISSION TO CENTRAL AFRICA.

On the 12th of December, 1856, Dr Livingstone arrived in England to tell his countrymen of his discoveries in Africa, and to stir up a feeling of interest on behalf of the natives of that country. In the course of 1857 he published his volume of *Missionary Travels in South Africa,* which excited much attention, and may undoubtedly be regarded as amongst the most remarkable records of personal enterprise. Looking upon Dr Livingstone's adventures, with reference to the addition which they have made to our geographical knowledge, and to science in general, or with reference to the prospect which they have opened of increased commerce with Africa, it is impossible not to assign them a very high value: but it is clear that Dr Livingstone himself regarded his own labours in a higher than either a scientific or a commercial light: he called his travels in South Africa emphatically *Missionary* travels, and he considered all other views of his work as subordinate to that of improving the spiritual condition of those illused and depressed races amongst whom he had spent a considerable portion of his life.

Accordingly, he was not content with publishing his book of travels, or with the ordinary modes of making known to his countrymen his views concerning England's duty to Africa. He determined to make an attempt to stir the hearts of the two ancient Universities. The attempt was very characteristic: it was frank, open, and free from all narrow jealousies. Livingstone, himself a Scotchman, and a Presbyterian, and employed as a missionary by the London Missionary Society, having persuaded himself that there was an immense amount of power and zeal in the Church of England, which might be called forth for the benefit of Africa, asked leave to tell his tale in each of the great centres of Church of England education.

It will be sufficient in this place to speak of Cambridge. On December 4, 1857, Dr Livingstone appeared in the Senate-house, for the purpose of giving a lecture on his African travels. The Bishop of Worcester, Dr Philpott, then Master of S. Catharine's College, and Vice-Chancellor, was in the chair, and introduced the missionary traveller: his reception was enthusiastic: the undergraduates cheered as only undergraduates can cheer; and after a lecture of great interest[1], adapted with great tact to the audience, Professor Sedgwick, at the Vice-Chancellor's request, in a warmhearted speech, expressed the satisfaction which every one present felt. The conclusion of the lecture was very emphatic, and

[1] The Lecture has been published, together with one delivered on the same day at the Town-hall, with the title, "Dr Livingstone's Cambridge Lectures," by the Rev. William Monk. Deighton, Bell, and Co. Cambridge.

could hardly be forgotten by any who heard it: "I go back," said Dr Livingstone, "to Africa, to try to make an open path for commerce and Christianity. Do you carry out the work which I have begun. I LEAVE IT WITH YOU." As he uttered these words, he looked up to the galleries, crowded with undergraduates, and seemed to imply that this moral of his tale was intended especially for them.

In 1858 the Bishop of Cape Town visited England. He came to Cambridge, and there explained the plans which he had formed for the further spread of the Gospel in Africa. He proposed to send missions, consisting of clergy, with a Bishop at the head, into some of those countries which bordered upon the South African Dioceses, and so to make the country already occupied by Christian Bishops a basis for further operations in the adjoining heathen lands. It may, I think, be fairly argued that this scheme, as propounded by the Bishop of Cape Town, is the true method of spreading the kingdom of Christ; and if so, it might also be argued, that it is unwise to desert an established and safe base-line, and to commence other detached missions in distant parts. But the Bishop of Cape Town found that a scheme for an African Mission, different from his own, and more immediately connected with the scene of Livingstone's travels and discoveries, had already been talked over in Cambridge, and had assumed something like a definite form. Livingstone's last words had taken effect, and it was thought that an effort to plant a mission in Central Africa, which should attempt at once to introduce civilization and Christianity, and check the abomination of slave-trade by facilitating lawful commerce, would commend itself to the feelings of the University, and would be taken up with enthusiasm. The Bishop of Cape Town accordingly forbore to press his own schemes upon Cambridge, and announced with frankness, that in the event of the Central African scheme being carried out, he would give to it all his own influence and support.

I think I cannot chronicle the early history of the mission, with which Mackenzie's name was afterwards so closely associated, in any better way than by introducing here the Report which was presented to the great meeting held in the Senate-house, on November 1, 1859, of which I shall have something more to say presently. It will be observed that the Mission was planned without any reference to Mackenzie, that for some time after the scheme had been set on foot, and after the question had been asked, Who shall head the Mission? his name had not been mentioned, and that even in the Report itself no allusion is made to him as the probable leader in the work.

REPORT.

In presenting a Report of their proceedings up to the present time, the Cambridge Committee of the Oxford and Cambridge Mission to Central Africa wish first to recall the special circumstances which have led members of this and the sister University to undertake the work of establishing a mission to those regions—a work well befitting the two great centres of Christian education in this country.

The Mission owes its origin, under God, to the impression produced by the visit of Dr Livingstone to this

University, revived and strengthened by the subsequent visit of the Bishop of Cape Town.

The feelings awakened by these visits resulted in the formation of a Committee, pledged to take steps towards establishing a Mission to Central Africa.

The first step taken by this Committee was to invite the co-operation of the University of Oxford. This was promptly and heartily accorded.

A highly influential Committee was immediately formed in that University, and large subscriptions were promised. A public meeting was also held in the Sheldonian Theatre on May 17th, at which the Bishop of Oxford presided, and which was attended by a deputation from the Cambridge Committee.

These proceedings were followed by a meeting held on May 26th, at No. 79, Pall-mall, at which a London Committee was formed, consisting of members of both Universities. Thenceforth all measures taken for effecting the objects in view have resulted from the correspondence and concurrence of the three committees.

In adopting the name of "The Oxford and Cambridge Mission to Central Africa," the committees are far from intending to imply that they do not seek the co-operation of those who are not members of either University—on the contrary, they earnestly trust that their design will call forth active sympathy and aid from all classes throughout the country, and that the clergy generally will give their cordial assistance to the secretaries in making arrangements for sermons and meetings in behalf of the Mission.

They also wish it to be distinctly understood that they disclaim any intention of founding a new Missionary Society, or of interfering with the operations of those already existing. It is their hope that in a short time they will be able to hand over to the Society for the Propagation of the Gospel in Foreign Parts the management of the Mission: but it is necessary that its establishment and maintenance, for the first few years, should be provided for by means of a special organisation.

The Committees hope to be able at an early period to send out not fewer than six Missionaries under the direction, if possible, of a Bishop.

With reference to the field of labour in which they shall be employed, the Committees have agreed that it shall be selected so as not to interfere with existing Missionary operations. The Bishop of Capetown has engaged to open communications on this subject with Dr Livingstone, who on his part has kindly promised to aid the undertaking.

From a comparison of statements furnished by the Society for the Propagation of the Gospel in Foreign Parts, the Church Missionary Society, and the London Missionary Society, of the expense of sending out Missionaries to South Africa, and of maintaining them there, it has been estimated that a sum of not less than £1,000 will be requisite for the outfit of a Bishop and six other Missionaries, and that the annual expense of maintaining the Mission cannot be less than £2000. The amount actually promised up to the present time in donations is £1,610. 7*s.* 4*d.*, and in annual subscriptions for a term of years £176. 3*s.* 6*d.*

It will thus be seen that great efforts are necessary to raise the requisite funds.

It will be understood that the great object of the Mission is to make known the Gospel of Christ; but as the Committees are well aware that, in Dr Livingstone's own words, "civilisation and Christianity must go on together," they think it advisable to state that it will be their aim to encourage the advancement of science and the useful arts, and to direct especial attention to all questions connected with the slave-trade as carried on in the interior of Africa.

In conclusion, the Committees beg earnestly to commend this great work of evangelizing the heathen in Central Africa to the earnest sympathy of all. They venture once more to repeat the appeal of Dr Livingstone, that now the way is open—but that it may be shut again—and they pray that it may please God to bless and prosper their undertaking, and to raise up men to go out as labourers into the fields which "are white already to harvest."

Having now sufficiently for the purposes of this Memoir explained the origin of the Mission to Central Africa, we will return to Mackenzie, whom we left on the point of leaving Natal for a visit to England, having, as it seemed, no very definite purpose. Here is a letter, written between Natal and Cape Town, to his sister, whom he had left behind in Natal.

LETTER LV.

WALDENSIAN, *June* 17, 1859.

DEAR ——,

We have got on very well so far. This is Friday, and we are lying at anchor during a high head-wind, which we hope will moderate soon. We got over the bar last Saturday about 2 P.M., just ploughing the top of it for about our own length, and thanked our captain for his pluck in trying it. It was a little unpleasant, almost all a little sick. On Sunday we had service on deck, I being afraid of tying myself up in the cabin for so long a time. We have had service every day since, except Tuesday. On that day we came to an anchor in Algoa Bay early. We went ashore just in time for service, (Whitsun-Tuesday). * * * Saw the Grey Institute, also S. Paul's Church, a pretty, nice building. We dined, and returned to the vessel at three. * * * We were in hope of being at Capetown during this night, and landing to-morrow morning: but about midnight the wind got up ahead, and we have been making so little way that we have stopped in a bay just east of Cape Agulhas. So here we are.

Things are going well. I have been so glad in having

service, and I have had opportunity of being kind to some who had need of help. I have not had so much reading as I should have liked: it will probably be the same for the first week on board the English steamer: after that I shall be more settled. We are still in good hopes of catching the *Athens*: her day is Monday: but she is more likely to sail on Tuesday or Wednesday.

* * * * *

June 20. This is our last evening on land. We got here, Capetown, on Trinity Sunday in time for church. * * * We sail to-morrow, and hope to reach England about the 27th of next month. The Bishop of Capetown will not leave till August; so we shall see him for a week or so.

God bless you in all your work, and water you also yourself, while you are watering others.

Your affectionate brother,

C. F. M.

The steamer *Waldensian*, on board which the preceding letter was written, was terribly crowded, and the discomfort of the passengers was increased by the roughness of the weather. An American missionary, with his wife and six children, who were amongst the passengers, were all ill; Mackenzie waited upon them, and dressed the little ones. The troubles of another family, whom he treated in like manner, were further intensified by the confinement of the mother: when the poor woman felt that her hour was come, she said no one could be of any comfort to her except the Archdeacon: he was with her directly, prayed by her side, and then went to superintend the getting of her boxes out of the hold. A few days afterwards he baptized the infant at the parents' request, giving it the name Charles Frederick

Mackenzie, himself and his sister standing as sponsors. These are some of the "opportunities of being kind," to which a passing allusion is made above.

I find just one short letter, written between the Cape and England, to his sister in Edinburgh, which I will insert as a record of that voyage, and as indicating the uncertainty of his future plans, to which I have already alluded.

LETTER LVI.

SHIP ATHENS, *July* 20, 1859.
About 43° *N.* 26° *W.* 1364 miles from Lizard Point.

DEAREST ——,

* * * * *

We sailed from Capetown on Tuesday June 21st, and had a good run as far as about 10° N. Since that we have been delayed by northerly winds. We are now looking forward to landing about Friday week, the 29th. I am very anxious to see the Bishop of Capetown as soon as possible. He will probably be leaving England by the steamer in August. I shall have a good deal to say to him. It is not to be generally spoken of yet, but the Bishop of Natal has written by this mail to the Bishop of Capetown, to say that as soon as he sees his way clear he will go himself to the Zulu country, giving up the Bishoprick of Natal. I think it most likely that it will be a consequence of this that I shall not go to Zulu land at all. But this last is in the doubtful things yet. Pray for me, dear one, and for all of us, that we may judge rightly.

Wednesday, July 27th. We are getting on well, and hope to be at Plymouth, where this will be posted, by noon to-morrow, and to land at Southampton on Friday, and be in London on that night. It will be most pleasant to see you all again.

*　　*　　*　　*　　*

The return of Mackenzie to England brought joy to many hearts, to none more so than his friends in Cambridge. The visit took us very much by surprise: in fact, I believe that the first intimation which we received, was the announcement that he was actually on English soil. He was very little changed: in manner and bearing I think not at all, and there was no visible diminution of physical strength caused by the laborious life which he had been leading: he was the same simple-hearted loving friend that he had ever been, as modest as ever, and even his joyousness of spirit seemed in no degree diminished.

Soon after his arrival in England I had the pleasure of seeing him on his way to Scotland. I said to him, "Well, what has brought you to England?" to which he replied with a laugh, "Upon my word, I am unable to tell you." He then explained to me the doubtful character of his future plans, whether he should be required as the head of a Mission into the Zulu country, or whether he should continue to work in Natal. On the whole, he seemed to think it probable that his visit would turn out to be merely a short one, in which he would be able to see his family and friends, and that then he would go back to his parish at the Umhlali.

I lay stress upon this indefiniteness of purpose in his visit, because his subsequent connection with the Mission to Central Africa could not fail to appear to his friends and to himself all the more clearly to be directed by the finger of God. The state of the case was just this. The Mission had been planned without reference to any particular person as head: an efficient head was manifestly essential to success: just at the moment when it was necessary to make a choice, Mackenzie seemed to be thrown in the way, his connection with Natal partially broken, his previous life and training, and his own personal character, suggesting him at once to the Committee of the Mission as the man of whom they were in search.

I here insert two scraps of letters which will illustrate what I have now said, and will exhibit the state of Mackenzie's own mind, previous to the proposal that he should undertake the Central African Mission. The first is written to his sister in Natal, the second, to his sister in Edinburgh.

LETTER LVII.

August 4, 1859.

* * * * *

It is August 4. We have been on shore close upon a week, which has flown like a bird. You will hear from the Bishop about S. P. G. They say if all other difficulties are removed there will be money forthcoming to support a Missionary Bishop in Zulu land. It is pretty clear—quite, in fact—that I shall not be at the head of either. So I don't see what I have to do in this country, and I think two months, or three at the outside, will be the extent of our stay. All goes well. We are happy, and I trust God is guiding us.

* * * * *

LETTER LVIII.

29, King Street,
August 5, 1859.

* * * * *

The Bishopricks are virtually settled, and I am very thankful to say that I get neither, and shall return to my old place in Natal. This is quite right.

Mackenzie had not, as has been formerly mentioned, any special gift of public speaking; and the danger of unreality in religious meetings, a danger which every one must have felt, would make the work of a deputation for a Missionary Society distasteful to his practical mind. Nevertheless, he had not been long at home before he placed himself at the disposal of the Society for the Propagation of the Gospel, and for some months laboured vigorously at the task which he had undertaken. His family urged him to take rest; but he replied, "Work, not rest, is the thing that I want."

And so matters went on until the time of the great meeting in Cambridge, to which reference has been already made. It was held in the Senate-house, and was called at the time, the "Great Zambesi Meeting." Amongst the speakers were the Bishop of Oxford, Mr Gladstone, Mr Walpole, and Sir George Grey. Mackenzie was asked to preach at Great S. Mary's on the day of the meeting, but at the meeting itself he was only a listener and spectator.

The meeting was certainly a very remarkable one; remarkable on account of the place in which it was held, remarkable on account of its purpose, and remarkable for the zeal and heartiness with which it was conducted: perhaps also it was not a little remarkable that such a stirring of the heart of the University should have been the fruit of the unambitious lecture, which Dr Livingstone had delivered in the same place not quite two years before[1]: the Vice-Chancellor, Dr Bateson, Master of S. John's College, in opening the proceedings, very properly referred to Dr Livingstone as the origin of the meeting: he quoted Dr Livingstone's parting words, given in page 206, and added, "Such was the text, and this grand meeting is the commentary." In ordinary language, the meeting was a great success: the oratory of the Bishop of Oxford and Mr Gladstone, the calm wisdom of Sir George Grey, the heartiness of all left nothing to be desired.

Mackenzie, as has been already said, did not take part in this meeting: he was however present, and during the enthusiasm of the proceedings he made a remark which was sufficiently characteristic to be worthy of being recorded. He was in the gallery of the Senate-house in company with some friends: presently he said gently to one of them, "I am *afraid* of this: most great works of this kind have been carried on by one

[1] It is only right to say that the introduction of Dr Livingstone to the University, and the subsequent missionary movement, were due very much to the efforts of the Rev. W. Monk, then Assistant Curate of Christ's Church, Cambridge. Professor Sedgwick said at the Meeting, "The map now before you was constructed by Mr Monk, a gentleman with whom rests the honour of having first introduced Dr Livingstone to to this University—a gentleman, too, who has toiled as no other man has toiled, in the promotion of the objects of this meeting. Mr Monk's task may, in some respects, have been a humble one; but humble tasks must be performed, and without the performance of such tasks even the most powerful might fail."

or two men in a quieter way, and have had a more humble beginning[1]."

He was not however to be permitted to remain as a spectator much longer. There was a feeling in the minds of almost all those who took an interest in the proposed mission, that Mackenzie was beyond all others the right man to undertake the work. Those who are willing to see the hand of God in small things as well as great, might well see in the circumstance of his unexpected return from Africa, the entire evanescence of the purposes which had brought him home, the breaking up of the ties which bound him to Natal, and above all, the fact that he was here on the spot to answer for himself, an indication that he was the man whom God would send upon this honourable but perilous mission. It was impossible also not to feel that he had, independently of his African experience and his previous missionary training, great and special qualifications for this particular work: going as it was proposed that the missionaries should, into a new and barbarous country, with everything to learn, even as to the mode of getting the necessary supplies of food, it was essential that the head of the party should be a man possessed at once of great personal vigour, and of those gentle qualities of heart which gain confidence and submission under circumstances of trial and danger. Mackenzie had precisely the qualities required: every one felt it.

Accordingly, at a Conference of Delegates of the

[1] It was not a little striking that Bishop Tozer, in his visit to Cambridge, thought it right to warn Cambridge men against resting too much upon the recollection of this one great demonstration.

Oxford and London Committees with the Cambridge Committee, held on the 2nd of November, the day succeeding the Meeting in the Senate-house, at which the Bishop of Oxford presided, and Sir George Grey was present, the following resolutions were adopted :—

1. That the plan of this Association be the establishment of one or more stations in Southern Central Africa, which may serve as centres of Christianity and civilisation, for the promotion of the spread of true religion, agriculture, and lawful commerce, and the ultimate extirpation of the slave-trade.

2. That to carry out this plan successfully, the Association desire to send out a body of men, including the following:—

Six clergymen with a Bishop at their head, to be consecrated either in this country, or by the three Bishops of Southern Africa; a physician, surgeon, or medical practitioner, and a number of artificers, English and native, capable of conducting the various works of building, husbandry, and especially of the cultivation of the cotton plant.

3. The Association contemplate that the cost of establishing such a Mission cannot be estimated at less than £20,000, with £2000 a year, promised as annual subscriptions to support the Mission for five years to come.

4. That the Secretaries be desired to open communications at once with the other Universities, with the clergy and friends of missions at large, and with the great centres of manufacture and commerce, to invite them to aid by their funds, counsel, and co-operation, in carrying out this great work for the mutual benefit of Africa and of England.

5. That the Ven. Charles Frederick Mackenzie, M.A., Fellow of Gonville and Caius College, Cambridge, Archdeacon of Pietermaritzburgh (Natal), who is now in England, be invited to head the intended Mission.

6. That the Bishop of Oxford be requested to convey this invitation to Archdeacon Mackenzie.

The invitation was given, and speedily accepted. He seems to have considered it unnecessary to consult his friends with regard to his conduct: concerning the sacrifice of himself he never entertained a doubt: the only point which required consideration, was the condition in which his departure to Central Africa would leave his sisters, whom he had been the means of taking out to Natal: he felt himself bound to them; but if they could go, he had no ground of hesitation.

The deliberate purpose with which he undertook the work may be judged from the following anecdote. He was staying at the time, with his sister, in the house of his friend Dr Paget in Cambridge. It seemed to Dr Paget right that they should both estimate at its true value the personal risk of the undertaking: accordingly he said to Miss Mackenzie, "Consider what would be the view taken by a Life Assurance Company. If your brother should wish to insure his life before going on this enterprise and were to apply to any Insurance Company, I feel sure they would not estimate his chance of life at more than *two* years." Miss Mackenzie was much shocked at first by this plain statement; but just then Mackenzie himself came into the room, and when his sister told him what Dr Paget had said, he took it as a matter of course, not treating it lightly, but as a subject which he had already well considered, and on which he had come to the same conclusion.

The following letter was written to his sister in Edinburgh, the day after receiving the invitation to lead the Mission.

LETTER LIX.

CAIUS COLLEGE, CAMBRIDGE,
Nov. 3, 1859.

DEAR ——,

The past is swallowed up in the present. I hope you got my letter from London, but now I must speak of the present. They want me to go at the head of the Zambesi Mission. (The question of the head being consecrated or not is not settled, and need not affect my decision.) I am ready if —— can go: if not, I must think what to do. But I think and believe she can, and —— of course can, and I fully believe will. So we shall have no difficulty in seeing our way. I have not given an answer yet, as we felt we did not like to decide on such a step for —— without you all advising. If you agree, I would at once accept. If not, we would come down to Scotland and talk it all over. I am much interested in this mission. Sir George Grey is most hearty in his promises of help. God bless us all in this and every thing.

Good bye.
Your affectionate brother,
C. F. M.

The next letter, to his sister in Natal, was commenced several days before the great Cambridge meeting; but it will be seen that the latter part of it was written three days after that meeting, and that he then regarded in his own mind the whole matter as fixed.

LETTER LX.

LONDON, *Oct.* 31, 1859.

DEAR ——,

* * * * *

We have determined to postpone our return for a month. I thought as my hand was in, in the way of begging for S. P. G., and as my personal experience of colonial work gave me an advantage over a better speaker, I would offer to the Society to stay another month and work for them. This they have accepted, and have already spoken of my going into the diocese of Bath and Wells, from the 10th to the 22nd of December.

* * * * *

Nov. 4. Dear ——. A—— has told you something about the proposal to go to the Zambesi. The fact of the offer having been made to me need be no secret; only I should like it to be understood correctly that it is the *Headship* of the Mission which has been offered me: the question of *Bishopricks* among the heathen, or rather outside Her Majesty's dominions, being in abeyance till the Committee of Convocation has expressed its opinion. But now as to the real thing: it will be a great work, and if you and —— can come with me, I do not hesitate to go. —— seems clear herself, but as we have not heard from Scotland since the offer arose, we do not consider it settled. * * * * I hope to be able myself to take a real charge and oversight, more firmly now that my sphere is extended, not forgetting to consult the actual workers, from whom good suggestions often come, but still keeping the reins in my own hands. Dear one, I need not say that I trust to your praying for me in this new and most responsible office. (I have undertaken to give an answer as soon as I can: but in my mind I am thinking of it as settled.) We shall now, I suppose, have to stay in England for something less than another year, trying to raise the necessary funds. I expect to be able to come up, and spend (I hope) a month at Natal, and shall be *so* glad to see you all again.

* * * * *

The Mission, which began by being the Oxford and Cambridge Mission, soon became the Oxford, Cambridge, Dublin and Durham Mission to Central Africa. It will be observed that in the fourth of the resolutions, given on page 218, the Secretaries were desired to open communications with the other Universities; this was done, and the response was very cordial. The arrangement was that each university should have its own local committee, that there should be in addition a central London committee, and that the acts of these several committees should stand to each other in certain definite relations, which need not be here explained or dwelt upon: though perhaps it may be permissible to express a doubt in passing, whether any such system of co-ordinate committees can be regarded as more than a temporary arrangement, which must yield eventually to something more simple and compact.

The great work which at once pressed upon the friends of the Mission was the raising of the necessary funds. A capital sum of £20,000, and a guaranteed income of £2000 for five years, could not possibly be secured without a very considerable effort. Much of the effort, it was clear, must come from Mackenzie himself; and he was willing to give himself up to this preliminary labour on behalf of his Mission, as soon as he should have completed his existing engagements to the Society for the Propagation of the Gospel. His time was, in fact, chiefly devoted to travelling through the country, for the purpose of making known the Mission and raising funds, until his final departure in the autumn of the next year. He was assisted in this work by several friends, amongst them the Bishop of Oxford, of whose kindness Mackenzie was wont to speak in warm terms of gratitude and affection.

The following letter was written to a sister before he had commenced work on account of his own mission.

LETTER LXI.

BURY ST EDMUND'S,
Nov. 7, 1859.

DEAR ——,

I came here to the railway, and find I am half-an-hour too soon; so I have made friends with the cloak-room clerk for room to sit, and for ink.

* * * * *

It is a great undertaking, this of the Zambesi, and rather unknown country that one is going to; but still I am prepared to undertake it with —— and ——.

* * * * *

Where we should settle is of course a thing to be decided; we are at present the "Central South African Mission." I suppose it would be where Livingstone first struck the river at Linyanti, but it might not. I fancy our first object would be to find Livingstone, and get his advice. But before even that, there will be the work of raising funds. With its present intentions the Committee is behindhand in funds. But, dear ——, think what a grand work may grow out of this, if God prosper it! I am loth, it is true, to leave my own parish unprovided for: but as before, in leaving Cambridge, I think my present work can be more easily provided for, than the proposed. I must find some one to take my place, and for immediate wants I think —— will go to the Umhlali, to be busy there till we are ready to sail for the Cape; and by that time I think we may find some one to relieve him by taking up that work permanently.

My dear ——, good bye.

Your affectionate brother,

C. F. M.

The next two letters are written to the same sister in pencil.

LETTER LXII.

GREAT WESTERN RAILWAY,
Nov. 22, 1859.

DEAR ——,

It is not so hard to write in a railway.

* * * * *

It does my heart and soul good to get a letter from you like the one I got to-day. It is indeed a glorious work, and my trust is that He who has called me to it will give me grace to carry it out.

Aye, dear ——, who can tell which of us may be gone before another year is over? How comforting it is to think of —— being so comforted and guided in her last days.

* * * * *

LETTER LXIII.

L. AND B. R.
Nov. 26, 1859.

DEAR ——,

I am on my way from Oxford to Leeds.

* * * * *

I went to Clerkenwell prison, and talked for 20 minutes to a Zulu, who has been spoken of in the newspapers. He was wild in the *Bush* near London, and was taken up for stealing a sheep. He will be leniently dealt with, I believe. I wish some one would engage him in service. I have written to Mrs —— about him, hoping that with her knowledge of Zulus she might be willing to try him. Poor fellow, he has such a lively remembrance of the horrors of sea-sickness that he will not agree to go back to Natal.

Thank you, dear ——, for the freedom of your letter. I don't think freedom to myself ever distresses me: freedom of expression about other people does sometimes, when I think things are said or thought which had better not be either said or thought.

* * * * *

God bless us all, and lead us into all truth.

* * * * *

The interest taken by Mackenzie in the Zulu referred to in the preceding letter was very characteristic of him. A mutual friend writing to me says: "Do you remember any particulars about *Ned,* the Kafir, who was prosecuted for sheep-stealing at a police-court in London? Mackenzie took a deep interest in his case, and maintained that he had mistaken a tame sheep for a wild 'bok:' on Ned's release, he intended to take him for his servant, and so preserve him from further difficulties with the policemen and magistrates. He was staying with us at the time, and arranged for the poor Kafir to come to him at ——; and on the night on which he was to arrive we all sat up late expecting him by the last train, but some other friend had adopted the Kafir and given him a lodging, and so my house was denied the honour. Poor fellow! he was shortly afterwards killed by the buffer of an engine, on the railway near Rugby. You may imagine with how much interest our whole party, including Miss Mackenzie, sat up, expecting Ned's arrival. Our house is not a large one, and Mackenzie with his sister and another visitor occupied all our spare rooms: the question therefore was, Where was Ned to sleep? for domestic difficulties, like all other difficulties which opposed themselves to what he considered his plain duty, never once entered his mind until they were encountered and overcome. The only place which we could arrange for our expected guest was the floor of the day-nursery, which created a strange combination of curiosity and alarm in the minds of our children, who were nevertheless more disappointed than relieved when it was discovered in the morning that Ned had not arrived."

With one more letter, written to his sister in Natal, I bring to a close the, to him, eventful year 1859.

LETTER LXIV.

LEEDS, *Dec.* 2, 1859.

DEAR ——,

You will have been for the last month gradually becoming more sure that our work is to be in Central Africa; and so it is. We found that the people at home did not wish to throw any obstacles in the way, and Sir George Grey's opinion was so distinct, that though it would not do well for —— (what did for her did for you, so you were not named,) to go up with the first expedition, yet that she might certainly, so far as he could see, join the mission after it had settled itself, that I determined on the 8th of November to accept the post of head of the mission.

I try not to let my head be turned: but it is a little dizzy to be on what I believe is one of the highest Church pinnacles at this moment in England. Livingstone's name adds interest to the scene. The two Universities having joined to start the mission gives great weight to the undertaking, and the warm interest taken in it by the Bishop of Oxford excites people's enthusiasm. I feel a little like what you felt when you went to Ekukanyeni, expecting the time when people will *find me out.* But then the calming, sobering thought is: Be more and more conscious that the work is for One who has nothing to find out, from whom no secrets are hid, and who has called me to this work, knowing that I am frail and foolish, and who expects, indeed, that we shall do all and give up all for Him, but does not expect more.

I have been working for S. P. G. these last two months, and shall go on till Christmas. Next year I shall be working for my own mission: now I am fulfilling promises made before Nov. 2. I do not so much dislike this pleading as I was sure I should. It is a sort of preaching, and I think quite as much of the good of the people I speak to as of the good I expect to get from them for those abroad.

* * * * *

Dear ——, how wonderfully He has made our way plain before our face. Not even the Bishop could foresee what would be the end of my coming home.

* * * * *

The year 1860 was pre-eminently one of bustling and exciting labour. He now fairly began to work on account of his own mission, and was almost constantly travelling, preaching, and speaking, until his departure in the autumn for his distant field of work. Letters, therefore, except of a purely business character, were of necessity rare: at all events very few have come into my hands.

One question of great and very general interest was raised by the scheme for a mission in Central Africa, namely, the propriety of sending out such missions under the direction of a bishop. The question was not a very simple one, and different opinions were entertained concerning its solution. In the first place the expediency and propriety of sending a bishop under such circumstances might be regarded as open to discussion; and supposing this point resolved in the affirmative, it would be open to doubt what the status of such a missionary bishop should be with regard to his Episcopal brethren, and with regard to his canonical obedience to a metropolitan; while the peculiar relation of the Church to the State in England threw in the additional question as to the power of the bishops of the Church of England to consecrate without license of the Crown. It was agreed to refer the whole matter to the judgment of the Convocation of the Province of Canterbury.

At the session of January 25, 1860, the committee of the Lower House of Convocation presented a report, which, having been adopted, was sent up as a representation from the Lower to the Upper House. I think I shall put this important proceeding in the clearest light by recording what took place subsequently in the Upper House of Convocation, namely, at their session of June 8. The Bishop of Oxford presented on that occasion the following report of the committee of the Upper House, moving at the same time that the report be printed and communicated to the Lower House.

Report.

The committee of the Upper House of Convocation of the Province of Canterbury, appointed to consider the report of the Lower House on missionary Bishops, have met and considered the same, and resolved to report—

1. That we highly approve of the course pursued by the committee of the Lower House in endeavouring to ascertain the practice of the primitive Church, as it may be inferred from Holy Scripture and from early ecclesiastical records.

2. That we do not feel it needful to make any special remarks on paragraphs 2 to 8.

3. That in giving a modified assent to paragraphs 8 and 12, we must observe that in many cases the adjacent Church, however anxious to evangelise the native heathen, will be unable, in its own infant condition, to supply men or funds for the work, but must throw the burden on the mother Church at home, whatever aid may be rendered to it by the Bishops of the contiguous dioceses or province.

4. That we deem it undesirable to divert from a yet unestablished and feeble diocese the energy and attention which are absolutely needful for its own development, by leading the Bishop of such a diocese to undertake arduous duties and indefinite responsibilities beyond its proper limits.

5. That as in such cases it may often be most convenient that the missionary Bishop should be sent out by the Church at home, it is expedient to ascertain whether any impediment exists to the power of the Archbishops and Bishops at home to consecrate Bishops for missionary service in heathen countries external to her Majesty's diminions.

6. That the consecration of missionary Bishops, the sphere of whose labour is virtually the extension of a previously established province, should be regulated in accord-

ance with ancient rule; and that such missionary Bishops should owe canonical obedience to the local Metropolitan, if any, the local Metropolitan owing canonical obedience to the Archbishop of Canterbury.

7. That in addition to the guarantees named in paragraph 16, every missionary Bishop should engage to maintain the doctrine and discipline of our Reformed Apostolical Church, as contained in her Articles and Liturgy, and that, so far as may be, the authorised version of the Holy Scriptures should be adopted as the basis of translations of the same.

8. That, looking first to the fact that where dioceses have been or may be constituted in foreign parts not subject to the statute law of the United Kingdom, the Bishops, though they may be held to be bound by the decrees of the mother Church which were in force at the time of their consecration, and by the Canons of 1603, so far as those canons apply to the circumstances of their dioceses, are yet in no way subject to new decrees and canons to which they have not assented; and secondly, looking to the great and continually advancing development of the Colonial Church, to the several peculiarities under which it is beginning in many districts to assume a fixed shape, to its want of endowments, and to the time which must elapse before its clergy or laity can enjoy the advantages of the Church at home as to fixity of institutions or familiarity with ecclesiastical law; there seems to us to be special need of combined counsels to maintain in unity the Church as it extends. That by a regular gradation of duly constituted Synods all questions affecting unity might be duly settled; Diocesan Synods determining all matters not ordered by the Synod of the province; Provincial Synods determining all matters not ordered by a National Synod; a National Synod ordering all matters not determined by a General Council. Unity with necessary variety might thus be secured to our spreading branch of the Holy Catholic Church.

Whereupon the President stated that he had received the following representation of the Lower House on the same subject :—

Representation of the Lower House of Convocation on the Subject of Missionary Bishops.

1. We have first considered what were the principles by which the primitive Church was guided with respect to planting missions, so far as they may be inferred from Holy Scripture and from early ecclesiastical records, and we have then endeavoured to apply these principles to the present condition and circumstances of the Church of England.

2. We gather from the New Testament that the Apostles were missionary Bishops in the fullest sense of the term; that they went about from place to place preaching the Gospel, planting Churches, and giving directions for their government.

3. As the Church increased, the Apostles conferred Episcopal authority on others, whom, under Divine guidance, they invested with the government of certain Churches—as Timothy at Ephesus and Titus in Crete.

4. Passing from the New Testament to the uninspired records of the early Church, it appears that the practice of primitive Christian antiquity with regard to the organization of missions is involved in considerable obscurity.

5. The Church grew and was extended continually by the power of the indwelling Spirit; but the manner of her extension does not appear to have been uniform or invariable. Ecclesiastical history fails to supply us with any certain or precise information upon this point. We find that Bishops frequently preached the Gospel to the heathen, and that the other orders of the ministry and even laymen were instrumental in sowing the first seeds of the Gospel in countries where it had before been unknown. There is abundant evidence, however, to shew that when Christian congregations had been gathered out of heathendom, and by

whatever instrumentality, they were placed as soon as possible under the care of a Bishop.

6. We proceed to apply these general principles to the present circumstances of our Church.

7. In considering the mode of the extension of Christian missions amongst the heathen external to her Majesty's dominions, a distinction should be drawn between the case of heathen tribes lying contiguous to a Christian people and that of heathen isolated and removed from any Christian Church, to whom an opening may be made along the pathway of science or of commerce, or by any other leading of God's providence.

8. We trust that our Church will be always zealous to act upon the ancient practice that the Bishops should endeavour to convert the heathen adjacent to their dioceses, and where these efforts are blessed with success and new congregations are gathered, or where the blessing of the Gospel is sought from our hands in any considerable numbers by the heathen lying beyond our borders, or by rulers desirous of evangelizing their subjects, we further trust that the uniform practice of Christian antiquity will be followed in the providing of additional chief pastors of the Church to minister among them.

9. There are cases in which it may be expedient to send out presbyters in the first instance as evangelists, as for example, where the Church has to originate missions to the heathen lying in close contiguity to the existing diocese.

10. But we think also that there are cases in which it may be desirable to send forth a Bishop at once as the head of a mission; as for example—

I. Where a large staff of missionaries is necessary; or

II. Where a large and imposing organisation has to be confronted, especially in regions lying remote from any diocese of our Church.

11. The expediency or inexpediency of sending out a missionary Bishop in the first instance can, however, only be

determined by the particular circumstances of the case as it may arise.

12. With regard to the heathen bordering upon a Christian people, we think that the converts should, in the first instance, be provisionally under the care of the Bishop of an adjacent diocese; and that all further arrangements respecting the government of such missions should be determined by a Synod of the adjacent province.

13. With regard to the more remote missions, we consider that the proper authority for determining when it is expedient to send out a Bishop would be that of an Archbishop, or other Metropolitan, with his Suffragans; and that during the missionary condition of such Episcopate, the Bishop sent out should owe canonical obedience to the consecrating Metropolitan.

14. Our instructions not requiring us to enter upon the legal question whether the Church of England has the power to send forth Bishops into heathen territories beyond the limits of the British dominions, we have framed our report upon the supposition that she has this power.

15. In the entire uncertainty which necessarily exists as to the relations in which any new Churches formed in foreign countries may stand to the civil and temporal rulers of those countries, we feel it impossible to lay down any rules for the permanent relations of the mother Church.

16. The guarantees for the future orthodoxy and good discipline of Churches not yet existing must be found chiefly, under the Divine blessing, in the prudence and enlightened wisdom of the Bishop and presbyters who may form any particular mission. We conceive that, with regard to the admission of converts, they would guide themselves by the analogy of such precautions as the Church has taken in her forms for the baptism of infants and adults, and that, with regard to the transmission of spiritual authority, they would, in like manner, adopt the analogy of similar precautions to be found in the Ordinal of the Book of Common Prayer.

17. In conclusion, we earnestly pray that abundant supplies of wisdom, as well as zeal, may be vouchsafed to all those who are endeavouring to extend the kingdom of our Lord and Saviour Jesus Christ throughout the world.

The following resolution was then put and agreed to, on the motion of the Bishop of Oxford :—

That this house has read the representation made to it by the Lower House : that in reply thereto they inform the Lower House that a committee of the Upper House have considered upon a report on the same subject made to the Lower House, and by it communicated to this house; that the report so made to this house has this day been received and adopted; that this house having taken into consideration the representation of the Lower House, considers it can best reply thereto by communicating to the Lower House its own report, since that report deals with the subject contained in the representation.

The Bishop of Oxford then moved further :—

That this house having heard, with thankfulness to God, of the prospect of a mission being led by the Venerable Archdeacon Mackenzie into Southern Central Africa, desire to express their deep interest therein, and their hope that the Bishop of Capetown and his Comprovincials may be able to see fit to admit the head of this mission into the Episcopal order before he be sent forth to the heathen.

This resolution gave rise to a discussion, but was eventually put and carried.

I have thought it well to give in detail the history of this question in connection with Convocation, because it undoubtedly marks an important epoch in the history of the Church of England, and because the hope expressed by the Bishops at home concerning the conduct which the Bishops in South Africa might see fit to adopt, was subsequently realized, and was the means, under God, of giving to the Church of England her first Missionary Bishop.

The next three letters contain not much important matter, but I cannot refrain from giving them a place in this memoir, as being almost the only record by Mackenzie's own hand of this very laborious portion of his life.

LETTER LXV.

(*To a Sister.*)

THE IRISH CHANNEL,
Jan. 28, 1860.

DEAR ——,

Here I go across the water to Dublin. I left London yesterday morning, and got to Kidderminster, where I was kindly received by the clergyman, Mr Claughton. He had arranged to have four services with sermons on Missions on the four Fridays of the Epiphany season, and offered me any one I liked, saying that I should have a collection at mine, and that there should be none at the others. * * * We got £38, which is almost the best weekday collection I have had.

* * * * *

Dear ——, I am sometimes low, and not without reason, I think, when I find myself doing my work, especially preaching, badly for want of preparation, and still more for want of earnestness and faith at the moment. Last Wednesday I was very angry with myself on that score, and was more disturbed at the Communion which we had than I think I ever was since my first; but yesterday encouraged me again.

Here is Dublin. I have a difficult work to do. I hardly expect to bring it to a successful issue. I came to preach three sermons on Sunday for S. P. G., but I went also to arrange with the authorities of the University about their co-operation with us. We want to get their warm and hearty support; we would have a separate list for the contributions of Dublin University, and they would, I suppose, canvass for us in Ireland.

* * * * *

LETTER LXVI.

(*To a Sister.*)

NEWARK,
Feb. 4, 1860.

* * * * *

It is a grand scheme. I often quail to think I am at the head of it, but I oftener thank God that this work, which He determined to be done, He has entrusted to me. And I look to Him to give me grace to carry it out. It is a sore blow to be removed from all those friends whom we have made in Natal. But then the scope is so enormous, and I think the hopes of success very bright. We have Livingstone to help and advise us. We have a very strong interest in our favour throughout the country, stronger I believe than ever a mission had before: and I seldom end my address to the meetings I attend without solemnly asking them for their prayers, and saying that success is as much dependent on their endeavours in this way as on ours upon the spot.

Good bye.
Your affectionate brother,
C. F. M.

LETTER LXVII.

(*To a Sister.*)

MANCHESTER,
May 23, 1860.

DEAR ——,

The meeting here has been, so far as we have yet seen, a great success; and I am most thankful. The huge room perfectly crowded: ladies standing the whole time: about 4,000 people must have been there. For myself, I felt not flurried, but able to say what I wanted, though in these large assemblages I seldom feel able to speak to people's religious sentiments as I can in a smaller body. I mean to make that a special object to-morrow. * * * Then came Lord Brougham, for 35 minutes or so, full of energy. It was a lesson in speaking which was not thrown away upon me, I hope.

* * * * *

The meeting referred to in the preceding letter was one of three, namely, at Manchester, Liverpool, and Leeds, which were attended by Lord Brougham. It was certainly not the least striking feature of the movement connected with the Central African Mission, that it should induce Lord Brougham to appear as a speaker upon a missionary platform. But, in truth, his conduct was thoroughly intelligible and consistent: he saw in it only the continuation of the war which he had waged strenuously for many years against the slave-trade: it was one of the professed features of the mission, that it was to appear in Africa as the antagonist to and witness against the accursed traffic, which has so long pressed and still presses as a heavy weight upon that afflicted country: and therefore it was no eccentricity, but a natural sequel to much of his earlier conduct, that Lord Brougham should commend to the support of all those who felt with him on the subject of the slave-trade, an honest and brave effort in the direction of African emancipation. The three meetings, at Manchester, Liverpool, and Leeds, were the largest and most striking of those in which Mackenzie took a part, and I think I shall do them no more than justice if I introduce here a report taken from a newspaper, (*The Guardian*) of the period.

OXFORD AND CAMBRIDGE MISSION TO CENTRAL AFRICA.

Last week will ever be a memorable one in the annals of this mission, and we believe of Church Missions in general. A deputation, consisting of the Right Rev. the Lord Bishop of Oxford, the Right Hon. Lord Brougham, and the Ven. Archdeacon Mackenzie, visited our three greatest centres of commerce and manufacture on three successive days, the 23rd, 24th, and 25th of the present month. Their reception in each place was as cordial and hearty as can well be conceived. Manchester was first visited, and there the deputation, during its stay, was most hospitably entertained by Mr Robert Barnes, one of the wealthiest merchants of that city.

The meeting was held in the afternoon, and never do we remember to have seen a goodlier sight. The enormous Free Trade Hall was literally crammed, and it is estimated that at least 5,000 persons were present. Lord Brougham commenced his speech by saying that it was "by very much the largest meeting he had ever yet seen assembled within doors;" and we believe it was the largest meeting that was ever gathered together in Manchester in the daytime.

This multitude listened with the liveliest attention and apparent interest to the plain, straightforward, earnest statement of the head of the mission, the powerful and energetic speech of the veteran ex-Chancellor, and the thrilling eloquence of the Bishop of Oxford.

The Hon. Algernon Egerton, M.P. for South Lancashire, presided, and the Rev. Richard Gresswell, of Worcester College, Oxford, T. Bazley, Esq., M.P., the Rev. Canon Clifton, and Robert Barnes, Esq., likewise addressed the meeting. About £150 was collected in the room, and four donations of £100 each were received. These, we hope, are a mere instalment of the large sum which may reasonably be expected from the wealthy and liberal men of Manchester.

On Thursday the members of the deputation went to Liverpool, and became the guests of Mr William Brown[1], so well known for his munificent gifts for the benefit of the working classes of the town.

The meeting was held in the evening in the Philharmonic Hall, and about 3,000 persons were present. The chair was taken by the Right Rev. the Lord Bishop of Chester. Here the Bishop of Oxford almost surpassed himself, and was peculiarly happy in some of his remarks, especially in the opening part of his speech. The following is the conclusion of his lordship's speech:

"I walked to-day with my kind host, your honoured townsman, Mr Brown—I walked with him to-day upon your noble quays. I heard from him something of the tale of wonder of this your wonderful community. He told me of the fifty years which had elapsed since he had first known the town, and of the growth of its population from 90,000 people to half a million. He told me of the yearly addition now to its numbers of some 10,000 more. He told me how these quays had grown, as commerce from every part of the earth had flowed into them with such increasing abundance, so that now it would take a man a walk of fourteen miles to go along the whole of these quays of yours, upon which are now disembarked all the wealth of every wealthy part of the globe. I looked around upon your town, and saw its buildings rising in magnificence—saw how God had put it into the heart of this man to give that noble library upon that noble site—aye, and I felt, and I know you will feel, that great as is that material gift, the gift of the heart that planned it was a greater gift to Liverpool than the gift of the library it furnished. I looked and I saw your churches rising upon every side, and testifying everywhere that you were caring for the souls of men, and ministering to them the unsearchable riches of Christ. I saw, even in the poor parts of the town, what, when I came to inquire about them, I was told were the buildings furnished, in order that the most abject of your people might be delivered from their cellar life, and might live in health and comfort above the earth. I saw

[1] Now Sir William Brown, Bart.

this, and I thanked God that He had given to the people of Liverpool not only great wealth and great opportunity, but a wise and understanding heart to appreciate and to use its gifts. I saw it, and as I stood upon the quay that good man said to me, 'Look at that arm of the sea flowing in round yonder point; see all this massing of wealth, these forests of masts filling the mighty docks; and there are no ships of war guarding it; an enemy might come in, and what should we do to resist him?' What a tale was it, after all, of God's gift of peace and security, and of righteous confidence in themselves, because they believed that their God would be with them. Well, I went on, and the thought rose within me, Are we using these gifts for the Giver; are we returning to Him according to His gift to us? Now, that is the question I would ask you to put to yourselves. Ah! my friends, it is not the first time, nor is it the hundredth time that these blessings of God have been showered upon a people, and because that people upon whom they were showered used them selfishly for themselves, the very gifts became their ruin, turned into poison under them, both as to their bodies and as to their souls. You remember how it is written in His Word, that the sins of Sodom grew from fulness of bread, and abundance of idleness. And yet what can that 'idleness' mean? There could not have been this 'fulness of bread' if there had not been a good deal of activity in raising the fruits of the earth and storing them. Therefore, in God's Word idleness cannot mean sitting with the hands folded and doing nothing. There is another and a higher meaning in it; it is the not using for the Giver the Giver's gifts: that is the 'idleness' meant in God's Word. And so, I ask you, if God has given us the faith in its purity, His Word in our own tongue, aye, and in the raciest accents of our own beloved fathers; if He has given us formularies with which to worship Him, venerable for their antiquity, and beloved by us for their devotion; if He has given to us His ministry in the completeness of its organization, and His Church in the perfect sense of its beauty, I ask you has He given us all this that we may rejoice before Him in spiritual selfishness and fold our hands in spiritual idleness? No, but He has given it to us for Him, to bless others in its use. There is an oath on high, that he who doeth not the will of his God shall be put down from the post to which he was lifted up that he might perform it. Ah, and this very country of Africa may give one fearful lesson to us this night. Cast your eyes one single moment, in thought, over the whole of the northern coast of Africa. What is it now? The Mussulman possesses it. Its goodly fields are laid waste, and the French wrangle with and slay the Arab in cruel fight again to possess it: and the name of Christ is hardly heard upon it. And what was it?

A Church in which once 500 Bishops met together in their solemn Synod: a land which fed the neighbouring Italy with the abundance of its harvests, and which, looked down upon by a favouring heaven, rendered back again to it every fruit that maketh man's heart glad and man's labour productive. And why has this change come upon it? My friends, it came from this—that they had, without imparting anything, clutched in spiritual selfishness what God meant them to distribute. They allowed the neighbouring people of Northern Africa to live on in their ignorance, without making any attempt to evangelize them, and so when the flood of Mohammedan invasion swept upon them, what were they? A handful upon the sea-border, instead of being the evangelizers of the people reaching on into the centre of Africa, who might have swept that invading wave across the sands into the sea, if only they had used their opportunity and united that people to Christ. There is a lesson, then, for us, and God forbid that we should not learn it. And I thought, after all, if that great arm of the sea upon which I looked in its beauty to-day, sparkling like a brilliant under the sunbeam, as the western wind chafed it into a little mimicry of motion—if the whole of that space was crowded with ships of war, if it was commanded from every part by your Armstrong guns, is it not written on high that 'it is in vain to keep the city except the Lord keepeth it'? and if He looked in anger upon it, what would become of your best fortifications and most watchful defences? O, there are still, depend upon it, for the eye of faith, angel squadrons encamping round about God's people, and prayers, in mighty phalanxes, defending His Church. Let England be true to England's mission; let her understand that it is hers to keep the faith in its purity, and to spread the faith in its truth; that it is hers to teach her people to love Christ, not to wrangle about Him, and then leave the Cross of Christ in the face of the world, longing in its dumb agony for the enfranchisement which that alone can give to it. Let England in this way rise indeed to the mightiness of her opportunity; and the God of wisdom and the God of battles will preserve her virgin soil from being tainted with the foot of an enemy, and enable us to hand on to our children's children what we have received from our venerated fathers—the lower gifts of prosperity and power, and the higher gifts of the purity of the faith and the abundance of worship."

Leeds came last in order, and here also the meeting took place in the evening, and was held in that magnificent Town Hall of which the people of Leeds are so justly proud. The large room was filled to overflowing, and the reception given to their former representative, Henry Brougham, and to their brother Yorkshireman, the son of Wilberforce, must have gladdened the hearts of those illustrious men.

We believe that about £11,000 in donations, and £1000 in annual subscriptions, have been already gathered. Surely these three wealthy cities will speedily set at rest all doubt about the remaining portion required.

There is little more to be said concerning Bishop Mackenzie's life and work till he left England: it was a very busy and anxious time, but it must, I think, on the whole, have been a happy time, proving to him as it must have done, how much the work to which he had devoted himself was esteemed, and how much love he had gained, both for his own and for his work's sake. He had, as will be readily believed, abundant practice, both in preaching and speaking, and at this period his preaching was usually without book: he acquired thus a readiness of speech, and his addresses were very telling from their extreme simplicity and manifest sincerity.

One of Mackenzie's companions in his journeys on account of the mission was the Rev. George Williams, Fellow of King's College, Cambridge; he has been kind enough to write the following.

"You have asked me to give some account of him, as we travelled together for the object to which he had deliberately devoted his life. No one will understand better than yourself, who knew him so well, that I can recall nothing specially worth recording. The same lovely simplicity of character, the same utter forgetfulness of self, the same simplicity of devotion, of which he was himself so wholly unconscious, attended him everywhere, and drew all hearts to him.

"It was impossible to travel so far with such an object, without encountering some *contretemps* and disappointments, more or less vexatious, particularly in thin meetings and unsympathetic audiences. But I never saw his equanimity disturbed for one moment, never heard one impatient expression pass his lips, but ever found in him a bright and beautiful example of that charity which 'seeketh not her own, is not easily provoked, thinketh no evil,...beareth all things, believeth all things, hopeth all things, endureth all things.'

"The memory of those days passed in his society will ever be among the brightest of my life."

For some time before he left England it became quite an understood thing, that Mackenzie was to be consecrated Bishop after his arrival at the Cape of Good Hope. The proceedings of the Convocation of the Province of Canterbury had cleared away, as was believed, every difficulty, and it was held to be beyond a doubt, that the Bishops of South Africa would follow the manifest wish of their brethren in England, and consecrate the Missionary Bishop. All arrangements were therefore made upon the supposition that Mackenzie was Bishop-designate. It was thought convenient that he should sail with a first party of missionaries to the Cape of Good Hope, towards the end of the year.

The last meeting which he attended in England, was at Brighton. The Bishop of Oxford was with him upon this occasion, and urged the cause of the mission with his usual earnestness: they travelled from Brighton together, to attend the farewell service in Canterbury cathedral, of which I shall have more to say presently. With regard to the Brighton meeting, I have nothing to record save that it was his last.

From Brighton also Mackenzie wrote the last letter in England that has come to my hands. It is addressed to a young man in deacon's orders, who had thought of joining the Central African Mission; the gentleness of its tone, and the period at which it was written, seem to entitle it to a place in these pages.

LETTER LXVIII.

BRIGHTON,
Sept. 29, 1860.

MY DEAR ——,

We thought of you much during last week and on Sunday, and I now write a single line to say, God bless you in your work.

I think the Collect for the first Sunday after the Epiphany expresses what I would pray for you and myself, that we may be taught what He would have us to do, and that we may be made willing in the day of His Power.

Be not discouraged if you do not quite fulfil your own hopes. They would be too low if you could. Neither be elated if you seem to succeed: it is He that worketh in us: but ever strive to work in His strength. Good bye.

Yours affectionately,
C. F. M.

We go on board at Southampton on the 4th, and sail from Plymouth on the 6th, God willing.

On Tuesday, October 2, there was a farewell service at Canterbury. A large number of friends of the Mission and personal friends of Mackenzie were gathered together for the purpose of joining with him in solemn worship, and wishing God-speed to him and his work. The service commenced at half-past ten: the spacious choir of the cathedral was crowded: the Holy Communion was administered to several hundreds: the offertory amounted to £400. The sermon was preached by the Bishop of Oxford, from Jeremiah xxxix. 15—17, "Now the word of the Lord came unto Jeremiah, while he was shut up in the court of the prison, saying, Go and speak to Ebed-melech the Ethiopian, saying, Thus saith the Lord of hosts, the God of Israel; Behold, I will bring My words upon this city for evil, and not for good; and they shall be accomplished in that day before thee. But I will deliver thee in that day, saith the Lord: and thou shalt not be given into the hand of the men of whom thou art afraid." I will produce here the concluding passage, not merely for its own sake, but because Mackenzie referred to it afterwards in conversation, as having really cheered his heart, and as having been the means of giving him a support which he felt at the time that he much required. I had the privilege of being placed next to him in the cathedral, and could not but notice his calm resigned expression of countenance during the whole service. Here is the passage:

And for THEE, true yoke-fellow and brother well beloved, who leadest forth this following; to THEE in this our parting hour—whilst yet the grasped hand tarries in the embrace of love—to THEE what shall we say? Surely what, before he gave over to younger hands his rod and staff, God's great prophet said of old to his successor,—"Be strong and of a good courage: for thou must go with this people unto the land which the Lord hath sworn unto their fathers to give them; and *Thou shalt cause them to inherit it.* And the Lord, He it is that doth go before thee; He will be with thee, He will not fail thee, neither forsake thee: fear not, neither be dismayed[1]."

What can man's voice add to that solace? He at whose dear call thou goest forth, HE shall be with thee; thou shalt know the secret of His presence; thou shalt see, as men see not here in their peaceful homes, the nail-pierced hands, and the thorn-crowned brow. Thou shalt find, as His great saints have found before thee, when He has lured them into the desert wilderness, that He alone is better than all beside Himself. When thy heart is weakest, He shall make it strong; when all others leave thee, He shall be closest to thee; and the revelation of His love shall turn danger into peace, labour into rest, suffering into ease, anguish into joy, and martyrdom, if so He order it, into the prophet's fiery chariot, bearing thee by the straightest course to thy most desired home.

In the afternoon there was a luncheon in the crypt of S. Augustine's College, speeches were made by the Warden of S. Augustine's, the Bishop of Oxford, the Dean of Canterbury, and others. In the course of his address, the Dean of Canterbury said: "The service of this day must, I am sure, have gone to all hearts, and called forth, I had almost said, tears from every eye. There is a little circumstance connected with this day's gathering, which, though trifling in itself, may be not inappropriately mentioned here. A tree has recently been brought to this country of a size surpassing all former growths; and Archdeacon Mackenzie has done me to-day the honour of planting in my garden, a specimen of the *Wellingtonea Gigantea.* May our Mis-

[1] Deut. xxxi. 7, 8.

sion resemble it in its growth and in its greatness, fulfilling the emblem of Him who said of the least of all seeds, that when it is grown it is the greatest among herbs, and becometh a tree, and covereth all the nations of the earth with its branches. May this be typical of our Mission!" The Bishop of Oxford made a happy allusion to the African blood of the man who was "chosen by the providence of God to bear up the hill of shame the Cross of Salvation, under which the Saviour fainted. They laid hold of one Simon, *of Cyrene;* him they compelled to bear His Cross." Mackenzie expressed himself somewhat as follows.

I would very gladly on this day have kept my seat, and been content with listening to what others had to say for our encouragement, warning, and instruction. But I cannot do so, because I represent not merely myself, but my fellow-workers, who have given up themselves to go forth with me to carry on the work of the Lord. For their sake I feel that I must not keep silence, and I return you the best thanks in my power for all that you have done for us, for the welcome you have given us personally, and for your efforts in favour of the cause in which we are embarked. I thank the Warden of this venerable place, whose walls have received us, only a young branch of the Church, and inspired us with greater strength for the work that awaits us in Africa. To the other friends, whether now present or not, we give our sincerest thanks for the trouble they have all taken to secure our comfort, and the kind welcome that has everywhere greeted us. This opportunity of publicly acknowledging our obligations is the more welcome, by reason of its being the last one that we shall have before our leaving England. Let all, then, of those hearty friends in Canterbury, or in the other parts of England which we have visited, take this assurance, on my word—

that often and often the thought of their kindness will rise up to our memory in days to come, refreshing us by our knowledge of their interest in our well-being, and conscious that we have their prayers for our success. Yes, and many, too, whose names I could not now mention, will be restored to our memory in those distant parts, and we shall often think with gratitude of the kind farewell they gave us in England. Before sitting down, let me make one more remark. It is well on this, as on all other occasions like the present, to have some definite and fixed object, by which we may settle in our minds the remembrance of this day's gathering. It seems to me that the most practical way of doing this will be by imitating an example which was set in another part of England some years ago, and which met with a very satisfactory success. They formed an association of the friends of the cause, and named one day in the year for a general meeting, when an account of what had been done during the past twelve months was produced. Besides this, they subscribed to a special fund for some particular object having to do with the cause; and, in the case which I am mentioning, they raised as much as £50 a-year, and sometimes £70. It may be objected that this is not a large amount. But the money is not the prime object of the association. It is rather to keep alive the interest in the cause, and to maintain the list of friends to it. Now I think that if an association of such a kind, or similar to it, were established here, it would have a very good effect. The particulars I presume not to arrange. The day of meeting, the object for which a special fund should be raised, and other details, could be easily settled in committee. I simply throw out the hint; and leave it to you to take it up, or not, as you think proper. Once more, I thank you heartily for all you have done for our cause, which may God prosper!

In the evening the students of S. Augustine's College were assembled in the hall to hear addresses from

Archdeacon Mackenzie and from the Bishops of Chichester and Oxford. It was the last public occasion upon which Mackenzie spoke in England; I have no report of his speech; but I remember that it was very practical and earnest, and seemed to me to carry great weight with it in consequence of the entire self-forgetfulness which characterized it. In the *Colonial Church Chronicle* I find it stated, that "Archdeacon Mackenzie impressed on his hearers the absolute necessity of possessing a strong and living faith, upon which, he said, the whole of a man's usefulness depended. They must look entirely to God-given strength, if they would bear up against the obstacles that pressed upon them in their upward and onward course."

From the hall the whole company adjourned to the chapel, where the proceedings of the day were brought to a close by Evening Prayer. It was a day which no one can forget; it was memorable for its own sake, as exhibiting a great outburst of Christian life from the very heart of the Church of England; it would have been among the most pleasing of the reminiscences of Mackenzie's friends, had he been permitted to revisit this country and to talk over past times; as it is, we may still venture to put it amongst our pleasing though sad recollections, and to rejoice that we were permitted to take such a parting leave of one whom in this world we were not to see again.

The day after the Canterbury farewell service I had the pleasure of travelling with Mackenzie to London. Several other intimate friends were of the party. He was happy and merry as ever; he was more than calm and collected; he gave lookers-on the impression that the sacrifice was nothing, and that there was nothing in the work to oppress his spirits. It would have been easy to make the party grave and serious, but in his sunshiny presence it seemed impossible to be otherwise than joyous.

In London we attended a meeting of the Committee at the house of the Society for the Propagation of the Gospel, and in the evening he started with his sister and a party of considerable magnitude, consisting chiefly of members of the mission, for Southampton. It was impossible not to feel that in all probability we had seen him for the last time on earth; happily, it may be thought, the bustle and hurry of parting, and the necessity for attending to small matters of business, prevent the mind on such occasions from dwelling upon melancholy forebodings. But what if we did not meet again? he had counted the cost: who could desire to hold him back?

Mr Hutt, his faithful friend and secretary, accompanied him to Southampton. He has been kind enough to furnish me with the following notice of Mackenzie's last hours in England.

"I will try and sketch as nearly as I can the proceedings of the 3rd and 4th of October, 1860. It was on the 3rd that we all dined together in London. You saw me start with two cabs heavily laden with luggage. I was commissioned to take tickets for all the party, in order to have as little extra luggage as possible to pay for. Mackenzie came as the train was starting, and we only just scrambled into the carriages in time.

Bacon's Railway Hotel was the place at which we lodged at Southampton. Mackenzie and I, at his particular request, had a double-bedded room, as he thought I might help him. We sat up till three in the morning: during most of the time after midnight he was letter-writing, or giving me directions for the settlement of various little matters which he had not had time to attend to. Three or four times he ceased for a few minutes from his work, and wondered when he should be in England again; then, checking himself, he would say, "Well, I wish to place myself altogether in God's hands: He knows what is best for me, and I trust that what we call *the worst* will be but a summons to our lasting home." (I would say that Mackenzie seemed to have a kind of presentiment that he should never return to England. I remember that at Brighton, on October 1st, he came to my bedside at about seven in the morning, and asked me to go down to the beach, and bathe with him. I did not care to do so: when he said very earnestly, Do come: I shall probably never ask you again, and you may feel sorry to have refused me my last request. He was so sad and earnest that I could not refrain from doing as he wished.) We were up by seven in the morning, and went to the docks to see the vessel and inquire about two puppies that had been sent from Scotland. Though he was very much pressed for time, he took pains to see that his dumb friends were made as comfortable as possible. Fancying that they were hungry, he hurried back to the inn, procured a large basin of bread and milk, and carried it in his own hands through the streets of Southampton, because a messenger was not at once obtainable. The whole party breakfasted together. From that time till going on board he was comforting the friends of those who were going with him. He asked me not to remain with him till the last, as he would like to have 'quiet thoughts with his own heart' when he was actually starting. I was so busily engaged in looking after luggage and paying fares and dock-charges, that I had not very much time for talking with dear Mackenzie, but there seemed to be an undercurrent of sadness, which at times almost carried him away from what he was endeavouring to do with his whole heart."

The mission party which sailed with Bishop Mackenzie consisted of the following persons: the Rev. L. J. Procter; the Rev. H. C. Scudamore; Mr Horace Waller, the lay superintendent; S. A. Gamble, a carpenter; and Alfred Adams, an agricultural labourer. The sister, who accompanied him in his first voyage to Africa, was again his companion in this second and (as it proved) final voyage.

CHAPTER IX.

CONSECRATION AT CAPE TOWN.

THE *Cambrian* steamer, which carried the mission party, left Plymouth for the Cape of Good Hope, on the 6th of October, and arrived after an uneventful voyage, on November 12.

There is little to be said concerning the voyage. Public worship was celebrated on board every morning; and, in the evening, the mission party had family prayers; on Sunday, two services with sermon; and on one Sunday the Holy Communion was administered. The Missionaries employed themselves in studying the Sechuana language, not because they had much hope that this dialect would be intelligible in the valley of the Shire, but because it appears to be more generally known than any other, and therefore almost certain to prove of utility in Southern Africa, either directly or indirectly. It has been called the *French* of South Africa. They did not however make much progress: their time was short, and their appliances imperfect, no dictionary, and no complete grammar; still, with a Bible, and Concordance, they managed to learn something.

Mackenzie also prepared himself for his future life by accustoming himself to take astronomical observations.

It is unnecessary to say that the party was cordially received by the Bishop of Cape Town. The Bishop had most kindly arranged for receiving all, some at his own residence of Bishopscourt, and some at the Kafir College. Thus the Missionaries found one more quiet and peaceful resting-place, before their more active labours should commence. It was necessary to make a sojourn of some length; arrangements were to be made for the consecration of Mackenzie as Bishop, and these arrangements involved the arrival at the Cape of at least two out of the Bishops of Graham's Town, Natal, and S. Helena; and in fact, as will be seen, Mackenzie was not able to proceed on his voyage till the commencement of the following year.

This delay was of course a source of grief to the missionary party; they had, however, the great satisfaction of finding on their arrival at Cape Town that news had been received from Dr Livingstone, who had heard of the mission, and had undertaken to meet the Bishop and his party at the Kongone mouth of the Zambesi, and conduct them himself to the scene of their future labours. Moreover, the time spent at the Cape was not lost: they were able to consult more definitely than hitherto as to the details of their plans, and to take advice from the Bishop of Cape Town, and the Governor, Sir George Grey. One question, which the Missionaries discussed earnestly at this time, must be recorded, on account of its bearing upon some events which will be subsequently related. The question was asked, what should the Missionaries do, if they should find that the people amongst whom they should settle should after a time prove unfriendly? Should they hold their position by force? Should they defend themselves against attack? It was agreed that it would not be their duty to hold forcible possession, that they were preachers of the Gospel of peace, and that if they found their position untenable, except by violence, it would be their duty to abandon it, and seek another. The reader is particularly requested to observe that a collision with the natives was contemplated from the first as a possible contingency, and that in case of such a misfortune a pacific retreat was agreed upon as the right course of conduct to be pursued.

During the delay at the Cape, Mackenzie wrote a few letters, some of which I will here produce. The first is to his sister in Natal.

LETTER LXIX.

Bishopscourt, Cape Town,
Nov. 17, 1860.

Dear ——,

I am very thankful for the very prosperous voyage with which our good Father has blessed us, pleasant and (I trust) not unprofitable. We have been studying Sechuana, without previous knowledge, without dictionary, and almost without grammar. The sketch which Livingstone left behind him, and of which Murray the publisher sent me a copy as a present, though it was not a published book, was not a grammar. Our mainstay was Moffat's Bible and a Concordance. So that our knowledge is as imperfect as ——, and not nearly so full. Still we got through eight or ten verses of II Chronicles and forty-five of Psalm lxxviii., leaving not many points unclarified,—unbotanized,—really it is very like *botanizing* the language. We must keep this up, though the value of it will be only like that of knowing French in Italy. I believe Sechuana is more generally understood by an individual here and there than any other dialect. Livingstone speaks of the "Kafir or Zulu family extending right up to the Zambesi. They are known there as Landeens or Landuns." He means up to the river along the coast. I do not expect however that they speak pure Zulu. Livingstone's letters are most hearty. He says for want of a better steamer he was compelled to go up the Shire. "Cautious reverence is required in ascribing human movements to the influences of Divine Providence: but having been prevented ascending to the Makololo country, and led very much against our will into a region we never contemplated exploring, and there found a field exactly suited for your mission, I really think that the prayerful movement of so many pious hearts at the Universities has had something to do with the direction of our steps." That is good: is it not?

* * * * *

The next letter is a long one, but I think of sufficient interest to claim a place here. It contains an account of a visit made by some of the mission party to a Moravian mission station. The account is interesting in itself, and may also be interesting to the reader, (doubtless it was regarded in this light by Mackenzie,) as an example of successful work, carried out upon the principle of combining the higher truths of Christian faith and worship with a systematic education of the African mind in the arts of civilized life.

LETTER LXX.

GNADENDAL, CAPE OF GOOD HOPE,
December 5, Wednesday.

I write a few lines in anticipation of the mail. This is a Moravian mission station, probably the most flourishing which they have in any part of the world.

We left Cape Town on Monday morning and got here (eighty miles) yesterday afternoon. Our party was the Dean of Cape Town, Procter, Scudamore, Waller, myself, and Bell, the last a lad of 16, our fellow-passenger in the *Cambrian.* For thirty-five miles we went over a flat sandy tract, leaving the wonderful view of Table Mountain behind us, and as we went about East we passed False Bay on our right. About thirty miles from Cape Town is Somerset, a village chiefly Dutch, where we dined. We were all, (seven, including the driver,) in a covered light cart, with three seats, one behind another, and all on two wheels, with four horses, which have come all the way, and are to take us back. We outspanned halfway to Somerset, and then started again about four P. M., first over a pass 900 or 1000 feet high, and then on rising and falling ground, till about nine at night. You may fancy how we tried the springs, and how often we came down *bump* upon the axletree, having compressed the springs as far as they could go. We started in first-rate spirits, and ended cheerful, but subdued. After supper and prayers we retired, two to a bed-room, four to shake-downs in the parlour, but not all to rest. I slept well myself; but in the morning there was a joke against those who had been half-devoured, that they would require only half a breakfast. We started at 7.30: earlier this time than the day before, when four of us had to come from Bishop's Court, six miles, before starting. We off-saddled half way, and got here about three or four P. M.

As you approach you pass some hundreds of acres of oats, &c., the produce of the labour of the people. Then the valley lies before you; the hills become higher; till at length the valley becomes a *kloof*, that is, quite a narrow spacc between high rocks. From this kloof, aided by two little valleys one on each side, flows the stream to which the place owes the goodness of its situation. The fresh green foliage of countless trees and green crops, which quite cover the ground, was most refreshing after the two days' drive through the dry burnt-up country we had passed. As we drove up the right-hand side of the valley we continued for more than a mile passing on our left the cultivated gardens of the people, which occupy the centre, and on our right houses, which improved in appearance as we approached the head of the valley, where are the church and school and the dwellings of the brethren. The doors in the first cottages we saw were made of reeds, kept together by three horizontal spars in front and as many behind, fastened at their ends to the hinge-posts; these were replaced half a mile further on by neatly made doors in cottages having well-finished windows and a framework stretching some five feet from the eaves, with festoons of vines, the clusters giving promise of good grapes in two or three months. When we got to the head place, we found before us a lofty building, large enough for 1000 persons, the church.

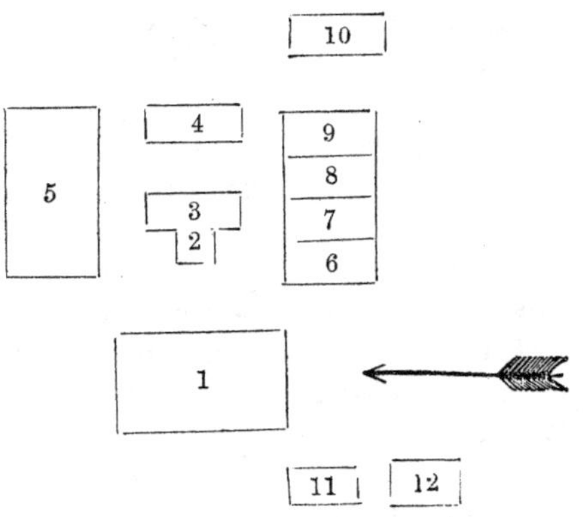

The sketch gives the different buildings; the arrow shewing where we alighted, and how we were facing

1. The church.
2. The dining-room.
3. Room behind it.
4. The kitchen.
5. A set of dwellings for the brethren: each family has two or three rooms.
6. The boys' and girls' school.
7. The carpenter's shop.
8. Wheelwright.
9. Blacksmith.
10. Mill.
11. Training-school.
12. Guest-house.

This last consists of a large common-room, twenty-two feet square, with four bed-rooms. We were at once welcomed by the Warden, had coffee, and saw the workshops. In the carpenter's shop were three lads of 18, under the instruction of a paid coloured artizan, the whole being under the direction of one of the brethren, of whom there are nine. In the blacksmith's shop, a tall man with two assistants was welding the tire of a wheel. Thence we went to the garden, about an acre of ground, in beautifully clean order. They commonly grow three crops of potatoes in a year on the same ground, sometimes four. In the middle was a pear-tree, under which we heard some of the early history of the mission.

It was founded by George Schmidt in 1737. For seven years he worked, and then returned home to stir up greater interest in the mission. The Dutch Government refused him permission to return, having a jealousy of missions in general. It was not till 1792 that missionaries were allowed to come. Schmidt was then dead, but the three brethren who came found an old woman, now blind, who nevertheless treasured the Dutch New Testament, which

Schmidt had given her, and which she had read till her sight failed her. I saw to-day that New Testament, kept in a wooden box, made of the wood of the old pear-tree which Schmidt planted, and which lived till 1836, (100 years,) when it was replaced by another, under which we stood. Thence we went to their burial ground,—graves marked No. 2367, and such numbers. They have now a population of 3000 coloured people, chiefly Hottentots: during two months lately they had sixty burials, chiefly children, owing to measles. There was an open grave, and we learned that two children were to be buried at sundown, and obtained permission to be present. Thence to the training school: nineteen lads, some from other mission stations. The school was not at work: but we saw the printing press and some of its later productions: this has been here for a year only: we saw also the room in which the lads sleep, their dining-room, sitting-room, &c. I have omitted the mill and the tannery. The former is used not only for the brethren, and for the people of the valley, who bring sacks of wheat and receive a tally, the duplicate of which is put on the sack, paying so much for the grinding; but also some of the farmers are glad to send several miles to have their wheat ground. In the tannery is used the bark not only of oak,—the quality is not so good as in England,—but also of mimosa and of a small plant called protea. They tan chiefly sheep-skins.

About sunset several of us went to the funeral. We entered the lofty church: in the middle of one long side, between the windows, is a kind of dais, with a principal seat in the middle: here sits the brother, who is to conduct the service, a table in front of him, and the brethren on each side. In the body of the building seats for the people, occupying the whole space, except the bases of two large pillars, which help to support the roof. A gallery runs round three sides: an organ was played by a Kafir boy. First they sang a hymn, all sitting: it was in Dutch, so

I could not understand it: but the sight of sixty or seventy natives, joining in the singing,—the thought that here in the time of their deep distress they were being brought to the source of all comfort, and that we (please God) were going soon to preach the same glad tidings to the poor natives of the Shire valleys,—brought tears to my eyes. The address was on the 21st or 22nd chapter of Revelation: the name of the Lamb coming often in the reading of it, and the name of Jesus oftener in the exposition. It was the Warden who officiated,—a simple, earnest man. Then a hymn: then they all rose, formed a semicircle in the court, with the minister at the apex, the men and women at the two sides, the two little coffins, each on its own bier, at the centre, touching the wall. Again they sang: this time only four lines: and then proceeded to the grave-yard. We went another way. They laid the coffins on the ground beside the graves, the minister standing on the western side of the graveyard, the people standing upon the path which surrounded it, the whole space within being thickly covered with mounds. Again a service, with responses from the congregation, and during the latter of two verses of a hymn the coffins were lowered, one after the other, by the lads from the training-school, who had been the bearers. After the service the mothers came near: one, taking a spade, threw three or four spadefulls which fell heavily on the coffin; then the other did the same. We came away, and I had hardly firmness to speak to Scudamore, as we passed through the old churchyard, of the joy of leading men and women in life and death to Him! We soon had supper, and were glad immediately after to go to bed.

It is their custom to meet in their common-room about 5.30, for short family prayers and a cup of coffee before church at 5.45. This morning, my watch being a quarter slower than their time, and having slept soundly till I was awakened, I was too late for their family prayers; but we joined them at church. None of the sisters were present, and not all the brethren: about sixty or seventy people. It is harvest time, and many are out at work for the farmers.

We returned to the guest-house till eight, when we were to be summoned to breakfast: I fell asleep again. This principle of the guest-house pleased me much. We are here not wasting their time when they are busy. They can devote as much time as they please to entertaining us, and they have not allowed us to feel solitary.

After breakfast we saw the retail Shop, which sells about £800 worth of goods per annum, the Dispensary, and the working of the Training School. This is supported by a separate foundation, some German Prince having about twenty-five years ago given money for the purpose, with the condition that they should always take at least five boys from other stations besides their own. The whole costs the Moravian funds nothing. Excellent and wonderful answers in Scripture and Geography were given. Some of them played on the piano well: on the violin, not so well. They sang some songs—such as "Rule Britannia," which they understood.

After this we climbed a shoulder of the hill to look at the village from above. There are about 400 acres cultivated as gardens, irrigated on a regular system, each man having the water for a certain time during the week. The general view of the village was very pretty: below us the long row of houses, each with its garden beyond it, with neatly arranged beds of mealies, beans, wheat, oats, or potatoes: the hedgerows of quince, or roses, and a great number of fruit-trees, which only needed to be in bloom to complete the picture of rich abundance. Descending the hill, we went into one or two of the houses: in one was a tailor, busy with a waistcoat for one of his neighbours: of course he was paid for his work, and the brother who was with us pointed to his own waistcoat and lower garments as specimens of this man's skill. In another house we found three women, one baking in the huge Dutch oven'; the produce to be divided between herself and the owner of the house. In another was a girl of ten on a sofa, having an attack of fever.

The floors were all of clay. The ceilings were of strong reeds laid above the beams; over these a layer of clay, two or three inches thick, which formed the floor of a granary and store-room in the roof. Each house had two or three rooms: the sitting-room about ten feet square, and the walls about nine feet high.

The dinner, at 12, was a substantial meal: soup, small joints and roulettes of minced meat, with potatoes and beans, stewed preserved apples and peaches, a roly-poly pudding, good brownish bread, with water or a glass or two of local wine. It was a long table, for we were ourselves an addition of six persons, besides Mr ——, the botanical professor in Cape Town, to their regular party of fourteen. They usually arrange themselves so that husband and wife shall sit together; while we were there, the chief brethren sat with us at the upper end, leaving the other almost exclusively for the ladies. The wives take it in turns to superintend the kitchen department.

But the most striking part of the arrangement was the grace. As at the Umlazi, where I so liked to join in the chanted Kafir grace, so here, at dinner and supper they began and ended by singing a grace. The Warden, who took the top of the table, and on whose left hand I always found myself, started the air, which was immediately taken up by the women, but almost overpowered by the deep bass notes of all the men. I am sorry I forgot to ask for the words and meaning of these acts of thanksgiving. I should have liked to have joined with them, and to have remembered them afterwards. After dinner most of us returned to the guest-house, and I began this letter to you. It received some additions this morning (Friday, December 7) at Somerset, on our way home, and is now being finished at Bishop's Court.

After tea, to which we were summoned at 4 by the bell, we again strolled out to see the irrigation of some of the gardens, and the condition of one or two of the best of them. I do not know whether the ground was originally chosen with a view to the irrigation, but certainly the water may be said to be the life of the place. I made further acquaintance with it by bathing in a shaded pool, much to my comfort and refreshment, before Church, for which the bell rang about sundown. There were about the same number as before of the coloured people, with one or two of the brethren, and our whole party, but none of the sisters. I was disappointed in not seeing them more anxious to join in worship. The service consists chiefly of singing and reading. This evening the 22nd chapter of Genesis was the subject, and a longish discourse was founded upon it, lasting 15 or 20 minutes. The music was touching: there was a short prayer before the dismissal.

I had thought once or twice, during our short stay at this Mission, whether it would be worth while for us to get one or two of their trained lads to join our mission to the Shire. I spoke to the Warden, asking whether if I wished it, it would be likely to be possible. He did not encourage the idea, saying he did not know whether the boys would like it: some of them were being educated for other Christian bodies, and in fact of those who were now being taught trades none were eligible.

By this time it was time for supper, 8 o'clock: after this we parted for the night. I received, besides two specimens of their printing, a copy of the rules of the institution, a lithograph of the view of the valley from the hill, and a photograph of the 19 boys in the training school: besides which I bought a knife and fork, the handles of which were made from the wood of the old pear-tree. We were to start next morning by 6, and were ready by 6.30. By this time the brethren had come from Church, and their earnest parting words of "God bless you, give you a good journey," will live with us, I trust. I believe they were in earnest, when they said that our visit had been a pleasure to them.

On the whole this has been a most enjoyable visit, and we have seen and heard many things which will be useful. I found myself two or three times thinking of Gnadendal as a realization of the Happy Valley: not that I forgot that there was still much of contact with the outer world, and also much sin and unhappiness in the midst of them: but when one compared their present state with their state in heathenism and barbarism, one could not help blessing God, and praying that we might be allowed to reclaim some of the wandering sheep further north, and give them the blessings of order and holiness. Certainly much is done at wonderfully little expense. The brethren are sent out from Europe, but receive nothing from home for their maintenance. Gnadendal is not only self-supporting, but contributes to the support of the younger and less flourishing missions of South Africa: so that as a body they are self-supporting. This is brought about by the profits on the workshops and the retail shop. In the former, pupils and hired men of colour work under the superintendence of the white men, thus learning the trade and at the same time bringing revenue to the Institution. Then work is done for the inhabitants of the valley, and for the Dutch farmers in the neighbourhood; and their work is so good that I am told pruning-knives have been made in Birmingham, with the Gnadendal stamp to secure them a better sale among the farmers. In the retail shop there is of course a profit, which may come to something on sales to the amount of £800 a-year. Then there is the doctor, who on suitable occasions charges for his drugs, and the fees which the farmers pay for his visits go to the general fund. This is exactly the scheme I had in my mind for our work: every workman a source of revenue. Again, the economy is considerable. The expense of supplying the table is at £40 a-year for each couple, (putting with each a proportion of the children;) so that, including everything, even the £1 a-year which each couple receives in cash, the cost is about £90, and this in a country in which a clergyman and his wife find it hard to get on with less than £250. The difference is perhaps partly due to the simplicity of their manners, but partly to their living in common, as well as to the excellent domestic economy of the sisters. I hope we shall find an estimate of £100 a-year for each European to be over the mark. The main secret of the success of these men, I think, is that they are well chosen for their work, and that their heart is in it. They have no visions of returning home, no dreams of rising to something higher. I believe it may be truly said that their aim is to promote the glory of God, and to advance the happiness and good of their fellowmen. May we go and do likewise!

I give one more letter written at this period. It is to a very dear friend in Cambridge. It is a good specimen of the warmth of Mackenzie's feelings, and at the same time shews with how much pleasure to himself he could have resumed a life, which he had thought right to abandon for the sake of Christ and His Gospel.

LETTER LXXI.

Bishop's Court, Cape Town,
Dec. 12, 1860.

My dear ——,

Though we are so far parted, and are likely to be so long, this seems to me only to bring you the closer to me in my heart, and in my longing desire for your happiness and highest good. And first, I may pray for you, as I do, that God our Father would keep you in His safe protection and guide you. But I am also anxious you should get into some really useful and directly ministerial work: the more I think of it, the more I think College is not the place for you, and though the College and University have a claim on their sons, yet not to the injury or real loss of the persons themselves. * * * It is one of the hardest places to be a clergyman in. Elsewhere people expect you to be a clergyman: the influence of the atmosphere around you helps to brace you up. In Cambridge there are many clergy who don't care to live as such, and this has lowered the standard of public opinion. —— would say, they ought not to be obliged to take orders. Well, that is not the question now: *you* will ask gently, "but Mackenzie, is that a reason for my running away?" I think in your case it is. I do really and honestly think you want country work, parish work, the work of feeding yourself and the flock which the Great Shepherd through the agency of His Church shall commit to you, with the food you will draw practically from the Bible. I know what it is to pass from Cambridge to actual ministerial duty, engaging undivided attention. I like mathematics; I liked teaching; and yet I felt the change like a breathing of fresh air, like working at a thing my heart was engaged upon; I am still fond of mathematics, (I came across Childer's *Caustics of Reflexion and Ray Surfaces*, and worked out some of the propositions yesterday, for ten minutes before dinner,) but my real best self is wrapped up in the hope of rescuing some of God's wandering sheep, with souls to rejoice in Him and glorify Him, from the darkness and the sin in which they now are. And I want you to be actively and simply and humbly working in the same sort of way, not only because it is so blessed, but because I do really think it would be good for you, and would be the way to make you see clearly and rejoice in the light of God's countenance. Please think carefully of this, and God guide you aright.

* * * * *

Did you ever think of this easy problem? "Compare the spaces described by two points on the rims of the fore and hind wheels of a carriage, running on a road such a distance that the points start together from the ground, and arrive together on the ground." The spaces are evidently equal.

"What is the locus of the foci of reflected pencils of light, the incident pencils being small parallel pencils, and falling in any direction on a reflecting curve?" (I mean all in one plane). Answer: A circle touching the reflecting curve, and passing through its principal focus. (How wretchedly confused I am in expressing these things !)

Again: "The shaft by which rotatory motion is carried from an engine of given horse-power to the work to be done, must be made stronger, in inverse proportion to its rate of revolution." Prove this. Answer: The strain on such a shaft depends on the couple (of forces) exerted upon it at one end, and which it exerts upon the machinery driven at its other end. That is to say, supposing it moved by a wheel of given radius, the strain is proportional to the force exerted tangentially on such wheel. But horse-power is proportional to such force multiplied by speed of such circumference: therefore the strain is inversely proportional to the number of revolutions per minute. The result is, that if rotatory motion is to be conveyed from one place to another, the final wheels revolving more rapidly than the engine crank, it will require a stronger shaft to convey it, if the speed be obtained by multiplying wheels after the shaft, than if it be multiplied first and the transmitted motion be of great rapidity.

You will say, how do your own affairs prosper? You must ask ——. If he does not hear from me by this mail, don't tell him that *you* have—but he will hear from others.

Good bye, my dear fellow,

Yours affectionately,

C. F. M.

One circumstance of a singularly interesting kind, and of great importance in its bearings on the subsequent action of the missionaries, occurred during Mackenzie's residence at the Cape. A coloured congregation existed in Cape Town, under the charge of an English clergyman, Mr Lightfoot: the congregation consisted of liberated slaves, persons who had been captured by British cruisers from slave vessels, on the Eastern coast of Africa, and set free at Cape Town. Many of these liberated slaves had been resident in the Cape colony for a long period, and had acquired the English language, while at the same time intercourse with each other had prevented them from losing their own. Mackenzie was very desirous of obtaining the aid of some native converts as guides and interpreters to the mission, and this coloured congregation at the Cape appeared to afford him the means of doing so. Accordingly, he was invited to preach one Sunday evening to these black people: he did so, and after explaining his plans, he asked how many of those present were willing to volunteer to accompany him and help him in the work which he was undertaking for their countrymen. Not less than twelve stood up; and it was encouraging to find that out of those twelve, six had been already mentioned by Mr Lightfoot to the Bishop of Cape Town as amongst the most suitable men in his opinion to join and assist the mission. Several of these volunteers did in fact give themselves to the work, and we shall find in the sequel, that they were of incalculable service. "I do think," said Mackenzie, in a speech which he made at a large meeting held at Cape Town, "that it is most encouraging to see men, natives of the far interior of the continent, liberated slaves, coming forward as they have done, ready to devote their energy and their peculiar qualifications, to the work we have in hand."

The meeting, which has just been mentioned, demands a little further notice. Nothing could exceed the interest taken in the Central African Mission by the inhabitants of Cape Town. It was in truth a most interesting occasion; Cape Town was about to be the scene of the first consecration of a strictly missionary Bishop of the Church of England; the people of the Cape perceived that they had a special and honourable share in the work; and as occupying the chief home of Christianity in South Africa, and being therefore the chief witnesses for Christ in that dark continent, they could not but feel that the missionaries might receive God speed upon their work with great propriety from themselves.

Accordingly, a large meeting was held, at which the Governor, Sir George Grey, took the chair, and the Bishop of Cape Town was present; the room was crowded to overflowing. The proceedings were of a most hearty kind, and only saddened by the news which had just arrived of the death of the missionaries of the London Missionary Society[1]. Mackenzie's speech

[1] Mr R. Moffat, the South African Missionary, wrote to Sir George Grey, under date Kuruman, Nov. 12: "Three hunters, sons of an old man named Aaron, of this place, have arrived with the melancholy news that the members of the Makololo mission have nearly all perished. The Aarons arrived at the Great Waterfall on the 18th of July, and crossed to the opposite bank. Here they ascertained that Mr Helmore, his devoted wife, their two children, and the infant of the Rev. Roger Price, had successively fallen victims to the fever; also three native

was a plain and simple statement of the history of the mission, and of the plans of himself and his brother missionaries. A few sentences will shew what his views at that time were. He said, "I suppose that we shall in about two months have arrived at the mouth of the Zambesi, and that we shall there meet Dr Livingstone, who, according to accounts dated Aug. 8, was at the Victoria Falls, but who promises to be at the mouth of the Zambesi by the end of the year, to meet the steamer *Pioneer,* the use of which has been given him by the Government. This vessel, as he himself has told us, is entirely at our service. I hope we shall not trespass too much on his kindness, but I am very thankful for the offer, as it will convey us through the malarious district at the mouth of the river, for sixty or seventy miles, to the valley of the Shire, whither we at present believe our work will lead us. I use this vague phrase *at present believe,* because we are unable to fix with exactness the spot where we shall commence; we intend to leave it to Dr Livingstone's advice. When we get there our first object will be to establish ourselves in a proper manner in the eyes of the natives, and for that purpose we have determined carefully to carry out our undertaking in such a manner as every Christian would desire to see it carried out, and so as not to lead the natives to suppose that we are mere adventurers or mere commercial men, far less slave-dealers, but a body of Christian men, professing a religion which we come not only to teach them, but

servants; and that in the preceding *moon* Sekeletu had insisted on Mr and Mrs Price leaving, or they too would go."

to practise ourselves. With this view, we have provided ourselves with a large church-tent, well furnished and appointed, through the kindness of friends in England. In this tent we hope, morning and evening, to join in prayer with the churches of other lands, with your own cathedral service here, and throughout the world. In the next place, we shall engage in such occupations as may strike the natives as useful, and may be likely to draw them to join us. I am not speaking now of the religious teaching of the natives, because we may be told, that these natives have a language which we cannot speak, and that we can do hardly anything in the way of teaching them the Christian religion. We shall however teach a great deal that is preparatory; and therefore, in our garden-work, in our building, in our carpentering, in all our industrial occupations, we shall endeavour to instruct some natives to work under us, not only to swell our own number of hands, but in order that they may learn how such things are done; we shall accustom them to the use of tools, and so endeavour to acquire an influence over them, leading them to see how a civilized nation like England produces those marvellous works, which the natives look upon with so much surprise."

With regard to the loss of the London Society's missionaries, he spoke with his usual simplicity, but in language which must have made a deep impression upon those who heard it, as coming from one who was not only making a speech, but also about to put his words of courage to the test of practice. "I would next refer," said he, "to something which has been already alluded to-day: I mean the sad destruction of life and the loss of Christian energy and zeal in the persons of those, who have been lately cut off in the interior of the country. It has been said, that we who are going are not to be daunted by that. No: rather should it be the opposite. Rather should we go up now with a more firm determination and intention, God helping us, of carrying on the work. We did think that we were going to the valley of the Zambesi, to carry on our own work in our own place, and that others would work higher up the stream, and that thus, at different points, Christ's name would be preached. We hear now that that mission has been destroyed, for the present at least. Must we not therefore work the more earnestly? Ought we not to go up more determinedly, humbly but faithfully trusting in God's strength to help us, that we may be enabled to work in His Vineyard, to carry His Name boldly and faithfully before the people of that land, and to bring in some at least, who, in the event of our destruction, our earlier or later death, may be ready to take our places, and carry forward the sound of the Gospel into the regions round about? * * * Thus it may be, that in the course of years we may become, what I have sometimes thought we were like, the original and early sprouts that rise from the seed in the ground, and which serve but to give life and vigour and energy to the shoots which rise above the ground afterwards. * * * That is the prospect we have before us; a prospect which does not depend upon our life or death, which does not depend upon our successes during our lifetime, but depends entirely upon the grace of God; a prospect which will undoubtedly be realised in God's good time, for we know that 'the knowledge of the Lord shall cover the earth as the waters cover the sea;' and therefore it is a prospect to which we may confidently look forward, trusting and believing that God's work will prosper, and that His Name and saving grace will be known among all nations."

The spirit, which expressed itself in such words as those just quoted, made Mackenzie impatient of the delay caused by the necessity of waiting at the Cape for consecration. His impatience was increased by the arrival of the *Pioneer*, which called at the Cape on its way to the Zambesi and Dr Livingstone. It seemed impossible to allow the opportunity to be lost, and yet it was impossible for Mackenzie himself to take a passage in the *Pioneer*. His doubts as to the best course of action are thus expressed in a letter to his sister at Natal.

LETTER LXXII.

BISHOPSCOURT,
Dec. 12, 1860.

DEAR ——,

* * * * *

The *Pioneer*, Livingstone's river steamer, has come out, casting anchor last week. She will probably leave again this day week or so. I don't know what I would not give to go in her, or rather in the steamer that will accompany her; but I do not see a chance of this. I am just hesitating whether to send my tail or a part of it, before I go myself; but it feels so awkward to back into a country, stern foremost, as it were; and I am not clear that I could (in my ignorance of so much that is there) give them any instructions that would be satisfactory. I shall probably have settled this point before the *Waldensian* leaves again.

* * * * *

The doubt was at length resolved in favour of sending a portion of the missionary party in advance by the *Pioneer*, or rather by H.M.S. *Sidon*, which accompanied it. Accordingly, Mr Scudamore and Mr Waller were thus sent in advance, the consecration being still delayed by the necessity of awaiting the arrival of the Bishops, who were to take part with the Metropolitan in the service. At length, on January 1, 1861, the Feast of the Circumcision, all was ready for the consecration. The Bishops of Natal and S. Helena had arrived; the Bishop of Graham's Town unfortunately lost his passage by the steamer, and so was unable to be present.

As the consecration of the first Missionary Bishop of the Church of England in modern times is an event of great historical value, beyond the interest attaching to it as having taken place in the person of Bishop Mackenzie, I shall give the account of the ceremony at some length, quoting from a report furnished by an eye-witness[1].

Although the first two or three days of the new year are exclusively devoted to holiday-making, all business being suspended, and the panting inhabitants of Table Valley being only too glad to escape from the boiling heat and dust to breathe the pure fresh air of the country, still the great interest taken in the forthcoming ceremony attracted a large

[1] The account is taken from a letter of the correspondent of the *Guardian* newspaper.

congregation to the cathedral. At half-past ten the bells of the Cathedral chimed out merrily, S. George's being the only church in the colony possessing a peal, which, though imperfect, are sufficient to remind one of home. The regular attendants at the cathedral were admitted by the south door, and at a quarter to eleven the great doors were thrown open at the western porch, and the church was soon filled. The order of ceremony observed followed as closely as possible that of the use of Westminster Abbey. The Dean, Canons, and Clergy met the Metropolitan and his assistants in the vestry at the right of the vestibule at the western entrance; the choristers and gentlemen of the choir in the baptistery on the opposite side. The procession formed in the following order, and proceeded up the church to the chancel:—

A Verger.
The Choristers in surplices.
Gentlemen of the Choir.
Eighteen Parochial Clergy of Cape Town and neighbourhood.
Canons and Cathedral Clergy.
A Verger.
The Very Rev. the Dean of Cape Town.
The Registrar of the Diocese.
The Venerable C. F. Mackenzie, Bishop-elect, and Chaplain.
Bishop of Natal. Bishop of S. Helena.
The Metropolitan's Verger, bearing mitre-staff.
Rev. Albert Wood, bearing the crozier.
The Right Rev. the Metropolitan Bishop.
His Lordship's Chaplain, the Rev. E. Glover, bearing the pastoral staff.

Arrived at the chancel the procession opened right and left. The Metropolitan proceeded to his throne on the north side; the Bishops of S. Helena and Natal to seats on the other side. The Dean, Canons, Precentor, and Bishop's chaplain also passed into their respective seats, and the other cathedral clergy to their stalls; the parochial clergy to the daily service chapel on the southside of the altar behind the parclose, the Bishop-elect, vested in surplice, kneeling at a faldstool at the entrance of the chancel.

The voluntary being finished, a hymn was given out, during the singing of which the Metropolitan moved to his place at the altar, and the Bishops of Natal and S. Helena to their places, north and south, as Epistoler and Gospeller.

The Nicene Creed ended, the Dean was conducted to the pulpit, and preached from Ephesians ii. 19—22.

After the sermon the Dean returned to his place; and whilst the hymn, "Christ is made the sure Foundation," was being sung, the Bishop-designate retired to the vestry, where he put on his rochet. Returning down the central passage, he was met at the chancel-steps by the assistant Bishops; who, taking him by the hand, led him towards the Metropolitan. The following words were then spoken by the Bishop of Natal:—

Right Reverend Father in God, we present unto you this godly and well-learned man to be ordained and consecrated Bishop.

The rubric demanding the Queen's mandate, was, of course, not observed. The word *charge* was substituted for *diocese*. The oath of supremacy was administered by the Registrar, and then the oath following by the Metropolitan:—

The Oath of Obedience to the Metropolitan Bishop.

In the name of God, Amen. I, Charles Frederick Mackenzie, chosen Bishop of the Mission to the tribes dwelling in the neighbourhood of the Lake Nyassa and River Shire, do profess and promise all due reverence and obedience to the Metropolitan Bishop and Metropolitical Church of Cape Town, and to their successors. So help me God, through Jesus Christ.

After the invitation to prayer, the Metropolitan knelt down at his seat, with the Precentor on his right hand, Chaplain on his left, the Bishop-elect and Bishops-assistant a few seats lower. The Litany was then sung; after which, the interrogations having being put, the Bishop-elect was conducted as before to the vestry, where he assumed the customary Episcopal vestments. During his absence, the anthem, "O, pray for the peace of Jerusalem," was sung; and on his return, whilst he knelt at the feet of the Metropolitan, Palestrina's *Veni Creator Spiritus.* The imposition of hands followed, in which the three Bishops joined. A large and beautifully-bound copy of the Holy Scriptures was then presented by the Metropolitan, which the new Bishop delivered to the care of his chaplain; he was then conducted to his seat next that of the junior Suffragan.

The Offertory was then collected. The clergy from the stalls and from the south chapel came forward and made their offerings, and remained at the altar-rails till they had communicated. The Dean received the alms, and brought the elements of bread and wine to the Metropolitan. The four Bishops administered the Communion. About 100 of the laity remained and communicated. The service concluded, the Dean, preceded by the vergers, conducted the Metropolitan, and the rest, to the vestry, the procession following, in reverse order to that in which it entered the church.

Thus concluded one of the most memorable services ever celebrated in South Africa. Thus ended the consecration of the first Missionary Bishop of England's Church since the Reformation. Let us hope it will be but the beginning of great and glorious things, that this *little one may become a thousand,* till, in the words of the Bishop of Natal, a "chain of Bishops, missionary and colonial, may extend from Cape Point to the Abyssinian Church in Northern Africa."

On the day after his consecration Bishop Mackenzie wrote as follows to a brother at home:

LETTER LXXIII.

January 2, Wednesday.

My dear Brother ——,

I think I am right in saying that on taking my degree, or on getting my fellowship, or on both occasions, I wrote first to you. Anyhow, I will write to you first this time, to tell you from myself that yesterday in S. George's, the Cathedral of Cape Town, the Metropolitan, with the Bishops of Natal and S. Helena, laid their hands on my head, and made me a Bishop of the Church, to lead a Mission to Nyassa and the Shire. I am very thankful that this has ended as we all hoped. I have said several times, that if I was to go at the head of this mission, as it was in any case the work of a Bishop, I ought not to be sent without the authority, and still more the grace of God, given in consecration. Besides this, I feel strongly that it is the right course, and that, whether there be any marked success in this mission or not, on the whole, we may hope for more rapid, sound, and united progress.

Some of my party, Waller, Scudamore, Adams, Gamble, and three blacks, including Lorenzo Johnson, the cook, started yesterday from Simon's Bay: at least, our latest news was that the vessel was getting up steam at seven A.M., when the mail left, and that mail brought us no letter from them: so I conclude, and shall probably hear to-day for certain, that they are off. It is a pity, after being delayed so long that they should not have stayed one day longer: they might then have been present at the consecration: and I, with Procter and the other two black men, might have gone with them. But I would not delay for an hour, by any request of mine, the vessel which was taking up the *Pioneer* to Livingstone.

* * * * *

On the seventh of January a large meeting was held in Cape Town, for the purpose of taking public leave of the missionary party, who shortly after went down to Simon's Bay to join H.M.S. *Lyra,* which was waiting to take back the Bishop of Natal to his diocese, and to convey Bishop Mackenzie, with the remainder of his party, to the scene of their future labours. At the farewell meeting the Bishops of Natal and of S. Helena spoke of the work which was being carried on in their respective dioceses. Bishop Mackenzie also spoke, and concluded his speech as follows: "And so it is that we have confidence to go forth on this mission, a small body indeed amongst the mass of heathenism, but trusting for God's blessing on what we do, on the work to be done in some measure through our agency, and in a still greater measure through the agency of native converts; so that by degrees the truth may be received among the nations of the interior, and may widely and more widely extend hereafter. Let us pray for God's blessing on this and all such works, not for success for our own honour and glory, for that is of no matter, but for the honour and glory of our Heavenly Father, for the honour and glory of His Son, who came into the world to redeem the heathen, to purchase for Himself an inheritance, and for the sake of those whom He so purchased, that they may have the blessing of God in His infinite mercy given to them, that they may lead Christian lives, may die Christian deaths, and may so be ushered into the presence of the Eternal King above."

No words can better express the spirit in which Bishop Mackenzie left the Cape of Good Hope, and which indeed breathed through his whole life.

CHAPTER X.

FROM CAPE TOWN TO THE SHIRE.

BISHOP MACKENZIE is now nearing the scene of his labours. He will have but one more halt, namely, at his old home, Natal, and then he will enter upon that field in which he was appointed to labour for so short a time. The mission party were on board H.M.S. *Lyra* on the morning of January 8, in Simon's Bay, but the ship was compelled by the South-East wind to wait till January 12, before she could get out. The party consisted of Bishop Mackenzie, the Rev. L. J. Procter, and three black men. Of these, one will especially come before our notice hereafter, Charles Thomas, of whom the Bishop says in one of his letters, "Charles Thomas was one of the pillars of Lightfoot's native congregation at Cape Town. It is twenty years since he came to the Cape. He was in the house of a Captain and Mrs Thomas, and owes to his mistress (or adopted mother, for he was quite a lad) his first knowledge and feelings of a religious kind. He is an active, intelligent man, speaking English well, and some dialects of Makoa, his native tongue, fluently." These black men left their wives at Cape Town, to follow them with the next mission party. In addition to the missionaries for the Zambesi, the *Lyra* also carried back to his own diocese the Bishop of Natal.

The voyage to Natal was made as pleasant as might be by the extreme kindness of Captain Oldfield, who made arrangements for receiving into his own cabin the two Bishops and Mr Procter. On Sunday, January 13, divine service was performed on deck; Bishop Mackenzie read prayers, and the Bishop of Natal preached; one of the sailors said he would walk twenty miles to hear him again. With reference to this voyage, Bishop Mackenzie writes in one of his letters as follows:

LETTER LXXIV.

H. M. S. *Lyra* S. Lat. 23° 48′.
E. Long. 36° 36′.
Feb. 4, Monday.

DEAR ——,

My memory will not serve me as to whether I have written to you since I left England: but in any case I am glad to be obliged to take up my pen, and say a few words to you, before leaving this the first man-of-war to which I was ever indebted for a passage. The Bishop of Natal, who came from Cape Town with us, agreed with me that we had seen a specimen of discipline, and of regular activity, and constancy of employment, which we ought not to forget. I spoke of being obliged to take up my pen to you, and part of the obligation consists in this, that I must ask you and any friends of the mission, in the event of their having any opportunity of being civil to Captain Oldfield of this vessel, to do so, on account of his great kindness and consideration for us on board. He has not only made this by far the most comfortable passage across the seas that I have made, and that at considerable inconvenience to himself,—taking three persons into his own cabin, &c.,—but has also offered to provide us with anything we want, or to let his men make anything for us. I am glad to say we are so well provided, that we have not been obliged to avail ourselves of his offer, to the extent at least that he intended and wished: but the kindness and interest he has shewn are the same.

We are having beautiful weather, and have had ever since we left Plymouth, with the exception of one night of wind, two or three days after leaving the Cape. I am thankful for this, on account of others as much as or more than myself.

* * * * *

The visit to Natal could scarcely fail to be one of great interest. Natal had been certainly the scene of the most painful days of Mackenzie's life, perhaps also the scene of the happiest. Many would welcome him there with great joy, and even those who had formerly been regarded as his adversaries had probably been brought by this time to appreciate the real nobility of his character, and to grieve that they had ever been found to oppose him. There is every reason to believe that the visit did in fact heal old wounds, and strengthen the bands of Christian charity. But, however this might be, the visit to Natal gave the Bishop the opportunity of seeing and consulting with the sister, whom he used playfully to call his *black* sister, from her love to the black people and successful work amongst them, and upon whose cooperation he now reckoned in his more distant mission. It may be well to explain here that this cooperation was not only reckoned upon by the Bishop, but intended by his sister at this time; subsequently, however, her own marriage with the Archdeacon of Maritzburg disturbed the arrangements, and compelled her to continue her useful missionary work amongst the Zulus of Natal. I shall give the reader an account of the Bishop's visit to his old country, as I find it in a very interesting home-letter, written by this sister.

Jan. 23, Wednesday. On Monday morning we were at the Point by 7 o'clock, and found them more than doubtful about going out, at any rate not till 9. * * * At last another message came from the flags at the ship that if they would not go out, the captain would come ashore in his boat; so orders were given to light the tug-fires, and off we set. We had a good toss on the bar, and then we neared the ship, and they sent out a boat and took us all on board. There were the two Bishops, and I was so happy. I hardly dared to ask how long we should have, for I feared to hear only twenty minutes; but our time was not to be so short. "Till Saturday, at any rate," said the captain, who has been most kind to the whole party. He with some of his officers and Mr Procter have gone to P. M. B., and our Natal Bishop started within a few hours.

The way in which he (Bishop Mackenzie) has been received has been quite heart-warming. One man, who was strong in opposition, came immediately and said how much he regretted what had passed, and how glad they would be now could they have him amongst them once more. He is to open and consecrate the pretty little church at the Point, and also to hold a Confirmation at the Umlazi.

All that afternoon people came and went, and came and went; but at last we made our escape, and had a little stroll on the shore, which was most pleasant.

* * * * *

January 31, Thursday. It is already more than a week since I wrote, and here I am quietly sitting *at home.* * * * I shall go on with my story as well as I can. On Wednesday I wrote with perpetual interruptions and callers: this lasted till dinner-time; after which we went to the photographer's, then home to tea, and then to church, where he preached. It was on the ten virgins,—earnest and rousing, and yet so tender that at the end I fairly got my head down and sobbed. * * * Next day *was* a day, work, work, work: packing and unpacking, dividing and sorting, interrupted with visitors. * * * Next morning to work again, for we had to clear the room for an entertainment, and at half-past ten to go off by the train to the little Point Church. It was beautiful. The new Bishop in his robes, with six of the Natal clergy after him, came up the centre of the little church, chanting the 24th Psalm. Then the prayers for the Consecration, so exquisitely beautiful; then his sermon. He began with Solomon's temple, wherein our churches differ from it, resemble it, and exceed it in glory; the duties of the worshippers because of their privileges; and then a most home-touching appeal to us all, as being ourselves temples consecrated to God. It was most earnest, and most profitable, and most sweet to listen to. Then came the Holy Communion. * * * Then home to our entertainment, which went off remarkably well. Then came speeches, and in the deep, earnest, loving words which fell from one after another, I was not the only one who was overcome. Strong men fairly cried, then and afterwards, as they spoke of the kind heart and loving deeds and earnest Christian life of him who was going from among them, and of the noble self-sacrificing spirit in which he goes forth. I cannot tell you all that passed: how he took blame to himself for some share in the troubles of past days, and begged those who heard him to tell his former opponents what he said, and how his friends repudiated the idea with horror, and declared that if all was to do again, they would again stand by him through thick and thin, and how the Bishop of Natal's health was proposed by one who is deeply indebted to him and most gratefully affectionate in his feelings to him, and at last how thankful I was to get away.

* * * * *

Next morning arrived the captain from P. M. B., and said if the mail did not come before two he would wait till Monday.

* * * * *

On Sunday off the first thing to Claremont riding. The ride was delightful. The whole road so full of associations. The river where I sat on my horse alone on the first night after my arrival, &c. The little church at Claremont was well filled. Seven were confirmed. The Bishop's address and sermon seemed to reach the children's hearts. The Litany seemed more full of meaning than I had ever heard it. Then the hymn, "Put thou thy trust in God," though chosen for the candidates, seemed every word to suit ourselves. * * * After church we rode to the Umlazi * * * and so back to town, just in time for the evening service. The Bishop preached again. He found a missionary sermon was expected. The church was crowded. He spoke most openly on the treatment of the natives here as a shame to the white people, only taking as much work out of them as possible, without caring for their interests in any way; no Church-school for them in the town; no sympathy with their home-joys or sorrows; hardly credit given them for having within them deeper thoughts and feelings, than they care to reveal to those who seem to have so little human sympathy with them. He said while this was the state of things among us here, to raise an interest in the tribes further off would be something unreal, and could lead to no good. Even before we left the church, as well as several times afterwards, people came to me to speak of the sermon, and say how it had smitten their consciences, and made them desire that the reproach should be upon them no longer. Indeed, we had a kind of meeting in our room after church, and I have good hope something may be done in the way of evening teaching for the people.

As we were returning we saw a rocket from the sea: a gun fired: the mail was in: and the captain, who was with us, said he would let us know the first thing in the morning what hour he would sail. Well, after this there was little peace or quiet. We were too tired to sit up that night, and next morning there was so much to arrange, and everybody was coming and going, and we heard we were to go by the half-past two train. A great many friends went with us; but on the shore we slipped away. * * * We went on board the tug, and stood together high up on the captain's place; we were washed again and again by the great waves. * * * When he went, and I had his last kiss and blessing, his own bright beautiful spirit infected mine, and I could return his parting words without flinching; I saw him go without even a tear dimming my eye, so that I could watch him to the last, looking after our little boat again crossing the bar, till we could distinguish each other no more.

In speaking one day of happiness, he said, "I have given up looking for that altogether. Now till death my post is one of unrest and care. To be the sharer of every one's sorrows, the comforter of every one's griefs, the strengthener of every one's weakness—to do this as much as in me lies is now my aim and object: for you know when the members suffer, the pain must always fly to the head." He said this with a smile, and O! the peace in his face! it seemed as if nothing *could* shake it.

The vessel which brought the mail for which the *Lyra* waited, brought also another missionary, the Rev. H. Rowley, who joined the Bishop's party. The plan now was to meet Dr Livingstone at the Kongone mouth of the Zambesi, pick up the first portion of the mission party, who had already gone forward in the *Sidon*, and then immediately proceed up the Zambesi and Shire in the *Pioneer* with Dr Livingstone.

The *Lyra* arrived off Kongone on February 7, and found that the *Sidon*, with the *Pioneer*, had arrived eight days previously. The *Pioneer* had gone in on Feb. 5, only two days before the Bishop's arrival. On Saturday, February 9, Captain Oldfield kindly took Bishop Mackenzie over the bar, in order that he might be no longer prevented from meeting Dr Livingstone and concerting future measures with him. The result of the consultation was rather disappointing; Dr Livingstone strongly dissuaded an immediate ascent of the Zambesi; the season was not favourable; there was no chief to whom he felt that he could at this time confidently commend the mission party, and he was very anxious to explore what he believed would be a better route to the future scene of the labours of the missionaries by way of the Rovuma, a river which enters the sea at a considerable distance north of Kongone. Bishop Mackenzie's position was one of much difficulty: he dreaded the thought of several months' further delay, and the possible forced idleness of a large portion of the mission party; on the other hand, it seemed impossible to insist upon a step opposed to the mature judgment of Dr Livingstone. The result was, that he consented to Dr Livingstone's plan, and the actual work of the mission was thus postponed. I will here introduce a letter from the Bishop to one of the secretaries of the mission, in which the position of affairs is explained.

LETTER LXXV.

MAYOTTA,
Feb. 27, *Wednesday.*

DEAR STRONG,

I have lately written, but as it is not unlikely that this letter may anticipate the last, I will tell you shortly what has happened since we left Natal. We sailed on Tuesday, July 29th, from Natal, having Rowley on board. We got to Kongone after a fair passage of nine days, and found the *Sidon* at anchor, having been there eight days; the *Pioneer* had crossed the bar on Feb. 5. On Saturday, Feb. 9, the *Pioneer* not having come out, as I thought she would, Captain Oldfield most kindly took me over the bar, when we fell in with not only Waller, Scudamore, Gamble, Adams, May and his party, but also Livingstone, Kirk, and Charles Livingstone. We had arranged to return to the ship on the Sunday morning, but again Captain Oldfield arranged his movements so as to suit me, and put off his return to his ship till Monday morning. This was rendered necessary by Livingstone's proposing a plan, which required some thought on my part. He proposed that instead of going up the Zambesi and Shire at once, to settle in such a place as he should advise, which was the plan we had all along considered our only one, we should postpone going up till he had explored the Rovuma, and ascertained whether or not it would give a better road to the district of the Shire and Nyassa than that afforded by the Zambesi. I objected to this proposal, that it would involve considerable and indefinite delay to us, and would transform us from a missionary body, ready to attempt at once to overcome the difficulties attending a settlement in a new country, into an exploring party, that we should be not only losing our time but embarrassing him by our presence, and that I did not see that our going up from Kongone and settling on the banks of the Shire was in any way opposed to his plan of exploring the Rovuma; for if he found a good entrance there, we could communicate with him in the interior. To meet my objection that we should be encumbering him, an objection that was not mine alone, he answered that the mass of our party might remain at some such place as Johanna, one of the Comoro Islands, which lie between the northern end of Madagascar and the continent, while I and perhaps another might go with him. I at once objected to this that we had had separations enough, as well as delays, and I thought this modification made the plan more distasteful to me than before. After speaking to Waller and Scudamore on the Sunday, and consulting Captain Oldfield, I determined to ask Livingstone to let us adhere to our plan, and to go with us, and see us settled, before he went to the Rovuma. Accordingly I wrote him my decision, not being able to see him before our early start to the ship on Monday morning (Feb. 11).

Next morning the *Pioneer* came out, and Livingstone begged me to reconsider my decision: he put more strongly than I expected the difficulties of doing as I proposed, repeating what he had written to England the previous May, that he did not know a single chief to whom he could commend us with confidence, now that Chibisa had gone; and besides, that before we could settle on any healthy spot, we must leave our goods on the low ground close to the Shire, and that the one who remained in charge, while we attempted to remove them gradually to a place of safety, would be sure to take the fever. In short, he spoke so strongly that I felt I had no right to force him to take part in a plan, of which he so distinctly disapproved; and yet my own objections to his plan were as great as ever. At last we agreed that we would do as he advised, with this proviso, that he should not keep us waiting more than three months, but would then, if not sooner, decide between our going up by Kongone or by the Rovuma. I further followed his advice by determining to go with him myself and take Rowley, but leave the rest at Johanna. I found that they all agreed to this as a disagreeable necessity, but in a way that left me no misgiving in adopting it. Johanna was chosen as being the head-quarters of the cruising squadron on this coast. It is a naval coaling station, and seemed the most suitable place both for present need and future contingencies.

Accordingly we again parted company: the *Pioneer*, taking May's and Livingstone's parties, proceeded direct to the Rovuma. The *Sidon* taking her old complement, excepting Waller, (that is to say, Scudamore, Gamble, Adams, Job, and Apollos,) was to convoy the *Pioneer* some part of the way, and then come on to Johanna, while the *Lyra* came away first to Johanna (with Rowley, Waller, Procter, Charles, Thomas, Roby, and myself) to coal, and then to meet the *Pioneer* at the Rovuma mouth, carrying to her five tons of coal, and handing over to her Rowley and myself, having previously deposited the rest of our party at Johanna. Waller had wisely brought out from Kongone on Tuesday morning all his detachment, and Livingstone his whole party; so that we were ready to be off. Accordingly that same afternoon we were all on our several routes. We fell in with the *Pioneer* two days after on the high seas, and were near enough to exchange visits by means of boats: also on the 16th, Saturday, we sighted them again. They had lost sight of the *Sidon* on the first night, and were making their way alone.

I ought to have said above, what will I think have been taken for granted, that during the discussion Livingstone continued as friendly and kind as possible, and was most willing to help in carrying out the plan we had thought of, if decided upon. He is an excellent fellow, and I have no fear of any difficulty at any time arising between us.

We reached Johanna on the morning of February 21.

*　　*　　*　　*　　*

The following letters will carry on the story:

LETTER LXXVI.

H. M. S. *Lyra*, OFF THE COAST, 50 MILES S. OF CAPE DELGADO,
March 4, *Monday*.

DEAR STRONG,

* * * * *

My last date was, I think, Feb. 22. On that evening news reached us confirming the report of the *Wasp* being on shore on the mainland, and also of the *Enchantress* having struck a reef off Mayotta, one of the Comoro Islands. Next morning, Feb. 23rd, we sailed for the spot and spent the next five days in saving goods from the wreck.

* * * * *

On Saturday morning, March 2, we left Johanna, passing for the fourth time safely through the passage between reefs, which is the only entrance to the harbour. * * * We are now (about one P.M., Monday, March 4) in sight of the *Wasp* and *Persian*, though not near enough to see what is being, or has been, done. Should the *Lyra* be obliged, as we have thought most probable, to remain and help here, the captain most kindly promises to send the 2nd lieutenant in the pinnace to take Rowley and myself to the Rovuma. If not, he will take us up in this ship. On parting from the *Pioneer* we said they might look for us about March 1. We may now hope to be not more than five days behind our time, notwithstanding the accumulation of obstacles that we did not foresee; and even this is of the less consequence, inasmuch as from the light winds we have had we do not think the *Pioneer* will be much, if at all, sooner than ourselves in reaching the rendezvous.

March 5, *Tuesday*.
At Anchor, Long. 40° 30′ E. Lat. 11° 10′ S.

We came to anchor yesterday, about one. Found the *Wasp* got off, though it is still a question what state she is in. As far as we are concerned our connection with her will cease to-night. We start for the Rovuma to-morrow morning. We expect to be out one night. (How little we think now of a voyage to last two days! It seems a mere step.) And then we quite hope to meet Livingstone. News of other kinds I have none. I am tired of saying I shall be glad to be at work.

* * * * *

LETTER LXXVII.

H. M. S. *Lyra, March 9th,* 1861,
Mouth of the Rovuma, Lat. 10° 30′.

DEAR STRONG,

I wrote to you by the Cape a letter which I sent on board the *Persian* three days ago. I was then on board this vessel, about 100 miles further south, in company with the *Persian* and the *Wasp*. We weighed anchor on the morning of the 6th, and rounded Cape Delgado and got into this bay, whose headlands are about ten miles apart—a shallow bay into which all the mouths of the Rovuma discharge themselves. We soon saw the *Pioneer* lying near the shore at anchor, and, steering for her, cast anchor some 300 or 400 yards from her. Dr Livingstone, Mr May, R.N., and Dr Kirk, were soon aboard of us. They had been here eleven days. They had gone up a narrow outlet to see to what it led, and returned, confirmed in the idea that the great mouth, in the jaws of which we are now at anchor, is *the one.* They spent a day on this also, and say that it is one mile broad between high water-mark on the two sides, and that in sounding they had no bottom at seventeen fathoms. There is no bar, only a rippling on the water at high tide. They went up about eight miles, and found themselves then at the entrance upon higher lands, about 300 feet high. This leads to the hope that vessels may easily anchor here, and that a very short time will suffice to carry a party through the delta, which is always found to be the most feverish place. They saw a good deal of cultivation. Many of the gardens of the natives near the river were flooded, the river being now about its highest. These natives spoke languages akin to those on the Zambesi, and, though much surprised, were not afraid. They had made up their minds to start up the river on Monday without us if we did not appear, and had already buried a bottle with this intelligence for us. They had suspended a large barrel, painted white, to a tree on the beach, to direct us to this simple *poste restante.* Now we propose to start on Monday about noon, the morning of that day being required for transferring coals and provisions to the *Pioneer*. They have been quite well, and were very glad to see us. Livingstone says they have been thinking that if this river looks well, they may, when a land exploring party leaves the ship, send her for the rest of our party to Johanna.

* * * * *

March 12, 1861, about 15 miles up the Rovuma.

It is more than I expected, being able to write to you by this opportunity from a point so far up the river. Capt. Oldfield determined to spend a day and a half, which have now grown into two days, in accompanying us part of the way up this river, and we shall send this away by him. Monday morning (yesterday) was spent by us in transferring some coals and provisions from the *Lyra* to the *Pioneer*, and finally, about one o'clock, we transhipped ourselves. I had formed some acquaintance with all on board the *Lyra*. Rowley also knew them all—I mean sailors as well as officers—and the cheer they gave us from the rigging, when our boat had pulled off from the ship's side, makes my heart leap to my mouth still by the mere remembrance.

We steamed up the right bank of the river, for two or three hours. The stream is about a mile wide, in many places five to six fathoms deep, in some one fathom and less; once we had to anchor, as we were in water less than a fathom deep, and we draw over four feet, and there did not seem to be any passage above. A boat went out to explore, and after some delay we retraced our course a little, and then got an opportunity of passing into another channel. It is interesting work watching this operation of seeking a channel, hearing the conversation between May, Livingstone, Charles Livingstone, and Kirk, or some of them, or getting an actual lesson when Livingstone shows us the signs of a bank, which we should not have seen. Last night we anchored in the full channel, stream running as usual two or three miles an hour. In the morning a boat pulled across the stream before the anchor was raised, to open or renew communications with the natives. I say "renew," because the *Pioneer's* boat had come up nearly as high a week ago, and had made friends, and begun a system of barter with one village. On landing we found it was not the same spot; one or two dark figures were just disappearing among the shrubs and trees. Dr Livingstone told one of the party (Joseph, who was engaged at Cape Town) to tell them not to run away, and the result of his shouting was that a man soon returned.

The language here is so much akin to that on the Lower Zambesi, that even Dr Livingstone holds a (somewhat broken) communication with them. The result of the interview was the purchase of some fowls and vegetables for cloth; a promise on the part of the native that he would tell all his neighbours that we are merciful and good Englishmen; and an attempt to express to him that we have come to teach the black people. We had not much time to spend, but were well satisfied with the result of our first interview with natives of the country. It is true this man is a stranger; the appearance of his garden corroborated his own account that he had not cultivated there long; still he will tell his neighbours, and so the effect of our visit will be the same.

The scenery is now becoming beautiful—hills two or

three hundred feet high within two or three miles of us, and the river winding majestically in its wide bed, sometimes washing the foot of the ridge that bounds the valley, on one side or the other; sometimes widening to a mile and a half, and forming islands, generally low and grassy, but occasionally of size and importance enough to carry trees with fresh and luxuriant foliage. The mangroves have all been left behind; now we have baobabs, flat-crowned palms, wild date, wild fig, &c. There has not as yet been either any tributary, or any stream branching off to form another mouth. It is clear this is the main mouth, though no doubt there are connections with other mouths near this one. In one or two places, within four miles of the sea, there were sluggish channels, fifty or sixty yards wide, leaving the stream and almost immediately escaping sight in the closer vegetation of that part. These might continue independent channels to the sea, or quite as likely might fine away altogether, or return shortly to the main stream.

So far as we can see, this river is answering the expectations formed of it. Of course we cannot tell what its upper part may be, but it is something to have got up fifteen miles (or at least twelve) with such ease. Good bye.

Yours affectionately,

C. F. M.

LETTER LXXVIII.

River Rovuma, 20 *miles from Sea,*
March 23, *Saturday.*

Dear Strong,

* * * * *

We ascended this river for five days. At first we had deep water, but very soon began to find it shoal. On the first day we had to stop (finding only one fathom), and cross to the other side. On the second, the navigation was in one or two places intricate. On the third, we had to return some distance, finding our channel fail us: so that we began to perceive that we should be compelled to return in a few days, instead of spending a couple of months, to secure our getting out before the fall of the water should make some of our difficulties become impossibilities, and so cut me off from a return to my party at Johanna, and indeed from any actual mission work. * * * It was by this time clear that we could not hope this season to explore far enough to give a favourable account of this river, *and* go to Johanna for our men. We were not 30 miles (probably about 25) from the sea, and could not be sure that before we had gone 20 miles further we should not find a cataract or something that would irremediably impede water-carriage. The natives indeed, on the whole, give a good account of it. They say that a canoe can come out of Lake Nyassa, where the Manganja live (they knew both these names before we suggested them), and reach the sea by the Rovuma: but no one of them has been far enough to quote his own experience on this point, nor have they seen any one who has; so that the matter is still in doubt. Besides, there is the important consideration that the steamer cannot go wherever a canoe can. We had no hesitation on this point, that the steamer must lose no time in reaching the sea, so that she may call at Johanna, and proceed up the Shire this year to place us where we may begin our work.

* * * * *

But *non facilis descensus Ovuma,* (the natives pronounce it as often without the R as with it;) the current, which would be of the greatest service if the channel were broad, makes it much more dangerous to thread the way down through shoals, than to go up over the same ground. We have already spent five days, and have not made good twice as many miles. We have spent two nights grounded on the sand, and have all had much hard work.

* * * * *

LETTER LXXIX.

(*To the same.*)

April 1, *Monday*.
Lat. 11° S. Long. 41° E.

WHEN I last wrote, I spoke of continuing to cut wood all that Saturday (March 23), and not lifting our anchor till the following Monday. However, about two P.M. it was decided that we should call all on board and start, a boat preceding us in doubtful places: partly by its aid, though more by the gain of a foot from the late rains, we ran down with less trouble than we had come up. Within a couple of hours we were in sight of the sea. * * * Thus ended a fortnight's voyage in the river.

The results of the exploration have not been great; chiefly this, that the hopes founded upon the appearance of the mouth have been to a considerable extent disappointed, while there is room left for hope as to the effect of trying a vessel drawing (say) two feet, and also the effect of the falling of the flood in deepening the channel when the river shall spread less unrestrainedly from bank to bank.

We proposed to spend two or three days in cutting wood, and preparing the vessel for sea, and hoped to get to Johanna in time to spend Easter-day (March 31) in reunion, and with Holy Communion with our friends there. But in this we have been disappointed. On the Monday or Tuesday I resigned myself into the doctor's hands, to be treated for fever: it was a very mild attack, certainly no worse than a slight influenza cold, and I was all right again in a day or two. Unfortunately, I was only the first of several, and before the engine was put into gear, after some parts had been repaired, an engineer was on his back; and in all, half the whites on board were attacked. It was clear that the sooner we could leave the coast the better. Accordingly, as soon as the engine could be connected, which was on Good-Friday morning, we were rejoiced to hear the order, "All hands, up anchor;" and we were soon out of sight of land.

* * * * *

The crew are beginning to return to work one after another: we have taken turns to supply their place at the wheel, and on the look-out. There has not been much else to be done.

* * * * *

As to the fever, they say that they think the Rovuma worse than the Zambesi. My experience would lead me to say that the cure is worse than the disease, but my attack was a slight one.

LETTER LXXX.

(*To the same.*)

April 18, *Thursday.*
JOHANNA.

THE day following that on which I last wrote, we reached, not Johanna, as we had wished, but another island of the group, Mohella. We cast anchor when the fuel remaining was not more than would have served to keep up the steam for one hour longer. We could not but feel a little anxious as we gradually neared the island: for had the coal failed before we could anchor, we should have been drifted back by wind and currents. We were detained for six days, merely getting enough wood and water to take us across to Johanna, which was now in full sight. At last, on April 8, we crossed, and found that though our friends had had severe attacks of fever, they were now all well, or with slight ailments.

* * * * *

Thus ended the expedition to the Rovuma. As it turned out, little advantage, or none, was gained for the missionary work; but I think it is clear that Bishop

Mackenzie could not have acted otherwise than he did, without exhibiting a confidence in his own opinion, when opposed to that of Dr Livingstone, which might have been justly described as not wise but headstrong.

It was in getting ready for sea, at the mouth of the Rovuma, that Bishop Mackenzie had his first attack of African fever; it will be seen from his mention of the attack, in the preceding page, that his illness was but slight, and that he was already tempted to think too little of the power of the disease; the strength of his constitution, and the readiness with which he rallied, tended perhaps to foster the notion more than he himself suspected, that the dangerous character of the fever had been exaggerated. To this underrating of the fever may to a certain extent be attributed the conduct, which afterwards, as we shall see, led to so lamentable a result.

In the Rovuma also, Bishop Mackenzie appears to have run a risk of his life, to which I find no allusion in his own letters; in a letter to a friend, Mr Charles Livingstone writes, "He worked very hard while we were in the river; and once, to our utter horror, gave a Rovuma alligator an opportunity (the like of which no alligator ever had before) of immortalising himself by devouring a live Bishop! Fortunately, the monster was not ambitious of such renown."

The next letter does not add to the narrative, but will be acceptable as a token of the gentle affectionate feelings of the writer. It is to a brother in Scotland.

LETTER LXXXI.

On Board the *Pioneer*,
Lat. 11° S. Long. 41° E.
April 1, Monday.

Dear ——

Every happiness and every blessing to you in the year that opens upon you on this day. I thought of you early this morning, before in fact it was your birthday to you at home. I was on watch on deck from one to half-past two this morning, as four of us agreed to relieve the crew for the night, many of them being down with fever. It is a dull day, and we have had rather a dreary week; but things are looking up, and we are now steaming rapidly (six or seven knots an hour) towards Johanna, where we hope to find our party in health and strength. It is this day three months since I was made a Bishop, and received mission to preach to the tribes of Nyassa and Shire; and since that time, I have been almost without interruption at sea. I do not think this has been my own fault; and even now Livingstone speaks of the advantage of our not having gone up to the Shire in February, when we were at Kongone. I am still of opinion that it would have been better if we had, but I do not think I could withstand the weight of advice that was pressed on me. Now, however, I trust that this month will not end before we are at the foot of the Murchison Cataract. It is very pleasant being on the easy terms we are with Livingstone; and as for Dr Kirk, we are the greatest possible cronies. He encouraged me to try my hand at botanizing, a thing which has been open to me any time as long as I can remember, but for which I never thought I had any turn; but now, with his help, I have settled the order to which each of some ten or twelve plants belong, of whose nature I had no notion to begin with. He is an excellent teacher.

There are a few things, which I have in constant use: your wrist-studs; the watch you gave me, which goes well;

the clock with alarum, which is at present acting as ship's clock; the writing-case I begged from —— in the *Cambrian;* the sextant —— gave me; ——'s Prayer-book; Mrs ——'s *Christian Year:* and, by the bye, as I may not be writing to Portmore immediately, please tell —— the cheese was not opened till we were in the Rovuma, and was found in excellent condition, thanks to your friend the tinman; indeed, Livingstone and all the party begged me to give their best thanks to the lady donor for a cheese, which had evidently not been made for sale. It was really very good; Englishmen allowed that Scotland could match them even in pasture produce, and we esteemed it so highly, that we laid by half till our whole party should be together: it will come out in the Zambesi.

* * * * *

I insert the following, because it contains one of the few confessions that (I believe) Bishop Mackenzie ever made of being overdone and out of spirits. It is to his sister in Scotland. It is amusing to observe the reason assigned for this confession of weakness.

LETTER LXXXII.

JOHANNA,
April 20, Saturday.

I HAVE been very well since I wrote last, excepting a fit of lowness and weakness from over-work a week ago. I had returned to this island a little below the mark, but thought a good walk would do me good. I arranged with Kirk that we should go together: we started at 7.30, instead of 5.30 or 6, as we were advised. The climb, 3000 feet, was very steep. I felt knocked-up, could hardly touch breakfast, and almost came back for fear I should break down. However, fortunately an hour's rest in the shade by a stream did me good. I went on, and got home tired. Next day I felt well, but the day after knocked-up; and my spirits gave way. I lay on the bed, or in an arm-chair, as weak as water for two days: but Kirk set me right, and now I am quite well. I tell you all this, because I wish you to believe me when I tell you that I have been quite well.

* * * * *

The delays which had been so wearisome to the missionary party were now at length at an end. The Rovuma had been tried, and for the present at all events had proved a failure; the missionaries were assembled at Johanna, and all was ready for a start towards the Zambesi. Speaking of the residence of himself and the rest of the party left at Johanna during the exploration of the Rovuma, Mr Waller says, "Our stay here would have been one of the utmost enjoyment, surrounded as we have been by extreme kindness on the part of the inhabitants, and benefiting by the unbounded hospitality and attention of Mr Sunley, the British Consul for the Comoro Islands. Unfortunately, however, we have suffered a good deal from fever, and I think but one out of the party of ten has escaped it." Speaking of the work in which they had employed themselves during their enforced residence at Johanna, he adds, "The Arabs of the islands are a most interesting set. They nearly all speak English a little, and were anxious beyond measure to learn it; kings, lords, and commons were our pupils; and right sorry we were to leave them. They are not at all disposed to quarrel on points of religion: on the contrary, nothing interested them more than comparing our stories of the Old

Testament with their Koran. Of course, when it came to the main points of our faith, the same disbelief which makes Mahometanism so antagonistic to our religion was present. One of the young princes has become a staunch Christian; and report says, the Sultan himself is mainly anxious to know English thoroughly, that he may read the Bible. He says it is 'more better' than the 'other book,' meaning the Koran. Still reading it for its poetry and searching it for its faith are two different things. Yet with a people so eminently susceptible of the power of language, and really religiously inclined, I cannot help thinking very much might be done. I mentioned the subject of a missionary to several of them. Nothing would delight them more than to have some one who would teach them English, and the king promises a piece of land and his personal aid to any one who would come out for this purpose; but, as a good Mahomedan, he cannot ask point blank for a missionary. Still, any energetic man would find here that the thin end of the wedge is inserted, and he would stand a better chance of causing a rift in this wretched infatuation than others less fortunate in finding a people disposed most favourably to everything English."

On the last day of April the *Pioneer* was off Kongone; the bar was too rough to permit the vessel to cross; on the morning of May 1, the passage was effected without difficulty, and on that day the Bishop reported his party "all well;" though he adds, that in the course of the voyage about half of those on board had been down with attacks of fever.

It is unnecessary to dwell upon the arrangements for ascending the river. We will suppose these to have been made, and will allow Bishop Mackenzie to tell his own story.

LETTER LXXXIII.

(To his Sister at the Cape.)

May 8, *Wednesday.*

DEAR ——,

*   *   *   *   *

We are now steaming up through the delta, without a single case of sickness on board.

This is a fine river; and we have this advantage over the Rovuma, that Livingstone knows the river, and we never stick as we did there.

*   *   *   *   *

The responsibility and difficulty of the work seem to increase as it comes nearer. I have been reading Moffat's missionary labours, and it has made me think more of the difficulties, not only of a practical outward kind, but still more of a spiritual kind. It has helped me also to remember that in God is our help, and that we attempt nothing in our own name.

Livingstone is most kind and excellent. He promises to make a tour with us, as soon as we leave the ship, to look out for a site. We hope to reach the Murchison Cataract in about seventeen days, that is, about Trinity Sunday. Then a party of us, perhaps all of *us*, with Livingstone Kirk and others, will start to look at the country between the Shire and Shirwa: high table land, south of the top of Zomba, where Livingstone thinks we shall find a suitable spot. After that, he proposes to take a boat up the side of the river, for thirty-three miles, and putting it on the water again spend four or five months exploring Nyassa, especially with the view of finding how near the Rovuma comes to the lake, or whether it actually runs out of Nyassa, which I do not believe. He will be back in time to take the *Pioneer* down to meet you on December 15. You may on getting this think of us as heard of as high as Mazaro, where it will leave my hands. God bless you.

Notice in the next two letters the unfortunately slight opinion, which Bishop Mackenzie had already been led to form of the dangerous character of African fever.

LETTER LXXXIV.

(*To a Sister.*)

River Shire,
May 16, Wednesday.

* * * * *

We are lying moored to the bank of the river, about three miles above its confluence with the Zambesi. Half our river voyage is thus finished. We are all in fine health; I myself in perfect health. We think very little of fever; but take fifteen or twenty grains of the mixture of calomel, quinine, &c., which Livingstone has found efficacious, lie by for a day or so, and then get up, a little weakened. In about a couple of days we are entirely set up: during these there is a great tendency to lassitude, which hangs about and retards recovery, unless an effort be made to throw it off.

* * * * *

We expect to settle somewhere on the high plateau between the Shire and Shirwa, which ends northwards in the high mountain Zomba. Our settlement will very likely be about thirty miles from where we disembark. Of course, *cœteris paribus*, the nearer the river we are the better: but we must choose our site partly with a view to health, and the heights are less feverish than the low valley of the Shire, and still more with a view to our work, for which a friendly chief will be a great help. However, we shall see in the course of our first month, that is, I hope, before the end of June, where we can best locate ourselves. Then getting to know the people, putting up buildings, beginning a garden and a field beyond it, bringing a stream of water to the house, these will fully occupy us till about Nov. 15, when the *Pioneer* will go down to the mouth for our ladies. We shall all rejoice very much to see them again.

* * * * *

LETTER LXXXV.

(*To a Sister.*)

May 25, *Tuesday.*

* * * * *

I amused Livingstone the other day by saying I knew that his engine burnt wood in the river, but had never reckoned the time required for cutting it. They cut down dead trees, and then have to saw them into lengths of about four feet for the furnaces, and split the thicker blocks. This often takes two days at a place, furnishing a supply for about as long. This time we also spent two days and nights aground. This was a serious matter, as the water was not rising, but gradually falling. With some difficulty we got off: it was not exactly mission-work, but was a necessary antecedent to it.

I have had another specimen of the fever since we anchored here, but it seems slighter and slighter every time: it came on Saturday morning without interfering with my breakfast, except by making it lighter than usual, and on the next day I was able to take part in the service. It would be worth some people's while to come out here, to get so easily through a fever.

* * * * *

The reader will conclude from these letters that the ascent of the Shire in the *Pioneer* was a very wearisome and laborious matter; in addition to the difficulties arising from the necessity of cutting wood for fuel, there were others arising from the numerous sand-banks, and the imperfect knowledge of the river possessed by those who were navigating it. One source of trouble was inherent in the *Pioneer* herself; she drew too much water; and occasionally a slight deviation from the channel would throw her upon a bank, upon which she would remain fixed for hours or even days. These difficulties brought out the finest parts of the Bishop's character; he was ready for all emergencies, and would help to cut wood, or assist in pushing off the boat, with as much vigour and earnestness as he could possibly exhibit in his own more peculiar duties. I do not wonder that he should have made a deep impression upon Dr Livingstone, who, in several of his letters, speaks in the highest terms of his character and his fitness for the work.

In a letter which I shall give presently, Bishop Mackenzie writes under date June 1, "We are not more than twenty miles from the end of our river voyage:" but in the letter which will next come before the reader, under date June 16, the party are still in the river Shire. This will give some notion of the extremely tedious character of the voyage. I do not wish that it should be equally tedious to the reader, but I cannot refrain from inserting the following letter, which is addressed to the Cambridge friend to whom was written Letter XLVIII.; the letter, to a certain extent, repeats what the reader already knows, but it contains also some expressions of warm brotherly feeling, which, under the circumstances of his own labours and anxieties, are very noticeable, and which I think the reader would be sorry to lose.

LETTER LXXXVI.

(*To a Friend in Cambridge.*)

RIVER SHIRE,
Sunday, June 16, 1861.

MY DEAR ——,

You will hear probably from others what tedious delays have arisen in our going up to the place of our work.

On Feb. 7 we anchored off the mouth of this river, and there met Livingstone, who persuaded us to delay our going up, till he had tried to ascertain the feasibility of a road by the Rovuma.

March 1 found us at Johanna, one of the Comoro Islands, delayed in reaching the Rovuma by disasters which befell two of H. M. ships.

April 1 found us returning from the Rovuma, which had encouraged us at first to believe that it might be an open way to the inland country, but from which we were glad to escape before the falling of the water should make this impossible. On April 2 we were near the Comoro Islands again, where we had to pick up those of our party whom we had left there, not to encumber the vessel in the exploration of the Rovuma.

May 1 found us crossing the bar of the Zambesi, and the month and a half since have been spent in labouring up the Zambesi and Shire. We are now constantly going aground from the narrow and winding channel, which alone is deep enough to float us; and a *stick* generally costs us three days' hard work, to be followed probably by a few hours' motion, in which we proceed a few miles. This is the more distressing, as I have written to Cape Town for our party left there to come to the Kongone and meet Livingstone and myself on December 15; and we have much to do, before we can call ourselves ready for them.

On the other hand, there is the all-comforting assurance that the work is not our own, but God's: that we did not seek it for ourselves, but were sent: that we have the prayers of those at home, and those in South Africa, for our preservation: and that if only we love God, all things will turn out for our good. I cannot but be most thankful for the spirit which God has given to all my fellow-workers, lay as well as clerical, of patient waiting on God: "Blessed is the man that trusteth in the Lord, and whose hope the Lord is: for he shall be as a tree planted by the waters, and that spreadeth out her roots by the river, and shall not see when heat cometh, but her leaf shall be green; and shall not be careful in the year of drought, neither shall cease from yielding fruit." Jer. xvii. 7, 8.

And all this time we have no news from home. The last letters we got were those that left England by last December mail: we cannot expect to get others till August or September next, or perhaps the end of the year. I am anxious to hear news that may affect the Mission, whether all those who purposed to come are still in the same mind, and other such like things. Perhaps I shall hear from you. You remember how I urged you to get into practical parochial work: I still think this more wholesome for you than College life. It will bring you into contact with those who feel the need of religion, and when the great fundamental truths are not merely propositions to which you assent, nor only the foundations of your own life and hope, but when you have fed others too, encouraged the timid, warned the over-confident, instructed the young, you will find other points take their subordinate place firmly and distinctly. You have qualities of intelligence and gentleness, which would enable you for this work. God bless you, my dear fellow. Write to me.

Yours affectionately,
C. F. M.

One more letter will carry us to the end of this tiresome river expedition. It is written to a sister in Scotland.

LETTER LXXXVII.

SHIRE,
June 1, 1861.

DEAR ——

* * * * *

We are now not more than twenty miles from the end of our river voyage at Chibisa's. It is just a month since we crossed the bar. We have come up much more slowly than we expected. This has been a week of misfortunes. We have not made more than ten miles since Sunday, and this is Saturday noon. The fact is, we have been aground about as many hours as we have been afloat, and the last stick has been one of the most troublesome we have had since I first came on board. She was aground midships, both bow and stern being almost or quite afloat. Accordingly, when we laid out an anchor from her bow she swung round that way, and when we laid out an anchor from the stern she just swung back, turning on her middle as on a pivot, but not coming off. It has been hard work. My hands are sore and cramped with hauling cables and handling chains and anchors. They say this vessel must never come up this river again, and they will be thankful if she ever gets down.

* * * * *

We are proposing now, that as soon as may be after reaching Chibisa's we should all (except Rowley and Gamble) go with Livingstone to choose a site, and that Waller alone should return to the ship and make successive journeys to bring up goods, while we remain on the spot, and begin our work. Rowley and Gamble will stay to get up a shed on the bank of the river for the reception of goods.

June 13. Well here we are, not having made more than 6 or 7 miles in the last three weeks. We have had serious fears that this vessel might be unable to reach Chibisa's. But yesterday we got out of a difficulty we had been in for two nights, and we are to-day steaming up with more hope.

* * * * *

You know I am of a sanguine temperament, and always believe that things will go well. Some of our party are not quite so much so: and even I foresee the probability of our being in some difficulties often. I was glad therefore to read the other day S. Paul's words, "perplexed but not in despair," and I mean to steep my mind in them in preparation. Besides, our Lord's promise is for us too, "It shall be given you in that same hour what ye shall say and do;" and those other words we may claim, I think, even more than clergymen at home, "Lo, I am with you always, even to the end of the world."

July 6. Since I last wrote, we have passed the great chief of the district, *Rondo*, and have got his consent to our going up and settling in the hills; which is well, though his consent is obtained more as a matter of form than anything else: he has little real power with the subordinate chiefs.

We are now within half a mile of Chibisa's, the place where the steamer anchored last year (but one), and where the vessel will lie this year.

At length then the *Pioneer* has arrived at her anchorage, and the missionaries at the end of their wanderings upon the water. The reader will observe that I have told the story of the voyage from the Cape of Good Hope very briefly, or rather have allowed Bishop Mackenzie himself to do so; the materials are in my hands from which the account might have been made much more full, and perhaps in one sense more interesting; but I have endeavoured to bear in mind that my business is not to write a history of the Universities' Mission to Central Africa, but a memoir of Bishop Mackenzie, and that this will be done most effectively by confining myself to a narrative of which his thoughts and doings shall be the principal or almost sole constituent. Moreover, much might have been said concerning the incidents of adventure on the way, concerning the inconveniences and hardships suffered, and concerning many other matters; but I think that a narrative, which passes by all these things, does in reality give the truest and most faithful picture of Bishop Mackenzie. I notice in all his communications a desire to be at his work, a tendency to pass by all other considerations as of little value compared with the great end of settling his party and commencing missionary operations: and so I think that the view of the voyage from the Cape to Chibisa's, which the reader will have gathered from this chapter, will be a faithful view of that voyage as it presented itself to Bishop Mackenzie's own mind.

It may however be interesting to remark, that even in this voyage his old love for mathematical investigation did not desert him. I have before me a memoir of considerable ingenuity on the *Method of Least Squares;* it is dated March 7, 1861; probably it was the last mathematical paper he ever wrote, and doubtless it served as an amusement in some weary hour. The mathematical reader will appreciate the taste and ability which could find pastime in so difficult a field of investigation; the ordinary reader may be satisfied with being informed, that the subject of the memoir in question belongs to the highest and most refined region of mathematical science. Mr Scudamore was also a mathematician, though his place in the Cambridge Tripos was not so distinguished as that gained by the Bishop, and frequently a mathematical discussion (so delightful to the initiated, though so dry and unintelligible to the rest of the world) formed a pleasant recreation for both.

Perhaps also I ought to observe, before concluding my account of the long voyage from the Cape, that the pressing anxiety of his own work did not prevent Bishop Mackenzie from taking a lively interest in the welfare of those with whom he was brought in contact. From Mohella, he wrote a long letter concerning the inhabitants of the Comoro Islands, especially those of Mohella[1]. It seems that the people of this island have a great dread of French influence, and a great desire to receive an English consul; they opened their hearts to the Bishop and Dr Livingstone, who spoke many kind words to them, but were able to do little more. "If I had not other work on hand," wrote Bishop Mackenzie, "I could find in my heart to settle here."

[1] The letter was published at length in the *Guardian* newspaper of Nov. 20, 1861.

The letter from Mohella, to which I have just referred, was accompanied by the following. It was written to one, for whom he had a very great regard, and exhibits that earnestness of devotion to his work, coupled with a playfulness of expression, and at the same time a depth of tender and affectionate feeling, which were increasingly characteristic of Mackenzie as his life advanced.

LETTER LXXXVIII.

Pioneer, April 5, 1861.
MOHELLA, ONE OF THE COMORO ISLANDS.

* * * * *

It is one of the pains attending this kind of work that our efforts seem to be partly wasted. We are gathering out the stones, while others are ploughing; but this preliminary state must be gone through. It is just six months since I left England, and I have not yet seen my work, nor do I expect to be on the ground for another month. Well, it is not wasted: it is the road to our work.

I am glad to say that the prospect of our expenses is not great. There seems every prospect of our being able to grow our own wheat; vegetables are common; and there is no reason why we should not have flocks and herds. This will take a year or two, or more likely three: but at the end of three years I hope to be, to a considerable extent, independent of such supplies. Materials for clothing will always come from England. The shoes and boots we brought are first-rate: the trousers have not stood the work (in my case it has been, and always will be, heavy) so well as I hoped. Our ordinary costume is simply flannel-shirt, trousers, shoes and socks: so there is no complication when things go to the wash. We have few wants, and no cares, except when we thought it possible that this vessel might not get out of the Rovuma, in which case we should not have got up the Shire for many months, or that we might be out at sea without water or fuel in this vessel, which does not *sail* well, having no keel. With these (*little*[1]) exceptions,—I wrote the word *little* in joke, and strike it out in earnest,—which made us pray at the time and be thankful afterwards, we have had no cares. And if we shall not soon, perhaps in some cases never, meet our old friends on earth, we have a sure and certain hope of a better meeting. It is pleasant to look forward to the one: it is Life and Joy to be sure of the other.

God bless you all.

Your affectionate brother in Christ,

C. F. M.

We must now return to the Shire. We left the *Pioneer* at her anchorage. The missionaries, it will not be doubted, lost as little time as possible in making preparations for their journey in search of a settlement. We will suppose these preparations to have been made, and the missionary party landed on the left bank of the Shire. The commencement of the journey shall be given in the words of Letter LXXXVII., which continues as follows.

LETTER LXXXVII. (*continuation*).

CHIBABA'S VILLAGE,
July 20, 1861.

I am now writing on a Saturday morning. Last Monday we left the vessel, and took to our feet. It is a beautiful country this, as fine as Natal.

You would like to see our picturesque appearance on march. From 50 to 100 we have been at different times this week. Livingstone in his jacket and trousers of blue

[1] In the original the pen has been drawn through the word.

serge and his blue cloth cap. His brother, a taller man, in something of the same dress. I with trousers of Oxford grey and a coat like a shooting-coat, a broad-brimmed wide-awake with white cover, which Livingstone laughs at, but which, all the same, keeps the sun off. *He* is a Salamander. Then some thirty natives carrying bundles. My large red carpet-bag, loosely packed, contains my kit, including two blankets and a rug for bedding: (I sleep on a cork bed, weighing 7 lbs., an excellent invention). A sack contains the pots and pans, betrayed by a handle sticking out through some hole. Livingstone's black people, many of them with guns; Mobita, who acts as lieutenant, and Charlie, who is interpreter. All these winding along the narrow path, sometimes admiring the glorious hills, Chiradzula which we left behind yesterday, Zomba with its flat top, or the distant peaks and precipices of the Milanje mountains on our right, beyond Shirwa. We have not seen its blue waters yet: we are about 1000 feet above it, on a plateau, but there must be many rising grounds on this plateau from which the lake will be visible.

* * * * *

We are later this morning than usual in making a start. We generally get two or three hours' walk before breakfast; but yesterday on getting here it was discovered that one basket was missing. One of Livingstone's people went back alone, without giving notice, to look for it, and has not yet returned, and, in the present state of the country, Livingstone is anxious about him. I hear this moment that the man has returned, but four others who went to look for him are still out. I suppose we shall be off immediately. Good bye, then, for the present.

The missionary party are now finally on African soil, and on their way to choose a settlement. The important events connected with this choice shall be reserved for another chapter.

CHAPTER XI.

SETTLEMENT AT MAGOMERO.

WE now come to the most eventful portion of Bishop Mackenzie's life.

The *Pioneer* cast anchor at a point of the river Shire, marked in the map as *Chibisa's*, on July 8. It is the spot at which Dr Livingstone left the *Ma Robert* on his former trips to Shirwa and Nyassa. Bishop Mackenzie says of it, "it is a beautiful place, on the right bank of the river: from the ship you can see the smoke and tops of the huts of the village, still called Chibisa's, though that chief has returned to his former place near Tette."

Some time was taken up in landing baggage and stowing it in a tent, which was erected for the purpose on an island between the ship and the eastern or left bank of the river; and when all necessary arrangements had been made, the party started on a land expedition, with Dr Livingstone at their head, and a train of bearers, as we have seen in the preceding chapter. The design was to find some healthy situation on the high ground, where the party might form a settlement, under the protection and patronage of some friendly chief. The people inhabiting the district in which the mis-

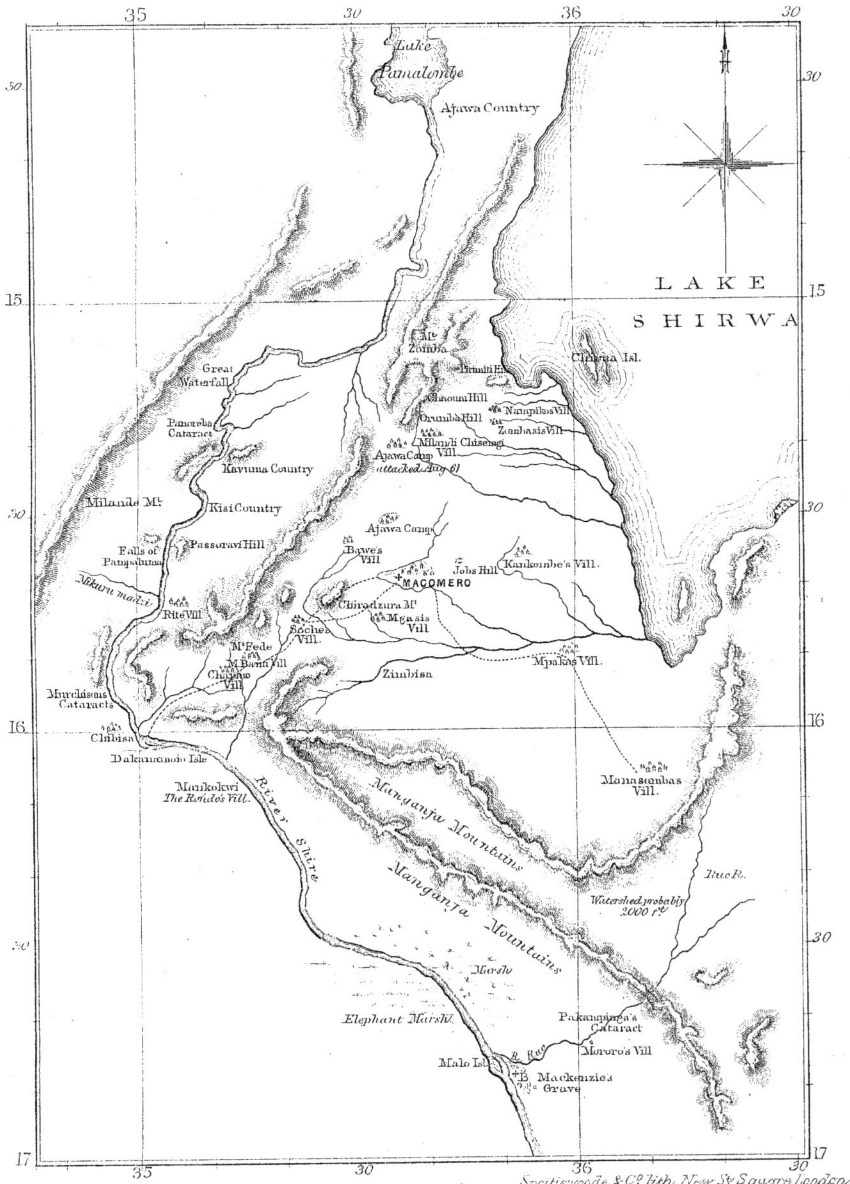

35
30
36
30
Lake Pamalombe
Ajawa Country
LAKE SHIRWA
15
16
17
Mt Zomba
Great Waterfall
Cataract
Kavuma Country
Milanje Mt
Kisi Country
Passoravi Hill
Falls of
Rite Vill
Murchison's Cataracts
Chibisa
Manikokwi
The Rondo's Vill.
River Shire
Manganja Mountains
Manganja Mountains
Marsh
Elephant Marsh
Malo Isl
R. Ruo
Mackenzie's Grave
Cataract
Mororo's Vill
Watershed probably 2000 ft
Ruo R.
Mpaka's Vill.
Zimbisa
MACOMERO
Jobs Hill
Kankombe's Vill.
Ajawa Camp
Bawe's Vill
Chiradzura Mt
Mgasis Vill
Soche's Vill.
Mt Fede
Ajawa Camp attacked Aug 61
Orumba Hill
Chaoum Hill
Nampilos Vill
Zonbasis Vill
Spottiswoode & Co lith. New St Square London.

sionaries now found themselves are known as Mang-anja; they appear to be not a very powerful race, at all events they are inferior in strength and courage to another tribe, or set of tribes, who occupy the neighbouring country, and who are known as the Ajawa. It is a slave-hunting, slave-dealing district, and is full of the evils which belong to that vile traffic. The Mang-anja, as the weaker folk, are the greater sufferers; they are not themselves by any means guiltless, and though they feel the inconvenience of living near to a people fiercer and stronger than themselves, they are full of the brutality of savage life, and have undoubtedly been engaged in the traffic from which they themselves suffer so severely. It was amongst these Mang-anja, that the missionary party intended, by Dr Livingstone's advice, to settle themselves, and that they did actually settle.

Just before starting on their expedition, a little circumstance brought before the eyes of the missionaries the first view of difficulties in which they might possibly be involved. Four men came down to Chibisa's to represent that the Ajawa were making war upon the Mang-anja people, and to seek assistance. This brought the question of the attitude which the missionaries should assume with regard to the slave-trade very close home. "The question," says Bishop Mackenzie in a letter to the Bishop of Oxford, "had been raised before, whether it would be right to use guns in self-defense, if by any possibility our own people should attack us. And we were nearly unanimous in thinking that we had better let matters go to any extremities, even to the loss of our own lives, than take the life of one of those for whose conversion we had come. We agreed that anything short of taking life was allowable in self-defense." The question, which was raised by the request for assistance against the oppression of the Ajawa, was however manifestly different from that which the missionaries had discussed. They had agreed that they would not hold by force their position amongst the tribes whom they came to teach and evangelize; but what should they do in case of being asked to assist tribes who received them gladly, supposing there should be such, in repelling aggression from neighbouring hostile tribes? It would not follow that because they ought not to defend themselves in a warlike manner against their own flock, therefore they ought not to help the weak against the strong, and prevent their mission work amongst friendly people from being stopped by the interference of mischievous and depraved neighbours. Bishop Mackenzie at once saw that questions might possibly arise, which would require his most anxious and prayerful consideration. For the present, he was content to leave such questions unanswered. He says in the letter just above referred to, "I thought I should be guided to a right course, if the emergency should occur, which did not seem very likely; and praying for such guidance, I went on without coming to a decision on the point."

I have given this account of what passed through Bishop Mackenzie's mind, when the first appearance of the possibility of a conflict with the Ajawa tribes presented itself, in order that we may fully understand that the policy of the missionary party was essentially pacific, and that we may be prepared to believe that nothing but overwhelming necessity (in the Bishop's judgment) could have induced him to adopt a policy of an opposite kind.

The foundation of this pacific policy was destroyed, (as we shall see), before the entire responsibility of the conduct of the party devolved upon the Bishop. It may perhaps be questioned, whether, under any circumstances, a thoroughly pacific course would have been understood and appreciated by men situated as the Mang-anja people were; I mean, whether they would have been able to comprehend the conduct of men who professed their desire to teach a more excellent way than the slave traffic, and yet sat with their guns by their sides while the Ajawa were hunting them down and selling them for slaves; but anyhow, such a course of conduct to be effective and impressive must be severely consistent; it must begin with non-intervention, and end with non-intervention; as soon as the first blow has been struck for the purpose of regenerating the country by physical force, the pacific policy can hardly fail to be mistaken for indifference or cowardice.

In saying this, I intend to cast no blame upon the conduct of Dr Livingstone, which will be related presently; that he acted with the best intention no one will doubt, and I think that it would be a bold thing to say that his conduct was not wise and justifiable; I only desire that it should be thoroughly understood to what extent that conduct committed the Bishop and his party, and that in any judgment which may be formed of his subsequent dealings with the natives due weight may be given to the first step, for which he was in fact not responsible.

Of course it may be said, that in a country in which the slave-trade is rampant, and the more powerful are preying upon the weaker and hunting them down for slaves, there is no proper missionary field: it may be said that the true Christian policy, however difficult it may be to practise, is to wait patiently until either the progress of civilization and the entrance of lawful commerce, or the undisputed possession of the more powerful tribes, have taken away from the list of missionary difficulties those which arise from the minds of the people being disturbed by the constant presence of war: and a very good argument may be based upon these premisses against interfering in any manner with the intestine troubles of savage tribes. But the reader ought to bear in mind that however good such a line of argument may be, it was not open to Bishop Mackenzie. It was not open to him to consider whether the tribes on the banks of the Shire were in a fit state for missions: he was sent as a missionary to them after the circumstances of the case had been weighed, and an opinion in favour of a mission had been formed: he could not retreat without changing the character of the mission or giving it up altogether; and therefore he had to determine what course of conduct he should pursue, when he found himself in friendly communication with tribes, whom the neighbouring Ajawa were willing to oppress, and persecute, and sell into slavery.

Having made these preliminary observations, I will now continue the narrative; and I cannot do so in any better way than by quoting the Bishop's own account, as contained in the letter to the Bishop of Oxford, from which I have already made an extract.

LETTER LXXXIX.

* * * * *

It was on Monday last, July 15, that we left the ship. We had been in some anxiety how we should get our things carried up. You know that there is no four-footed beast here larger than a goat; so luggage must be carried by men. We were thankful to find on the Monday morning that we had fifteen bearers, in addition to the six coloured men from the ship, whom Livingstone had most kindly assigned to us. We were prepared to start if we could get ten men to carry. How rich we were now with twice as many! and before the end of the day we had twenty-seven.

We were a strange party. Livingstone tramping along with a steady heavy tread, which kept one in mind that he had walked across Africa. * * * We were all loaded. I had myself in my left-hand a loaded gun, in my right the crozier which they gave me at Cape Town, in front a can of oil, and behind a bag of seeds, (together weighing about twenty-five pounds,) which I carried the greater part of the day. I thought of the contrast between my weapon and my staff, the one like Jacob, the other like Abraham, who armed his trained servants to rescue Lot. I thought also of the seed which we must sow in the hearts of the people, and of the oil of the Spirit that must strengthen us in all we do.

We got to that day's end most of us stiff and tired, and found that the last three miles had not only been more than was intended, but being off the road had not shortened our march. The people of the village refused to sell anything. For ourselves we had biscuit and salt beef to eat with our tea and coffee, but the people that were with us had eaten nothing since morning, and many of our bearers had probably fasted all day. We followed Livingstone's example, giving the party a piece of cloth, that they might try their success in bartering, and that if they failed they might at least not blame us, and might console themselves by a division of the stuff. It was but two yards of calico among twenty-one persons.

In the morning on calling our bearers it seemed that five had gone off to try and buy meal at a neighbouring village. We took a cup of coffee, but were to breakfast at the next village. The sun was up, and Livingstone was anxious not to detain the whole party (in all forty-seven); so Procter remained with me to bring up the rear. We sat on one of the packages in the middle of that heathen village, and read the Psalms for the day, chanting the doxologies; partly because we are both fond of music, partly that the people might become aware of our occupation, as they doubtless would from one of our Christian blacks who stayed with us. At last the men appeared, and we started. We knew the general direction, and at every place where the path branched one of the leaders of the party made a scrape with his shoe across the path which we were to avoid, or laid a fresh twig across to mark it. We got to the village of Mambame about an hour after the others, and learned that by going out of the way the previous day, we had this morning reached this village by a much easier path than that which Livingstone already knew, a discovery of far more importance for the future than simply for the ease of that morning's walk. With what appetites we sat down to breakfast about eleven, you may imagine.

But now comes the important part of my story. Livingstone being not quite well, and this village being large, and the head man, Mambame, friendly, it was decided to stay for the day. I went down to the stream with Procter and Scudamore to bathe. We heard a sound of penny trumpets, and thought Livingstone had been giving away presents:

when shortly Dr Kirk came and told us that a party of six men with muskets had come flourishing into the village, with a train of eighty-four slaves; that the men had run away and the slaves were free; that our guns had all been out, though the conscience-stricken wretches had needed no firing to hasten their flight. There had been five or ten minutes' notice of their approach, so that Livingstone had time deliberately to take his course,—a course which no one can blame; but surely all will join in blessing God that we have such a fellow-countryman.

When I came up from the stream I found the whole party that had been freed sitting in groups round fires, which they had lighted and were feeding with the sticks which had been fastened round the necks of some to reduce them to obedience. There was a preponderance of children; not many men. In answer to Livingstone's inquiries, they said they had been brought from Zomba, that is, near the place where we thought of settling ourselves. One little boy looked up at Livingstone and said, "They starved us: and you tell us to cook food for ourselves: where do you come from?"

It seems that Mambame gave Livingstone notice that a large slave-party was coming, and would reach his village that day. * * * The party arrived. Livingstone at once recognized amongst the drivers a slaver whom he had known at Tette. He took him by the wrist and said, "What are you doing here, killing people? I shall kill you to-day." The man (Keturah) answered, "I do not kill; I am not making war; I bought these people." Livingstone then inquired of the slaves. Two men said, "We were bought:" six said, "We were captured:" and several of the women said, "Our husbands and relatives were killed, and here we are." By this time some of Livingstone's people, (Makololo and others,) had begun to plunder the party and tear the clothing from the backs of the drivers. Keturah said, "May I have my gun again?" Livingstone said,

"Yes, if I am satisfied about you:" he then added, "We will free these people," and began himself to cut their bonds and loose them. They were tied together as usual in gangs of two or three or five or six, by strong cords fastened to a cord round the neck, so that they can walk in Indian file along the path. Livingstone then explained to the late captives that they were free, that those who liked might go on to Tette, and those who liked might return home, or stay for the present under the protection of the English. Of course all stayed. All this time they were expressing gratitude and respect in the native fashion, by a slow clapping of the hands. Livingstone told them to cook and eat, but they said, "These things have taken us by surprise; we will eat presently." Some of the captives told us, that two women who had been trying to escape had been shot as an example, and that an infant who was too heavy to be carried by its mother, along with the burden assigned to her, had its brains dashed out before her eyes to solve the difficulty. There is something awful in being brought so near to the cruelties of which we have heard so much.

The following day we proceeded and kept a look out as we walked, having heard that another party of slaves was a-head on its way to the Shire (that is, coming to meet us). About an hour after we started we found six captives, three women and three boys. The captors ran away and left them in our hands.

* * * * *

Yesterday we had a long march. We split our body in order to follow two paths, and on arriving at night at Mangazi, we found that Waller and Charles Livingstone had surprised two Tette men, with four guns and six captives. The captives were free, the captors were bound. This made our number ninety-eight. The villains made their escape during the night, though guarded by five trusty men.

To-day we came on to this place, known as Chibaba's, though Chibaba has died since Livingstone was here two years ago. We learn here that the Ajawa are near us, perhaps five or ten miles from this, in what the people here call considerable force, that yesterday they attacked and burned a village near this, and made captives, and that yesterday calico went up to them from men of Tette in our rear to buy captives.

The Ajawa live on the south-west of Shirwa, about 100 miles from this, but Livingstone heard when he was here before that they come over here to fight, and it seems that a few of them have settled in villages on this side of Shirwa. * * * * I ought to have said, that whereas our plan was to come up here to Chibaba's, where we are, and to Chinsunzi, who is the next chief in the neighbourhood, and with Livingstone's advice select a site near to some largish village, it was suggested when these eighty-four captives were rescued that we should plant ourselves in some convenient place with these people to begin with. Accordingly it is now under consideration where we shall settle. In the meantime we have left our ninety freed people at Soche's, under the care of Procter and Scudamore.

July 20. This morning some light was thrown upon the question of our future settlement, by the chief of this village (Chigunda) asking how long Livingstone would stay in this country. He answered that he himself would go this month, but that some would stay altogether with our freed people. Chigunda said, "Will they not stay here? All the chiefs around have fled before the Ajawa; Chinsunzi has hid himself for fear. I only remain; and I will not run away, if the English will stay with me." Livingstone said, "But there are so many people, and there may be more: and they will want gardens." Chigunda said, "There is plenty of room for them here." It was only last night that I determined to ask this man if he would like us to be near him with our freed people, and to be guided partly by his answer. The objections to this place are, that it is nearly twice as far from the ship as the plain we selected on our way up, and does not seem so fertile and beautiful, or to have such facilities for water-power: but we have not seen enough of either to make a fair comparison.

I ought to say a word about the principle of using force, and even firing, if necessary, upon the captors of these poor creatures, in order to free them. The objection lay chiefly in this, that having been sent out to this country to bring blessing and peace to the people, I could not reconcile it to myself to kill them even in self-defense: and I still think that if by any possibility the people of this land should attack us, to drive us away or to rob us, we ought not to kill our own sheep. But this is a different case. These are strangers from Tette and beyond Shirwa, coming to make war on our people and carry them off as slaves. This we must help them to resist by every means. Livingstone is right to go with loaded gun and free the poor slaves; and there being so few English here, we are right, though clergymen and preachers of the Gospel to go with him, and by our presence, and the sight of our guns, and their use, if necessary (which may God avert), to strengthen his hands in procuring the liberation of these people. When Kirk went down last Thursday to the ship, where Rowley is, I wrote to Rowley to say, "Do as you think right yourself; but my advice is, that you volunteer to help Kirk by going armed in the boat or by staying armed on board, and use your gun, if necessary: but if you are not required, be glad that you are spared so painful a position. I intend to act on that principle here." I believe some will blame Livingstone, and more will blame me: but I can only act as I think right, after often using the Collect for the first Sunday after Epiphany and similar prayers.

*　　*　　*　　*　　*

July 22. I take out my letter, not to detail the events of this day, for that would weary you; but I will only say that being on our way towards the Ajawa, and meeting many persons running away from the war, we learned at one village that some Tette people who had come up to buy captives yesterday, were on their return, with a great many slaves, and were close at hand: having got one or two natives to shew us where they were, we turned aside, and after two miles' march came upon them, freed more than forty captives, and took three Tette slavers prisoners. One of these says that he was sent by his master, and that the Government of Tette knew of his going.

* * * * *

I am now writing with two groups of these freed people before me, dressed (elaborately, almost extravagantly, according to native ideas, having from one to two yards of white calico wrapped round them) with the stuff intended by their captors to increase the number of miserables. In the middle of each group is a fire, with two or three black earthenware native pots, cooking porridge of fine white native meal, almost as fine and white as flour, or pieces of goat-meat. This food was captured with them. On my right-hand are the three prisoners, their own necks now confined in the forked sticks we took from the captured men, of

which I have made a rough sketch: a stick as thick as one's thigh, six or eight feet long, with a natural fork, and with an iron pin passing through in front of the neck. A man with such a thing on is very helpless.

* * * * *

It will be seen from this narrative, that even before a settlement had been fixed upon, a character had been impressed upon the Mission party, which they had not contemplated at first. They had come to preach the Gospel, and to instruct and civilize the natives, and by indirect moral means to raise a protest against slave-taking and slave-selling: but now they stood before the country as slave-liberators, and it is manifest that this character would be in the eyes of the natives a very different one from that of mere preachers and teachers. I am not at all condemning the conduct of the party, nor do I see how Englishmen, situated as Dr Livingstone and the Bishop were, could very well have acted in a different way: but certainly it was a way which led the Mission party out of the intended track, and which if it promised greater usefulness, at the same time entailed greater responsibility.

Moreover, the liberation of the slaves had an important influence upon determining the settlement of the Missionaries. They had now a tribe, as it were, of their own; the Bishop had become an African Chief, and he could settle down not as a visitor in a native village, but as the head of his own population, the father of his own family. This is the character in which we must henceforth view him; and the missionary problem which was given him to solve was this, whether with a number of natives attached to him by the bonds of gratitude and affection, he could hold his position in the country, civilize and convert those brought into immediate contact with him and his party, and make the settlement a centre of light and freedom to the country round.

Towards the end of July the missionaries settled themselves down at a spot called Magomero. The reader will see its position upon the map. The chief advantage of its situation seems to have been, that it is included by the bend of a river in such manner that by running a stockade across from bank to bank over the promontory, the settlement would become safe from any hostile attack. On the other hand, the sanitary circumstances of the place were not good; it was low and covered with trees, so that the party found by sad experience that it did not secure for them that immunity from fever which they had been led to expect in the high land. It was also inconveniently distant from the river station, Chibisa's,—about 60 miles; this length of journey, up hill, with a bad road and no beasts of burden, was certainly a great drawback, and might have seemed to those, who did not know all the circumstances of the case, an objection which should have been fatal. However, Magomero was chosen as the Mission Station, and there Dr Livingstone and his party left the missionaries while he pursued his own journey of exploration.

The first consideration was the erection of huts for residences. The reader will see in the drawing opposite to this page the appearance of the settlement in its complete state. It was a matter of much labour, however, for some months to bring things to a condition of such apparent comfort; all laboured vigorously, none more so than the Bishop himself; and, indeed, it seems wonderful how the missionary village could have been built so well and so speedily.

But the erection of the village was not the only labour. A population of more than 100 had been thrown upon the hands of the missionaries by the emancipation of the slaves. These had to be provided for; many of them were women and children. The children must be educated; and it was thought that in the absence of perfect communication with them by language, it would be well to attempt the foundation of their education by bodily discipline. Accordingly, under the direction of Mr Scudamore, they were drilled and taught the first lessons of order and submission to authority. One portion of the drill was amusing: the small regiment of boys were drawn up in line by the side of the river; then at the word of command given, the whole body plunged into the water, no doubt with the best results. The women it was more difficult to deal with. The Bishop often sighed for the female part of the mission party, feeling that the presence amongst themselves of some Christian women was, under God, the only means of purifying the minds of the female portion of the Magomero heathen settlers. He sincerely hoped that this defect in the missionary staff would be corrected towards the end of the year, when Dr Livingstone had arranged, having returned from his own journey of discovery, to descend the river in the *Pioneer*, and bring up the first party of ladies who were to meet him by appointment at Kongone.

I shall presently give a more full account of the peaceful and happy occupations of Magomero, as described by the Bishop himself. Indeed, I may say here, that the life of the missionaries appears to have been most peaceful and most happy: in one of his letters the Bishop declares with most affectionate earnestness, that he believes there never was a man so fortunate in his fellow-workers as himself, and they on their part appear to have felt to the full extent that personal influence of Mackenzie's character, and that warm love towards himself, of which I have had occasion to speak in a former part of this memoir. I would willingly dwell only on this portion of the mission work, but unfortunately it is necessary at once to describe events which were of a different kind,—events which I will endeavour to describe simply and fairly, and then leave the reader to form his own candid judgment concerning them.

The reader has seen that the principles, upon which the missionaries took up their position at Magomero, were of necessity affected by the liberation of the captives on their way thither. The emancipation not only surrounded them with a native population attached to them by a strong bond of interest, and threw an unexpected responsibility upon the Mission, but (as I have already observed,) it published the advent of the missionaries, to the apprehension of the natives, as an engagement to protect the weak against the strong, and to defend the friendly tribes against their slave-hunting neighbours. I do not intend to assert that Dr Livingstone, in liberating the captives, or the missionaries in co-operating with him, at all desired to pledge themselves to a war against slave-hunters; it would clearly have been most impolitic and unwise and unsuitable to do this; but I think it cannot admit of a doubt, that the interpretation which would be put by the natives upon the first acts of emancipation would be something of this kind—"here are men who will not permit slave-dealing to be carried on: they have power and will on their side: henceforth, if we want help, we shall know where to seek it."

Dr Livingstone evidently perceived that such an interpretation was possible, and of course he equally perceived that it was an interpretation, the fallacy of which could not be demonstrated too soon. Accordingly, when he took his leave of the missionary party at Magomero, at the end of July, he warned them against taking any part in defending the Mang-anja tribes against the Ajawa: he said, they must expect to have constant applications for help, but they must not yield to them. Applications, as he had predicted, soon arrived from various quarters, all in most urgent terms stating that the enemy was close at hand, and that they expected to be destroyed in a day or two. These stories the Bishop and his party did not wholly believe; indeed, there were inconsistencies in the accounts which made it impossible to give credence to them all. Nevertheless, they found it painful to be compelled to turn a deaf ear daily to men, who told them that their wives and children were sleeping in the bush, and that no one dared to cultivate the ground for fear of being seized and sold into slavery.

At length a more formal application was made. On August 7 ambassadors came from Chinsunzi and Kankomba, the two greatest chiefs in the country, to inquire whether they might themselves come and state their case and ask for help. To this application the Bishop did not think it right to say no; and accordingly, on August 9 the two chiefs arrived, with about one hundred attendants. The mission party was strengthened by two officers of the *Pioneer,* and altogether mustered ten white and three black.

Before admitting the chiefs to a conference, the Bishop debated with his friends the general question, Could they, under any circumstances, entertain the petition? or must they at once give a refusal, as they had hitherto done?

The answer to these questions was based upon two principles. In the first place, the missionaries considered that had they been an ordinary body of English Christians settling amongst the Mang-anja as friends and neighbours, and had these friends and neighbours been in danger from a fierce enemy, who would destroy the strong men and sell the rest into slavery, they, the English Christians, would be justified in putting themselves at the head of the Mang-anja, and so giving them their support against an enemy, otherwise invincible. But, secondly, they concluded, and that without a dissentient voice, that if the circumstances were such as to make it their duty, regarded simply as English Christians, to head their Mang-anja friends, there was nothing in the fact of the clerical character of the party to annul the duty. No doubt, they argued, such work is best left to lay hands, as it would be in a civilized country; but so also in a civilized country a clergyman would not build his own parsonage, nor perform a number of duties which must fall upon missionaries in a wild country like central Africa: and if it should be said, that no clergyman should be engaged in shedding human blood, it might be replied that neither should any Christian be so engaged; but as there are conditions which render scenes of bloodshed the right scenes for Christian duty, so there may be conditions which render such scenes not unsuitable even for a Bishop and his clergy.

These considerations led the missionaries to agree not to give a decided negative to the application from the Mang-anja. It may be open to doubt whether the conclusion to which they came was the wisest and best: of course the natural tendency of the minds of Christians at home, removed from the actual scene of operations, and enabled to contemplate it upon abstract principles, is to condemn the conclusion as unsound; and it may be added, on this side of the argument, that Dr Livingstone had himself warned the missionaries that they would receive applications, and that they must not attend to them. But, on the other hand, I think that we are bound to regard with great respect a conclusion arrived at on the spot, by men whose every feeling would draw them away from the conclusion to which their judgment brought them, and in the soundness of which (as will be seen hereafter) Dr Livingstone ultimately expressed his belief. I am certain that no person who was acquainted with Bishop Mackenzie would believe, that anything less than a very strong conviction of the duty and necessity of assisting their friends would have induced him to adopt a course of conduct, from which his gentle heart would shrink; and I shall be much disappointed if those who know him only through the medium of this memoir, have not gained sufficient confidence in him to adopt the same view. We have seen already, that in the first collision with slave-takers he anticipated much blame for his conduct from friends at home, but he counted the cost, and believed that he was doing right; and in the present instance, he must still more surely have seen that his conduct would be severely criticized; the ground was less clear, the responsibility was greater; yet, with all this before him, he considered that it would be unworthy of the place which they had assumed amongst the friendly tribes, if they should stand by as idle spectators of the destruction of their friends. He again counted the cost, and did what he believed to be his duty; I would ask, therefore, at the hands of the reader, for one so good and gentle, placed in such strange and painful circumstances, a kindly and considerate judgment.

There was one point which does not seem to have entered into the calculations of the Bishop and his friends, but which was certainly worthy of consideration, as the event proved:—I mean the real relations in which the Mang-anja tribes stood to the Ajawa. The missionaries seem to have assumed that the district in which they were settled was Mang-anja ground, that the Ajawa ground was at a distance from them, and that the incursion of the Ajawa, which was now causing so much terror, was (as it were) an accidental raid, which might be checked by showing a firm front, and would then subside and leave the Mang-anja in peace. It was clearly impossible that they could be for ever fighting native battles; and if the ground upon which they had fixed themselves were such as could be held only by such a course, then it would be obvious that the ground was unfit for missionary work. Now the truth appeared to be, though the missionaries were not aware of it at the time, that they had made their settlement at Magomero just at the time of the approach of a more powerful tribe: the Ajawa attack was not a casual outbreak of a stationary people, but the indication of an aggressive policy on the part of a race who felt themselves to be stronger than the present occupiers of the country. This process of conquest, of the possession of weaker tribes by more powerful, has, as we well know, been going on from the beginning; it is, as it were, a law of the world's progress, and though the process may be productive of much misery, and may be a very painful spectacle for Christian eyes, and may bring to mind the thought that the whole creation groaneth and travaileth in pain, still it is one against which it is useless to contend; and it is after the healing of the wounds caused by this terrible natural surgery, that the missionary work of the Gospel of peace has its proper point of commencement. It was after the Saxons had conquered their position in Britain, and become undisputed lords of the soil, that they were converted to the faith by Christian missionaries. Had Bishop Mackenzie and his party known at the time as much as they knew afterwards, they might possibly have come to the conclusion that Magomero was the wrong spot for their settlement, and they might have effected at once that migration which was carried out afterwards; but if they were to hold their position in the neighbourhood of the Ajawa tribes, I think that nothing would have persuaded them that any line of policy was feasible other than that which they adopted.

But to return to our story. Having come to the conclusion which has been above explained, the missionaries went and received the petition of the chiefs. They declined to give them an immediate answer; but explained that some of their party had just come from the vessel at Chibisa's, and were weary with their journey, so that it would be necessary to defer their final answer till Monday. Meanwhile, however, they wished to ask the chiefs a few questions. Would the Mang-anja people join together, if the missionaries headed them? Yes. Who would join? Chinsunzi, Kankomba, and some ten or twelve subordinate persons, in lively speeches, expressed their willingness. How many followers could they bring? Many more than were there present. Had they any guns? Yes, they had some.

On Saturday night, the missionaries discussed the answer which they should finally give; and they determined to go. But in coming to this determination, it was necessary to have some settlement of the terms on which they should assist the Mang-anja; they were to help these men against those who would take them and sell them as slaves; but how if the Mang-anja should indulge in slave-dealing themselves, as doubtless they had done in former times? There was no native law against it, and custom was in its favour: would it not be a grand step in the missionary work, if the assistance given to the Mang-anja against their enemies could be made the occasion for enacting a law against slave-taking amongst themselves? This seemed to be the right basis for the defensive alliance; accordingly, on Monday, when the chiefs came for their final answer, the Bishop said to them, "We will head you against the Ajawa on certain terms:

I. The captives in the hands of the Ajawa are to be set free. No one shall claim them as his. They shall go where they please.

II. You will all promise not to buy or sell men any more.

III. You will all promise to join in punishing any chief who sells men.

IV. If any persons come to buy men, you will not let them stay, but will drive them away, and tell us."

To these conditions the chiefs agreed; to the second they replied that they never did such a thing, but the Bishop told them not to deny it, but to promise for the future; to the third Kankomba declared that if he ever found any one selling men, he would bind him. The chiefs having agreed, the Bishop invited all those who would promise to stand up: they all stood up: and so the alliance was made. The natives applauded the result with three slow united deep-sounding claps of the hands.

On August 13, the Bishop and his party arrived at Chinsunzi's, but not sufficiently early to see where the hostile Ajawa were situated. Soon after six o'clock the next morning they started, followed by a large body of natives, probably nearly a thousand. In about two hours they came in sight of the Ajawa villages.

It was determined that before anything else was done, a parley should be attempted by two of the English going unarmed towards the Ajawa camp, and requesting an interview with the chiefs, also unarmed. The Bishop himself, with Mr Waller, undertook this task; they were accompanied by Charles Thomas, one of the Capetown men, and by one of the Mang-anja: this arrangement was necessary, inasmuch as the Bishop was compelled to speak in English, which was translated into Makao, his own language, by Charles, and so made intelligible to the Mang-anja man, who finally acted as interpreter to the Ajawa.

The terms proposed to the Ajawa were as follows:

I. They must liberate all their captives.

II. They must give up all Tette men and others, who might be with them to buy slaves.

III. They must give up all their guns, and go right away out of the country.

It was hardly expected that these terms would be accepted, but it was thought right to offer them. The parley turned out to be a more dangerous affair than was anticipated: the Bishop and his small unarmed party went somewhat rashly (as it would seem) out of sight of their friends, and had an interview with half a dozen of the Ajawa, who were armed with bows and arrows, and one with a gun: indeed, as Charles Thomas afterwards informed the Bishop, they only escaped with their lives by the fact of the parleying party disobeying orders, which were shouted to them from head-quarters, to fire upon them at once. The result was nothing: when the Ajawa heard that the Bishop and his friends were English, they said, "We do not want to have anything to do with the English; they help the Mang-anja against us."

Having performed their perilous task, the parleying party retired, first walking, and then at length, when the thought of a musket-ball in their rear had had time (as the Bishop expresses it) to produce in their legs a sufficient amount of nervous irritation, running.

It was now clear that the hostile measures must proceed. Before the parley above described, the Bishop with his friends and Mang-anja allies had gained a commanding situation, overlooking the Ajawa encampment; soon after ten they were marching down the hill under the direction of Mr Waller, to whom the Bishop had wisely given the chief command. The result of the conflict appears never to have been doubtful; the few English were as a host on the side of the Mang-anja, who, though inferior to the Ajawa when left to themselves, fought with sufficient courage under English auspices. In one hour the victory was gained; but it was more than three before the affair was entirely over, and the victorious party brought back from the pursuit.

It must have been a very painful day for Bishop Mackenzie. War, in its most civilized form, is sufficiently revolting to gentle minds; but the war of barbarous people is utterly horrible; and the Bishop found that he had the double work of assisting the oppressed against the oppressors, and then of restraining the savage zeal of the oppressed in their flush of victory.

When the victory was complete, and the Mang-anja

restrained from pursuit, other cares opened upon the missionaries. It was necessary to see that the regulations were enforced respecting the captives: the Bishop had given assistance on certain terms; he was bound to see that those terms were fulfilled. A number of captives who were in the hands of the Ajawa were taken in charge by the Bishop, while others of the party led back the body of natives who had gone to the war.

It was a weary march home; many were foot-sore, many leg-sore. On the way a touching incident took place. Passing through a deserted village, the Bishop observed a little boy, looking very ill, sitting in the door of a hut. He desired a man to take the child up, and bring him along with the party: the man objected, saying that the child was sickly, and that it was of no use to take him. The Bishop, however, insisted, and the child was carried as he had desired. When they got to Chinsunzi's, the village in which they were to halt for the night, the child was deadly cold: the Bishop took him into his own hut, wrapped him in a blanket, and tried, though in vain, to administer some brandy: he lay by the Bishop's side all night: in the course of it brandy was tried again, but with no better success. In the morning the child died: the Bishop had baptized him the evening before, giving him the name of Charles Henry: he was buried in a place assigned by the chief, the English funeral service being read over his remains.

On the evening of the engagement they counted eighty women and children of rescued captives. Next day, the chiefs of the allied army met, and the Bishop reminded them of the conditions of the alliance, namely, that all rescued captives should be allowed to go where they pleased. These were separated from the captured Ajawa, and each woman was allowed to name some Mang-anja man with whom she wished to go, he promising to be kind to her, and not to sell her. All were disposed of on these terms, which seemed to give general satisfaction; the missionaries alone felt a little disappointed, that after the part they had taken in the rescue, none cared to come with them and settle at Magomero. The Ajawa women and children had not been included in the treaty; but these the missionaries took under their own charge, rightly considering that it would be impossible to entrust them to the tender mercies of the Mang-anja, even with a promise of good behaviour towards them. They also took the Mang-anja orphan children who were too young to choose for themselves. They then told the Mang-anja people, that the Ajawa having been driven away, it behoved them to work diligently in their fields, lest a famine should come upon the land.

The adjudication lasted four hours, and was very laborious. Then came the burial of the little boy already mentioned, and then the march home. They started at about two P.M. The march was very wearisome, and was still further complicated by rain. The Bishop would not leave his charge, and many of them were not more than ten years old. It seemed likely that they would have to spend another night upon the road, and there was no village in which to shelter; happily, some of the Mang-anja came up, and, at the Bishop's instigation, consented to carry some of the little ones. He himself set the example, and walked into Magomero at eight o'clock in the evening, with a little girl on his back, amid three cheers from those of the party who had already returned. Charles Thomas remained to bring up the rear, and did not reach home till half-past nine. This man had been out for fifteen hours, without sitting down and without eating, yet never grumbling or complaining of his position, but rejoicing in the opportunity of doing something for people, with whom, as a rescued slave himself, he knew so well how to sympathise. As they walked home together, the Bishop said to him, "Charles, it is wonderful those men did not fire on us this morning, when we asked them to send the chief to a parley." He said, "Yes, sir, I have been thinking that it was God that protected us."

This expedition added about forty to the population at Magomero, dependent upon the missionaries; it having been no less than 111 previously. Here was a serious increase of responsibility; but the Bishop looked upon it with his usual cheerful hopefulness. Speaking of the general results of the expedition, he says, "The results are, that we have freed at least forty (probably three or four times as many) captives who were in the Ajawa camp, ready to be sold into slavery to men from Tette, who were in the camp at the very time: and, on the other hand, we have captured about forty (perhaps many more) of the Ajawa, but have brought them not into slavery, but into more perfect freedom, and besides, brought them within hearing of the Gospel, which we hope soon to be able to preach to them. Then we have given peace and security, which I trust will be lasting, to a large tract of country, which was gradually melting away into a desert, as the flames of Ajawa war spread across it; and we have given, I trust, a decisive second blow to the slave-trade in these parts,—Livingstone having given the first. We have also got the chiefs (at least the most influential in these parts) to agree to abstain from and abolish the buying and selling of people, and have made it legitimate for those who hate such traffic to use force to prevent it; and I believe that these results, combined with the steady influence of Christian teaching and example, and the introduction of legitimate trade, will soon make slavery unknown here, at one of its freely flowing sources."

"But if," he continues, "the stream is to be dried up, it is not enough to dry up one of its springs. We cannot at present exercise an influence to much effect beyond thirty or forty miles on every side. There is an opening for other efforts of the same kind as ours. In a year or two I shall hope to have split up all the men I have, or expect, so as to cover a wider extent of country than I have just named, and then I shall be compelled to call on you at home to make another great effort, and send us out further reinforcements. I speak of this at once, that you may be prepared for the appeal when it comes. In the mean time, may God bless our efforts here, and give us peace, that we may learn the language and the habits of this people, and may proceed with the moral and religious training of those whom God may put within our reach."

Having done what they deemed right for the protection of their friendly neighbours, and for the repression of slave-hunting, the missionaries now hoped to be able to give their undivided attention to home work at Magomero. I will here introduce a description of their daily life, as given by the Bishop, in a letter to his sister in Scotland: the letter is the continuation of that which was partly given in the preceding chapter: it was the Bishop's habit to commence letters to his friends, and then add to them from time to time, after the manner of a journal: hence it is, that in the present instance the date of the latter part is considerably later than the period at which we have now arrived: but as the subject is one, I have thought it well to introduce the whole in this place.

LETTER LXXXVII.

(*Continuation.*)

Aug. 29. I have not said much to others of our domestic life. At 6 A.M. we are all called by the cook. The summons arouses us to varied scenes. I wake to the consciousness of lying in a round hut, 9 feet in diameter and 10 feet high in the middle, with the cheerful light of the breaking day twinkling through innumerable openings in its straw roof and walls. I am full length on a cork bed, which avoids all fear of damp, and weighs only seven pounds, with (don't be shocked) my clothes on, and a blanket over my legs, another round my shoulders and head. The upper end of my bed resting on my carpet-bag makes my pillow.

On the other side of the hut is Waller, nearly a facsimile of myself in his circumstances. The floor is strewn with dry grass (grass here is about five feet long), and in the strip between our beds is a stick, about two feet high, on the top of which is the oil-lamp which has been in use the night before. Between me and the round side of the hut is a deal-box, containing a few rockets and spare ammunition; above my head my double-barrelled gun loaded; a revolver also loaded. Above all, a shelf, made by thrusting the ends of bamboos through the roof at both ends, on which are my Bible, *Christian Year*, *Thomas à Kempis*, Wordsworth's New Testament, Trench, and one or two others.

After taking advantage of the quiet for my prayer, I get up, put on my shoes and cap, fold up my blankets, roll up my bed, take my towel, and go to bathe and wash in the river. By the time I come back, Charles has tidied the hut, and is probably sweeping the carpet, that is, stroking the grass smooth with a stick. I have now about twenty minutes or half-an-hour to read quietly before our morning prayers, the full Church service, at seven: every one attends once a day: most of us twice. Then there is a quarter of an hour before breakfast: perhaps I look up some one of our party who is ill: for it is unusual for all our thirteen to be well at once, so far as our present experience goes. Breakfast consists of meat, (fowls or goat), vegetables, (yam or sweet potatoes, beans or peas,) and porridge of ground Indian corn. Once or twice a week we have a loaf. We drink coffee or tea, and have one goat in milk. Our plates and cups belong to a canteen for six persons, bought in London. They are iron, enamelled inside, and don't break. During our breakfast Charles has been gathering the men and boys together. The list is called over as they stand in a ring, and answer to their names "Kuno," (*here*). Then I tell them what work they have to do, and make any address through William which may be required. By this time the men have finished breakfast, and we get to work about 9.30. I have 75 men and boys on my list, of whom about 30 or 35 may be employed, the rest being too small, or there being no tools for them. These latter then have their breakfast. Two women have been appointed to receive every night the next day's food for two lots of little ones, and to give them their breakfast about 10, and their supper about 5. It consists of porridge, and sometimes a few beans to give it a taste. We have no plates or spoons for them; we shall acquire that luxury, I hope, soon. They sit down in a row, and a fat motherly woman, with an infant on her back (which she adopted, because it had no mother), gives to each a handful. They sit and eat well pleased, and when each has had some, she gives the remainder among them as extra mouthfuls. This is more orderly than at first, when there was always a scramble for every meal, like one for nuts at a school-feast.

Then the work of the day proceeds till one. One doctors the sick and sore. One buys the food which comes in daily, baskets of meal, or bunches of corn-cobs, or nuts, or beans, or huge yam-roots, some weighing fifty pounds: or goats are led in, or fowls hung upon sticks or in the hand: and for these we usually give white calico, sometimes coloured, or beads. One drills the boys; part of their drilling consisting in being marched into the river. The order, "Off clouts," being by most obeyed in laughter, by one or two with slow hand and mournful face. Some work at our new house, which is within ten days of completion.

We dine at 1, and amuse ourselves till 3. Dinner is a facsimile of breakfast, only that out of the same cups we drink native beer, here called "moa," instead of tea or coffee. From 3 to 5 we go to work again. The sun sets near 6, just now: in the longest days it will never be quite so late as half-past six. We have tea with porridge, and nuts or eggs;

and at about half-past seven prayers. Soon after that we part for the night.

Saturdays and Saints' days are half-holidays.

* * * * *

One of the curious customs of this country is their way of giving presents. They always expect to receive a present of at least equal value in return. One morning a woman brought us three large baskets of beer, each as heavy as a person could carry: we did not want so much: it would spoil before we could drink it: but we did not like to refuse it, lest she should be offended. So we sent her just what we thought its value. She considered our present too small, and took away the largest basket, saying we had not given enough.

Oct. 22. I take up my pen, that there may not be too long intervals between my paragraphs.

* * * * *

Dr Mellor, the medical man of the *Pioneer*, is here on a visit, having leave of absence with two of the men, to recruit their health by change of air.

I am so longing for our ladies to come up. It is not a week since we got an increase of fifty people, only ten boys and no men. Here is more work for them. It is impossible for us men to do what I trust God will do by them. The women are some of them wild and rude, and some of them worse, but I hope the influence of our ladies will tell upon them.

There is one girl in whom I feel great interest. She is deaf and dumb. The rest treat her kindly, but her poor mind must be sadly wearied by the want of communication with others. She is ten years old, good-tempered, and obedient whenever she knows what you want her to do. When she sees me passing she claps her hands together. One day I wanted to fold up a great sheet, and made her take one end, just as a table-cloth is folded: she watched what I did, and did the same, as neatly as she could, with the greatest gravity. Four or five times I have brought her into my hut, and made her sit at the door while I shewed her a picture. I took one of the large coloured Scripture-prints, the raising of the Shunammite's son: she pointed to some limb, and then pointed to the same part of herself. I have followed this hint, and each time we have gone through every part. We are keeping patiently to the one picture. There are four figures, which is variety enough. From the earnestness with which she does this I am sure it is a pleasure to her, as indeed it must be, breaking in on the vacuity of her mind. I do not know any one of my charge with so gentle, manageable and amiable disposition; and that is better than all brightness of intellect, or keenness of perception. I do not know that she ever had a name; but the one by which she commonly goes is *Kana nena*, "she cannot speak."

Our people are singing and dancing outside the hut; not the fierce dances of the Zulus, nor with their deep, panting noises. I do not know that the Mang-anja have any war-dance; it is more like the dance "all round the hawthorn-bush," or such simple games as they have at school-feasts. The music consists of three or four drums, played with great vigour and perfect time, while the dancers move slowly round in a ring. Sometimes there is a rapid movement of the feet, like that in a hornpipe, only each step is not more than an inch or two, while the body is nearly still, reminding one of the graceful motion of a good skater. Sometimes one or more make a diversion into the space within, turning once round rapidly and moving the arms over the head, and all this time they sing a strain consisting of but few notes, with clapping of hands in time, and the sound of cymbals, which are fastened, I think, to the ankles of one of the circle.

October 28. We have jokes among us, notwithstanding the seriousness of our profession. Last Saturday night there was very little to eat at tea. There was no porridge, because the people had not brought any meal for sale all day. So I went out, got some heads of *chimanga* (mealies, under another name), had them shelled, ground them myself in the mill, ordered some water to be boiled, made some porridge, and reappeared in twenty minutes with the dish. They did not know what I had gone for, and my dish was highly praised: it was not quite enough boiled; but by common consent we use now meal from our own mill, instead of the *ufa* or meal, which the people bring.

* * * * *

The quiet of the missionary station was not secured by the successful expedition against the Ajawa, which has been described in this chapter. Reports soon began to circulate of Ajawa incursions, and of the terror caused to the minds of the Mang-anja in the neighbourhood. These reports the Bishop did not feel inclined wholly to believe; he knew the unfortunate readiness of the natives to lie if it suited their purpose, and he found so much inconsistency in the tales told concerning Ajawa atrocities, that he perceived it was impossible to believe everything, and therefore doubted how much was true, or whether there was any truth in the tales at all. Accordingly, he determined to go and see for himself, and started on September 9, with Mr Scudamore, three Makololo, William, (the Cape Town man,) as interpreter, and some guides, to reconnoitre. The application for help in this case had come from a certain chief, named Bawi, who represented that the Ajawa were burning his villages, murdering his men, and taking the women and children into captivity. They very soon found that the doings of the Ajawa had been much exaggerated; and they quarrelled with their friend Bawi, who turned sulky because the Bishop refused to go with him and his followers, and forthwith give battle to the enemy. The reconnoitring expedition was continued several days, during which, notwithstanding the exaggerations referred to, they saw abundant evidence that an enemy was in the neighbourhood, villages burnt, others deserted, and the inhabitants of those not deserted manifestly living in daily terror of an attack from an enemy whom they dared not face. On one occasion, they fell in with some of the Ajawa foe, and endeavoured to catch one or two of them, in order that they might send a message to the rest, and warn them to mend their manners or depart; but the Ajawa were too fleet for them. William, the interpreter, who suggested this scheme, described the effect which he hoped to produce in a very amusing manner. "One will say, I saw him myself! another, I was in his hands! they will say, there were a great many of them, and all had guns: the news will spread, just like a newspaper." However, William's plan could not be carried out, and the Bishop had to return home with the general result of knowing that the Ajawa were near, but not knowing their numbers or exact situation, and of being pestered with applications to go once more at the head of the friendly tribes, and endeavour to clear the country finally of the lawless and cruel Ajawa.

Soon after the return to Magomero, a messenger came to say that two days after the Bishop and his party had been at the village of the chief Nampeko, the Ajawa had come down and burnt it. A discussion was held as to what should be done, and it was determined to go and drive the marauders away. The chiefs in the neighbourhood were called together, and the injured man himself confirmed the account of the destruction of his village. Conditions were made concerning the freeing of captives, and putting a stop to the slave-trade, as on the former occasion, and the arrangements were nearly complete, when something was said about meeting at the chief's village. What village? "The village in which you slept," was the reply. The Bishop asked, "Is it not burned then?" "No." "Did you lie then, when you said it was burned?" To which the chief replied, with a smile upon his face, "I lied." "I am not," writes the Bishop, "naturally excitable, but I have once or twice since I came here thought it necessary to make a demonstration. I shook my fist in his face, and said, 'If a dog could do as you have done, I should kick it. I cannot speak to you any more to-day.' Very soon, after a few moments' consultation, I said I could not go to fight at all; that I wanted them to feel how bad a thing it is to lie."

However, after a fortnight, the chiefs began to come again. He who had told the lie about his village expressed his sorrow; he promised to tell truth for the future, and began by confessing that they had seen nothing of the Ajawa since the Bishop's visit: still he represented that they were in constant fear. The Bishop thought that the purpose of keeping the Ajawa at peace might be effected by sending them a message, to say that if they attacked the Mang-anja, they would certainly be punished: none of the Mang-anja folks however could be found courageous enough to carry the message; in fact, the vices of cowardice and lying seemed in their case, as in many others, to go closely coupled together.

What was to be done? The Bishop was extremely anxious to avoid further warlike proceedings; but soon after, he received reliable information of villages burned in the neighbourhood; he felt that such marauding habits must be stopped, and therefore he again headed a party against the Ajawa trespassers. I shall not give this expedition in so much detail as the former; in fact, there was little or no actual fighting; the Ajawa retreated at once at the approach of the Mang-anja with their English allies. Here is the Bishop's own account.

"October 17. Noon. We got away at six: which was a wonderful thing, as loading more than thirty Mang-anja guns took an hour, I suppose. We walked slowly for nearly four hours, with a large body of Mang-anja, and a weak force of English. Dr Mellor was what would be called in England quite unfit for anything. Two others of our party were far from well. So that it seemed almost rashness to go to war in such a state; but it would not have been easy to put off the fight, and I trusted partly to the influence of our presence, but I trusted more in the verse which I repeated to myself several times, 'The battle is the Lord's, and He is the governor among the people.'

"October 18. Friday evening. (On the banks of Shirwa.) As on former occasions, we the Christians stood together to ask Him to direct all things according to His will. It was near ten when we found we were getting near. The Mang-anja kept running on before, and on the smallest alarm falling back. One time, when we came to the edge of the river, close to the Ajawa, they all stopped and allowed Adams, who was the foremost Christian, to go on twenty or thirty yards alone, and only followed him when we came up. I asked two or three times for Nampeko, and was told that he was behind; so he was, for I never saw him all day. It is unsatisfactory, acting in alliance with such people, on whom you can rely only for cowardice and falsehood. Adams, in the act of crossing the water, fired two shots at Ajawa, two of whom had guns. They immediately ran away, and this was all the opposition we met with: when we arrived, we found the huts empty, which we burned."

The arrangements concerning the captives were carried out as on the former occasion; the result was a still further addition to the population of Magomero. "This addition," says the Bishop, at the close of the letter in which he describes the expedition, "makes our number exceed two hundred. We might be tempted to fear about the supply of food: but we cannot refuse to take care of people who thus throw themselves upon us; and we trust that He, who has given us the charge of them, will give us the means."

The reader has now before him the history of what may be called the Ajawa wars, in which Bishop Mackenzie and his party were engaged. His conduct has been severely criticized, as himself anticipated; and of course, if we adopt the principle that under no conceivable circumstances can a minister of the Gospel be justified in taking up arms, his conduct must be condemned. But I think it is very difficult to establish any such general principle; and unless it be established beyond the possibility of a doubt, it is an ungracious thing for us in England to sit in judgment upon the conduct of men placed in such peculiar circumstances as were the missionaries of Magomero. Certainly it is a point to which great importance should be assigned, that these good and holy men, having weighed upon the spot all the responsibility of the course to which they were committing themselves, should have adopted the course unanimously. It is irrelevant to say that the measures adopted did not eventually succeed; success was in God's hands; and I have said before that there was an element in the case, of which the missionaries took no account, and which tended to make their policy a failure; I refer to the fact, that the Ajawa tribes were spreading over the country as a more powerful race, and that they were not merely mischievous neighbours who could be kept within their own bounds by a little boldness. It is clear that Bishop Mackenzie's conduct can be condemned, only upon the general principle of the impropriety of war on the part of the missionaries under all circumstances; and supposing this principle not conceded, it may well be asked whether the conception of the missionary settlement as the head-quarters of a tribe of emancipated persons was not a very noble one, and whether the existence of such a settlement might not be the most effective means of preaching the kingdom of heaven. It would be very difficult, as missionaries always find it to be, to reach the intellect of the poor savages; it would be very difficult even with all the facilities afforded by a thorough knowledge of their language, the vehicle of their thoughts; it would be infinitely more difficult for preachers, whose powers of oral communication were so small as those of Bishop Mackenzie and his party must have long continued to be; but suppose that the natives found amongst them a settlement of men emancipated by the missionaries, and knew that in this settlement truth was cultivated and brutality of all kinds discouraged, that in this settlement there was constant worship of God, and that the white men would not allow the black population under their government to be molested and alarmed, would not this be a practical preaching of the kingdom of God and of Christ, which the native mind could understand, and which would attract and move towards itself the native heart? This seems to have been Bishop Mackenzie's conception: who will say that it was not a noble one?

I have said more than once, that if the missionaries had realized in the first instance the true relations of the Ajawa to the Mang-anja, they might possibly have come to a different conclusion with regard to the course to be pursued, when they were requested to defend one against the other. This statement seems to be justified by such a passage as the following, which I extract from a letter written to the Bishop of Cape Town in May, 1862. The letter was written in explanation of the reasons which induced the mission party subsequently to leave Magomero, and settle themselves at Chibisa's; besides elucidating the point for which it is adduced, it will also confirm the statements made in this volume as to the unhealthy character of Magomero. "We had intended," writes Mr Procter, "to leave Magomero, and seek a new site somewhat nearer the Shire, among the hills, ever since our sad experience of the last rainy season, in which so many of our people died, and we suffered ourselves so much from sickness. The place lying low, and surrounded with thick vegetation, had been pronounced decidedly unfit for our further habitation by Dickinson; and as soon as the *Pioneer* arrived with a fresh supply of cloth, to enable us to pay bearers, we had decided to make a removal. In the meantime, however, we heard that the Ajawa were again busy ravaging the country, in various parties, to the North-West of us; and applications for help against them kept coming in from several Mang-anja chiefs, who declared themselves to be sufferers from their incursions. I have not time to go into the many reasons for our constant refusals to listen to these requests; but chiefly because we saw from our experience of last year, that we had made a mistake in becoming the warriors instead of the teachers of the Mang-anja, who, weak and cowardly, were learning to value us only because we could defend them, and because we were making enemies of a powerful tribe, or rather nation, *who clearly must in time become masters of all the North-West corner of the Mang-anja territory between Mount Zomba and the Shire.* At last we determined to go and fight for the Mang-anja no more." This shews the views of the missionaries founded upon their experience; at the same time it is right to add, that some persons well acquainted with the country have held, and still hold, that if Bishop Mackenzie's policy had been consistently carried out, the terrible devastation of the country, which afterwards took place, might very possibly have been prevented. This is a point, however, upon which it is unnecessary, perhaps it would be presumptuous, to express an opinion.

There is one other point which I would ask the reader to bear in mind, in order that he may estimate fairly the conduct of the missionaries with regard to these Ajawa troubles. He must bear in mind, that although in the history they seem to occupy so large a space, yet in reality they occupied a very small portion of the time spent by Bishop Mackenzie at Magomero. One or two stirring days of warlike expedition make a great figure in a narrative, whereas ten times the number of days spent in the works of peace make little show. The reader therefore must not give too much weight to the Ajawa wars, as though the missionaries were always fighting, but rather regard the missionaries as given up to the peaceful and holy labours of Magomero, with the exception of some few days, in which, under an imperious and painful sense of duty, they assisted their Mang-anja friends against their Ajawa oppressors.

I have said that the conception of the kingdom of God, come among the poor natives of central Africa, in the form of a colony of emancipated blacks under the government of a white Christian Bishop and his clergy, was a very noble one; the drawback was the difficulty which the Bishop felt, but which his strong faith in God enabled him to tolerate, of finding food for the people. Moreover, even if food should be forthcoming, the police regulations (if I may so call them) necessary to make the condition of Magomero healthful, would be difficult of execution.

This difficulty of knowing how to deal with their friends was (as I apprehend) quite as formidable as that of dealing with their enemies: in fact, the colony grew too rapidly, and it seems inconceivable that a population such as that of the blacks at Magomero could be supported permanently, and that Magomero with such a population could be a suitable residence for white men.

This is a question, however, which need not be further discussed now; my purpose in the remarks which I have made is rather to restrain the reader from hasty condemnation of Bishop Mackenzie, and to suggest that the policy adopted by him was not wrong and bad in itself, might have been necessary, and may even now be blessed by God to the benefit of the oppressed Africans. If any corroboration of this view be required, it will be found in the following testimony from Dr Livingstone. The letter which I here produce, and which has been published before, was addressed to the late Sir Culling Eardley. It was written, as will be seen, long after the Ajawa troubles, and when the country had been reduced to famine and misery by those internal wars, which Bishop Mackenzie endeavoured to bring to an end. With this testimony from one so competent to form a judgment, I shall leave the case in the reader's hands.

RIVER SHIRE, *Jan.* 23, 1863.

I have just been visiting Bishop Mackenzie's grave. At first I thought him wrong in fighting, but don't think so now. He defended his 140 orphan children when there was no human arm besides to invoke. To fight even in self-defense must always be but a sad necessity; but to sit still, and let bloodthirsty slave-hunters tear away those orphans who cleave to us for protection, must be suffering martyrdom for our own folly. In coming up the Shire we have met fifteen dead bodies floating down. The whole country on the east of the river is devastated by a half-caste Portuguese, called Marianno, with about 1000 armed slaves. You would not credit the enormities of which this fellow has been guilty; the poor people have fled to the reedy banks of the river, and having left all their grain behind, famine and death (of which we are every now and then compelled to see sickening evidence) have followed as a matter of course. The same evils have been produced higher up the river by the people of Tette, of whom the governor is the leader; and besides those carried into slavery, an untold number perish of hunger. The Tette people put arms into the hands of the Ajawa, to be wielded against a tribe named Mang-anja. The passions of one body of blacks are employed against another. Both suffer grievously. We have tried, and still try, to stop the evil at its origin in the Portuguese slave-hunter. The greatest evil of all is, that this legalized system of slave-hunting has prevented the influences of Her Majesty's squadron being felt inland through missionaries. On the west coast comparative quiet has been produced by the presence of men-of-war. About twenty missions have been established; the means have been brought into play which the government hoped for, while here the only mission that has been tried is in danger of being worried out by slave-hunting. On the side of the oppressor there is power. Let us hope that ye, who have power with the Almighty, will let your prayers prevail on behalf of this wretched trodden-down country.

With Christian salutations, I am, &c.

DAVID LIVINGSTONE.

That the Bishop's mind was not wholly absorbed in warlike matters during his residence at Magomero, will be seen from the following letter written to a very dear friend, whose name has already appeared several times in the course of this memoir.

LETTER XC.

MAGOMERO, *Nov.* 3, 1861.
E. Long. 35° 35′, S. Lat. 15° 35′.

DEAR HOPKINS,

I have been writing a good many letters through the week about what has been passing here, and what state we are in, till I am sick of it; and this is Sunday—so I shall leave you to get your information about the mission from other sources, and return to the old days when we could chat in that inner room of yours at Catharine Hall.

* * * * *

On the whole my life here is most happy. There is everything to make it so, and you know I am not much given to *moping:* but just occasionally for an hour or so I get low, and can always trace it to my own fault, letting this lower world send up a mist to obscure the bright clear sunshine of God's loving presence, in which we might always live. It was in such a mood, a little, that I sat down to chat with you just now: but it has gone. I was thinking of you this morning. You will have forgotten a walk I had with you on the Ely road before my degree, when I said

I thought sorrow and mourning need never be in this world: and you said you thought there was good cause for them. I was reading Archer Butler's Sermon on the daily imitation of Christ, in taking up our cross daily. How beautiful his sermons are!

I thought I had such a deal to say; but I am afraid I have got out of the habit of thinking lately: though by the bye it is a severe restriction which I laid on myself, not to allude to anything that is going on among us here. I wish we could meet, (or rather how nice it would be, for I do not wish it really,) and have a chat about everything. When I come back, shall I find you in Wisbeach still? I think I shall, and I hope I shall. There is always to me a great charm in the idea of an aged clergyman, in a parish in which he has been for thirty years, half of his people having known no other pastor, and loving and respecting him as he deserves, and better. To be sure my vision of such an old age was laid in a country parish, not too large to be worked with something like satisfaction, but the principle would be the same. Stop: I shall be late for evening prayers.

Nov. 4. We are looking now for the return of Dr Livingstone from Nyassa. He has been gone more than three months: he was to be back about the middle of this month. So he may turn up any day. You will hear by this same mail the news of this exploration of his, which we have not yet got. It will be interesting to you, but doubly so to us, as influencing our movements and plans. I know now where I should like to plant our first branch-mission, supposing his discoveries do not affect the question, namely, at Nampeka's: but it is quite possible that what we may learn, as to our future route of communication with the sea, may affect the planting of the first branch. We have plenty of room here for setting down six or eight missions: in one or two places we know that the chief would welcome us: in others, I have no doubt he would; but we have avoided asking too definitely, for fear of raising false hopes. I shall be able in a week or two, I hope, to mature my ideas about the future, when I have seen Livingstone, and to write accordingly to the Committee.

We have just got up the last part of our baggage from the landing-place. Charles, one of our Cape men, went away last Monday morning taking some twenty men from hence: he returned this morning, having these and about sixty-three more, each with a load of from forty to fifty pounds. Each is to be paid by a scarf about five feet by three, worth one shilling in England. So you see we get our things by luggage-train. This was rapid work: we took five days to come up; and they have gone and come in six days.

I told you I should not write you a missionary letter, and neither have I. So good bye.

Yours affectionately,

C. F. M.

It will be seen, that at the period of writing the preceding letter, Bishop Mackenzie's mind was full of hope with regard to his work. The position of the mission appeared to be pretty well established; his policy, in shewing himself the active enemy of the slave trade and the energetic protector of those who trusted themselves to his guardianship, appeared crowned with success; and he looked forward to a system of missionary colonization, which should bring the whole neighbouring district under Christian influences. Meanwhile the work of Magomero went quietly on, and the chief drawback was the growing sense of the unhealthiness of the place; it was too low, too much surrounded by thick vegetation, and the uncleanly habits of the native population which the missionaries had gathered round them tended to make the habitation pestilential. I may state by way of confirmation, though the circumstance lies beyond the limit of Bishop Mackenzie's life, that about six months afterwards the missionaries found themselves compelled to leave Magomero, and to seek another settlement.

Nothing more, I think, need be said concerning this portion of Bishop Mackenzie's life. It is the portion which will be most canvassed; by some, perhaps, it will be condemned. I have no right to dictate a verdict to the kindly hearted Christian reader, and I have already said all that I deem necessary in the way of defense. I shall conclude this chapter with some very energetic words written by Mr Waller, for which I would bespeak the attention which they deserve. "I do so hope and trust," says Mr Waller, "that the news of our doings with the Ajawas may get the shrewd and candid investigation they require. *To us* it is palpable that it was perfectly right and necessary: whilst the end has been so blessed to us, in the love and respect gained from the fatherless, the child, and the widow,—the rescued human merchandise, for which we risked so much. The means were, and are, in our estimation, quite justifiable,—the helping those who had no friends, the trusting in God's strength to stay the most accursed state of things I ever came across. Our enemies have found the nerve gone from their arm, and the blow cannot be struck at those, who they see come to do good. 'You came and helped us,' say chiefs from afar, reinstated in their villages, 'and we thank you.' 'We want to come and to live with you,' say the Ajawas. Who shall say we did wrong? But we care not: some must cavil: we will forgive them. Six thousand miles requires a long and clear sight to scan facts and circumstances. Far from the spot, far from the land that fills the slave ships, theirs may well be a cramped and one-sided view. Do not let us be run over roughshod. I know that there are heads and hearts in plenty to do battle for us."

CHAPTER XII.

LAST DAYS AND DEATH.

ON the sixth of April, 1860, the second detachment of the mission party sailed from Plymouth. It consisted of the Rev. H. De Wint Burrup and his wife, Mr John Dickinson, M.B., the medical officer of the mission, John Andrew Blair, a printer, and Thomas Clarke, a tanner. They reached Cape Town on May 14, and were received by the Bishop and Mrs Gray with their accustomed kindness. The Admiral of the station, Sir Baldwin Walker, offered to send them to their destination in H.M.S. *Gorgon* and *Penguin*, in the latter of which Mr Dickinson proceeded at the end of May; Mr Burrup, with the two mechanics, followed in the *Gorgon* on June 14; and Mrs Burrup remained at the Cape, to follow with Miss Mackenzie, when the mission arrangements should be reported as suitable for the arrival of ladies.

Mr Burrup fell in with Mr Dickinson at Johanna, on August 3, and sailed with him for Mozambique, where they landed on August 9; Blair unfortunately was compelled to return to the Cape for the recovery of his health. At Mozambique they were detained

for a fortnight, and in the middle of September arrived safely at Quilimane. The expedition from Quilimane to Magomero deserves to be recorded in Mr Burrup's own words; it was an expedition which was most successful, inasmuch as the party arrived safely at their journey's end, but unfortunate inasmuch as it tended to do away with the force of the lessons of caution, which Dr Livingstone and those who had had experience of African climate had endeavoured to impress upon the missionaries. "My cautions to the Bishop," wrote Dr Livingstone afterwards, "were unfortunately all nullified by Mr Burrup's wonderful feat." Here is his own account.

We started from Quilimane on the 12th Oct. Mr Dickinson had just been ill of fever, but was able to start. I had also felt an attack, but had taken medicine and would not lie by, and so, although weak, was able to look to things. We had two large river-boats and six canoes: one, Major Tito had to himself; and I, Dickinson, Clarke, and young Tito, were in the other. I should tell you that what is called the Quilimane river, named likewise the Mutu, is a large branch of the Zambesi, the bed of which is dry to the extent of about twelve miles in the dry season. It is a very fine river in itself, even when cut off from the Zambesi, because it has many fine streams which support it. We started up the Mutu, and used to land, sleep, breakfast, and dine at villages or huts. In one or two instances there are regular places for accommodation. Instead of going to the extreme point of the Mutu, we turned up one of its tributaries called the "Quar-quar." We landed from this river on Friday, the 19th, and had our baggage carried twelve miles to the Zambesi by fifty-two bearers. This was our first African walk across country, and I assure you it was piping hot. Thanks to our kind friend Tito, we found a capital house ready for us close to the left bank of the glorious Zambesi. It certainly had many inhabitants in the shape of a determined colony of cobras, one of which emerged from Dickinson's bedding one night just as he was unfolding it. We had an offer here from the Governor of Quilimane to escort us up to Livingstone, as he was going with his Portuguese and native soldiers after a man who does not choose to own the Portuguese authority. This we gladly accepted, and made an appointment to meet him up the river; in consequence, neither Major Tito nor his son went with us, as the latter was going to Tette, on the Zambesi. We started on Tuesday, 22nd Oct. We also lost Major Tito's private slaves, a crew, &c., by this change, which was a great loss. We had two canoes—one a large one, about two and a half feet broad—two-thirds covered by straw to secure our luggage, most of which was in this boat; the rest was in another small canoe, about a foot and a half broad. In one were ten natives, whom we had never seen before, for crew, and in the small one, four natives. We had not gone far before the men in the big canoe refused to go any further, as it was sunset. They had not gone three miles; they were close to home; and to-morrow there would be all the trouble of getting them off again. I insisted on their not stopping. They got out of the boat. I gesticulated, vociferated, declaimed in broken jargon of Portuguese, &c. At last I got them in, and off again. They were continually, however, turning the head of the boat round, and letting her drift back. Fortunately, as the sun set I had noticed the course, and with a punt-pole at the bow, and the assistance of Dickinson and Clarke at the stern, we managed to keep the boat right. I so far conquered them, that, with the fear of crocodiles, they pulled the boat up to their middles in water for an hour or two that night. Meanwhile, we had missed the small canoe; but at length, much to our delight, we rejoined her, and I allowed my unruly crew to land and sleep, about midnight, at Mazaro, at Mr Vienna's, which we took by storm. The first trial over, I remained master of the position to the end of the journey. We were four days in the Zambesi, and then came to its confluence with the Shire, where was a Portuguese fort, and at which the Isle of Monoconga was the rendezvous appointed by our friend the Governor, four days from starting. We met him with eight boats full of men coming down the river, on the third day. He said he was going to Quilimane. I said I was going up the Shire. We rather coolly shook hands, and went our different ways. The Commandant here was very civil; he wanted us to stay; tried to frighten us with lions, tigers, &c., up the Shire. He did us one good turn. He threw into the canoes, just as we were off, two strong ropes, which did us a good turn afterwards. We slept under shelter in a house twice out of the four nights on the Zambesi, otherwise in the open air. Our routine was to rise at daybreak, get a cup of coffee, and be ready to start by broad daylight; about 10 o'clock we used to land in the open air, make fire and have breakfast; about 12.30 or 1 o'clock start again, and go on until sunset. We slept, as you may suppose, in some very rough places, but during the whole time were never once attacked by man or beast.

On the 26th we entered the Shire; it is a fine broad, deep, and, in some places, rapid river. The range of the Morambala skirt the whole left bank up to the Elephant Marsh. We went on without any mishap up to this time, when a change took place. You must know that our first point was to get to Livingstone, who was at anchor in the *Pioneer*, at a place called Chibisa's; our party was we knew not where. Livingstone, therefore, became our rendezvous; but not Tito, nor anybody at Quilimane, nor Portuguese on the river, could give us any but the vaguest idea about the locality. Worse still, when we got on the Shire, where we hoped, as we got further, to get a little more certain information, we found that the natives all knew too well the great "Puff, puff," which had so startled them when first it went up, but they gave the most inconsistent and vague accounts of the distance and position. The consequence of this was, that our crew were in danger of being disaffected, and leaving us in the lurch. They had already asked for the full payment they were to receive at the end of the journey, and I had given it them, and had engaged them on; but there was no knowing when they might take it into their heads to say their engagement was at an end. Dickinson and Clarke thought that if we could only communicate some certain information of our being on the river, it would be very well. I therefore started off ahead in the small and light canoe, with a crew of four black men, to get, if possible, quickly up to Livingstone, tell him we were on the river, and then return. This was Tuesday, November 5th. We went on capitally, soon lost sight of the big canoe, but at night we stopped at a large village to get rice. The object of the crew evidently was to delay and sleep there. I was determined not to do so if possible, and pushed off two or three times, but could not get them all into the boat at once. It was now become quite dark, and I was afraid of the inhabitants of the villages sympathising with them if I went *too* far; so I was forced to yield; but I sulkily made myself a bed on the luggage in the boat, with my revolver at hand.

The men made a fire close by the boat, and were visited repeatedly during the night by villagers: one, a kind of jester or singer of the village, remained the whole night, singing to the accompaniment of a very extraordinary instrument, which he played with his mouth and hands, being some rude combination between a fiddle and bagpipes. My attempts to get him to leave off were of no use. This is the only incident of this part of the journey (not a good beginning), and I soon got them to shake down into implicit obedience. They often tried to entice me to stay at a village when they heard 'Tom-toms' and drums sounding—signs of a night dance, and where they knew they would get 'Pombi,' the native beer; but they never again succeeded, and we reached the ship safely on Wednesday, November 13th.

The last day was very wet; it rained the whole day; and was the first day of the rains, which we had feared, as swelling and making the river too rapid for the large canoe to stem it, besides being an additional risk of disaffecting its crew. I can tell you, when we hailed the *Pioneer*, and saw English faces looking over the side at us, wondering who we were, and then among those on deck recognised the hard-worn face of Livingstone, I felt a considerable thrill of pleasure and satisfaction pass through me. They were very kind and hospitable. In my hurry to get away I had forgotten to put Dr Livingstone's letter-bag into my canoe; this certainly disappointed them much. I slept on board, in the next berth to Livingstone. On Thursday morning, to my very great satisfaction, who should appear but Bishop Mackenzie himself, from Magomero, our home. He greeted me most warmly; was, of course, most surprised, as he had never expected us. He had come to see Livingstone, before he left Chibisa's to go down the river to meet a vessel at the mouth on the 1st of January. As Livingstone was going down the river, I was released from the obligation of going back myself, and so I remained. On Friday morning the *Pioneer* weighed anchor, and was soon out of sight going down the river. Directly afterwards the Bishop and I started with a train of bearers overland for Magomero; it is a hilly rough road the first part of the journey, and the hills were covered with mist. We slept at a village, having walked about twenty miles. We ought to have reached Magomero in about three days or less; but I was not quite up to walking, in consequence of not having walked much lately, and also as the river, cold at night, &c., had chilled my stomach. We therefore delayed on my account a good deal, and did not reach Magomero until November 19th.

Having welcomed Mr Burrup at Magomero, after this truly wonderful expedition, we must now pass to events which led directly or indirectly to the premature termination of Bishop Mackenzie's labours. It will be remembered that Miss Mackenzie remained at the Cape, intending to follow her brother as soon as news should be received that the settlement was suitable for the accommodation of ladies. Mrs Burrup also was left by her husband at the Cape, to follow on the same conditions. The Bishop had written to say that the ladies might come, and it was arranged that Dr Livingstone should meet them at the mouth of the Zambesi, in the *Pioneer*, and bring them up to Chibisa's. The *Pioneer* left her moorings at Chibisa's on Nov. 15.

It could not but be doubtful whether the arrangements would all fit in with each other,—whether the ladies would have received the Bishop's letters, and whether they would have been able to obtain a passage from the Cape to Kongone. However, so far as this was concerned, all was well. Mrs Burrup and Miss Mackenzie, together with the Rev. E. Hawkins, and Mrs Livingstone, took their passage in December, by a small vessel called the *Hetty Ellen:* it was a very rough and uncomfortable passage, but on January 8 they reached Kongone, where they threw up rockets and made signals, hoping that the *Pioneer* would shew herself. There was no sign of life, and the vessel again put out to sea, intending to make for Mozambique. The weather became very bad, and the voyage miserable; they reached Mozambique however on January 21, where they happily fell in with H.M.S. *Gorgon*. Captain Wilson, of the *Gorgon*, kindly took Miss Mackenzie and Mrs Burrup on board, and taking the *Hetty Ellen* in tow, they sailed on the afternoon of January 22, in greater comfort and with better prospects than they had had hitherto. On the 27th the ship anchored about three miles from the bar of Quilimane, where at present I must leave the party, in order to relate the doings of Bishop Mackenzie.

It has been already stated, that the *Pioneer* left her moorings at Chibisa's on Nov. 15; the arrangement was, that Dr Livingstone should bring up the ladies, who it was thought might arrive at Kongone in the beginning of January, and that the Bishop and Mr Burrup should meet them at the confluence of the Shire and the Ruo. The map will at once shew the reader, that there ought to be some more direct road from Magomero to this point of confluence than by way of Chibisa's and the river. Accordingly, on December 2, Mr Procter and Mr Scudamore started to explore a road. What happened to them can be best described by the following letter from the Bishop.

LETTER XCI.

MAGOMERO, *Dec.* 7, 1861.

DEAR STRONG,

This is a day we shall not easily forget; and, as our friends at home cannot fail to be interested in the events of the last week, I shall write to-night while some of them are fresh in my mind, and enclose a fuller account of those which did not pass under my own eye.

When Livingstone left his anchorage on November 15, he arranged with me that I should be ready to meet him on January 1 at the mouth of the Ruo, about half-way between the anchorage and the confluence of the Shire and Zambesi. He would there hand me over the party. We expect to meet him at the bar, and we should proceed to this place by land. Of course it was necessary to ascertain that there was a practicable road this way; and I proposed to explore the way first, and then start from this with a sufficient party in time to keep the appointment. He said he thought it would be better to make one trip of it, starting in sufficient time to allow for unforeseen delays; and he also advised me to try a line more to the west than that which I had thought of.

On returning home, I considered the whole matter, and, after consulting the others, I determined to abide by my own opinion, have an exploring party first, and try the line of country stretching from this to the southern end of Shirwa, and thence to the Ruo mouth—probably down the valley of that stream itself. My reason for preferring this line was, that it would set at rest the question of having a main line of communication from north to south on Shirwa.

I intended to have gone on the exploring party myself, but there were one or two things to be done at home which I could not well commit to any one else, and I had gone on almost every trip; so I arranged with Procter and Scudamore, to their complete satisfaction, that they should go with Charles to find the road, and return before Christmas, or, failing that, "let me hear from them." We only waited for the arrival of the mail with Dickinson and Clarke. They got here all right on Friday, November 29; and last Monday (December 2) Procter and Scudamore set off, having some hastily-written letters to be given to Livingstone in the event of their seeing him.

* * * * *

This afternoon I was sitting out, trying to improve in knowledge of the language by talking to one of the natives, and was in the act of endeavouring to get the word for "hope," by saying that I *thought* Procter and Scudamore would soon be back, and that I should be *glad* when they came home safe, when I saw a strange figure coming in at the gate; it was some time before I recognised that it was Charles—haggard, in rags, foot-sore, and looking wretched to the last degree. He was soon surrounded, and said faintly, "I am the only one that has escaped—I and one of the bearers. The Mang-anja attacked us." Finding he had had nothing to eat for eight-and-forty hours, some soup was made ready for him at once. He then told us his story.

They had got on well for three days; on the third the chief whom they passed at midday went with them to their resting-place, *Manga.* On Thursday they started with two additional guides, intending to sleep at Tombondira's, whom Chigunda had named as a great chief of those parts. At a fork of the path their old guide pointed to the right, which was the direction they would have preferred from the compass; but the two guides maintained that the left-hand path was the better one, and their local knowledge gave weight to their counsel, which was accordingly followed. By midday they reached a large village, strongly defended, as some villages in this country are, with hedges and thorns. On entering they were almost at once asked if they wanted to buy slaves—a pretty clear indication of the kind of white people they were accustomed to see. Of course they said they did not come to buy slaves, that the English set their faces against such trade, and that they were English. "Well, then, what will you buy?" Answer—"We are only passing through to look at the path, and are anxious to lose no time that we may meet our friends at the mouth of this river (the Ruo). Where is the chief?" "He is coming; you must wait for him." "Very well; only we want to get on to Tombondira's to-night." After a delay of an hour or two, no chief appearing, they determined to go on; so they packed up, and set off. They were followed out of the village by a number of men with bows and arrows, who became loud in their calls and threats if they did not return. When they had got about two miles from the village, the violence and ill-feeling was such that they stopped to consider whether they were not needlessly making enemies of these people, and whether it might not be best to see the chief, instead of breaking the etiquette of the country by running through his village. They asked if the chief were returned, and, being assured he was in the village, agreed to return and cook food, and then to set off, as they were really in haste.

When they got back they found the chief, who treated them civilly, giving them beer and wishing to trade. They bought what they wanted, which seemed, however, very small to the people, who unfortunately saw their cash for three weeks' absence (consisting of about 140 yards of calico), and evidently thought themselves ill-treated in not getting a good share of it. Stragglers were dropping into the village, and things were not looking quite pleasant. Their host was not surprised at several European articles they produced, saying he had been at Quilimane and Senna. Still he was civil, and pressed them to remain all night. They went down to bathe, and on their return Charles told them that their bearers had overheard plans for burning their hut in the night, killing them, and taking their goods. This determined them to be off. They called the chief, and while they occupied him by giving him a fine bright-coloured scarf, Charles was instructed to get the bearers into motion, and Procter and Scudamore would follow them out of the gate. The chief seemed taken by surprise, on hearing they were going to start at once, but the scarf occupied his attention in some degree. The men in the open space of the village, on seeing the movement, cried out, *Atawa!* ("they are running away"), and some of them tried to block up the gate; but Charles dashed forward, and made them fall back, and the flight became general. Charles escaped into the bush; he heard two shots fired, which must have been by our friends,—our dear brothers, as we felt more than ever they were; but what had become of them he did not know.

He had been almost caught once or twice, had heard the pursuers say, "Here he is! here he is!" but, thank God, he had been hid in the darkness. They had left the village just at sunset, and night had set in very soon. He avoided all paths, but was stopped by a large river, which they had crossed that morning at a village; so that he was forced to seek a new place for crossing. He sat down on the bank till morning. He was then obliged to ask where he could cross, and with difficulty persuaded the people to guide him. That day he avoided villages still, and got here on the following day, as I have described, hungry and weary.

You may perhaps imagine our state of mind. We anxiously made inquiry, from which to form conjectures where our two friends might be; but first we gave Charles some soup, and then we joined together in our temporary church in prayer for them, whether in suffering or fear, or wherever they might be, that God would be their support and strength; and for ourselves, that we might have wisdom to act with thought and charity towards the persecutors, and yet for the safety of our brethren. Then we consulted what was to be done. Rowley was on his bed, unable to move from the place; some of the rest were a little out of sorts; but, besides, we had sufficient accounts of Ajawa fighting on our west, within twenty miles, to make us feel the necessity of leaving an adequate strength here, while we went towards the south-east. On the other hand, to go to a strong village, in the centre perhaps of a populous district, only four or five of us, seemed likely to increase the mischief; yet we could not depend on the Mang-anja going with us in a case in which they were not concerned, still less on their standing by us in case of need. Our only course was to get the help of the Makololo, who would not be disposed to take the part of any of the natives against us, and would be glad to go with us anywhere if there was any chance of plunder. They were most of them at the anchorage of the *Pioneer* (Chibisa's), and Job must be sent for them. This settled, the sorrow, and the trying to be simply trusting in our Father, returned as before. We thought how sad it was to have to wait some days before setting off to look for them. I could not drive from my imagination the picture of what I saw in August—a man in the act of being stabbed to death. Just then one of our women came running to say, that the English were returning: and so indeed they were. They looked in better heart than Charles, for whom they asked immediately, not knowing whether he was safe. They, too, were hungry, having lived on a single fowl each for eight-and-forty hours, in which time they had walked about eighty-five miles. They were supplied with soup, and then we again assembled with very different feelings in our place of worship, to thank Him who had been guiding them while we in our anxiety were praying for them, and to pray that we might be bound together now in still closer bonds in carrying out our great common end.

By degrees we heard their account. They had passed through the gate close after Charles. Some of the bearers had their loads taken from them, others threw theirs down. They were followed, and crowded on each side, by a mass of men armed with bows and poisoned arrows. They shouted for Charles, but got no answer. Two or three of the natives got hold of Procter's gun and tried to wrest it from him; afterwards they got him down, and he had to defend himself with his heels as he lay on his back. Scudamore, who was a few steps in advance, came to the rescue, and fired on the man who was most busy. On this they ran away. At one time an arrow was discharged at Procter, which must have passed through his thigh, and, laming him, most probably have cost them both their lives, had it not *most* providentially been received by the *stock of his gun.* He broke it off afterwards, but the point is still deeply bedded in the wood. Procter also fired both barrels; and this and Scudamore's shot having cleared a space behind and round them, they struck off into the trackless bush on the left of the path. In a minute or two they stopped, deliberated, and prayed for guidance, and then set off homewards.

It was slow work, treading over the burnt grass, the stalks of which stood up crisp and black, about a foot high; but it was better than long grass higher than their heads, or thick underwood, while the darknes ssufficiently concealed them: thus "all things worked together for good for them." About twenty miles they went that night, guided by a fire on the Milanje mountains on their right. But for this fire they must in all probability have wandered, and perhaps fallen back into the village they had left. Their next difficulty was the river. Three times Scudamore (who is a good swimmer) stripped to find a crossing: twice he was carried down by the stream, and obliged to land on the same side. At the third place he got across, and then they carried their clothes above their heads to keep them dry. For half an hour about sunrise they rested, half-dozing, on the top of an ant-hill, concealed by the bushes which grew upon it, and discussed the plan of hiding there till night. It was well, however, that they went on. That day, Friday, they got over forty miles, finding it safe now to keep the path, but avoiding a village here and there. They asked a man who was hoeing in his garden to shew them the path to a hill which they had passed, and which they named, telling him they had no cloth to pay him. The man put his hoe on his shoulder, and went with them some miles. Afterwards they thought of their pocket-handkerchiefs. One was torn up and used as cash; a quarter of it remained on their return. On the Saturday they walked about twenty-five miles, making the whole distance eighty-five, which tallies with other estimates. They were both looking much fagged; Procter has a scratch on his face, made by an arrow in the tussle. Now, after four nights have passed, they are more like themselves.

In looking back on all this, some people will blame me for not exactly following Livingstone's advice. He said:

"Send no separate exploring party, but start in sufficiently good time to explore and arrive on the 1st of January at the Ruo mouth. Take the old road as far as Soche, and then keep the mountain Choro on your right." Livingstone had never been on the road, but thought that the best way. He also advised me not to weaken our home party too much, for fear of attack from the Ajawa on our west. My reasons for not acting on this advice were, that by the route actually taken we could get guides on whom we could depend from Chigunda, who spoke at one time of going himself; whereas guides from Soche might, I thought, be as likely to mislead us as to guide us rightly. Besides, I thought it a good opportunity to explore a new route, and one which, if successful, would probably be better than the one named by Livingstone; and I thought he had given the advice he did, because he wished us to keep the old safe road, so far as it would serve. How far I am condemned by the result will not be clear till we have tried his path, which I now propose to do.

Dec. 13.—There have now returned six of the men who went with Procter and Scudamore, leaving two, together with Nkuto, one of our boys who went with them. The sixth came here this morning, and made a formal report to Chigunda and us. He was caught on that Thursday night, on the path, some men having gone on before to secure all who tried to escape. Our friends and the others struck off the path, anticipating the danger. They bound all the four, and kept himself and our boy Nkuto in the great village, the other two in a neighbouring village. Our goods were all put into the large hut in which "the English" had been, and to which the two false guides had access. In the morning, these two, the sons (as it appears) of Chipoka, the chief from whose village they had started on the Wednesday morning, claimed the freedom of this man, and he was at once given up to them. With them he returned to Chipoka's village, Manga. In answer to the question whether these two had any share of the plunder, he said that he could not see what was inside their bags, nor hear what was said behind his back. Chipoka escorted him to the village of Saopa, and Saopa to a village near this. Chipoka sends an arrow to Chigunda, our chief, and says: "I am not in blame for this war; Manasomba has tried to kill the English, has stolen their baggage and their boy, and has kept two of your men. He says, If the English want the men, let them come and buy them out, or else fight for them." We asked why he supposed they had thought evil against us; he said, "Because you went about with much cloth, and refused to buy slaves, and would not buy much of anything else; so they thought it better to take it from you." We asked some questions about the nation of Manasomba, and the extent of his territory. It seems probable, though not certain, that he is not a Manganja; some say Auguru, some Amlache. If they had kept the right road they would not have come near him, and would have been well received by Tombondira, who is supreme over Saopa and Chipoka, and whose influence is said to extend to the Shire.

This treacherous attempt to murder the two missionaries, besides being extremely painful in itself, was also a source of anxiety to Bishop Mackenzie in another way. Could such an outrage be passed over without notice? especially as some of the party were still missing, and might possibly have been murdered? And if any notice should be taken, when and by whom? The Bishop would gladly, as he states in one of his letters, have left to Dr Livingstone the responsibility of calling the offenders to account in the Queen's name; but would it be likely that Dr Livingstone would be able to find time to take the matter in hand? and if it should prove that the work must fall upon the Bishop himself, would it not be much better to see to it at once and not defer the matter till his return from the rendezvous with Dr Livingstone, when he would probably have a party of ladies, and a large supply of goods, on his hands? But if so, there was no time to be lost; it would be necessary to go to Manasomba's, then perhaps return to Magomero, and then hasten with all speed to keep the appointment at the mouth of the Ruo, by way of Chibisa's and the Shire. This general explanation will be sufficient to introduce the following letter to his sister in Scotland; it carries the story of the Bishop's life very nearly to its conclusion, and is the last letter written home by him. Possibly, had it not been the last, I might have been tempted to abridge it.

LETTER XCII.

MAGOMERO, *Dec.* 22, 1860.
Fourth Sunday in Advent.

DEAR ——

I must write a few lines by this mail, though it may not be much. First, I asked you, in a letter despatched Dec. 2, 1861, which is probably lost, to send me three Bibles, like the one I have myself, in strong binding. I want also a copy of Boone's *Sermons*, late Incumbent of S. John's, Paddington. You may read them, if you like, first: let them be bound. Also please buy for yourself from me a copy of Archer Butler's *Sermons*, and for ——, from me, a copy of *The Faith Duty and Practice of a Christian Missionary* (Rivingtons'); also, for me, Thrupp *On the Psalms* (Macmillan).

Dear ——, I have much at times to depress me; more than ever I had. But I expected it, and must not complain.

The Dean of Cape Town, in his sermon at my consecration, told me I should. But the work is God's. I should not mind discouragement among the heathen; but it is among our Cape Town men. God help us all to grow in grace, and them especially in the grace of purity. Dear—— and ——, pray for them. They need also humility, and —— especially needs command of temper. I feel these sins in themselves as wounds to our Saviour and breaches in the walls of our Zion, and as positive hindrances, so far as they go, to our work, by lowering us among the heathen. But in all this I comfort myself that the work will live, and leaven the masses of this people by the power of the Holy Spirit, dwelling in and vivifying His Church.

Dec. 24. To come to events. This is the second day of our journey to the Ruo mouth to meet the *Pioneer* on Jan. 1. How strange that you probably know already whether I shall find our sisters in the *Pioneer* or not. There is a good deal to say on both sides from our point of view. The Bishop of Cape Town would know of the appointment as soon as the Admiral; and whether the Admiral sent a vessel from Cape Town, or sent word to one on the station, that is, near Johanna, to go to Kongone to meet Livingstone, in either case our party would have an opportunity of leaving Cape Town. But then it is urged here, that as I wrote for them from the Zambesi only, and have not had an opportunity of writing for them from Magomero in time for them to come this time, the Bishop of Cape Town and all prudent people would advise their staying at Cape Town till accounts of us are received from some fixed resting-place. This is quite natural; but I hope as against this that —— would be strong enough to say, "We yielded to his own (that is, my) decision, that the ladies could not go up at first: surely we ought not to be kept from going up, when Livingstone and he agree in saying, Come." Again, I say, if there was any difficulty about a man-of-war from Cape Town for them, still they would have to send us stores; at least I trust they know that we are depending on a fresh supply now, having brought from Johanna as little as we could possibly do with. If they do not send us stores, we shall have to hope that we may get some cloth through the Doctor from Senna, at three times the English price, and live on native produce till we can get more stores; and on this we shall probably be half of us ill all the time, on an average. But I am not afraid of this. The above discussion of probabilities may amuse you.

We meant originally to have left home on Thursday[1]. Then, to please Chigunda and accommodate ourselves to the assembling of the few hundred men he was gathering to go with us, we delayed till Friday. From Friday we delayed till Saturday from the impossibility of getting bearers; and the Makololo, whom we had asked to come with us, only arrived on Saturday, and there was not time to make a start after talking over the affair with them. So it was Monday, leaving eight week-days in this year, one of which is Christmas. Of these I expect six will be spent in walking, and there will be left two for the visit we intend to pay to Manasomba. You know already what is the cause; it is clear we can not do anything like making a demand to be backed by force when we have ladies on our hands, and it is likely that it will not suit Livingstone to keep our ladies till we can do this; though if I thought he could do this, I would much rather have his name and authority joined with my own in the matter.

I was not well in the morning, and the doctor gave me a little chalk and opium; I hoped the walk would quite set me up. It was a good day for walking; and we did a short journey, about fourteen miles. I bathed afterwards, which was perhaps unwise, and found at night that I was no better; but Waller has just (11 A.M.) given me some more medicine, and I shall enjoy my breakfast when it is ready. There is the chief of this village, and I must speak to him.

I have had my talk with him, and have had breakfast;

[1] December 19.

and now he is looking on in wonder while I write. He gave us a kid, and a basket of corn, and I have given him two yards of velvet, bright blue, with which he looks much pleased. His name is *Kwanji*, and also *Sata-Massira*, the latter of which means plenty of corn; a very appropriate name, for it is almost the only village I have seen for some time, in which the people have not been starving. We are going nearly due South, and are getting near to the grand range of the Milanje, nearer than Livingstone has been. To-night we sleep at Saopa's, and to-morrow go on to Chipoka's. We cannot afford, after so much loss of time, to sit still on Christmas Day, but we shall have our service of worship and communion with the whole Church, of which Christ is Head, notwithstanding. Now they are ready to start: it is about 12 or 1, I suppose.

Dec. 25. Christmas Day. You will be sorry to hear that we are walking to-day as usual. I was very anxious to get here (Saopa's village) last night, that our journey to-day might have been a short one, from this to Chipoka's. And then we should have had a communion service in the quiet part of the day, which would have been the morning. But some of the party were too tired to come on last night. So we have had more than three hours' walking this morning, and have about six before us.

Since I wrote the above we have had breakfast, and have had a long talk with the two chiefs, Chigunda, who came with us, and Saopa of this village. They say that Chipoka was here not long ago, to ask if we were coming. (Saopa also was at Kwanji's, and returned the day before yesterday.) Chipoka left directions that when we came he should be summoned, that we might talk over the whole matter quietly. This he thought better, because in his village are so many that have relations with Manasomba, who would be apt to call out *Nkondo* (war), on our appearing, and give notice at once to Manasomba, while here at Saopa's we may stay without his hearing of us. As it was by the two guides from Chipoka's that our party was led to Manasomba's, we ask whether he is to be trusted; they say, "Yes: he and Chigunda and Satawa and Saopa and Tombondira are brothers; they all look up to Chinsunzi and Kankomba, and they will all send some men with the English against Manasomba." It will be best, they think, to call Chipoka, as he wished. The messenger will go, so as to get to Chipoka's at night. The chief will come away in the darkness, and no one in his village will know where he is gone. I asked these two chiefs what they thought would be the resulting advice to-morrow: Chigunda answered, more by signs than by words, that we should go to Chipoka's from this perhaps to-morrow afternoon, as quietly as possible, trusty men guiding by a zigzag path, to avoid the main road; that early next morning we should go in silence (his lips all grasped in his hand to indicate silence) to Manasomba's, (his forefingers stepping stealthily along the mat on which we sat, till on getting to Manasomba's he made a spring forward with both hands so as to seize all that was there), and then return quietly to Chipoka's, (where his look of perfect innocence, and ignorance of having done anything remarkable, after the animated features of the march and attack, was inimitable). I asked how it would do to send a message to Manasomba that we were coming against him, and that his only way of averting an attack would be by meeting us on the path and bringing the stolen men and property, with a goat for each man wrongfully detained; if he did this, we should not touch him; if he did not, we should burn his village? They said, "O, he will take the people and the things, and will run away, and we shall never see them." I said, "Suppose then we go quietly as you propose, and on getting near the village tell the first men we see to tell the chief the same thing." They thought this might be done.

Dec. 26. I laid down my pen at this point yesterday, a fit of drowsiness having come over me. In a few minutes we had our evening prayers, followed by Communion. I thought there were innumerable Christian congregations joining in Communion, but probably none so far from the centre of earthly communion, I mean none in so out-of-the-way a place. How wondrous the feeling of actual instantaneous communion with all you dear ones, though the distance and the means of earthly communication are so great and so difficult! How great this boon which He instituted and in His Holy Gospel commanded us to continue, as a perpetual memory of Him until His coming again!

The chief of this village is Saopa, an old, thin, tallish man, with a pleasant face, with whom I think I get on better in trying to speak, than with any previous stranger. He sent for his neighbour *Satawa* (meaning, *not runaway; tawa* is to run away), to whom we gave two yards of blue velvet, as we had given Saopa the same quantity of scarlet. They were beautiful colours, though the stuff is narrow, and the fabric slight: it calls forth great admiration always. The site of this village is very good: on the east is the towering range of the Milanje, hiding the sun, it is true, till two or nearly three hours after he has begun his course to the zenith. These hills, whose summits are estimated by Livingstone as being about 8000 feet above the sea, (and we are here about 2000,) remind me of the Wetterhorn near the river Aar in Switzerland; so towering, such inaccessible precipices. There the avalanches are roaring down every hour; here the torrents pour down, tracing vertical lines on the rock, which remain when the supply of water fails, and give the precipice a curious striated look, which we can see from Magomero, forty or fifty miles off. In some parts the precipice gives place to a steep slope covered with the trees and other luxuriant vegetation, below which is precipice again; the streams from the top giving an almost daily supply of moisture to the slope, from which it drains again to supply the lower ground; and all along the foot of the precipice is the rapid descent to the level of the plain, formed by the débris of the cliffs above. On this descent are many villages, and well cultivated gardens, the early produce of which helped our simple meal yesterday; for we had new heads of Chimanga (the mealies, you remember, of Natal), Indian corn, a fortnight or three weeks earlier than I remember them in Natal. The village itself lies in the shade of its own large trees, Indian fig and others, the central space being vacant, and serving for the reception of visitors, and large bodies of men, and for the transaction of business. It is in this place that we have taken all our meals, and that I am now sitting on one of our boxes writing to you. I have said there is abundance of rain here, caused, I suppose, by the nearness of these lofty, precipitous hills: and this with the heat produces the luxuriant vegetation; but on the other hand the place is damp; all round the village the grass, as high as one's middle, is soaking; and under these trees the mossy mould of damp soil is spread, while the tops of the hills are shrouded in the level lying clouds, like the table-cloth on Table Mountain at the Cape. We have not seen the sun during the four-and-twenty hours we have been here. Even here the people are complaining of hunger; and one would have accused them of inconceivable idleness for being without food in such a land of plenty, but that we hear in this quarter also of inroads by other oppressors, like our friends the Ajawa on the other side. The poor Mang-anja seem hunted and oppressed on all sides. Perhaps these afflictions have been appointed as a means of their receiving the Gospel. Tontorua seems to have been a destroyer now for a long time. William, who has been twenty-one years at the Cape, remembers his name before he left his own country, though that may have been a former holder of the title. We are told that the present Ajawa chief, Kainka, is the son and successor of another of the same name.

Dec. 27, S. John's day. Dear ——, it is strange passing these Holy days in this secular way. It makes me often review my position and say, "If it feels strange to be on such an expedition on a Saint's day, is it right to go on it at all?" and the result is that I always feel that it is. Yesterday we stayed at Saopa's village till 12, and then sent word to the chiefs that as the messenger had not yet come back from Chipoka's, we should go immediately, and meet him on the road. At the same time we ordered a fire to be lighted, water to be boiled, and chocolate made, that we might have something to start upon, as it would probably be dark before we began to think of another meal. By *one, we* were ready to start: but they said our bearers had gone out to buy food, and the only guide who knew the way to Chipoka's was gone with them. I said to my party, "If you will go on, marking the road well (that is, making a line with a stick, or shoe, across every path that you do *not* take, to *bar* it), I will follow with the luggage as soon as I can. I can walk quicker, and do not mind being late out." This plan was not a good one, and met with no favour from my companions; but it seemed to me to be the only way to save, if possible, the day which was just slipping through our fingers. So I stuck to it. The baggage was made up. The bearers turned up, and some of the Makololo also who were out; the chiefs Chigunda and Saopa were induced to get off the ground, and the latter himself became our guide. We got off by *two;* a perfect triumph of determination over obstinacy and indolence.

We got here (Koronko, I think, is the chief's name) about seven, having crossed some troublesome streams, swollen by the heavy rain, which was dashing down the precipices on our left in beautiful cascades. The first of these we crossed by tucking up our trousers, and half wading, half springing from stone to stone: the second we were carried over; the rest we waded simply, being already drenched with rain; and at the last, which was the worst, we were obliged some of us to stand in the water holding each other up, and pass over baggage, and help some of the rest. Some of our bearers from Magomero were the worst; the old chief Saopa, a man of sixty perhaps, was very plucky: Chigunda came out in a way that surprised us all, and his nephew and heir-apparent, Zachurakamo, was the boldest and best.

The chief, Chipoka, has come here, and is in confabulation with Chigunda and Saopa. I let them alone for a little, on the principle that disturbing them would only be wasting time, as they would have their talk out before I heard anything. But after a little I sent William to say, that I should be glad to see Chipoka. He has been gone about a quarter of an hour, and I suppose is learning all the news.

This morning we heard the following account. A man of this village told Chigunda last night that he had been lately in Manasomba's village, and learned that three of Manasomba's men had been as spies at or near Magomero; he having ascertained that we were coming against him, had called his brother from the banks of the Shire to help

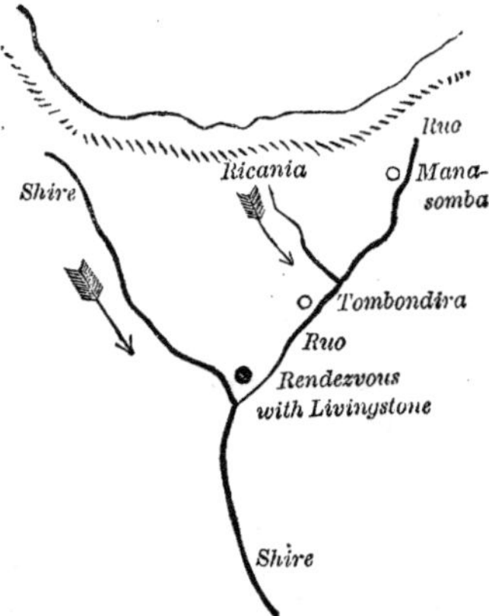

him, and had strengthened himself in a camp on the east (the left) bank of the Ricania, at the only ford where we could cross to get to Manasomba's. In the annexed sketch the line *in the writing*[1] may represent the outline of the Milanje mountains. The lines *in the map* are meant for the river Shire, its branch the Ruo, and *its* branch the Ricania. Tombondira's village is on the west side of the Ruo, as I have put it, and *probably* below the confluence of the Ricania. I do not believe the whole of this story: I do not believe that the spies ascertained, at or near Magomero, what our movements were. It was only three days before we left home that I told Chigunda what we were going to do. Men might guess before that, as I sent about a week earlier for the Makololo to come up; but I don't believe our intentions were at all generally known till this day last week. The other part of the story is possible enough: we have two other and independent sources of the information that Manasomba has relations on the Shire, or Ruo, or at the confluence. A further account says, that the camp is on this side of the Ricania, which is better for us, as we should have an opportunity of routing them before trying to cross the river in the face of them. This latter is, I think, a possible though certainly a difficult operation, as we may probably have to swim, and it will be difficult to obey Cromwell's injunction, to keep our powder dry.

1.30 P.M. We are just going to sit down to breakfast, (having, however, broken our fast on two cups of coffee and a biscuit at 7). We have had a long talk with Chipoka, and the rest. He said he was very sorry for what had happened, but Manasomba had done it himself. He (Chipoka) had sent our party there in good faith. We asked what character Manasomba had, and he said, that "though he had often ill-treated strangers, he had never done any harm to any one conducted by *his* messengers. It was their ordinary way of going back and forwards between Chipoka and Tombondira." "What did Tombondira think of it all?" Ans. "O, we are

[1] The Bishop has written over the upper part of his sketch; this cannot be reproduced in print, but the reader will find the map perfectly intelligible.

one : what is done to one is done to both." I said, "I think it right to punish such a man; so we will go together; but do not suppose that I am always going about with my gun to kill men, ("hear! hear!" from Chigunda;) my children came down peaceably to this place, but were detained and attacked by Manasomba. I live quietly at Magomero. Our wish is to do you good by exchanging cloth, beads, and other English goods for your goats and corn, ivory and cotton: and what is more than all, we come to you from God, of whom we have a better knowledge than you, whose laws we know, and we want to teach you these things. (All the chiefs said to this, "that is good.") So do not think I like bloodshed; but this man must be punished, and we must get back the three that are in his hands."

As to the time, we arranged that we should come to his village and sleep there; that he should go at once to call together his own and Tombondira's men, and that we should all be off early in the morning. He proposes that we should return to his village at night. Whether we do that, or go on to Tombondira's, will depend on circumstances. Now we must be off, 3.30 P.M.

Dec. 30, 10 A.M. Chipoka's village, called Manga. We got here on Friday sooner than I expected, soon enough to have a bath before dark in the sparkling rocky stream that we crossed just before we entered the village. This is a wonderfully beautiful situation. Under the overhanging precipices of the Milanje on the north, rising in two huge domes of the shape of a lemon standing erect on a plate, when the smaller half has been removed; the sides of the granite furrowed and gnarled by the torrents, that pour down when there is tropical rain. These domes guard the entrance of a steep-sided horse-shoe valley or scoop in the range, the back of which is thickly covered with trees on its inaccessible surface. From the foot of one of these domes the ground slopes pretty rapidly to the level of the southern plain; and it is on a part of this slope, just above the bank of the stream, the Malodza, (Marossa, as Procter and Scudamore have written it, and it is not much different, as *l* and *r* seem interchangeable in this language,) that the village of Manga is built. There are fine trees, among which the huts nestle in groups of four or five, so that it is difficult to know their number, but I suppose there are fifty: the one we are sleeping in is one of the largest: it is about sixteen feet in diameter, inside, the roof extending to a diameter of about twenty-four. There are numbers of beautiful banana trees, but there is little ripe fruit this year, the people having eaten a great deal unripe during the late scarcity. The view towards the south is extensive, seeming to reach for fifty miles or more, a wide rich plain, intersected by the Ruo and its tributaries, dotted with hills of six or eight hundred feet, and bounded, I believe, by the hills beyond the Shire, with perhaps a dip down on this side of it, like a sunk fence, concealed from this.

That night we had a talk with the chief, and finally arranged that we should start very early, so as to get to Manasomba's before people were awake. But when they came to wake us it was half-past twelve, and so dark a night, that no one would go down the bank of the stream to get us some water for coffee, till Scudamore went with them. We agreed that it was wild to start so early, and that they might come for us towards daybreak; and we lay down again to sleep. In the morning we started on a cup of coffee, carrying with us cold kid and a bottle of wine. Our only cup was the one —— gave me. The first stream we came to was so deep, that, though I was mounted high on the back of a man as tall as myself, I got wet up to the knee. The largest river we had to cross was the Ricania. It was this water that Scudamore had tried three times to ford before he succeeded *that* night in the dark. To our surprise we found a good bridge, consisting of a large tree thrown across. On the other side we halted for a quarter of an hour to refresh ourselves. We were in all about fifty, fifteen of whom were

English and Makololo, with guns, the rest Mang-anja from Chipoka and Saopa, with one or two guns among them: so that both in number of our own party and in smallness of our allies, we were more like the party of July under Livingstone than either of our own later bodies of August or October. About a quarter of an hour after this we stopped to pray for God's blessing, professing that we were not going in private revenge, but to free the captives, and to punish the robber and would-be murderer, in God's name, (having the good word, as you see, of the chiefs around, and their approval of our going,) and then I told them all that I wanted was to get my children back, and the stolen property, (more than 100 yards of cloth, besides change of clothing, food, pots and pans, &c.;) that I did not wish to kill any one, only to get these things, and to burn the village, that Manasomba might learn not to do so again, and others might fear; that if they defended their village we would drive them out, but on no account take women or children, or hurt them; that I wanted none of the plunder we might get, but they must bring it all together, and I would give shares of it.

After this we proceeded, expecting to reach the village in about an hour. Within ten minutes of our halt, (during the prayer all had been bowed to the ground except myself, standing up, with my eyes shut,) we saw a body of men nearly as large as our own coming to meet us. I called out, "Walk on, do not stop." I wished to know at once for myself what they said. As we afterwards learned, Chipoka, the chief of this village, had last Wednesday, (before he knew of our approach,) held a meeting with Manasomba, and arranged to have a *Minandu*, a discussion of their quarrel, on that very Saturday, that this was actually Manasomba and a few men coming to the Minandu, and not seeing at first that there were English or so many guns in our party, called out, "Stand still, do not come on:" but on our continuing to advance they left the path, and he stood on a huge ant-hill on our right. I found they were saying something about a *talk;* so I told William to call out, that if they wished to speak, five of them might come out and meet us. I did not know Manasomba was among them; but they ran away, and on asking where they had gone, I got answer that probably they had gone to *his* village. So we resumed our march, expecting to find the village defended: but when we got there, we found the entrance where the bearers some weeks ago had thrown down their burdens, and where Scudamore and Procter had had such a tussle, unguarded; and on passing through we found ourselves in a fine, but deserted village. I stayed at the centre, telling the rest to search the huts and bring everything to the centre. There were some fine Muscovy ducks, about half a dozen sheep and goats, and a little corn; of our own goods we recovered our valise, a pair of shoes, two or three pots, two tins of preserved meat, and a piece of soap. Then we set the huts on fire, most of the party carrying out the plunder.

I had left Burrup with Charlie (Makololo), Zachurakamo, and one or two others at the gate, to prevent our being surprised. We left the village in about half an hour; the sheep and goats were divided, three to the Makololo, two to Zachurakamo, (the nephew and heir of Chigunda,) two to Chipoka's people. Everything else I left as it had arranged itself, and we began our return. The live stock were much in our way; and Waller begged me to cut them adrift; and this had to be done at last. About an hour on our way home, as Scudamore and Burrup, who were in front, were in a narrow muddy place between masses of reeds, a shot was fired on them from the front. I heard the shot, where I was, behind, and hurried forward. I sent a party to go through, saying we from behind could now command the ground from which the shot had come. They went through this time without molestation. We found one man had been shot in the stomach by an arrow, which had to be cut out, as the first barb was buried, and another had flesh-wounds as from shot, or small stones. After this we tried to keep our party a little more in hand; but this was not easy, for after I had cut the sheep and goats adrift, the men would delay to kill and carry them: a time of no small anxiety, as the head of the column had got out of sight; I was in the middle waiting for Mobita to come up. However, at last we got into order, and went on slowly. The wounded man could not walk fast, and at last had to be carried. We were thankful to find the tree-bridge across the Ricania free, and got home rather tired about five. The day had been got through, to which we had looked forward with much doubt as to how we were to act. We had, indeed, failed to get back our people, (I forgot to say that we called out to Manasomba, that we wanted our people, when we met that party on the path,) but we had punished the robber, and had returned safe. We had vindicated the English name, and had shewn in this neighbourhood that it is not safe to attack an Englishman; and I hope the lesson may not be thrown away on these people.

Yesterday, being Sunday, we were a little disturbed by reports, which we did not believe, that Manasomba had come across the Ricania, and at one time that he was already at the foot of this village. I sent some of the Makololo to ascertain the truth, and in the mean time we had prayers. The chief Chipoka was attracted by the sound of the responses, and came to the door of the hut, where he stayed quietly, standing and sitting as he saw they did inside, all through the Morning Prayer and Litany: we reserved the Communion-service till the Makololo should report, and when they did it was late. Their report was, that Manasomba had never crossed the Ricania, but they saw a messenger professing to come from him, asking Chipoka to come next day to a *Minandu.* Chipoka sent back answer (on their return) to the messenger, who was to wait where they found him, that *he* would not cross the Ricania, that Manasomba must come to meet him at Coswe's, (a village we saw on Saturday;) he would meet him there.

Last night and this morning we have had much discussion what to do. The proposed plans were, to go across country to Soche, where (with your accurate geographical knowledge, you will know) we fall into our old route to the ship's anchorage, take that route, and go down the Shire by canoe, or go to Tombondira's from this, and so down the Ruo, or, as we have seen some reason to fear the chiefs on the Ruo, to keep a little more to the right, (the West,) say twenty or fifteen miles, and try to strike the confluence as nearly as possible, or to stay where we are and hear the end of the *Minandu*, sending Zachurakamo to it, to represent us, and in our name and Chigunda's demand the captives. Of these four plans Waller and Scudamore leaned to the first or last, the second was mine, the third Burrup's. I objected to the first, that we should be about a week too late in keeping our appointment. To the fourth, that I did not see that we should do any good to Chipoka by staying a day or two here: he must depend on himself at last, when we went; and as to demanding the captives, saying that was the condition of peace with us, it seemed neither true nor expedient to do so, unless we were prepared to do something to enforce the demand in case (as seemed very likely) it were refused; and we were all agreed that we could not and would not do more. Finally, we took this last course, with the modification of not making any threat: we told Chipoka we would wait till he came back from the *Minandu*, and we sent Zachurakamo, simply to demand the captives. That was, I suppose, about nine o'clock. It is now a quarter to two. The wounded man has died, and his companions have taken the body, in a piece of cloth which we gave, to bury him. Scudamore is very far from well, feverish all over. I think we shall not get away from this to-day. I imagine we shall be three days in getting to the Shire: if we start to-morrow we shall be there on the second instead of the first.

I have had a chat this morning with the old mother of

Chipoka: when she came yesterday I gave her a piece of cloth, and to-day she brought her acknowledgments in the shape of a fowl and three eggs.

Jan. 3, 1862. Dear ——. This is the first time I have written the name of this year: may it be to us and to you a year of greater grace and blessing than the last, and so may we abound more and more until the coming of our Lord and Saviour. How curious saying this to you, and probably the year will be far gone before you read it! But you are saying the same things, and God hears the prayers of both, and will shower down on each the showers of His blessing in answer to the distant prayer, just as the rain rises from the distant ocean, and falls on the thirsty ground, where He has appointed it. I am sitting in a hut on my way from Magomero to the *Pioneer's* anchorage: it is about six o'clock, and the light will soon fail me, and the fowl we have just bought will soon be ready: so I must make the best of my time to bring you up to date.

We meant to leave Chipoka's on Tuesday, and make our way with all speed to the Ruo mouth. Scudamore was looking so much unwell, that I determined he must go home, and Waller go to take care of him, while Burrup and I went on; but in the morning, when we asked for guides and bearers, Chipoka refused. He said, "All that country is occupied by Manasomba's friends: you will be killed if you go, and then the English who are behind (at Magomero) will come and blame me and burn my village. If you want to go back, I will give you guides and bearers; but forwards, I will not." It was vain to argue. He had made up his mind; and much against our will we turned homewards about eleven o'clock. Waller and Scudamore both said strongly, it was much better. Scudamore said it was natural he should wish to keep us behind him, while he was still treating with Manasomba. Waller said we had had enough of fighting: and that going down that way was only provoking more, and would make it more difficult for us to assert our character as ministers of the Gospel of peace. I said I did not expect any more fighting: my party would be too strong to allow them to think of touching us. Accordingly, I tried on the road to arrange that Waller and Scudamore should go on with the guides and[1] * * *

Jan. 8. I forget where I was, and what place I was at. O, I see; I was an hour or two from Magomero, and was describing our return from Chipoka's. I am now at Chibisa's, the anchorage of the *Pioneer*, and hope to get down the day after to-morrow, and to find that the *Pioneer* has not been staying long waiting. To make short work with the old story, I tried time after time to get down across country to the Ruo mouth, but always failed: generally there were at least three obstacles, and so it ended in my going on homewards day by day; actually turning my back on the spot I was making for, on the day I had appointed to meet Livingstone. I found, you see, that it was impossible to get down straight, and was obliged therefore to take a longer way round as the shortest in the end, and by coming down from home to Chibisa's here, to go down the river from this. I gave up the plan of going across from Soche, as being a tempting of hostilities lower down the river, which was undesirable on every ground. Well, on Thursday, January 2, I got to Magomero. Scudamore was very unwell from fatigue and exposure. We found them a sick house: Procter only on the turn to amend, after fever: Rowley very low: Dickinson a good deal pulled down with work. Burrup and Waller were both worse than myself; and I had been suffering from diarrhœa for three or four weeks. I had hoped to get a fresh companion out of the home stock. But this was impossible: and I think in any case Burrup would have objected to staying at home. So off we started next day.

We have established the custom of having a few prayers

[1] The letter here breaks off abruptly, as though the Bishop had been called away by sudden interruption.

at our Church before starting, and after return of any of our party on a journey: so we had prayers for those that remained and for those who were going, and we set off. It rained heavily, and we had hard work to get the Makololo into motion. But it is a good thing to get away, though we only made five or six miles that day. From that till this morning we have had almost incessant rain, and have slept five nights on the road, which I ran through in seventeen hours last time. Once we were detained two or three hours by a river, in a place where I think I have always stepped across. In two others some of us stood in the middle and on the banks to help others across. It was a great relief on Monday night to find ourselves more than half-way, at Soche: the chief was very civil, and gave us some *ufa* (native meal), for which we were very thankful. Yesterday we got on better, and this morning we got here: but so ill had we calculated the distance, that we took a couple of hard eggs with us, starting without even coffee, meaning to breakfast here, and it was two P.M. before we began that said early meal. But we are repaid for all our trouble by finding that it will not be difficult to get boats a little lower down, the chief here undertaking to send us there, which augurs well. Accordingly we are in better spirits, and are to start with volunteers from among the Makololo. This is good. Then we have seen the sun to-day; and this is a very beautiful place: a village perched on the top of a cliff of red clay over-hanging the stream, which is now swollen much, and commanding a view of the valley of the Shire, or at least of its lowest level, extending four or five miles to the eastern hills. The valley itself, in a freer sense, stretches many a mile behind us to the west,—fine fertile land, studded with shrubs and trees, and apparently fit for any cultivation. I suppose, however, it is not so healthy as the higher lands.

The men of this village are old friends, most of them: and all looks bright. I have been having many a laugh with them already. Thus it is that God gives us bright spots in our life at the darkest,—and how often bright tracts stretching over much of it!

I am all this time stopping to shew my watch to some of them, and to explain to another that if we do not agree on the price of his meal we need not quarrel; on which he comes back to take what I offered, and I give him a little more. But I must stop now. Thank God for this day.

Jan. 9. It is half-past 8. We have had breakfast; at least we are waiting for the tea. Burrup has taken but little. I hope he will be up to his work to-day. He will in spirit, I am sure. You may think we are in tolerable time; but that only shews your ignorance. We ought to have been off before this. However, it is no use hoping to go at railway speed here, or with railway punctuality. The delay now is on account of Mobita, whose mansion is at some distance, perhaps a mile, and who has not yet turned up. I read Burrup this morning the *Keble* for xxvth Sunday after Trinity. I do so admire the last verses.

Monday, Jan. 13. Our suspense is at an end. We got here, the Ruo mouth, on Saturday, to learn that Livingstone, by most trying delays, as they must have been to him, had passed downwards not many days before; so that, if we had kept our appointment, and been here by the first of January, we should have been in time to see him going down. This, though sadly trying to him, and running some risk of his losing the meeting at the bar, and also involving our staying here a good while, two or three weeks probably, seemed, and seems still, good news to me, inasmuch as we have not detained him by arriving ten days after time.

We had, on the whole, a prosperous journey down. The chief at Chibisa's, you know, undertook to send us down to a chief an hour or two down the stream, Turuma, where we should be likely to get a larger boat. His own he could not spare, as it is constantly wanted to cross the river, and for communication between the village and the island, on which are some of their gardens. Accordingly, on Thursday we set off at 3, and got to Turuma's in half an hour. It was delicious, the floating down that broad, green-banked river. The uncertainty as to the length of the voyage gave it a dreaminess, like some parts of Southey's *Thalaba*. But like *Thalaba* our difficulties were not at an end. Turuma refused to see us, returned our present, and declined to hire his boat to us, not, as I believe, from ill will, but, as he said himself, for fear of Mankokwe, whom (you remember) we saw on July 1 with Livingstone[1]. What was to be done? We thought of trying to persuade our boatmen to take us to another village, where we might have better luck; but before doing so, I thought it might be possible to borrow the boat we were in, (the men having positively refused to go so far as the Ruo,) by arranging to borrow Turuma's boat for them. They agreed to this, and so did he, a good deal to my surprise. The next question was about men. Chibisa's would not go on, Turuma was afraid to send his. Just then two of the Makololo, Zomba and Siseho, joined us, having walked down the bank. Mobita had in the morning refused to come, and I gave them all up except Charlie, who never hesitated. These three undertook to go down with us. So off we started, wondering at the way God was leading us.

In an hour or two we landed at Magunda's, where they received us well. The chief, not well enough to see us, sent us a goat, before we had sent him anything, which was unusually civil. Next morning we were off early. Burrup was far from well. About midday we stopped to cook; found a village a little back from the stream, where we stayed three hours: we carried our cooked food, as we were entering the Elephant Marsh, and should not come to another village before dark. At night we drew to the shore, made fast the boat to the grass on the bank, ate some cold goat, and prepared for bed. By this time the mosquitoes were very troublesome. I lent two pairs of trousers, and a blue coatie to the three men, wrapped my own head and

[1] The Bishop refers to a letter not printed in this volume.

shoulders in my mosquito curtains, and should soon have been asleep, when one of the men said, "We are going on." It was better, they thought, to work on in moonlight, rather than be eaten up by the insects. In less than a minute we were off. Sometimes I sat up, watching the guiding of the boat in the narrow winding channel, for before dark we had left the midstream on the chance of finding a village on the margin of the marsh. After half-an-hour or so we found ourselves stranded on the flooded bank, having been sucked out of the stream by the overflowing water. As we had taken a little water, and might have been upset, two of the men were for stopping here. I, who had been delighting in this way of turning mosquitoes to good account (by getting three or four hours at five or six miles an hour, a problem this which has, I believe, baffled all former travellers in mosquito countries,)—I was for going on, saying, "Let us see a second time," but gave in to the majority of the men.

In a few minutes Zomba, the bowman, gave his orders for a start, and off we were again in silence. This time we were sooner in coming to grief. A sudden turn, which our bowman did not see in time, landed us again on a point where the stream parted into two; the two men in the stern jumped out, up to their middles. I followed immediately; Burrup after me. But in vain; the canoe continued to fill, and we began to pull out our things. Unfortunately one piece of baggage, containing all Burrup's things, was washed out of the stern: all that was saved had to be laid on the bank, which consisted of long grass, two or three feet deep in water, till we could get the canoe raised and baled out. Then the things were put in again, all soaking; guns, powder-flasks, bags of sugar and coffee, books, mail-bag, watch, &c.; all from below the surface; and we wet up to our middles. We had to get into the boat, wringing the water from our trowser-legs, and then to lie down again, worse attacked by mosquitoes than at first. It was about ten, as my watch informed me in the morning, not having gone after this. I slept the best, I suspect. Burrup said he did not mind mosquitoes, and certainly never uttered a word. I took Charlie under the corner of my curtain. The rest switched themselves from time to time. No one proposed going on again: indeed, we were thankful our losses had been no worse, though it was not till next day we remembered that all our medicine was gone, and our spare powder; and all my powder was wet. Before the sun was up we were off. Fortunately the night was far from cold, or we must have taken harm: as it is, Burrup is none the better for it. I think I have escaped any ill consequences.

In the morning (Saturday, Jan. 11), about 9, I was wakened by being told we were at the Ruo mouth. We landed on an island where we saw a village, learned that the *Pioneer* had lately passed, (though it is evidently not a week ago, it is hopeless to make out the exact day), and I cannot learn that Livingstone has left any letter for me. I must get a canoe as soon as I can, and go and look for it among the neighbouring villages. In the meantime we have been led to a very nice village. A benign, oldish chief, Chikanzi, with a large population, occupying, I think, about a hundred huts, willing that we should remain here, warning us that the chiefs a little way up the Ruo would cut our throats if we tried to pay them a visit, which, whether true or not, at least removes all fear of his joining them, and betraying us. I have my hopes, in my own mind, that our being here in this way may be intended to prepare this village for being one of the stations to be worked by our Mission steamer (the University Boat), for which I hope to write by this mail.

So matters stand at present. Burrup is very low, and we have no medicine. Quinine, which we ought to be taking every day, there is none. But He who brought us here can take care of us without human means. If we *should* be down at once, Charlie will take care of us. The texts in Greek which we have learned day by day lately have been Rom. ii. "For he is not a Jew, which is one outwardly; neither is that circumcision, which is outward in the flesh: but he is a Jew, which is one inwardly; and circumcision is that of the heart, in the spirit, and not in the letter; whose praise is not of men, but of God." iii. "But now the righteousness of God without the law is manifested, being witnessed by the law and the prophets; even the righteousness of God which is by faith of Jesus Christ unto all and upon all them that believe: for there is no difference: for all have sinned, and come short of the kingdom of God." vi. "For the wages of sin is death; but the gift of God is eternal life through Jesus Christ our Lord." vii. "O wretched man that I am! who shall deliver me from the body of this death? I thank God through Jesus Christ our Lord. So then with the mind I myself serve the law of God; but with the flesh the law of sin." viii. "I am persuaded, that neither death, nor life, nor angels, nor principalities, nor powers, nor things present, nor things to come, nor height, nor depth, nor any other creature, shall be able to separate us from the love of God, which is in Christ Jesus our Lord." x. "Whosoever shall call upon the name of the Lord shall be saved. How then shall they call on Him in whom they have not believed? and how shall they believe in Him of whom they have not heard? and how shall they hear without a preacher? and how shall they preach, except they be sent? as it is written, How beautiful are the feet of them that preach the gospel of peace, and bring glad tidings of good things." Good bye for the present.

Here the letter terminates abruptly, for reasons which the reader will guess only too truly. I may add, the letter bears marks of having been immersed in water; some small portions of it have been rendered nearly illegible. It is a very precious document; and the concluding words, *Good bye for the present,* form as suitable a parting from his earthly friends as he himself could have desired.

The loss of medicines by the upsetting of the canoe was a matter of far more serious moment than the Bishop has represented it. Looking upon the matter coolly, one would feel disposed to say, that there were three courses which might have been adopted, and that the one actually taken was the only thoroughly bad one. The Bishop and Mr Burrup might either have gone back to Chibisa's and Magomero, and returned with a new supply of quinine, in which case active exercise might probably have preserved their health; and even then, judging from the former experience of the *Pioneer*, they could have been again at the rendezvous, before Dr Livingstone was likely to have returned: or they might have made a push to overtake the *Pioneer*, which had only recently passed, and which might in all probability have been overtaken: or lastly, they might remain where they were, in perfect bodily inaction after long severe bodily exercise, with no exciting mental occupation, and with no medicine, and consequently under the most favourable conditions for the action of African fever. But, unfortunately, the Bishop had hitherto seemed almost fever proof, and Mr Burrup had already been able to set all rules of African travel at defiance; as Dr Livingstone said, Mr Burrup's wonderful feat, which has been already recorded, had destroyed the effect of all his cautions; and so, in defiance of the apparent dictates of ordinary prudence, they determined to remain where they were.

No doubt one strong argument for remaining was

that the Bishop thought he could turn his time to good account. He could make friends with the chief of the island and his people, and so lay the foundation for future missionary work; and with this prospect before him, the rashness of the attempt would become invisible. The result, however, adds another to the list of melancholy proofs which have been furnished, of the need of not completely forgetting the necessities and the weaknesses of flesh and blood: let a man, placed in a responsible position, whether as a missionary or otherwise, first do all that human wisdom and prudence can suggest, and then humbly and devoutly leave the result in God's hands; but it is impossible to applaud the wisdom, though we may marvel at the exalted piety, of trusting for preservation to God's providence, under circumstances in which the laws of the natural world prove by experience that safety is not to be expected.

However, the Bishop determined to remain on the island. On January 16, he wrote as follows in a letter to Mr Strong: the date, it will be observed, brings it into immediate connection with the letter to his sister given above.

LETTER XCIII.

Jan. 16, 1862. I have written to my sister a full account, which you will see, of my journey with Scudamore, Burrup and Waller, to Manga and back, and subsequently with Burrup to this place, an island at the confluence of the Ruo with the Shire, where we are awaiting the return of Livingstone, in the *Pioneer*, from the sea. We left home on December 23. Spent Christmas at Saopa's village, under the precipices of the Milanje mountains. Found that Chipoka, whose guides led Procter and Scudamore to the village of Manasomba, disclaimed all complicity in the outrage. Accordingly, with a few of his men, who, together with our own, amounted to about fifty, we went on January 4, and finding the village of Manasomba deserted, burnt it, and returned to Chipoka's. We went with the avowed object of recovering the two remaining captives, one of whom was one of our own freed-people at Magomero, and punishing the perpetrators of so treacherous an act as that described above, in order that he might desist from such courses, especially in the case of Englishmen, and that others might fear. In this I feel that we did right. It is true our Lord said to His disciples, "They knew not what spirit they were of." But in this case we were not revenging ourselves. There was no ruler ordained of God (Rom. xiv.) to whom we could refer the matter, else we should have been only too glad to do so; but we believed that, being the only power in the place that could do it, *we* were ourselves God's ministers for the purpose.

I would gladly have left it for Livingstone to do in the Queen's name, but feared he would say his other duties were too pressing, and that he had no time. I should have preferred waiting for his approval of my doing it, which I am sure he would give; but by that time, with ten tons of goods, and probably a party of ladies, on my hands, it would have been impossible. As speedy a retribution as possible seemed the best; and in that belief, and with the approval of my associates, I acted. We marched peaceably among fields and villages belonging to Manasomba's people, and spared a village near his own, said to be the residence of his wife (equivalent to a second village belonging to himself), and were glad to find on our return that this moderation was appreciated, and was attributed to a desire not to shut out the possibility of a reconciliation with the offender. To this object Chipoka now devoted his energies, and, to avoid risk of failure, refused to help me in any way to make my way to the Ruo mouth in a straight line, as I believe I might easily have done in two days. Chipoka said we should pass through country occupied by Manasomba's friends, and that our doing so would frustrate his attempts to heal the breach. Besides, if we were killed, the English from behind (at Magomero) would come and blame him for guiding us into danger. With the greatest reluctance I yielded to necessity, and got here in eleven or twelve days, instead of two, going over about 230 miles instead of about fifty, and being ten days after our appointment with Livingstone. I ought to have said that in the attempt to recover the captives we utterly failed, but left that as an outstanding demand which Chipoka promised to make in my name.

The most painful part of the whole was the death of one of our bearers, who was wounded by an arrow on our way back, and the illness which repeated exposure brought back with increased force upon Scudamore. I left him, I am sorry to say, on January 3rd, in a high fever. There was not one of the party that I left really well (except perhaps Adams), though none of the rest were very seriously ill. Burrup and I had a very wet walk to the anchorage of the *Pioneer*, sleeping five nights on the way, and came down here in a canoe with no other mishap than being once upset and losing one of our bundles; it contained our spare powder, (so that we have only three or four charges dry,) all our medicines, which we miss as we are both in want of them, and all Burrup's bedding, change of clothes, and other private property. We had an uncomfortable night (it happened at 10 P.M. by moonlight), as we were soaked up to the waist (nothing whatever indeed was dry but the shirts we had on), and we were nearly at the mercy of an unusual number of mosquitoes. Burrup has not been well since. I am myself, thank God, in almost perfect health, and only regret, on my own account, the loss of the little packet of drugs, inasmuch as I shall probably have a touch of fever soon for want of quinine. We learned that Livingstone had gone down only a few days before we reached the rendezvous: his delays from sandbanks must have been as trying as on our way up. We do not expect him back for at least a fortnight (our cloth for purchasing will last perhaps three weeks).

At first sight it might seem that it would have been much better, could we have been here in time to see him before he went down. We could, it is true, have sent letters later by six or seven weeks, as an addition to our mail of November 15; and we should probably have gone to the sea with him, and so received our ladies. We *two* might also have answered the letters we hope to receive soon. On the other hand, by our stay here, we are making intimate friends of the inhabitants of this large village. There are, I believe, more than 100 huts, giving, I suppose, about 500 people. I do not know any Mang-anja village so large, and the importance of this friendship may be great, for I expect to add to this letter a request for a steamer to ply on this lower Shire, to constitute our connection with the civilised world. Livingstone warns me not to *depend* on the *Pioneer* to bring up stores, or occasional additions to our body; for it will not always be possible for him to do us this service at the time we require it, as he would be only too glad to do. There must, then, be a steamer on which we can depend for supplies and communication. I think I told you how I shrank from the responsibility of having such a vessel, which would have to lie idle for months together, periods injurious alike to body and soul. I thought of fevers on board, and, far worse, of quarrelling among its crew, and of conduct unbecoming our Christian name, and dishonouring to God, and undermining our mission work among the natives. But why should it be idle? Why not have mission work on this river, under the management of a priest, and perhaps a deacon, always on board? Why should not there be several, aye, from five to ten villages, on the banks, visited regularly, in which preaching, schooling, marketing, and general civilising influences might go on? The trip to the sea, once or twice in a year, would make little interruption in this, which would be the main work of the vessel; and if there were this constant passing up and down, at regular or irregular intervals, only not too long, there would be much greater difficulty than at present in transmitting slaves from the east to the west bank. In this way of looking at the matter, which has arisen in conversation at Magomero, all my objections vanish. There would be healthful occupation for the crew, and such employment for their minds as would, I hope, give the ship rather a good than a bad influence on their characters, while the whole would be under the command of a clergyman, who would consider that his parish included his fellow-voyagers, as well as the natives on the banks. And, in this view, may not our stopping here and making friends with this *island* chief be of importance, greater than all that we might have done if we had been here a week earlier?

Soon after writing the above the fever seized upon the Bishop, and made rapid progress. He became aware of his approaching end, and told his Makololo attendants that Jesus was coming to fetch him away. About the 20th or 21st of January, his intellectual faculties gave way, and he lay in his hut in a state of utter prostration, almost without uttering a word, or if he did speak, speaking incoherently. Sometimes, in going out of his hut, he would fall forward on his face, and lie on the ground without being able to move. On the 24th he appears to have ruptured a blood-vessel, and was henceforth weaker than before. Mr Burrup was almost as debilitated as himself, and was of course unable to render much assistance. The three Makololo, however, were faithful and attentive, and did all they could. So matters went on till January 31, when the Bishop died.

On the morning of that day, the chief, under the pretence that the hut was needed for some other purpose, insisted upon the Bishop being moved; Mr Burrup represented the impossibility of moving a man in such a condition; but in vain. The fact probably was, that the chief was afraid that the death would take place in his hut, and that afterwards, according to the native superstition, the presence of the departed spirit would render it uninhabitable. Fearing lest the chief should banish them from the island altogether, Mr Burrup at length consented, and the dying Bishop was removed to another hut. The change probably hastened the end, for in about an hour and a half after arriving in the new hut, the Bishop breathed his last.

It is needless to say that the position of Mr Burrup was a very painful one. Himself in a state of great exhaustion, he was compelled at once to take steps for removing the body from the island: the chief would not permit it to remain even till the following day: and accordingly, on the same evening, assisted by the three faithful Makololo, Mr Burrup conveyed the remains of Bishop Mackenzie to the main-land in the canoe, chose a secluded spot under a large tree, dug a grave, and after reading as much of the burial service as he was able in the dim evening light, left the dear remains in sure and certain hope of the resurrection of the just.

The reader will wish to know what became of Mr Burrup. The day after the Bishop's death, he made preparations for returning to Magomero; and leaving a letter with the chief to be given to Dr Livingstone, when he should return in the *Pioneer*, he started on his homeward journey on Sunday, February 2. The Makololo wished to leave the canoe and go to Chibisa's by land; but as the canoe had been lent by the people of that place, Mr Burrup would not consent. Accordingly, the party started in the canoe, but at the end of three days, when they had got through the Elephant Marsh, the navigation became so difficult, that the Makololo positively refused to continue with the boat, and landed; Mr Burrup was compelled to follow. On February 8, they arrived at Chibisa's: Mr Burrup's walking powers were by this time all expended, and from Chibisa's to Magomero he was carried.

It was on February 14 that the missionary party, who had begun to grow uneasy concerning the Bishop and Mr Burrup, were discussing the propriety of sending down to Chibisa's and making inquiries, when one of the Makololo suddenly appeared: his sad looks at once told them that something was wrong. They asked whether the Bishop was coming; he shook his head, looked on the ground, and answered in Mang-anja, "Bishop wa fra,"—the Bishop is dead. The truth could not be doubted: he himself had assisted at the burial.

Soon after Mr Burrup arrived. The first few days it was hoped that he would recover his strength, and in all probability this hope would have been realised had European comforts been at hand; his appetite was good, and he was able to walk; unfortunately, neither brandy, nor wine, nor wheaten bread were to be had, and on February 22 he rapidly sank, and died in the evening. On Sunday, February 23, he was buried in a quiet retired spot near Magomero.

The story of the Bishop's decease would hardly be complete, if I did not add some account of the party of ladies, to meet whom the disastrous journey down the Shire had been undertaken. The reader will remember that we left Miss Mackenzie and Mrs Burrup in charge of Captain Wilson of H.M.S. *Gorgon*, at Quilimane. They soon fell in with Dr Livingstone and the *Pioneer*, and arrangements were quickly commenced for taking the whole party up the country. There was a good deal of work to be done before the expedition could start; Dr Livingstone's new steamer, the *Lady Nyassa*, which was on board the *Hetty Ellen*, had to be transshipped to the *Pioneer*, besides smaller arrangements. However, on February 10 they entered the narrow channel which joins the Kongone mouth with the great Zambesi, and the difficulties of navigation soon began. On that very afternoon, they grounded on a sand-bank; two days afterwards, something went wrong with the machinery; and the next day all the coals were exhausted, and they were compelled to send out parties to cut wood. At length, Captain Wilson kindly proposed to take Miss Mackenzie and Mrs Burrup forward in his gig, and on Monday, Feb. 17, they started upon their journey. It would be beyond the scope of this memoir to attempt to narrate the details of this remarkable expedition, and I am unable to describe, in adequate terms, the chivalrous courtesy which the two lone ladies received from Captain Wilson, Dr Ramsay, and the crew. Suffice it to say, that the party reached in due time the place of rendezvous, at the junction of the Ruo and Shire, Miss Mackenzie at the time lying in a state of unconsciousness from fever; here they made inquiry concerning the Bishop, but the natives denied that they had seen or heard anything of him, the reason for their lie no doubt being this, that they feared lest they should be called to account for the Bishop's death. On March 4, they reached Chibisa's, where they heard of the sad calamity. From hence Captain Wilson, with Dr Kirk, made an expedition to Magomero, to hear all particulars; on arriving there, it was found that not only the Bishop, but Mr Burrup also, as the reader already knows, had been taken away. There was nothing to be done but to return to Chibisa's with the melancholy intelligence, and offer to the two sad-hearted women the means of leaving a country in which it was now impossible for them to remain.

They started on the return voyage at five A.M. on March 12, and at four P.M. reached the island where the Bishop died. Inquiry was made for the letter which had been left; the natives looked one at another, and saying, "It is all known," produced the letter. It ran thus:

MOUTH OF RUO, ISLAND AND VILLAGE MALO,
Saturday, Feb. 1, 1862.

MY DEAR DOCTOR,

I deplore to tell you that our good Bishop died on this island yesterday about 5 o'clock. We arrived here on Saturday, January 12. We had been upset in our canoe the night before, and the valise in which the medicines were with the quinine was lost. We had, therefore, none, with the exception of some made from your prescription, which had likewise suffered from the wet. He had been suffering from diarrhœa for some weeks before, but had got rid of it. He took the pills twice, once before he came here. He was quite well and strong notwithstanding, and shewed no signs of failing strength for ten days after our arrival, but from that time he shewed symptoms of wandering in the head, and at length mental and physical prostration, which continued up to the last. The Chief objected to his being buried on the island. We therefore, although sunset, went over and buried him as decently as the haste thought necessary made possible. The spot is under a large tree, which the natives will shew you. In consequence of my arrangements I shall not be able to do anything to the grave.

Captain Wilson had great difficulty in procuring a guide to shew him the grave; at last an old man consented to go, but on condition that he should go in his own canoe, not in the captain's gig. Captain Wilson and Dr Kirk found the spot, which had evidently not been disturbed; they made a cross of reeds, and placed it over the grave. This act of piety performed, the boat continued her sad voyage that same evening.

On April 2 the ladies were again on board the *Gorgon;* on April 26 they were safely landed at the Cape, and were once more hospitably received by the good Bishop of Cape Town.

Reference has already been made to the plan of having a steamer in the service of the mission. The Bishop conceived the notion of making an appeal for such a steamer to the members of the boat-clubs in Oxford and Cambridge. I now give the letter in which the appeal was contained. It is only a fragment, and is a rough draft written in pencil; but it will, if I mistake not, be read with great interest, partly as being one of the last productions of the Bishop's mind, partly because it will shew how nobly desirous he was, even to the last, of turning every advantage which his position gave him to the account of the great work which he had in hand.

LETTER XCIV.

River Shire (a Branch of the Zambesi),
January, 1862.

Sir,

I write to you as a member of the University Boat-Club, of which I am myself a member, to ask you to give attention to the matter which I now lay before you. Those were noble contests in which some of us took part, and all took interest, on the Isis or the Cam; but we are older men now, and may well turn to higher and nobler aims. There is on the river Shire a contest to be maintained with evil, both with sin, as the root, and with oppression, cruelty, and every other form of the fruits of sin. In order to engage in this contest, and to continue the mission already established on the high table-land fifty miles from its banks, we must have a steamer to ply on the stream, to connect and bring under our superintendence the several points along its course, where Christian and civilising influences may advantageously be applied; and also to keep up our communication with the sea, from which we must receive our letters and supplies for barter, and other necessaries. The Bishop of Cape Town first spoke of the need of such a vessel, and I am fully convinced it is absolutely required; I have delayed writing for one, only till we could see our way through one or two objections to the idea as it at first presented itself to me.

The following is a sketch of what I think would do the

work, and without which it could not be done. A steamer 80 feet long, 16 feet wide, drawing two and a half feet of water, when carrying her own spare gear, without crew or stores, and making easily (with wood in her furnaces) a speed of eight miles an hour when loaded so as to draw four feet of water. A master of the grade of the master of a merchantman, with boatswain and three seamen, an engineer with assistant, one stoker, and a doctor; the whole to be under the direction of one of the clergy of the mission. I would make it the duty of this vessel to take a trip down the river and back again, once in (say) two months (its head-quarters being at Chibisa's, the anchorage of the *Pioneer*), and stay two or three days at each of the five or six villages on the bank, which might by degrees be chosen as central points for their respective neighbourhoods. In the course of these two or three days, preaching, schooling, and general teaching would be the main objects, while the inhabitants of the vicinity might be tempted to swell the numbers in the villages by the opportunity they would have of getting cloth by bartering their goods. The vessel would in this way have a supply of fresh goods, and the first attempt would be made to establish a trade in cotton and other articles of export. To keep up foreign communication, the steamer would make a trip once a year or oftener to the bar, meeting some sea-going vessel by appointment. She would then discharge any cotton, ivory, &c., which she might have received in barter, at the same time that she received the year's supplies for the missions on the river and on the highlands. In case of necessity this vessel would, I conceive, be able to make a run to Johanna or Natal; but I would not contemplate this as any part of her duty. One future good result of the plying of such a vessel on this river, would be that, in concert with Livingstone's operations on the upper Shire and Lake Nyassa, the transfer of gangs of slaves from the east to the west side of this line would be very much impeded—probably entirely prevented

—and thus a slave path, apparently quite recently opened, would be closed. The cost of such a vessel would probably be £5,000, and the annual outlay not less than £1,700. Might not these sums be raised by the members of the University Boat-Clubs, and the boat be called the "University Boat?" Will you give a liberal share, and do what you can to urge others to do the same?

The appeal contained in the Bishop's letter has not met with a response so warm as might perhaps have been anticipated. Nevertheless, something has been done towards carrying out the scheme, though in a modified form. Further consideration, and the results of Dr Livingstone's experience, led those best fitted to judge into the opinion that a boat, manned by a native crew, would be far more practicable and more effective than a steamer; in fact, that a steamer could not be permanently worked, and that a boat, rowed by natives, possibly might. Accordingly, an attempt has been made to raise the funds for such a boat service; it is manifest, that if the mission is to hold its ground in the country, something of the kind must be done.

And now I come to the last document, left behind him by Bishop Mackenzie, which I shall think it necessary to preserve in these pages. It is Bishop Mackenzie's will; it has already been printed in a paper put forth by the Committee of the Mission, but deserves a place in this Memoir of his life, because it is so thoroughly like himself,—so manly, so considerate, so kind, so Christian. Before leaving Magomero on December 23, the Bishop put a paper into Mr Procter's hands, directing that it should be looked at in the event of his death. When that sad event did take place, the paper was examined, and contained the following.

MAGOMERO, *December* 23, 1861.

At my death I commend my soul to God, as unto a merciful Creator, Saviour, and Sanctifier, until *that day*.

As to the affairs of this world, I should wish the members of this Mission to act under the temporary headship of the Senior Priest, acting with the advice of the other Priests, or if there be no Priests, the Senior Deacon, or if there be no Deacon, the Senior Layman, acting with the advice of the others of their own degree respectively, reckoning seniority in the following order:—Procter, Scudamore, Burrup, Rowley, Waller, Dickinson, Gamble, Adams, Clarke, Charles, Johnson, Williams, Job. This temporary arrangement to hold until the arrival of my successor, or of instructions from the Metropolitan.

My personal property, such as has not been bought at the expense of the Mission, I leave to the Mission, with the exception of a few books, to be given to my family as reminiscences, such as my Consecration Bible, my Bible and Prayer Book, my Prayer Book, Greek Testament, Christian Year, Bishop Andrews' Devotions, Hickes' Devotions.

After payment of all dues, I give the remainder of my property to the Additional Bishopric's Fund, remitting the loan I made to the Cathedral at Maritzburg, in Natal, and acting with consideration for all my debtors.

This memorandum to be read here, and then sent

to my brother, John Mackenzie, Esq., 11 Abercromby Place, Edinburgh.

C. F. Mackenzie.

Witnesses {H. C. Scudamore,
H. Waller.

It is perhaps a little remarkable that the execution of this will did in reality precede by little more than a month the event, in anticipation of which it was prepared. To a looker-on the Bishop's life would have appeared to be in no greater peril at the time of starting for Manasomba's, than on several previous occasions; and there is, I think, no trace to be found in any of his letters of his having taken a less cheerful prospect of the future than formerly. The reader may possibly be disposed to think that the faithful servant had received some slight shadowy hint, which he could hardly explain or express, that the time of his departure was at hand. Anyhow, it is beautiful to see how, in the prospect of an event, which was always more or less probable, the good Bishop thought chiefly of his flock, and took care that, so far as he could ensure the result, the peace and harmony which had reigned in Magomero during his own lifetime should not be endangered by his departure.

What the feeling of loss and desolation would be at Magomero, when the news of the Bishop's death became known, possibly the reader may imagine; any one who knew Mackenzie as I knew him, will quite understand that the party would grieve over something more acutely painful even than the loss of their head;

every one would feel that he had lost a brother. I have avoided as much as possible in this Memoir mere commendation of him who is the subject of it, but I think that I may, without any breach of good taste, introduce in this place a passage from a letter written by Mr Procter to Miss Mackenzie, in which he speaks of his own feeling concerning the loss, and of the impression made upon his mind by Bishop Mackenzie's character.

Speaking of the troublous state of the country, subsequent to the Bishop's death, and the need of trust in God's protection, Mr Procter says, "Such thoughts as these never fail to remind me of him whom you and we have lost, our friend and Bishop, who was of all I have ever known the most calm and gentle, and whose spirit failed not to make itself felt on all around him. O! Miss Mackenzie, great as is the brother that you have lost, the father and friend that we have lost, and the careful shepherd that the poor wandering heathen have lost, I can never think of that calm quiet *man* in every sense of the word, that kindly heart which was ever ready with its sympathy and love, that lofty mind that soared so far from earth, and yet seemed not to soar at all, without feeling that the Christian world has lost more than all,—a benefactor whose influence extended far wherever he went, and with whom no one could converse even for a little time without feeling himself a better, and very often a wiser man. I cannot look upon him as a hero, as one standing out from and above all others, but as one moving amongst them, assuming nothing high or original, but a true and genial friend of the world,—in the sense of all men living in one common brotherhood. He has left us too soon as we may be inclined to feel, but not before his Father saw fit to summon him to the house of the angels and the blessed, whom he loved so well. And it seems as if a goodly string had been struck while he lived and spoke amongst us, and that, though broken and silent now, a sweet echo still comes as from the everlasting hills, 'Glory to God in the highest, and on earth peace, good will towards men!' I, as one only, loved your brother, and knew not how I loved him until he was gone."

Nor can I resist the temptation of adding here a few lines from one who had every opportunity of forming a judgment concerning Bishop Mackenzie—I mean Dr Livingstone. The Bishop's admiration for Dr Livingstone has been seen several times in this volume; it is a pleasure to be able to record that the admiration was mutual. The paragraph which follows is taken from a private letter written to General Hay.

"I regret exceedingly," writes Dr Livingstone, "having to report the death of your kinsman, Bishop Mackenzie, on the 31st of January last. He came down to meet his sister in a small canoe, which was unfortunately upset in the Shire, and bedding, clothing, and medicines lost. He arrived at the place of meeting twelve days after the date of the appointment, took fever, and without medicine or any proper treatment succumbed on the 31st, the very day that H. M. S. *Gorgon* appeared off the mouth of the Zambesi, with his sister on board. We had agreed to meet on New Year's Day, at the mouth of a feeder of the Shire, called the Ruo, but were ourselves so detained by a sudden fall of the river above that point, that we passed it on that same day on our way down. He came, as I have said, twelve days afterwards, and, unlike himself, remained there, instead of pushing on after us. It is a sad blow to us here, and his loss will be deeply deplored by all who knew him. He was utterly regardless of comfort in his work; he never spared himself; and we now grieve that he did not husband his strength, and avoid exposure. The low-lands are deadly, but he was so strong that he could not believe it. He used jokingly to say that our pills were worse than the fever. Mr Burrup, the next in strength, perished also about a fortnight after the Bishop; he left the Ruo ill of dysentery, and a few days after reaching the mission in the highlands died."

The fact to which reference is made in the preceding letter, namely that the strongest man in the mission died first, and the next in strength (in Dr Livingstone's judgment) second, is worthy of notice. It seems to give a warning to those who undertake missionary work, as to the absolute necessity, for the sake of those great interests which they have most at heart, of taking care of their own lives and of running no unnecessary risks. It is curious, but I believe cannot be accounted for by reference to any imprudence of conduct, that the next loss which the missionary party sustained was that of Mr Scudamore, who appears to have been pre-eminent in strength and activity. It would carry me out of my proper province if I should undertake to give an account of this devoted and good man: he was admirably fitted for his work, cheerful, unselfish, well-judging, and appears to have been specially dear to Bishop Mackenzie, and in many respects not unlike him. I could not mention Mr Scudamore's name in this place, without alluding to the fact of his subsequent death, and paying a slight passing tribute to his memory; but my chief reason for referring to him is that I wish to introduce a portion of a letter written by him some months after Bishop Mackenzie's death, in which he describes in a very interesting manner a visit made by himself to the Bishop's grave.

"After passing through the Elephant Marsh," so runs the letter, "two days in length, the Ruo enters the Shire, running from its source in the Milanje. As it enters the Shire it breaks into two streams, which form with the Shire what is called here a *Malo*. The island or *Malo*[1] is where the Bishop died. We did not stop in going down, but on our way back we spent a Sunday on the bank, opposite the island, and determined, if possible, to see the Bishop's grave. This was not easy; for the people are very superstitious, and always denied knowing anything about it. After trying several chance persons in a quiet way, we determined to go and see the chief, and ask him at once. It seemed almost hopeless, but at last by bribing and talking we managed it. The chief said all the men who knew where he was, who had buried him, had gone over the mountain. Then I asked him if *he* knew; he said he did, and I got him to point in the direction. At length he said it was on the opposite side of the river.

[1] I am informed that this is a mistake, and that *Malo* is the name of that particular island: but I do not wish to alter Mr Scudamore's letter.

Then a man undertook to shew me from the water's edge the place on the opposite bank; and finally, by the promise of a fathom and a half of cloth, to take us there. We took him into the canoe, but he was in a great state of excitement, and worked away to get the job over as quickly as possible. Presently he began to lap the water with his hand in a very hurried manner, which made Mr Stewart, who was with me, think that he would break down. We kept talking and laughing with him, in order to draw off his attention till we came to the place. It was very wild, desolate-looking, but quiet, and at a little distance seemed better fitted for his grave than any we could choose. There were several crocodiles lying under the bank, quite out of the water, and fast asleep.

"When we landed the guide took a paddle, and told us to take our guns because of wild beasts. We made our way to the grave, not more than fifty yards off. The grass and reeds were so tall and so dry, that they drooped and met over our heads, and sometimes we had to stop and crawl through the tangle which we could not pass in any other way. Every now and then we came to a dry gully, where the guide would rattle about with the paddle to frighten away the alligators. At the end of one of these tunnels of reeds the guide stepped on one side and said, 'There is the grave.' We could perceive nothing; but going a little further I saw something like a pole hidden in the grass; pushing the tangle aside I discovered it to be the cross put up by the sailors of the *Gorgon*.

"When we came away, and had emerged from the

long grass, Mr Stewart took a sketch of the place. The bank rises high from the river; two trees stand some little distance apart about two thirds of the way up, one I think an acacia, the other I don't know; the ground seems rather level at their feet. There is the grave. It will never be disturbed by the natives; they are too much afraid of the place; it is quite out of their haunts, and is never visited but by lions and wolves."

The Bishop's resting-place has since been visited by Dr Livingstone, as stated in the letter printed on page 362. On this occasion Dr Livingstone erected a more permanent cross over the grave, and a sketch was made by one of the party, from which has been copied the engraving, which will form the conclusion—I think, a very appropriate conclusion—of this volume. Is it too much to hope that a church may one day be built upon the spot, and that the inhabitants of this region of Africa may point to it as the place in which the Cross of Christ was first effectually planted in their dark land?

I must not speculate upon the future of the Mission in founding which Bishop Mackenzie sacrificed his life[1]. Troubles came thickly upon it after his departure; war and famine desolated the country, sickness afflicted their own party, while the difficulty of obtaining supplies was a constant source of anxiety. The Mission Station was

[1] I may however mention that on the news of Bishop Mackenzie's death reaching the Cape, Bishop Grey at once started for England, and that before he left this country a successor was found for the deceased Bishop in the Rev. W. G. Tozer. While these sheets are passing through the press, letters are anxiously expected from Bishop Tozer, which may explain his views concerning the future prospects of the Mission.

moved, as already mentioned incidentally, to Chibisa's; and there we must leave it, holding its ground nobly against unforeseen difficulties, and waiting for the arrival of the new Bishop from England. Whatever the future of the Mission may be, certainly it will have the advantage of having been led to the scene of its work, and watched over during its infancy, by one of the most noble and simple-hearted servants of Christ, who ever gave up his home, and his comforts, and his life, for the sake of that which was to him infinitely more precious than all.

Nor is it possible to believe that in any case can the life and death of Bishop Mackenzie have been in vain. It is not Central Africa only, but the whole world, that has an interest in such men. The immediate work to which they gave themselves may or may not appear to flourish; but the fruit of their example is certain. God will not permit it to perish. And so whatever may be the results of his labours to that afflicted country, for the evangelization of which he gave himself up so freely and so completely, I am convinced that hereafter Bishop Mackenzie will be to many,—more than he himself in his humility could have believed,—a witness for Christ and for Christian truth. Many who feel no call to the missionary life themselves will yet see in the missionary life of Bishop Mackenzie a pattern of that self-sacrifice and love to which all Christians are called, and perhaps some may be tempted to follow him even as he followed Christ.

CHAPTER XIII.

CONCLUSION.

Upon a review of what has been laid before the reader in the preceding pages, I have felt in doubt whether I should here close the memoir of Bishop Mackenzie's life, or whether I should add another chapter in which an attempt might be made to give a condensed and comprehensive view of that which has already been exhibited in detail, and to form something like an estimate of the Bishop's mind and character.

On the whole I have determined to add the chapter. It shall be very short, and I shall endeavour, as in the former part of the volume, so in this its conclusion, to abstain from the flattery of friendship, and from those exaggerations into which the biographers of good men are tempted to fall.

Be it observed in the first place, that the intellectual side of Bishop Mackenzie's character can, by the necessity of the case, be exhibited very imperfectly, and that it is in fact exhibited very unfairly and inadequately, in this volume. His intellectual superiority was chiefly confined to the domain of mathematical reasoning, and in this department he was undoubtedly very powerful;

but a missionary to the Kafirs of Natal, or to the Manganja of the river Shire, has small opportunity for exhibiting this mathematical pre-eminence; and therefore the distinguishing power of Bishop Mackenzie's mind never found any sufficient field of operation. The reader should bear this in mind while he peruses the memoir of the Bishop's life; and he should also bear in mind that the opportunity of indulging his mathematical taste, of indulging, in fact, the strongest intellectual passion that he possessed, was deliberately and knowingly sacrificed for the sake of Christ. If in this volume Bishop Mackenzie does not appear in all the strength of intellect that belonged to him, it is because he consented to put aside his strength and to become weak for the sake of his weak brethren.

But it was never as a man of high intellect that Mackenzie was specially valued by his friends. We all knew his powers, and appreciated them. His intellect was in his own peculiar sphere comprehensive, penetrating, manly. This last epithet expresses correctly, in my judgment, though some persons may think it strangely applied, the intellectual character of his mind. Mathematicians have their styles, and one differs much from another. When I examined Mackenzie for the Smith's Prize, as related in this volume, the thing which struck me was the straightforward manner in which he grappled with the problems he endeavoured to solve: his manner was not neat, and did his matter injustice: in one or two cases I was disposed to imagine at first sight that he had quite mistaken the problem, but I always found that however he might have failed to arrive at the result, he had always seized the principle, and with a consciousness of right on his side had worked vigourously and manfully, though perhaps not always successfully. But, as I have said, it was not emphatically as a clever man, or a man of intellect, that Mackenzie was chiefly estimated by his friends; if his powers had been tenfold what they were, they would never have given him that peculiar hold upon the hearts of those who knew him, which as a matter of fact he possessed. His special and peculiar attribute was that of loveableness. Those, who knew him, more than liked him: they felt themselves drawn towards him by strong bonds of affectionate and brotherly feeling. In saying this I am not speaking from a limited experience: I am convinced that my judgment would be supported by all his contemporaries.

If it be asked upon what features of his character was based this facility of being loved, I may refer to the pages of this volume, and say that they tell their tale but badly if they do not supply an answer to the question. But more particularly I may remark, that utter unselfishness and thoughtful kindness in small things and imperturbable good temper were perhaps the features of character which chiefly made it difficult or impossible to know Mackenzie without loving him.

Then, too, he was thoroughly humble; he never put himself forward, and even in giving up his home for foreign service, apologized as it were for his presumption by saying, that nobody else would go and therefore he would.

This humility was associated with, or rather was

identical with, a simplicity of demeanour, which was more remarkable in Mackenzie than in any man I ever knew. On one occasion, before his last voyage to Africa, he was receiving some hints from an old African traveller, I think Mr Galton. Speaking of some astronomical observations, Mr Galton said, "They will only require a little Algebra and Trigonometry; and I suppose you can manage that?" "O yes," replied Mackenzie, "I dare say I can," but with such perfect simplicity, that it would have been impossible for Mr Galton to detect the fact that he was talking to an accomplished mathematician. If the reader should say —which after perusing this memoir I am sure he will not—that this was pride aping humility, I can only record my conviction, founded on an intimate knowledge of Mackenzie's character, that it was nothing of the kind.

Being humble in his disposition it would be expected that Mackenzie would take patiently any reproof or advice given to him; but I think it right to add, that his humility did not prevent him from gently reproving others, when he thought himself called upon as a true friend to do so. Nothing is more difficult than to tell a friend of a fault, and this Mackenzie could do, so simply, so good-naturedly, so unaffectedly, as to ensure the rebuke being taken in good part, and to give it a chance of being useful.

From the very first Mackenzie regarded himself, as we have seen, in the light of a candidate for the sacred office of the ministry. To this he made all other purposes subservient, and if he did not receive so definite a training as might have been wished, it was the current in which he found himself that carried him away, and he himself expressed his regret that his clerical education had not been more complete. As a parish priest in England, however, I should doubt whether he left much to be desired in his qualifications for the office: nothing could exceed the love and reverence felt for him by the people of Haslingfield, and had his lot been cast permanently in an English parish, I think that he would have been a country parson after George Herbert's own heart.

At the same time I think that a country parish, during his younger days at least, was not the most useful sphere for his exertions. He would have made a good parish priest, but a college priest better still. He was singularly fitted to influence young men of ability, and notwithstanding his own feeling of disappointment, I am sure that his actual influence in Cambridge was most strong and valuable.

But it pleased God that neither English parish nor English college should have the principal portion of Mackenzie's life and labour. He gave himself up to foreign work, and the point to which I would wish to direct the mind of the reader of this Memoir, is not so much the sacrifice which Mackenzie made, as the spirit in which he made it. "Others will not go, so I will." "Christ's servants should consider themselves as labourers in the same field, and be ready to go to any part where there is work to be done." These were the principles upon which he went out, and if, like Henry Martyn, he was not permitted to labour long or with any very conspicuous results, still, like Henry Martyn, he has set an example of missionary spirit which cannot very easily, and by God's grace will not, be barren of fruit. If Mackenzie had left nothing behind him, except the letter numbered XIX., and printed at page 65 of this volume, I should hold that he had bequeathed a most precious legacy to the Church.

With regard to Mackenzie's conduct as a missionary, and specially as a missionary Bishop, in which capacity he was for the first time his own master, I think that we are not yet in a condition to form a thoroughly satisfactory judgment. So far as regards inspiring love and confidence into the hearts of his associates, and governing as an elder brother should govern, it is clear that he was thoroughly successful; so far as his general principles of establishing the Mission are concerned, we shall perhaps be able to form a better estimate at a later period of the history of the Mission. I shall be very glad if the reader of this Memoir should come to the conclusion, that Bishop Mackenzie attempted to carry out the great purposes committed to him in the wisest and best and most manly and practical way possible under the circumstances in which he was placed. But even if he should come to a different conclusion, he will not be prevented from admiring the spirit and zeal with which the Bishop laboured on behalf of those afflicted people, to whom he came to bring the glad news of salvation and liberty.

The point upon which of course hostile criticism

is likely to fix itself, is the troubles with the Ajawa tribes. I have already gone pretty fully into this matter, and have no desire to repeat what I have said; I would only add, that I cannot regard the Bishop's conduct as a mistake for which to apologize, and I trust that nothing which I have written will be regarded in this light. It was a conduct which he knew would be criticized, and which, having counted the cost, he determined to adopt. It was a conduct which all his associates approved. It was a conduct, which, after mature deliberation, and after forming a different opinion in the first instance, Dr Livingstone declared to be right.

There are two occasions on which I have ventured in this Memoir to say that the Bishop appeared to me to have acted with bad judgment. The first was with regard to the Church Council at Maritzburg, the second was his determination to stay on the island at the mouth of the Ruo without medicines. I bring these two together, and mention them here, because, different as the nature of the two errors was, (if errors they are adjudged to be,) yet the source was the same, and that a noble one: in each case it was the love of the native races, to whom he regarded himself as specially sent, that rightly or wrongly moved him to act as he did. Thus I apologize for Mackenzie's faults: I leave the reader to form his own estimate of his virtues.

One other subject I wish briefly to touch upon before I lay down my pen. I have said nothing in this volume concerning a point which in these days suggests itself very prominently to many minds, namely, the school of religious opinion to which Bishop Mackenzie belonged. Was he High Church, or was he Low Church, or what was his school? I shall be very glad, if, after perusing this volume, the reader should declare himself unable thoroughly to answer the question. To say the truth, Bishop Mackenzie could not be identified with any party: his doctrinal views were in loyal and affectionate conformity with the Book of Common Prayer, but I do not remember ever to have heard him discuss with earnestness any of the controversial questions of the day. The view of religion which commended itself to his mind, was the practical application of the Gospel of our Lord Jesus Christ to the wants of men; and the best method of doing this was, in his opinion, a simple and faithful adherence to the principles and rules of the Prayer-book. I never met with a more sincere Churchman, or with one who had less of the spirit of party. I never met with a man whose religious system seemed to lie more completely within the four corners of the Book of Common Prayer. For religious speculation he had little taste, for religious eccentricities he had an utter abhorrence; but if there was any Christian deed to be done, any work of mercy to be performed, either for the bodies or the souls of men, then Mackenzie's whole heart was engaged: to go about doing good was the only employment, which he thoroughly and unreservedly loved.

And he did go about, like his Master, doing good; and he grew in grace, and in the knowledge of the Lord Jesus Christ, so long as life was given him. Now

PART OF THE EASTERN COAST OF AFRICA.

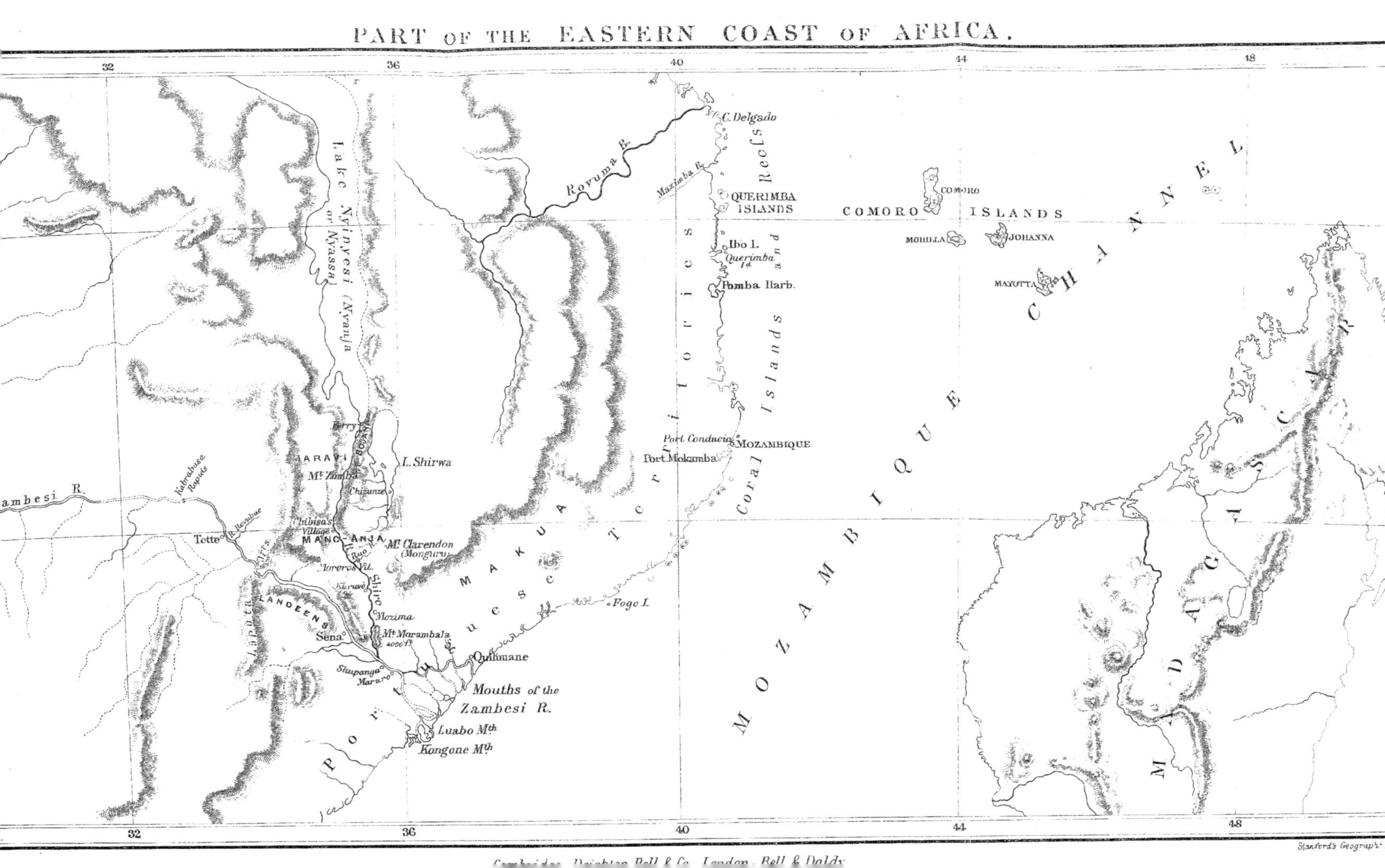

Cambridge, Deighton Bell & Co. London, Bell & Daldy.

he rests from his labours, in his quiet grave by the river Shire, under the symbol of that Gospel of salvation which he came to preach to his poor degraded brethren. His labours will not be in vain; and the Cross planted upon his grave may be the emblem and pledge to Central Africa of a great work of evangelization, which has been nobly commenced, and which it is to be hoped that the charity and the zeal of the Church of England will endeavour faithfully and vigorously to carry on.

Dr Livingstone planting the Cross on Bishop Mackenzie's Grave.
(From a sketch made on the spot.)

THE END.

Cambridge:
PRINTED BY C. J. CLAY, M.A.
AT THE UNIVERSITY PRESS.

CAMBRIDGE.
October, 1863.

BOOKS PUBLISHED BY

DEIGHTON, BELL, & CO. CAMBRIDGE.

(Agents to the University).

Jerusalem Explored: being a description of the Ancient and Modern City, with upwards of One Hundred Illustrations, consisting of Views, Ground-plans, and Sections. By ERMETE PIEROTTI, Doctor of Mathematics, Captain of the Corps of Engineers in the Army of Sardinia, Architect-Engineer to his Excellency Soorraya Pasha of Jerusalem, and Architect of the Holy Land. [*In the Press.*

Memoirs of the late Bishop Mackenzie. By the DEAN OF ELY. With portrait and illustrations. Dedicated by permission to the Lord Bishop of Oxford. [*In the Press.*

The Greek Testament: with a critically revised Text; a Digest of Various Readings; Marginal References to Verbal and Idiomatic Usage; Prolegomena; and a Critical and Exegetical Commentary. For the use of Theological Students and Ministers. By HENRY ALFORD, D.D., Dean of Canterbury.

Vol. I. Fifth Edition, containing the Four Gospels. 1*l.* 8*s.*

Vol. II. Fourth Edition, containing the Acts of the Apostles, the Epistles to the Romans and Corinthians. 1*l.* 4*s.*

Vol. III. Third Edition, containing the Epistles to the Galatians, Ephesians, Philippians, Colossians, Thessalonians,—to Timotheus, Titus, and Philemon. 18*s.*

Vol. IV. Part I. Second Edition, containing the Epistle to the Hebrews, and the Catholic Epistle of St. James and St. Peter. 18*s.*

Vol. IV. Part II. Second Edition, containing the Epistles of St. John and St. Jude, and the Revelation. 14*s.*

The New Testament for English Readers. Containing the authorized Version, with additional corrections of Readings and Renderings; Marginal References; and a Critical and Explanatory Commentary. By HENRY ALFORD, D.D., Dean of Canterbury. In two volumes.

Vol I. Part I. containining the first Three Gospels, price 12*s.* [*Now Ready.*

The Harmony of Revelation and Science. A Series of Essays on Theological Questions of the Day. By the Rev. J. DINGLE, M.A., F.A.S.L., Incumbent of Lanchester, Durham. Crown 8vo. 6*s.*

Hands, Head, and Heart; or the Christian Religion regarded Practically, Intellectually, and Devotionally. In Three Sermons preached before the University of Cambridge. By HARVEY GOODWIN, D.D., Dean of Ely. Fcp. 8vo. 2*s.* 6*d.*

The Appearing of Jesus Christ. A short Treatise by SYMON PATRICK, D.D., formerly Lord Bishop of Ely, now published for the first time from the Original MS. Edited by the Dean of Ely. 18mo. 3*s.*

Short Sermons on Old Testament Messianic Texts preached in the Chapel of Queens' College, Cambridge. By the Rev. GEORGE PHILLIPS, D.D., President of the College. 8vo. 5*s.*

Novum Testamentum Græcum, Textus Stephanici, 1500. Accedunt variæ lectiones editionum Bezæ, Elzeviri, Lachmanni, Tischendorfii, et Tregellesii. Curante F. H. SCRIVENER, A.M. 16mo. 4*s.* 6*d.*

An Edition on Writing-paper, for Notes. 4to. *half-bound.* 12*s.*

A Plain Introduction to the Criticism of the New Testament. With 40 facsimiles from Ancient Manuscripts. For the use of Biblical Students. By F. H. SCRIVENER, M.A., Trinity College, Cambridge. 8vo. 15*s.*

A Companion to the New Testament. Designed for the use of Theological Students and the Upper Forms in Schools. By A. C. BARRETT, M.A., Caius Coll. Fcap. 8vo. 5*s.*

Annotations on the Acts of the Apostles. Original and selected. Designed principally for the use of Candidates for the Ordinary B.A. Degree, Students for Holy Orders, &c., with College and Senate-House Examination Papers. By the Rev. T. R. MASKEW, M.A. Second Edition, enlarged. 12mo. 5*s*.

Hints for some Improvements in the Authorised Version of the New Testament. By the late J. SCHOLEFIELD, M.A. Fourth Edition. Fcp. 8vo. 4*s*.

Observations on the attempted Application of Pantheistic Principles to the Theory and Historic Criticism of the Gospels. By W. H. MILL, D.D., late Regius Professor of Hebrew in the University of Cambridge. *Second Edition, with the Author's latest notes and additions.* Edited by B. WEBB, M.A. 8vo. 14*s*.

Codex Bezæ Cantabrigiensis. Edited, with Prolegomena, Notes, and Facsimiles. By F. H. SCRIVENER, M.A. [*In the Press.*

An Exact Transcript of the CODEX AUGIENSIS, Græco-Latina Manuscript in Uncial Letters of S. Paul's Epistles, preserved in the Library of Trinity College, Cambridge. To which is added a full Collation of Fifty Manuscripts containing various portions of the Greek New Testament deposited in English Libraries: with a full Critical Introduction. By F. H. SCRIVENER, M.A. Royal 8vo. 26*s*.

THE CRITICAL INTRODUCTION *is issued separately, price* 5*s*.

Wieseler's Chronological Synopsis of the Four GOSPELS. Translated by the Rev. E. VENABLES, M.A. [*Preparing.*

The Historical and Descriptive Geography of the HOLY LAND. With an Alphabetical List of Places and Maps. By the Rev. GEORGE WILLIAMS, B.D., Fellow of King's College, Cambridge. [*Preparing.*

On The Imitation of Christ. A New Translation. By the Very Rev. the DEAN of ELY. *Second Edition.* 18mo. 3*s*. 6*d*.

Fcp. 8vo. An Edition printed on LARGE PAPER, 5*s*.

Messiah as Foretold and Expected. A Course of Sermons relating to the Messiah, as interpreted before the Coming of Christ. Preached before the University of Cambridge, in the months of February and March, 1862. By the Rev. HAROLD BROWNE, B.D., Norrisian Professor of Divinity, and Canon of Exeter Cathedral. 8vo. 4*s*.

A History of the Articles of Religion. To which is added a series of Documents from A.D. 1536 to A.D. 1615. Together with illustrations from contemporary sources. By CHARLES HARDWICK, B.D., late Archdeacon of Ely. *Second Edition, corrected and enlarged.* 8vo. 12*s*.

*** A considerable amount of fresh matter has been incorporated, especially in the two Chapters which relate to the construction and revision of our present code of Articles.

Commentaries on the Gospels, intended for the English Reader, and adapted either for Domestic or Private use. By the Very Rev. H. GOODWIN, D.D., Dean of Ely. Crown 8vo.

S. MATTHEW, 12*s*. S. MARK, 7*s*. 6*d*. S. LUKE, *in the Press*.

The Psalter, or Psalms of David in English Verse. With Preface and Notes. By a Member of the University of Cambridge. Dedicated by permission to the Lord Bishop of Ely, and the Reverend the Professors of Divinity in that University. 5*s*.

A General Introduction to the Apostolic Epistles, with a Table of St. Paul's Travels, and an Essay on the State after Death. *Second Edition, enlarged.* To which are added a Few Words on the Athanasian Creed, on Justification by Faith, and on the Ninth and Seventeenth Articles of the Church of England. By A BISHOP'S CHAPLAIN. 8vo. 8*s*. 6*d*.

Bentleii Critica Sacra. Notes on the Greek and Latin Text of the New Testament, extracted from the Bentley MSS. in Trinity College Library. With the Abbé Rulotta's Collation of the Vatican MS., a specimen of Bentley's intended Edition, and an account of all his Collations. Edited, with the permission of the Master and Seniors, by the Rev. A. A. ELLIS, M.A., late Fellow of Trinity College, Cambridge. 8vo. 8*s*. 6*d*.

Three Plain Sermons, preached in the Chapel of

Trinity College, Cambridge, in the course of the year 1859. By the Rev. E. W. BLORE, Fellow of Trinity College. 8vo. 1*s*. 6*d*.

Butler's Three Sermons on Human Nature, and

Dissertation on Virtue. Edited by W. WHEWELL, D.D. With a Preface and a Syllabus of the Work. *Third Edition.* Fcp. 8vo. 3*s*. 6*d*.

A Translation of the Epistles of Clement of Rome,

Polycarp, and Ignatius; and of the Apologies of Justin Martyr and Tertullian; with an Introduction and Brief Notes illustrative of the Ecclesiastical History of the First Two Centuries. By T. CHEVALLIER, B.D. *Second Edition.* 8vo. 12*s*.

On Sacrifice, Atonement, Vicarious Oblation, and

Example of Christ, and the Punishment of Sin. Five Sermons, preached before the University of Cambridge, March, 1856. By B. M. COWIE, B.D., St. John's College. 8vo. 5*s*.

Five Sermons preached before the University of

Cambridge. By the late J. J. BLUNT, B.D., Lady Margaret Professor of Divinity. 8vo. 5*s*. 6*d*.

CONTENTS:—1. The Nature of Sin.—2. The Church of the Apostles.—3. On Uniformity of Ritual.—4. The Value of Time.—5. Reflections on the General Fast-Day (March 1847).

Five Sermons preached before the University of

Cambridge. The first Four in November, 1851, the Fifth on Thursday, March 8th, 1849, being the Hundred and Fiftieth Anniversary of the Society for Promoting Christian Knowledge. By the late Rev. J. J. BLUNT, B.D.

CONTENTS: 1. Tests of the Truth of Revelation.—2. On Unfaithfulness to the Reformation.—3. On the Union of Church and State.—4. An Apology for the Prayer-Book.—5. Means and Method of National Reform.

Two Introductory Lectures on the Study of the

Early Fathers, delivered in the University of Cambridge. By the late J. J. BLUNT, B.D. *Second Edition.* With a brief Memoir of the Author, and a Table of Lectures delivered during his Professorship. 8vo. 4*s*. 6*d*.

The Example of Christ and the Service of Christ, Considered in Three Sermons preached before the University of Cambridge, in February, 1861. To which are appended, A Few Remarks upon the Present State of Religious Feeling. By FRANCIS FRANCE, B.D., Archdeacon of Ely, and Fellow of St. John's College. Crown 8vo. 2*s*. 6*d*.

Ecclesiæ Anglicanæ Vindex Catholicus, sive Articulorum Ecclesiæ Anglicanæ cum Scriptis SS. Patrum nova collatio. Cura G. W. HARVEY, Collegii Regalis Socii. 3 vols. 8vo. Reduced to 16*s*.

The Doctrines and Difficulties of the Christian Religion contemplated from the Standing-point afforded by the Catholic Doctrine of the Being of our Lord Jesus Christ. Being the Hulsean Lectures for the Year 1855. By H. GOODWIN, D.D. 8vo. 9*s*.

'The Glory of the Only Begotten of the Father seen in the Manhood of Christ.' Being the Hulsean Lectures for the year 1856. By H. GOODWIN, D.D. 8vo. 7*s*. 6*d*.

Four Sermons preached before the University of Cambridge in the Season of Advent, 1858. By H. GOODWIN, D.D. 12mo. 3*s*. 6*d*.

Four Sermons preached before the University of Cambridge in the month of November, 1853. By H. GOODWIN, D.D. 12mo. 4*s*.

CONTENTS :—1. The Young Man cleansing his way.—2. The Young Man in Religious Difficulties.—3. The Young Man as a Churchman .—4. The Young Man called by Christ.

Christ in the Wilderness. Four Sermons preached before the University of Cambridge in the month of February, 1855. By H. GOODWIN, D.D. 12mo. 4*s*.

Parish Sermons. By H. GOODWIN, D.D. 1st Series. *Third Edition.* 12mo. 6*s*.

——— **2nd Series.** *Third Edition.* 12mo. 6*s*.

——— **3rd Series.** *Second Edition.* 12mo. 7*s*.

——— **4th Series.** 12mo. 7*s*.

——— **5th Series.** With Preface on Sermons and Sermon Writing. 12mo. 7*s*.

Short Sermons at the Celebration of the Lord's Supper. By H. GOODWIN, D.D. *New Edition.* 12mo. 4*s.*

Lectures upon the Church Catechism. By H. GOODWIN, D.D. 12mo. 4*s.*

A Guide to the Parish Church. By H. GOODWIN, D.D. Price 1*s.* sewed; 1*s.* 6*d.* cloth.

Confirmation Day. Being a Book of Instruction for Young Persons how they ought to spend that solemn day, on which they renew the Vows of their Baptism, and are confirmed by the Bishop with prayer and the laying on of hands. By H. GOODWIN, D.D. *Second Edition,* 2*d.*, or 25 for 3*s.* 6*d.*

Plain Thoughts concerning the meaning of Holy Baptism. By H. GOODWIN, D.D. *Second Edition.* 2*d.*, or 25 for 3*s.* 6*d.*

The Worthy Communicant; or, 'Who may come to the Supper of the Lord?' By H. GOODWIN, D.D. *Second Edition,* 2*d.*, or 25 for 3*s.* 6*d.*

An Historical and Explanatory Treatise on the Book of Common Prayer. By W. G. HUMPHRY, B.D., late Fellow of Trinity College, Cambridge. *Second Edition, enlarged and revised.* Post 8vo. 7*s.* 6*d.*

Liturgiæ Britannicæ, or the several Editions of the Book of Common Prayer of the Church of England, from its compilation to the last revision, together with the Liturgy set forth for the use of the Church of Scotland, arranged to shew their respective variations. By W. KEELING, B.D., late Fellow of St. John's College. *Second Edition.* 8vo. 12*s.*

The Seven Words Spoken Against the Lord Jesus: or, an Investigation of the Motives which led His Contemporaries to reject Him. Being the Hulsean Lectures for the year 1860. By JOHN LAMB, M.A., Senior Fellow of Gonville and Caius College, and Minister of S. Edward's, Cambridge. 8vo. 5*s*. 6*d*.

Twelve Sermons preached on Various Occasions at the Church of St. Mary, Greenwich. By R. MAIN, M.A. Radcliffe Observer at Oxford. 12mo. 5*s*.

Lectures on the Catechism. Delivered in the Parish Church of Brasted, in the Diocese of Canterbury, By the late W. H. MILL, D.D., Regius Professor of Hebrew, Cambridge. Edited by his Son-in-Law, the Rev. B. WEBB, M.A. Fcp. 8vo. 6*s*. 6*d*.

Sermons preached in Lent 1845, and on several former occasions, before the University of Cambridge. By W. H. MILL, D.D. 8vo. 12*s*.

Four Sermons preached before the University on the Fifth of November, and the three Sundays preceding Advent, in the year 1848. By W. H. MILL, D.D. 8vo. 5*s*. 6*d*.

An Analysis of the Exposition of the Creed, written by the Right Reverend Father in God, J. PEARSON, D.D., late Lord Bishop of Chester. Compiled, with some additional matter occasionally interspersed, for the use of Students of Bishop's College, Calcutta. By W. H. MILL, D.D. *Third Edition, revised and corrected.* 8vo. 5*s*.

Horae Hebraicae. Critical and Expository Observations on the Prophecy of Messiah in Isaiah, Chapter IX. and on other Passages of Holy Scripture. By W. SELWYN, B.D., Lady Margaret's Reader in Theology. Revised Edition, with Continuation. 8*s*.

THE CONTINUATION, separately. 3*s*.

Excerpta ex Reliquiis Versionum, Aquilæ, Symmachi, Theodotionis, a Montefalconia aliisque collectis. GENESIS. Edidit GUL. SELWYN, S.T.B. 8vo. 1*s*.

Notæ Criticæ in Versionem Septuagintaviralem. EXODUS, Cap. I.—XXIV. Curante GUL. SELWYN, S.T.B. 8vo. 3*s*. 6*d*.

Notæ Criticæ in Versionem Septuagintaviralem. Liber NUMERORUM. Curante GUL. SELWYN, S.T.B. 8vo. 4*s*. 6*d*.

Notæ Criticæ in Versionem Septuagintaviralem. Liber DEUTERONOMII. Curante GUL. SELWYN, S.T.B. 8vo. 4*s*. 6*d*.

Origenis Contra Celsum. Liber I. Curante GUL. SELWYN, S.T.B. 8vo. 3*s*. 6*d*.

Testimonia Patrum in Veteres Interpretes, Septuaginta, Aquilam, Symmachum, Theodotionem, a Montefalconio aliisque collecta paucis Additis. Edidit GUL. SELWYN, S.T.B. 8vo. 6*d*.

The Will Divine and Human. By T. SOLLY, B.D., late of Caius College, Cambridge. 8vo. 10*s*. 6*d*.

Tertulliani Liber Apologeticus. The Apology of Tertullian. With English Notes and a Preface, intended as an Introduction to the Study of Patristical and Ecclesiastical Latinity. By H. A. WOODHAM, LL.D. *Second Edition.* 8vo. 8*s*. 6*d*.

Rational Godliness. After the Mind of Christ and the Written Voices of the Church. By ROWLAND WILLIAMS, D.D., Professor of Hebrew at Lampeter. Crown 8vo. 10*s*. 6*d*.

Paraméswara-jnyána-goshthi. A Dialogue of the Knowledge of the Supreme Lord, in which are compared the claims of Christianity and Hinduism, and various questions of Indian Religion and Literature fairly discussed. By ROWLAND WILLIAMS, D.D. 8vo. 12*s*.

MISCELLANEOUS.

Verses and Translations. By C. S. C. *Second Edition.* Fcp. 8vo. 5*s*.

A Lecture on Sculpture delivered in the Guildhall, Cambridge, before the Cambridge School of Art March 17, 1863. Price 1*s*.

The Student's Guide to the University of Cambridge. Fcap. 8vo. 5*s*. 6*d*.

Contents: INTRODUCTION, by J. R. SEELEY, M.A.—ON UNIVERSITY EXPENSES, by the Rev. H. LATHAM, M.A.—ON THE CHOICE OF A COLLEGE, by J. R. SEELEY, M.A.—ON THE COURSE OF READING FOR THE CLASSICAL TRIPOS, by the Rev. R. BURN, M.A.—ON THE COURSE OF READING FOR THE MATHEMATICAL TRIPOS, by the Rev. W. M. CAMPION, B.D.—ON THE COURSE OF READING FOR THE MORAL SCIENCES TRIPOS, by the Rev. J. B. MAYOR, M.A.—ON THE COURSE OF READING FOR THE NATURAL SCIENCES TRIPOS, by Professor LIVEING, M.A.—On LAW STUDIES AND LAW DEGREES, by Professor J. T. ABDY, LL.D.— MEDICAL STUDY AND DEGREES, by G. M. HUMPHRY, M.D.—ON THEOLOGICAL EXAMINATIONS, by Professor E. HAROLD BROWNE, B.D.—EXAMINATIONS FOR THE CIVIL SERVICE OF INDIA, by the Rev. H. LATHAM, M.A.—LOCAL EXAMINATIONS OF THE UNIVERSITY, by H. J. ROBY, M.A.—DIPLOMATIC SERVICE.—DETAILED ACCOUNT OF THE SEVERAL COLLEGES.

"Partly with the view of assisting parents, guardians, schoolmasters, and students intending to enter their names at the University—partly also for the benefit of undergraduates themselves—a very complete, though concise, volume has just been issued, which leaves little or nothing to be desired. For lucid arrangement, and a rigid adherence to what is positively useful, we know of few manuals that could compete with this Student's Guide. It reflects no little credit on the University to which it supplies an unpretending, but complete, introduction."—SATURDAY REVIEW.

The Mathematical and other Writings of ROBERT

LESLIE ELLIS, M.A., late Fellow of Trinity College, Cambridge. Edited by WILLIAM WALTON, M.A., Trinity College, with a Biographical Memoir by the Very Reverend HARVEY GOODWIN, D.D., Dean of Ely. [*In the Press.*

Lectures on the History of Moral Philosophy in

England. By the Rev. W. WHEWELL, D.D., Master of Trinity College, Cambridge. New and Improved Edition, with Additional Lectures. Crown 8vo. 8*s*.

The Additional Lectures are printed separately in Octavo for the convenience of those who have purchased the former Edition. Price 3*s*. 6*d*.

Athenae Cantabrigienses. By C. H. COOPER, F.S.A.

and THOMPSON COOPER, F.S.A.

This work, in illustration of the biography of notable and eminent men who have been members of the University of Cambridge, comprehends, notices of: 1. Authors. 2. Cardinals, archbishops, bishops, abbats, heads of religious houses and other Church dignitaries. 3. Statesmen, diplomatists, military and naval commanders. 4. Judges and eminent practitioners of the civil or common law. 5. Sufferers for religious and political opinions. 6. Persons distinguished for success in tuition. 7. Eminent physicians and medical practitioners. 8. Artists, musicians, and heralds. 9. Heads of Colleges, professors, and principal officers of the university. 10. Benefactors to the university and colleges or to the public at large.

Volume I. 1500—1585. 8vo. *cloth*. 18*s*. Volume II. 1586—1609. 18*s*.

Volume III. *Preparing*.

Cairo to Sinai and Sinai to Cairo. Being an

Account of a Journey in the Desert of Arabia, November and December, 1860. By W. J. BEAMONT, M.A., Fellow of Trinity College, Cambridge. With Maps and Illustrations. Fcp. 8vo. 5*s*.

A Concise Grammar of the Arabic Language.

Revised by SHEIKH ALI NADY EL BARRANY. By W. J. BEAMONT, M.A., Fellow of Trinity College, Cambridge, and Incumbent of St. Michael's' Cambridge, sometime Principal of the English College, Jerusalem. Price 7*s*.

Livingstone's Cambridge Lectures. With a Prefatory Letter by the Rev. Professor SEDGWICK, M.A., F.R.S., &c., Vice-Master of Trinity College, Cambridge. Edited, with Introduction, Life of Dr. LIVINGSTONE, Notes and Appendix, by the Rev. W. MONK, M.A., F.R.A.S., &c., of St. John's College, Cambridge. With a Portrait and Map, also a larger Map, by Arrowsmith, granted especially for this work by the President and Council of the Royal Geographical Society of London. Crown 8vo. 6*s*. 6*d*.

This Edition contains a New Introduction, an Account of Dr. Livingstone's New Expedition, a Series of Extracts from the Traveller's Letters received since he left this country, and a History of the Oxford and Cambridge Mission to Central Africa.

Newton (Sir Isaac) and Professor Cotes, Correspondence of, including Letters of other Eminent Men, now first published from the originals in the Library of Trinity College, Cambridge; together with an Appendix containing other unpublished Letters and Papers by Newton; with Notes, Synoptical View of the Philosopher's Life, and a variety of details illustrative of his history. Edited by the Rev. J. EDLESTON, M.A., Fellow of Trinity College. 8vo. 10*s*.

A Manual of the Roman Civil Law, arranged according to the Syllabus of Dr. HALLIFAX. By G. LEAPINGWELL, LL.D. Designed for the use of Students in the Universities and Inns of Court. 8vo. 12*s*.

The Study of the English Language an Essential Part of a University Course: An Extension of a Lecture delivered at the Royal Institution of Great Britain, February 1, 1861. With Coloured Language-Maps of the British Isles and Europe. By ALEXANDER J. D. D'ORSEY, B.D., English Lecturer at Corpus Christi College, Cambridge, late Head Master of the English Department in the High School of Glasgow. Crown 8vo. cloth. 2*s*. 6*d*.

Graduati Cantabrigienses: sive Catalogus exhibens nomina eorum quos ab anno academico admissionum 1760 usque ad decimum diem Octr. 1856. Gradu quocunque ornavit Academia Cantabrigienses, e libris subscriptionum desumptus. Cura J. ROMILLY, A.M., Coll. SS. Trin. Socii atque Academica Registrarii. 8vo. 10*s*.

JONATHAN PALMER, PRINTER, SIDNEY STREET, CAMBRIDGE.

www.ingramcontent.com/pod-product-compliance
Lightning Source LLC
LaVergne TN
LVHW020934110826
845150LV00004B/858
* 9 7 8 1 4 2 5 5 5 2 2 0 6 *